Beyond Expectations

Beyond Expectations

SECOND-GENERATION NIGERIANS
IN THE UNITED STATES
AND BRITAIN

Onoso Imoagene

UNIVERSITY OF CALIFORNIA PRESS

University of California Press, one of the most distinguished university presses in the United States, enriches lives around the world by advancing scholarship in the humanities, social sciences, and natural sciences. Its activities are supported by the UC Press Foundation and by philanthropic contributions from individuals and institutions. For more information, visit www.ucpress.edu.

University of California Press
Oakland, California

Library of Congress Cataloging-in-Publication Data

Names: Imoagene, Onoso, author.
Title: Beyond expectations : second-generation Nigerians in the United States and Britain / Onoso Imoagene.
Description: Oakland, California : University of California Press, 2017 | Includes bibliographical references and index.
Identifiers: LCCN 2016040311 (print) | LCCN 2016041889 (ebook) | ISBN 9780520292314 (cloth : alk. paper) | ISBN 9780520292321 (pbk. : alk. paper) | ISBN 9780520965881 (ePub)
Subjects: LCSH: Nigerians—United States—Social conditions. | Nigerians—Great Britain—Social conditions. | Children of immigrants—United States—Social conditions. | Children of immigrants—Great Britain—Social conditions.
Classification: LCC TE184.N55 I46 2017 (print) | LCC E184.N55 (ebook) | DDC 305.896/69073—dc23
LC record available at http://lccn.loc.gov/2016040311

Manufactured in the United States of America

25 24 23 22 21 20 19 18 17
10 9 8 7 6 5 4 3 2 1

CONTENTS

ACKNOWLEDGMENTS

There is an old saying: It takes a village to raise a child. Well, it has taken a village and a global effort on three continents—Africa, Europe, and North America—to bring this book to print.

I must thank my family, of particular note, my sister, Anikphe. I joked and wrote in the acknowledgment page of my doctoral dissertation that she deserved a quarter of my doctoral degree; I think it has increased to half of the degree now. Anikphe read and reread many drafts of this book and stayed awake into the wee hours of the morning across the pond challenging me on the arguments I was making. I thank my father, Prof. Oshomha Imoagene, who has always been a tower of support. I thank my mother, Eunice, and my other siblings, Jude, Oshoke, and Egbhabo, for their support and prayers. A special thank you to my brother-in-law, Adeoye, who has always had an encouraging word. Finally, we can all celebrate.

I thank my friends and colleagues who read the entire draft or chapters of the manuscript and offered tremendously helpful feedback. So thank you to Annette Lareau, Chenoa Flippen, Camille Zubrinsky Charles, Crystal Fleming, Chinyere Osuji, Van Tran, and Peter Blair. I thank the reviewers of the manuscript for pointing out what needed to be strengthened and pushing me to further develop my arguments. I thank my UC Press editor, Naomi Schneider, for her steadfast support. I thank Tamara Nopper, Jennifer Moore, and Carolyn Bond for helping me say what I wanted to say in more concise ways while keeping my own voice. I thank my dissertation committee members Orlando Patterson and Chris Winship. I especially thank Mary C. Waters for her support and mentorship. I thank the staff at the Nigerian embassies in New York and London for giving me access to their consular waiting rooms during my fieldwork and for being so helpful. I am sure there are some people I have omitted, always the danger in naming names. I am grateful to all for their assistance. Finally, I thank the individuals who participated in this study for being willing to take the time, for being gracious, and for being honest and forthcoming. Their stories about their lives in Britain and the United States made this book possible.

Introduction

Idowu Damola grew up in a poor family in a very bad neighborhood in a large New Jersey city.[1] He recalls walking along the glass-strewn block where he lived, "with people yelling and screaming and fighting. It was a pretty run-down place." His big break came when he won a full scholarship to an elite all-boys prep school in Connecticut. After he graduated, Idowu went on to study business and finance at Yale University, one of the top ten universities in the United States. At the time I spoke with him, Idowu had just started working as an investment broker on Wall Street. To get there, he had taken advantage of affirmative action opportunities available to black people in the United States. His progression from a "run-down" street in urban New Jersey to a coveted white-collar job on Wall Street is an American success story, a story that exemplifies the promise many immigrants see in America.

Idowu acknowledges that he has benefited from being black in America, but he does not identify as African American—even though he is of African ancestry. To him, being black does not mean the same thing as being African American.[2] He sees African immigrants, both the first and the second generation, as psychically and culturally different from African Americans. He says, "African Americans by and large in this country have had a very distinct experience, socially and culturally, and for whatever reason that experience [of slavery, Jim Crow] has become a sort of a chain, a weight to many African American individuals. They have a lot of problems that maybe are caused by external forces acting on them. But, you know, by and large it is also their fault in the immediate sense, but it might not necessarily be their fault when you take a cultural or social historical look at it. But I am just not associated with that. Those chains that are weighing them down don't weigh me down."

He continues, "I am obviously not a white American. I don't feel that I am an African American. I don't feel that I have strong cultural ties to that group, and I don't really, can't identify with them." He identifies as Nigerian but acknowledges that he is an ethnic hybrid: "I can't even claim to be a real Nigerian. I don't know enough. I don't appreciate enough about being Nigerian because, look, it isn't really my stuff." He is caught in between, a feeling shared by many of the second generation of Nigerian ancestry, especially those who were born in their parents' host country and who have not lived outside it except for brief vacations. Idowu concludes his commentary on his identity by saying, "I think of myself as a beast of no nation."[3]

Michelle Anoke is a barrister, a highly coveted profession in Britain.[4] She was born and has lived in Britain all her life. She is married to a first-generation Nigerian and has two children. I interviewed her in her home in an upper-middle-class neighborhood in London. Michelle was raised by a single mother whose finances were devastated after divorcing Michelle's wealthy father. She was forced to remove Michelle and her sister from the private elementary school they were attending and place them in the local comprehensive, which, according to Michelle, was "okay, not bad and not great." In school and in her neighborhood, Michelle had a "rough time" getting along with most of her black Caribbean peers. Growing up, she had attended a predominantly Caribbean school, and she quickly found "what seemed to be a very big difference between children who were of African parentage and Caribbean parentage," because "in the 1980s, it was not fashionable to be of African extraction at all." Africans were bullied by their Caribbean peers, and "the bullying took the form of name calling, lots of 'you're African,' laughing at our hair—my mom used to do our hair in thread and they would laugh at us. I was called 'spider head' throughout my years in secondary school."

Michelle sees discrimination as something black people face in Britain every day. Her experiences of discrimination were not confined to school, nor were Caribbeans the only people to treat her as a second-class citizen. "It doesn't surprise me," she said. "It doesn't particularly disappoint me [to be discriminated against] because I have a low expectation in terms of what I'm going to be given by white people. I don't expect anything. I don't even expect, on a day-to-day basis, a 'hello' because English people are notorious for saying hello, having a chat with you one day, and the next day they don't know you." Partly as a result of this, Michelle does not identify as British.

"'Black British' was not a phrase used in my house because you're not British. So I don't ever consider myself to be Black British. I tell people I am a British-born Nigerian."

Beyond Expectations examines the nature of second-generation Nigerians' incorporation in the United States and Britain.[5] Until this book, we knew relatively little about the incorporation of second-generation African adults into British and American society because second-generation assimilation theories and most existing research on the black second generation have focused on the Caribbean experience.[6] Furthermore, none of these studies fully explicated the processes and mechanisms that affect identity formation among second-generation blacks from highly selective immigrant populations. This book does this. The key objective of this book is to understand how, *in combination,* race, ethnicity, and class (both parental and individual)[7] affect the identity formation process and assimilation trajectories of the adult second generation of Nigerian ancestry in the United States and Britain.

Existing theories predict that children of black immigrants (the black second generation) will forge a reactive black ethnicity and black identity characterized by an oppositional culture that devalues schooling and work and stresses attitudes and behaviors antithetical and often hostile to success in the mainstream economy;[8] or form variable and situational identities, where the identity deployed depends on the individual's reading of what the situation demands;[9] or simultaneously hold racial and ethnic identities;[10] or choose a racelessness option, where the individual selects "Other," rather than black or white, on forms requiring racial information.[11] I find that the Nigerian second generation have not forged a reactive black ethnicity and black identity characterized by an oppositional culture but rather have formed a multifaceted identity that combines into more ethnic choices than were previously theorized. In this book, I describe this identity formation process, identify the key actors, factors, and mechanisms that have an impact on the process, and unpack what is going on at the intersections of race, class, and ethnicity for black people in the United States and Britain.

This study is comparative and global in nature. I examine how national context affects the ethnic identities of the second generation. I investigate how the ethnoracial context of the United States differs in its impact compared to the impact of the British ethnoracial system. In addition, I seek to uncover what other national factors impinge on the experiences of the second generation and influence their identity formation process. This involves examining how the histories of the United States and Britain—from the ethnoracial traumas of slavery, colonialism, and legal color segregation to the ways they have tried or failed to address these traumas to their national identities—influence the identities of the Nigerian second generation. I also examine how globalization and transnationalism give rise to a reflexive relationship between the local, foreign, and global that makes these individuals ethnic hybrids.

Nigerians, one of the most educated immigrant groups in the United States and the most educated group in Britain, present an excellent opportunity to examine the import of migrant selectivity on assimilation outcomes of children of black immigrants. I wanted to investigate the impact of the extreme immigrant selectivity of first-generation Nigerians in both countries on their children. The extent of their selectivity via these countries' immigration policies, crafted to allow entry to the brightest and best immigrants from sending countries in the developing world, is revealed in a stunning statistic: while only 7 percent of Nigerian adults over the age of twenty-five in Nigeria have at least a bachelor's degree, 63 percent of Nigerians in the United States over the age of twenty-five have at least a bachelor's degree. This educational profile far outpaces the U.S. national average of 29.3 percent and the black average of 19.7 percent. In Britain, we see the same thing: 61 percent of Nigerian immigrants over the age of twenty-five have at least a bachelor's degree. Again, their educational profile far outpaces the British national average of 28 percent and the black Caribbean average of 22 percent.[12]

Studying Nigerians presents an opportunity to understand how immigrant selectivity and pre-migration middle-class status converts into new ethnic forms as they encounter the ethnoracial systems and interact with other racial and ethnic groups in British and American society and how these adaptive ethnic forms affect the trajectories of their children. Put another way, studying Nigerians affords an opportunity to understand how race intersects with ethnicity, immigration, and class; how key ethnic elements within the Nigerian diaspora[13] influence the racial, ethnic, and transnational identities created in the host countries; and how all these factors working in combination influence the second generation's assimilation outcomes.

Nigerians form the largest African group in both countries. One of every five black Africans in Britain and one of every six in the United States is Nigerian.[14] Nigerians have the largest adult second generation of all sub-Saharan African nations; their population size is noteworthy because forty-eight countries make up sub-Saharan Africa. Consequently, their experiences are a significant part of the black African second-generation story in these two countries. Their experiences are also worthy of investigation because Nigeria holds a powerhouse status on the African continent. As the most populous nation with the largest economy in Africa, and one that has significant natural resources in comparison to other African nations,[15] Nigeria's social, cultural, political, and economic progress or lack thereof has a profound impact on the rest of the continent. Africans pay close attention to what is going on in Nigeria and with Nigerians in the diaspora. Nigerians, often, blaze a trail that other Africans copy. Thus Nigerians are viewed as one of Africa's main reference group in terms of how they construct and negotiate the complex terrains of ethnoracial systems and identities, whether locally in Africa or in the West and the rest of the world.[16]

Over the past quarter century, African immigrants have become both countries' fastest growing black population.[17] In the United States today, African immigrants, along with Caribbeans, are approximately 10 percent of the black population, whereas in 1980 they were less than 3 percent of the black population. In Britain, Africans are now the largest black group, overtaking Caribbeans during the first decade of the twenty-first century, even though Caribbeans, on the whole, have been in Britain for at least a generation longer than Africans. The increased presence of African immigrants has occurred in tandem with increasing immigration of people from nonwhite parts of the world to both countries. Given this, studying African immigrants and their children provides an opportunity to understand the breadth of and diversity in the black second-generation experience.[18] We can also identify unknown mechanisms operating among African immigrants and their children to understand divergent identity formation processes and socioeconomic outcomes among black communities.

While the Nigerian second generation remain within the black racial category because of the ethnoracial systems found in the United States and Britain, which also impact the ethnic boundaries they draw against African Americans in the United States and black Caribbeans in Britain,[19] their identity formation processes and incorporation reveal that they have more ethnic choices than what is predicted for the black second generation by key theories of second generation assimilation. I find that the adult second generation of Nigerian ancestry in both countries have developed a multifaceted identity that balances their racial status, a diasporic Nigerian ethnicity, and a pan-African identity, as national factors shape their identification with the country of destination. My detailed examination of the Nigerian second generation's experiences and identification practices significantly contributes to our understanding of the immigrant experience and the challenge of maintaining ethnic distinctiveness among nonwhites, who are typically neglected in considerations of ethnic options. Furthermore, their experiences, as I show in this book, are centered or, put another way, occur within the larger black experience and help showcase the diversity in the black experience in these countries.

INTERTWINING STORIES OF RACE, ETHNICITY, CLASS, AND NATION

The first story that *Beyond Expectations* tells is how the interplay of race and ethnicity along with social class (both parental and personal) for the black second generation necessitates a more nuanced understanding of their assimilation outcomes in both the United States and Britain. Among the second generation of Nigerian ancestry, relations with proximal hosts during adolescence were extremely influential in the fashioning of ethnic identities. Throughout this book, I refer to African Americans in the United States and black Caribbeans in Britain as the *proximal hosts* of the African second generation. Proximal hosts are the group to which new immigrants are assigned in the receiving country—or put another way, the group perceived as the new immigrants' coethnics based on criteria such as race and religion.[20]

Because they are of African ancestry and thus have been assigned to the black racial category, African Americans serve as the proximal hosts of black immigrants and their children in the United States and black Caribbeans as the proximal hosts of African immigrants and their children in Britain. Because the United States and Britain racialize ethnic minorities, especially black people, and positions them on one side of a stark racial divide opposite white people, little attention is paid to how the black second generation relate with the more established black groups in these countries. In both countries, respondents report that when they were younger, relations with proximal hosts were tense and fraught with conflict and that it was constantly communicated to them that they were different. They were told in various ways that, though black, they were a different kind of black. These tense intergroup relations put respondents on the path of defining blackness that would recognize being racialized[21] while simultaneously distinguishing themselves ethnically from proximal hosts.

As I show, even in the face of racial prejudice and discrimination, the Nigerian second generation are constructing a *diasporic Nigerian ethnicity* distinct from the reactive black ethnicity commonly discussed by segmented assimilation and other theorists.[22] I add *diasporic* to stress that the Nigerian ethnicity formed in the British and American diasporas reflects the extreme selectivity of the Nigerian populations in these countries. It is also diasporic because Nigerian as an ethnicity has gained salience only in the diaspora for principal organizing lines in Nigeria are usually based on ethnic group membership, religion, and sometimes social class.

Just as for other immigrant groups, especially Asians in both the United States and Britain, ethnicity is a resource for the Nigerian second generation. A powerful social norm among the ethnic group is that it is "un-Nigerian not to go to college," which fosters high educational and occupational attainment among the Nigerian second generation. This norm is an outgrowth of the extreme selectivity of first-generation Nigerians in the United States and Britain. Another mechanism is the multiplicity of highly educated professionals in their social networks who serve as role models and against whom the Nigerian second generation measure success. Different mechanisms that help the Nigerian second generation maintain ethnic distinctiveness from proximal hosts operate in both countries. An example is the transnational mechanism of *cultural embedding*—a process by which the second generation, during childhood, learn the symbolically significant elements Nigerians associate with ethnic group membership. In conjunction with several others, this process ensures ethnic distinction and a diasporic Nigerian ethnicity are transmitted to the second generation. Thus, for the Nigerian second generation, ethnicity is not a mark of subordination as asserted by segmented assimilation theory. Rather it is a source of progress, because from within their Nigerian communities several forms of social capital have emerged that foster high educational and occupational attainment.

An ethnic group is defined as "a collectivity within a larger society having real or putative common ancestry, memories of a shared historical past, and a cultural focus on one or more symbolic elements defined as the epitome of their peoplehood."[23] This definition is apt because it guides researchers to look for the symbolic elements that respondents, their parents, and members of their diasporic communities define as the epitome of their peoplehood. This definition also makes explicit the cultural origins of an ethnic group:

the claim of shared ancestry can be factually based or putative. So if members of a group believe that some cultural element is the epitome of their peoplehood, even if someone says, "I don't believe it," or argues that other groups and peoples can make similar claims, such assessments do not disturb this belief from strongly influencing members of the group. Thus what makes an ethnic group an ethnic group is not just shared culture, but a self-conscious belief on the part of ethnic group members that they have a sense of kinship and symbolic repertoires that make them who they are. I found several examples of symbolically important cultural elements selected as central markers of Nigerian ethnicity in both the United States and Britain.

However, even as the Nigerian second generation maintain ethnic distinctiveness from proximal hosts, their identity formation processes are circumscribed by their racial status. They are assimilating into the middle class in both countries, not as individuals who have exited the black category, but as blacks. They hold very meaningful middle-class identities that are entangled with their notions of what it means to be a Nigerian in the United States and Britain. It informs how they relate to Caribbeans in Britain and to African Americans in the United States. Because they have spent most of their lives in these countries and have become ethnic hybrids, they know they cannot fully distance themselves from their proximal hosts to the extent that their parents did. They have also grown up in these countries and understand the challenges that all black people face in terms of ongoing racial prejudice and racial discrimination. As a result, they use class considerations to know which members of their proximal host to relate to and which to shun. And as they use class in these two ways—as one of the multiple identities forming their multifaceted identity and as a way to order intraracial relations with proximal hosts—I find that there is an emerging, loose coalition of all middle-class blacks, regardless of ethnicity, in both countries. To summarize their position, they do not contest that they are of the black race, nor are they unmindful of the various ways race affects their lives, but they do not define themselves through the prism of race.

As a result of these key findings, I argue that the demographic changes being wrought in the United States and Britain from steady, large-scale migration from many parts of the world has opened up space for first- and second-generation African immigrants to assert their ethnic, cultural, and class differences from their proximal hosts. It is doubtful that contemporary black immigrants and their children can ever become deracialized or whitened in the same way as Europeans, and even to some extent successful Asian and Hispanic groups, largely because they do not have the right bodies to access whiteness and because of the persistence of in-group marriage patterns and - racial prejudice and discrimination.[24] But I argue that we are at a time in both societies when their racial status does not always have to be a stigma.

The second story this book tells is how national contexts matter. By taking into account the colonial histories, the construction of national identity as racial projects, and antiblack racism in both the United States and Britain, we gain a clearer picture of how race matters in different contexts. I find that the Nigerian second generation feels more accepted in many ways in the United States than they do in Britain. Those in the former country identify more strongly with the nation than do their counterparts in Britain. I found that Britain's colonial history was a critical element of understanding the racism Nigerians experience in Britain, as well as how the Nigerian second generation related to the nation and fashioned their ethnic identities. The Nigerian second generation in the United States also felt the impact of that country's history with black people and attempts to redress its racist past. They have entered a country that has made some racial progress. They have been able to piggyback on the infrastructure built to redress the generational disadvantages experienced by African Americans from slavery to Jim Crow and beyond. Most notably, they are beneficiaries of affirmative action policies, particularly in admission to tertiary institutions and being considered for and awarded minority fellowships and grants, to the extent that affirmative action has worked exceptionally well as a second-generation integration policy, and especially for black immigrants and their children.[25] Thus their collective memory of living race in the United States is quite different from, and less traumatic than, African Americans' collective memory of living race in the same country. Furthermore, though Britain's government is more supportive of multicultural policies than that of the United States, these findings show that multicultural policies by themselves cannot deliver better integrated citizens, as proponents claim; instead, countries have to invest in significantly reimagining national identities and national myths to emotively appeal to increasingly diverse populations.

Based on my close-up study of the Nigerian second generation, I develop and present in this book a new theory I term *beyond racialization theory* that helps explain why the Nigerian second generation did not forge a reactive blackness, why they did not become culturally indistinguishable from their proximal hosts, and why they have had more positive assimilation outcomes. This theory identifies three key contributing factors: relations with the proximal host; the role of ethnicity as a resource in multitudinous ways; and the role of transnational linkages and perspectives in transmitting a diasporic ethnicity and offering up more ethnic options.

The stories I tell in this book are not simple ones. They are fraught with complex plots, conflicting motives, and unsettling conclusions. The import of all these stories is that we need a more nuanced reading of the impact of race and racialization theory on black individuals, which argue that children of black immigrants because of racial discrimination and other structural realities of race "will be sorted into the bottom strata of classes"[26] in the United States and Britain. In sum, *Beyond Expectations* makes an argument for a more nuanced understanding of how the ethnoracial systems of each country interact with ethnicity, immigration, and class position to explain the assimilation outcomes and identity choices of the black second generation. And in doing this, we see that there is more than one identity formation process and assimilation pathway for them.

THE STUDY

I set out to answer my original research question, whether the experiences of the African second generation of middle-class parents mirror those of African Americans of middle-class parents—who it was found were not replicating their parents middle-class status[27]—by interviewing second-generation adults of Nigerian ancestry. I wanted to understand how their experiences would help us unpack the black box of what goes on at the intersections of race, ethnicity, immigration, and class. I had initially wanted to study intergenerational mobility of the Nigerian second generation compared to their parents but broadened the study to encompass their identity formation process because I realized this would garner more comprehensive understandings of their social mobility, their lived realities, and the nature of their incorporation in American and British society.

This book is based on semistructured in-depth interviews with 150 second-generation adults of Nigerian ancestry, 75 in Britain and 75 in the United States, which I conducted myself.[28] I spoke with some of them over the phone, while others welcomed me into their homes or met with me in coffee shops and cafés or their workplaces. I define the second generation as children born in the receiving country of at least one foreign-born parent. I include as part of the second generation the 1.75 and 1.5 generations, who are defined as persons born in a foreign country of at least one foreign-born parent but who arrived in the United States or Britain between the ages of 0 and 5 years or between the ages of 6 and 13 years, respectively.[29] Regarding the main issues discussed in this book, generational status did not make a difference.[30]

Because I was interested in questions of identity and wanted to examine a wider range of experiences affecting ethnic identity construction, I decided to study adults over the age of 22. This has given me the opportunity to examine a wider range of experiences affecting ethnic identity construction, the most critical being experiences with parents at home, with proximal hosts in schools and neighborhoods, and with white people in professional settings. Studies investigating the identity formation process of the black second generation in the United States and the few examining the identity formation process of the African second generation in Britain tend to study these processes among adolescents and teenagers. But at this stage, self-selected ethnic identities are very much in flux, and there is a limited range of experiences to draw from when theorizing the relationship between identity formation and assimilation trajectories.[31] The greater majority of my respondents were middle- and upper-class professionals with at least a college degree.[32] But a sizable number of respondents either were not college graduates and held manual or low-level nonmanual jobs and or had parents who were poorly educated and/ or working class (see table A in the methodological appendix for an overview of the general characteristics of the sample).

Because I wanted to understand the ethnic identification journey of the Nigerian second generation, during our conversations I asked them how they identify themselves and to describe what influenced the formation of their identities. Other questions followed my first two: In what ways have the presence of African Americans in the United States (and Caribbeans in Britain) and their relations with them from childhood to adulthood shaped their identities? How do they understand and live race and the interplay of race and ethnicity in a country where to be black is to be attributed certain racial meanings? How do they define blackness and respond to external definitions of blackness?

In addition to the formal interviews, I spent over three months in each country doing ethnographic observation in Nigerian embassies in London and New York and during an annual picnic for Nigerian youths in Boston. These sites gave me an opportunity to study second-generation Nigerians as they interacted with coethnics and consular staff. All names used in this book are pseudonyms. I gave respondents who had ethnic names pseudonyms drawn from their particular ethnic group. For example, a respondent with a Yoruba name is given a Yoruba pseudonym, and those with English names are given English pseudonyms. I have also changed some other identifying information to ensure respondents' anonymity. Some subheads in the book are quotations taken from respondents' interviews; they are placed in quotation marks for easy identification.

Getting a sample of second-generation Nigerian adults was not easy. They are not as visible as first-generation Nigerian immigrants (see the methodological appendix for a discussion on the many decisions I had to make to acquire my sample). My primary research sites were the Nigerian embassies in London and New York. After I exhausted the embassy as a site for interviews, I added snowball sampling. I had two points of entry in both countries: churches and Nigerian organizations. Key informants referred me to others in their organizations and social networks. I was careful to not oversample from any one social network. I diversified the sample so as not to sample on identity issues and to control variation in involvement in community. I also used my personal contacts within the Nigerian community. As a first-generation Nigerian immigrant, I was able to tap into the social networks of friends and family members on both sides of the pond.

There were no regional differences in how the respondents identify. In the United States, I interviewed respondents from four of the top five destination cities, states, and regions in which Nigerian immigrants are concentrated (New York, Boston, Texas, and Virginia-Maryland-Washington, DC). In Britain, almost all the respondents lived in London. I believe there were no regional differences in how they identify because the mechanism of cultural embedding was widespread and so powerful that the multiple identities held by the Nigerian second generation are strongly influenced by Nigerian values in both the United States and Britain.

The study was designed to be comparative in order to understand how race, racial framings, and other structural conditions matter. By observing and explaining divergent outcomes within an immigrant group in two national contexts while holding the immigrant group constant, my study reveals that observed differences in outcomes likely result from the structural conditions affecting the adjustment of the group to the host societies. Since this was not a randomly selected sample, the findings cannot be generalized to the wider population with any degree of statistical confidence. The sample was designed to establish an in-depth look at the lived realities of a sizable subpopulation of a rapidly growing African population in the United States and Britain. My objective was to understand their ethnic identification journey and the mechanisms that influenced their racial and ethnic identities.

My role as a researcher was that of an insider because I am a first-generation Nigerian immigrant. This was an advantage, as respondents were extremely candid with me about their experiences in the United States and Britain and about the challenges they have faced and continue to face. They were especially open when discussing their relations with their proximal hosts. Their narratives, especially when describing their ethnic differences from their proximal hosts, were often unsettling because often they were a regurgitation of views held by the dominant group (whites) and other non-blacks in both British and American society. I contextualize and evaluate these views, explaining why they are held within certain segments of the Nigerian community.

I decided to present these views in their totality, which might be upsetting to some readers and which some might say paint the Nigerian second generation in an unflattering light, not to place the cat among the doves and create friction between members of these groups. Nor do I wish to provide more ammunition to those who want to place the difficulties of African Americans in the United States and of Caribbeans in Britain at their feet, attributing them solely to personal and cultural failings without acknowledging the roles played by these countries' racial politics and persistent racial discrimination. Instead, in this book I want to achieve two things: first, start a discussion on why Nigerians, and as studies suggest other black immigrants, hold these views,[33] discover why stronger kinship ties, considering that Nigerians and their proximal hosts are part of different waves of the African diaspora, are not being built between Nigerians and their proximal hosts and how stronger coalitions might be built; and second, by reproducing these views, illustrate a dimension of the increasing diversity among blacks in both countries and the ways it manifests and is used in boundary work against the proximal host. The ways it manifests often do not sufficiently acknowledge the historical and sociopolitical contexts that have entrenched these countries' racial systems and racial meanings.

But beyond some critical narratives of their proximal hosts, the larger critique the Nigerian second generation were engaged in was criticizing the ethnoracial systems in their countries that equate blackness with poverty, a disadvantaged class experience, or criminality. They were aware of and trying to communicate, sometimes in an unartful manner, a critique of a racial system that views blackness as monolithic. None of them contested their racial status or claimed whiteness. I would summarize their position by paraphrasing the words of Dr. Martin Luther King Jr.: they are looking forward to a time when they and all blacks will be judged by the content of their character and not by the color of their skin.[34]

The only negative aspect of being an insider was my respondents' unwillingness to divulge their annual incomes, although I am not sure that they would have readily divulged this information to an outsider. Nigerians tend to be suspicious of such questions. After a few weeks in the field in Britain, I dropped the income question from my interview schedule. I compensated by getting detailed occupational and educational information. I was careful to ask respondents to fully explain their thoughts whenever they tried to convey them in shorthand form, thinking that I knew what they were talking about. For example, phrases like "You know how it is" were answered with "Please, can you fully elaborate what you mean?"

I did not find that the quality of my interviews differed by gender. I also believe that my position at the time as a graduate student at Harvard University conferred a high degree of legitimacy to my interactions with them. Respondents in the United States, both male and female, were very eager to tell me their stories. The questions I asked touched on issues they had been asking themselves and discussing with friends and family for many years. Respondents in Britain were just as happy to tell their stories. As I discuss in chapters 5 and 6, they were on the whole more cynical about Britain and what it meant to be a black person living there than were their U.S. counterparts with regard to the United States.

ASSIMILATION OF THE NONWHITE SECOND GENERATION

There is an ongoing debate about how the children of post-1960s immigrants will adjust to Western host societies. A key characteristic of contemporary immigrants to the United States is that the majority are from nonwhite parts of the world. In the United States, the question is whether they will be able to replicate the trajectory of earlier waves of European immigrants who ended up joining the American mainstream as "whites." Would they, like the second and subsequent generations of the earlier wave of white European immigrants, follow the straight-line assimilation model, where the more they lose their ancestral ethnic culture while culturally assimilating into America, the more successful they become? In particular, there is a question whether blacks can attain this default definition of success given their history as victims of racial discrimination. In some respects, the British situation is similar, but it is also very different because of Britain's history as an imperial power and its more recent history as a destination country for large-scale, nonwhite immigration.

To grapple with the role of race in second-generation assimilation, a new theory was born, segmented assimilation theory, which sought to understand how race along with other factors complicated the pathway of assimilation—a pathway heretofore thought to be straightforward, at least for white immigrants. The theory stressed that parental human capital, family structure, and the context of reception, which includes the size of the immigrant's coethnic community and governmental and societal responses to the immigrant's group, affected the adaptation outcomes of the second generation. The theory also stressed the role of race and ongoing racial discrimination in placing barriers to successful middle-class adaptation of the black and Hispanic second generation. And in doing so, the theory was quite pessimistic about the socioeconomic trajectories of many of the black and Hispanic second generation.

According to segmented assimilation theory, white groups, for whom ethnicity is a matter of choice, would have a smooth transition into the mainstream. For others, particularly certain Asian groups, ethnicity is a source of strength and social capital, helping them through selective acculturation—that is, deliberately choosing which cultural practices to accept from American culture and which to reject—to integrate as upwardly mobile individuals into the mainstream. However, for blacks, ethnicity is *not a matter of choice nor a source of progress but a mark of subordination.*[35] Their racial similarity to African Americans will cause them as well to be victims of racial prejudice and discrimination. And their response to this, and the frustrations of living in poor urban areas that condemn them to poor economic prospects, will lead them to develop a reactive black ethnicity and take on a black identity that the authors associate with self-destructive attitudes and behaviors that retard positive socioeconomic outcomes and a smooth entrance into the middle class and/or mainstream American society.

By linking ethnic identity to social mobility, segmented assimilation theory predicts that the black second generation are "at risk of joining the masses of the dispossessed, compounding the spectacle of inequality and despair in America's inner cities."[36] Such a prediction promotes the view that black culture is reducible to an oppositional culture that devalues schooling and work and valorizes attitudes and behaviors antithetical to and which imperil success in the mainstream economy. In sum, because segmented assimilation theory treats black people as a single ethnic group, it predicts that children of black immigrants will become culturally indistinguishable from African Americans and become "just black." Such a conclusion conflates race, ethnicity, and identity into a single matrix. The problem with predicting that the black second generation will become "just black" largely because of structural barriers imposed by racial discrimination is that the possibility of alternative trajectories among blacks is undertheorized. We know little of how differences in terms of national origin, ethnicity, parental resources, class status of the adult second generation themselves, and contexts of reception may result in varying assimilation pathways among blacks. In this book, I address these gaps in our knowledge.

In addition, I argue that the presence of a proximal host group and interactions with this group are further and important aspects of the context of reception for the black second generation that must be considered. This factor is one of three key factors identified in *beyond racialization theory*. The distinction I make here is that it is not just race, in this case being black, that affects the identity formation process of the second generation. The nature of interethnic relations of the groups, even as they all reside in countries that racialize them as black, is a key determinant of how the black second generation identify. Also, beyond racialization theory stresses how ethnicity can be a resource for second-generation groups theorized to be at risk of downward mobility. In this book, I show how ethnic resources in Nigerian communities in the United States and Britain affect the identities and assimilation trajectories of the Nigerian second generation. In so doing, I extend the ethnicity-as-capital framework to the black second generation.

Once we begin to pay attention to racial and ethnic differences in the assimilation outcomes of the second generation, the conversation often shifts to proffering cultural arguments to explain why members of a group do better or worse than another group. The model minority thesis is one such theory. The term *model minority* is used to refer to a minority (be it racial, ethnic, or religious) whose members are seen as high achieving on measures such as education, income, and low criminal rates. The model minority thesis, used commonly to explain why some Asian groups in the United States and Britain do better than other immigrant groups and native whites, posits that Asians have a family-mediated ethnic culture that fosters good academic performance. The popular narrative is that Asian American mothers are strict and drive their children very hard to excel academically, that Asian Americans are very studious, are extremely respectful of their parents and work hard to show this respect, and are respectful to teachers, who therefore treat them better and give them more opportunities to excel.[37] But a critical analysis of why many second-generation Asians do well in school compared to their black, white, and other ethnic minority counterparts reveals that what seem to be cultural explanations actually rest on structural factors, ranging from the hyper-selectivity[38] of the first generation to community-wide informational networks and supplementary educational programs.[39]

Furthermore, the origin story of the model minority thesis reveals that different Asian American groups, primarily Japanese and Chinese Americans, crafted this thesis purposely to advance their sociopolitical interests and gain inclusion and full citizenship in the United States while positioning themselves against African Americans.[40] Along with framing their success as due to strong and stable families and cultural elements such as hard work, respect, duty (obligation), honor, and nondelinquency, they positioned themselves and their culture as the antithesis of African Americans and their culture.[41] By promoting themselves as model minorities, Asian Americans helped sharpen the racial boundary between whites and blacks and placed themselves closer than blacks to whites in the racial hierarchy.[42] This history inflects the model minority thesis with antiblack sentiments that, alongside valorizing a (immigrant) group and their culture, place the blame for African Americans' difficulties and failure to achieve parity with whites on many indices at their own feet, attributing it to personal and cultural failings rather than rightly fingering the roles of institutional racism[43] and the United States as a racial state—a state that even after the gains of the civil rights era has reconfigured and promulgated new laws and technologies that continue to impede African Americans from achieving racial parity and full inclusion in American society. Moreover, valorizing Asian Americans is a way for white people to triangulate Asian Americans between whites and blacks and thereby subordinate Asians and especially blacks while maintaining their privilege.[44]

Some have suggested that first- and second-generation Nigerians can be viewed as a model minority or a black model minority. There have been several mass media stories and numerous blog postings that have called attention to first- and second-generation Nigerians' success, often in terms of education, in both the United States and Britain. For example, in Britain in 2012,

Nigerian students' performance in the GSCEs exam, which is largely equivalent to a high school diploma, is 18 points higher than the British national average. In a recent book, Nigerian Americans were identified as one of the most successful cultural groups in the United States, along with Mormons, Jews, Iranian and Lebanese Americans, Cuban Americans, and Indian Americans.[45] But as the history of the term *model minority* makes clear, applying the moniker to any group means not just supporting cultural arguments for success but also positioning the group against African Americans.

What I show in this book is that the supposition that the Nigerian second generation might be a model minority is problematic for several reasons. First, the mechanisms that have given the Nigerian second generation more ethnic choices and more positive assimilation outcomes than what key second-generation assimilation theories predicted have their genesis in the extreme selectivity of the Nigerian first generation and the social capital generated from the ethnic resources within their communities that have helped create human capital and ethnic-group consciousness in the second generation. Second, such an assessment neglects that Nigerians' racial status as black causes their experiences and assimilation trajectories in British and American society to significantly differ from that of some second-generation Asians. Thus I make clear that there is nothing intrinsically or inherently Nigerian about the cultural elements the Nigerian second generation use to delineate the ethnic boundaries between themselves and their proximal hosts. Rather, their experiences and identification practices demonstrate that culture is not intrinsic to groups but structurally generated.

ORGANIZATION OF THIS BOOK

It is a sociological truism that context matters. After all, identity is not created in a vacuum. Instead, people develop their identities as they interact with other groups while navigating the social, political, and economic milieu of the country they live in—a milieu greatly influenced by the country's specific racial history. In chapter 1, I present a succinct but thorough discussion of the social, political, and racial contexts in which the black second generation in the United States and Britain form their identities. This chapter provides the backdrop for understanding the observed national differences and their impact on the experiences of the second generation. I discuss key theories and studies on second-generation assimilation and how the black second generation identify, specifying how my study engages with and builds on existing literature. The chapter also provides more information on the African diaspora in both countries and the Nigerian communities in particular. And it briefly sketches the history of Nigeria and provides a sociodemographic profile of Nigerians. The chapter concludes with a discussion of the sociodemographic profile of the parents and second generation involved in this study.

Chapters 2 through 4 discuss the three key factors identified in beyond racialization theory that influenced how the Nigerian second generation in both the United States and Britain identify. Chapter 2 shows how the proximal host is a crucial actor influencing how the second generation of Nigerian ancestry identify. It details how relations with the proximal host in childhood, particularly feelings of rejection and exclusion based on perceived physical and cultural differences, laid the foundation for developing a distinct ethnicity in adulthood. In chapter 3 I examine how ethnicity serves as a source of capital for the Nigerian second generation in both countries. The discussion of ethnicity as capital being "a source of progress"[46] for the second generation has heretofore been largely limited to a discussion of certain Asian groups in both countries.[47] The chapter examines how ethnicity became a resource for the second generation of Nigerian ancestry that facilitated their good educational and occupational outcomes, outcomes that were ethnicized and used as an ethnic boundary between themselves and their proximal hosts. A larger discussion of how the Nigerian second generation negotiate their racial status while foregrounding their ethnicity in the United States and Britain begins in this chapter.

Chapter 4 details the important role played by the transnational mechanism of cultural embedding in shaping how the Nigerian second generation identify. It details how the Nigerian second generation are forging a diasporic Nigerian ethnicity in the United States and Britain via two simultaneous processes required in identity formation: signaling difference from members of other groups and establishing similarity to determine the boundaries of group membership. I discuss the cultural, moral, and socioeconomic boundaries established by the Nigerian second generation to delineate ethnic parameters between themselves and their proximal host. I also explain why the second generation in Britain do not draw as sharp a boundary between themselves and their proximal hosts compared to their U.S. counterparts.

Chapters 5 and 6 examine the endpoints of their ethnic identification journey and the import of national factors for the identities formed. Chapter 5 shows that a key endpoint is integration into the black middle class. It uses respondents' experiences of racial discrimination, exhibitions of racial solidarity, voting patterns, and use of class as a sorting mechanism to order interactions with proximal hosts and develop middle-class identities, and in the United States their views on whether black immigrants and their children should benefit from affirmative action policies, to illustrate how the Nigerian second generation balance race and ethnicity and how race intersects with ethnicity and class in British and American societies.

In chapter 6 I show how the specific history an immigrant group has with the receiving country is an important aspect of the context of reception that does not receive sufficient attention in segmented assimilation theory's discussion of the black second generation. I show how national contexts—specifically, how national identity and legacies of the past, from slavery to colonialism to color segregation—influence identificational assimilation, the development of a sense of peoplehood based exclusively on the host society, among the second generation. Engaging the multiculturalism literature, the chapter discusses how legacies of the past and national identity are two rarely considered factors affecting immigrants' integration over time. Given the increased linkages between immigration and national security in discourse and policy, these findings add to our knowledge of the factors impacting the degree of national identification among immigrants. The chapter concludes by comparing the ethnic identification patterns of the Nigerian second generation in the United States and Britain and discussing the multifaceted identity formed by the second generation of Nigerian ancestry.

In the conclusion, I articulate again the main points of beyond racialization theory. I discuss what the experiences of the adult second generation of Nigerian ancestry in the United States and Britain reveal about the intersections of race, class, national origin, and ethnicity in these countries. I discuss what their experiences tell us about the future of the color line and understandings of blackness in the United States and Britain. The experiences of the second generation of Nigerian ancestry show that the ethnic, cultural, and socioeconomic diversity among black people is being recognized and increasingly so. Their experiences suggest that their presence in the black middle class has the potential to change the largely negative ways black people are viewed and possibly help redefine what it means to be black in both countries.

ONE

Setting the Context

IMMIGRATION, ASSIMILATION VERSUS RACIALIZATION,
AND THE AFRICAN AND NIGERIAN DIASPORAS
IN THE UNITED STATES AND BRITAIN

Titi Ajayi, a twenty-nine-year-old researcher with a PhD, came to the United States when she was twelve years old. She learned to think of herself in racial terms only after her arrival. She experienced "culture shock" because, she said, "it was really my first time of thinking about white. I knew that there were white people and Asians in the world, but I didn't know that people actually called [other people] white. I was surprised that the color white is what you called somebody. That was a foreign thing to me. Because before wherever I lived people were just different, but it was never, you never just called somebody white." Titi continued, "I remember I had to learn, oh, when you say white you mean a person, that's actually a person. That black means a person. So, that was one of the big things I had to learn in the United States." Even as she has learned to think of herself as black, Titi also identifies as Nigerian as well as Nigerian American.

British respondents shared similar stories of racialization. Adex Malik, a thirty-year-old pharmacist, told me he was not treated as racially different when he was a child growing up in Britain. As he put it, "Everything was hunky-dory." But then: "As my friends used to say, when you are young, before the age of ten, you are a cute little boy. But when you become eleven you become a black person." When asked why he thought this happened, he told me: "You begin to get more aware of what is going on and you start to have different experiences at that point. You begin to feel the difference in the way people view you. Before I was no threat to anybody. I was just a little kid." Now, as a black man, he is perceived racially, as scary, hypersexual, and prone to violence:[1] "White people cross the street to avoid me. Elderly white people riding on buses look at me 'funny.'" As a child he "had no full understanding of race," but he does now. Like Titi, Adex is aware that racially he is black while simultaneously identifying in other ways, as Nigerian and African.

These vignettes underscore the importance of ethnoracial contexts in the process of identity formation among the Nigerian second generation. The objective of this chapter, then, is to delineate both the national contexts and the contexts of reception in which the Nigerian second generation form ethnic identities. Next, I turn to a discussion of the predicted assimilation outcomes for the black second generation that flow out of racialization and segmented assimilation theories and their conception of black identity and blackness that the experiences of the Nigerian second generation in both the United States and Britain have led me to challenge. Overall, the focus of this chapter is to understand how history, politics, and immigration shape the national context for black natives and black immigrants and how the composition of Nigerian communities in the United States and Britain impact the assimilation outcomes of their second generation.[2]

THE UNITED STATES AND BRITAIN
AS COMPARATIVE CASES

When studying identity formation among the Nigerian second generation, the United States and Britain provide an ideal comparison of national contexts. Both are advanced, English-speaking, Western democracies with racially and ethnoculturally diverse populations—populations projected to grow increasingly diverse due to immigration.[3] In both the United States and Britain, racial hierarchies exist, with white people placed at the top as the presumably superior race and black people placed at the bottom.[4] Racial boundaries are normally drawn on the basis of physical markers such as skin pigmentation, hair texture, and facial features, while ethnic boundaries are normally drawn on the basis of cultural markers such as language, religion, and shared customs.[5] Although notions of race as a meaningful biological category have been debunked, as has also racial science, which linked social outcomes to biological traits, race and racial categorization still hold great social and political power in contemporary British and American society. Consequently, race can be defined as "a concept, a representation or signification of identity that refers to different types of human bodies, to the perceived corporeal and phenotypic markers of difference and the meanings and social practices that are ascribed to these differences."[6] Both nations have long histories of racism and discrimination against black people. In the United States, antiblack discrimination has its roots in the ethnoracial traumas of trading and possessing enslaved Africans and legal segregation (Jim Crow). In Britain, the roots of antiblack discrimination are traced to the imperial history of slavery, colonialism, and color segregation. All of these practices were maintained and given legitimacy by the ideologies of white supremacy and black inferiority. The one big difference between the United States and Britain is that African Americans endured slavery and segregation on American soil, whereas black people in Britain are mostly immigrants from the West Indies, Africa, and other former British colonies. For Britain, trade in enslaved Africans and the practice of slavery occurred far away from the British motherland. Even though significant racial progress has been made since the abolition of the slave trade and slavery, with many laws being passed banning antiblack discrimination in public spaces and organizations, black people in both countries still experience significant racial prejudice and discrimination.

Past and present social policies and societal arrangements, such as the persistence of institutional racism in both countries, the ghettoization of inner cities in the United States, and mass incarceration that affects more ethnic minorities—and especially more blacks than whites—have created and maintained significant racial inequality in both societies. Black people on the whole lag behind whites on many measures, including education and health outcomes, employment and labor market experiences, housing and residential segregation, income and wealth, and judicial experiences and sentencing. Despite the prediction of traditional assimilation scholarship, which holds that social mobility is correlated with social acceptance, racism affects even middle-class blacks.[7] In the United States, the black middle class face housing segregation just like the black poor, with the average middle-class black person living in a neighborhood worse than those inhabited by the white poor. Thus the returns on socioeconomic status for blacks in terms of neighborhood quality are much lower than for other groups.[8] In both Britain and the United States, blacks do not perform as well as whites in school, are more likely to be in prison, have lower employment rates, have less wealth, have children as teenagers or out of wedlock, and are less likely than whites to marry.[9] These dreary statistics, when taken together, are evidence of racial discrimination and the deleterious effect of racism on black people's life chances. In short, in both countries antiblack racism still profoundly affects many aspects of black people's lives. And in both countries, the state is rearticulating these racialized ideologies, retreating from policies designed to relieve racial inequality.[10] And in both countries, many whites refuse to see how racial barriers and institutional racism in many sectors such as law and the judicial system maintain racial inequality between blacks and whites.[11] Their refusal to confront these issues also saps the political will to bring about change.[12]

Yet there are key differences between the two countries in terms of how race politics are articulated. While both the United States and Britain have color lines separating blacks from whites, the latter's ethnosomatic stratification system is not as rigid as the one found in the United States. Britain's ethnosomatic stratification system is described as one of proletarian incorporation, where society is not organized along racially constituted lines, whereas the United States has a dichotomous/binary code restricting blacks to one side of the color line.[13] There is no consensus among scholars on whether the U.S. color line has evolved from black/white to black/nonblack or a tri-racial system similar to those found in Latin America, but within this debate, black people are usually understood to be at the bottom of the racial hierarchy.[14] The less strict rigidity of Britain's ethnosomatic stratification system is revealed in the political usage of "black" as a broad category encompassing African, Caribbean, and South Asian groups in postwar Britain up until its reduced usage in the twenty-first century. The term has been the subject of some controversy, but it was used to call attention to ethnic minorities' "outsider" status, their similar proletarian structural position within British society "as workers performing predominantly unskilled and semi-skilled jobs on the lowest rungs of the economy," and to mobilize resistance to their treatment in Britain that is attributable largely to their non-whiteness.[15] Being black was an expression of political solidarity among Africans, Caribbeans, and South Asians. The emergence in Britain of the term *black* demonstrates the influence of the U.S.-based Black Power movement on British ethnic minorities and their fight for civil rights.[16] Similar political alliances between racialized groups in the United States where they fight under the umbrella term *black* have not occurred in the United States. While some nonwhites organize politically under the category "people of color," it has been argued that over the course of U.S. history, immigrant groups who have assimilated have done so at the expense, or on the backs of, native blacks.[17] As a result of these differing ethnoracial systems, I expect that

British respondents would draw less sharp boundaries between themselves and their proximal hosts than would U.S. respondents.

The United States and Britain hold differing views on the role of immigrants in their societies. Though both nations have long histories of immigration and are top destination countries for immigrants, they hold dissimilar views on the place of immigrants in their national identities. Immigration is part of the charter myth of the United States, which, despite its peaks of nativist sentiment and xenophobia, likes to claim it is a "nation of immigrants" and thus more welcoming to the foreign-born. Conversely, Britons are generally more hostile to immigrants, especially from its former colonies in Asia, the Caribbean, and Africa, with many white Britons perceiving immigration "as being akin to war and invasion."[18] Because of these differing views on immigrants and their role in nation building, my U.S. respondents should feel more welcomed in the United States than their counterparts do in Britain.

In both the United States and Britain, many of the native-born harbor anxieties about the new immigrants in their country: in the United States the fear is of the "browning," or Hispanicization, of America; in Britain the fear is the rise of nonassimilating ethno-Islamic groups and radicalized Islamic minorities who purportedly pose a threat to security and whose communities serve as breeding grounds for domestic terrorists. In Britain, Islam has become the immigration fault line, whereas in the United States Latinos are the immigration fault line.[19] Immigrants who represent these fault lines experience increasing xenophobia and hostility to their presence. Right-wing movements influence the politics of immigration and engender an environment for multiple racisms to occur. In Britain, the National Party runs on an anti-immigration policy platform. In the United States, the Republican Party on the whole and the Tea Party, which leans Republican, oppose any immigration law that includes a pathway to citizenship for undocumented immigrants, which disproportionately affects immigrants from Mexico. This comparative structural analysis of race relations is key to understanding the similarities and differences in the experiences of the Nigerian second generation in both countries. In short, national contexts of reception matter.

ETHNICITY AMONG BLACKS

There exists a view that that ethnic differences among blacks are of minimal sociological importance. This view is related to the prominence of the ethnicity paradigm as one of the major schools of thought in assimilation scholarship.[20] The ethnicity paradigm emerged as a challenge to the biologistic explanations of race and beliefs about racial superiority and inferiority.[21] Ethnicity theory, which was based on the experiences of white immigrants from Europe to the United States, sought to understand how these ethnic groups were assimilating and becoming American. *Assimilation* is the process whereby immigrants and their descendants become integrated into, and more like members of, their host society via prolonged exposure to and socialization in their institutions. It can also be viewed as the decline in ethnic differences.[22] The sociologists Michael Omi and Howard Winant argue that ethnicity theory "operated on cultural territory" and treated "race as a matter of ethnicity," pushing an understanding of race "in terms of culture."[23] This paradigm has been critiqued for promoting an image of an egalitarian society, rather than a discriminatory one, because it is suggested that all groups, irrespective of race, religion, or color, can succeed in the new country and become full citizens depending on their willingness or ability to acculturate.[24] The flipside of this belief is that if a certain group is not doing as well as others it must be due largely to deficiencies within the group—its cultural practices, family structure, lack of goal-oriented identities, attitudes, and so on. Consequently, according to the ethnicity paradigm, the significance of race and institutional racism is underplayed because race and thus racial inequality are reduced to being cultural phenomena.[25]

According to this logic, all black people are to be lumped into a single ethnic group, with race and ethnicity treated as interchangeable. The persisting significance of race, what blackness means in these countries, and the structural barriers imposed by racism that adversely affect black people more than all other groups, including other nonwhite groups who also experience forms of discrimination and exclusion, are underplayed. While the ethnicity paradigm is often employed to ethnicize whites, thus downplaying race when it comes to whites, black ethnic differences are generally treated as insignificant due to race. As Omi and Winant conclude, "The ethnicity approach views blacks as one ethnic group among others. It does not consider national origin, religion, language, or cultural differences among blacks as it does among whites, as sources of ethnicity.... [T]here is in fact, a subtly racist element in this substitution—in which whites are seen as variegated in terms of group identities, but blacks 'all look alike.'"[26]

Studies using ethnicity theory propose cultural explanations for why black people fail to fully assimilate.[27] These arguments are widely used to explain why African Americans, whose ancestors arrived in the United States long before those of white Europeans, who came in the great immigration wave of the nineteenth and early twentieth century, continue to lag behind according to most socioeconomic indicators of assimilation. Similar arguments are made about British blacks lagging behind other ethnic minorities in education and occupational outcomes.[28] Black people have come to be viewed as having "one recognizable set of behaviors and cultural practices that render them unassimilable": a pathological culture—a culture of poverty—characterized by "a sense of resignation or fatalism, an inability to delay gratification and plan for the future, low educational motivation, low social and economic aspiration, a trend toward female centered families, and an inadequate moral preparation for employment."[29] And in both the United States and Britain, blackness is seen as emblematic of criminality and economic disadvantage.[30]

Many scholars have critiqued this portrayal of black people where blackness connotes poverty and criminality. Some do not reject the conclusion that a culture of poverty exists but argue instead that the deleterious cultural behavior found in black communities is an adaptive response to key structural factors limiting economic opportunities.[31] These scholars point to institutional racism, residential segregation, and the concentration of poverty, poor-quality public schools in black neighborhoods, and a changing economic system in which well-paying manufacturing jobs have been replaced by poorly paid service jobs as key structural factors perpetuating black disadvantage and imperiling upward mobility among blacks.

Despite growing acknowledgment that ethnicity theory cannot satisfactorily explain the challenges to assimilation of nonwhite groups, including blacks, Asians, and Hispanics, many studies on the children of black immigrants operate with the assumption that native blacks possess a deleterious set of attitudes and behaviors.[32] One of the most notable examples of this in assimilation scholarship is segmented assimilation theory.

This view that black people are a single ethnic bloc with a deficient culture is also shared in Britain. Britain does not have as influential a theory of second-generation assimilation as segmented assimilation theory, but Tariq Modood, a premier immigration and race and ethnicity scholar in Britain, suggests that the theory is applicable. In an article examining why Indians, Pakistanis, and Chinese are overrepresented in higher education compared to white Britons and British blacks, he argues that "the motor of the British South Asians and Chinese overcoming of disadvantage lies in migrant parents getting their children to internalize high educational ambitions and to enforce appropriate behavior."[33] In contrast, he posits that British blacks have a working-class culture that fails to intergenerationally transmit goal-oriented identities to children. Black youth culture, in Modood's assessment, is characterized by "Hollywood, soap operas, music, clothes fashions, celebrities, football, pubs, clubs, and binge drinking."[34] He adds that British blacks not only personify this dominant working-class culture but also impress it on others, as they have "come to be a leading-edge presence, quite remarkable for a group that is less than 2 percent of the population, stigmatized, and economically disadvantaged."[35]

Like the authors of segmented assimilation theory, Modood conflates race and ethnicity for black people in Britain by not distinguishing between Caribbeans and Africans or the different national groups that fall under these broad regional and continental categories. As in the United States, national origin, specificity of the country and its historical links with Britain, ethnicity, religion, and social class status (for the group and the individual) are not seen as factors that can lead to disaggregation within the black category. Overall, Modood treats British blacks as a single ethnic group with a working-class culture that undermines their socioeconomic success in a way similar to the oppositional culture of American blacks. And similar to how Asian immigrants in the United States are depicted by segmented assimilation scholars as possessing social capital, Modood concludes that Asian parents "have little credence in this [working-class culture] domain and try to limit their children's exposure to it."[36] Modood implies that the working-class culture found among the black British is contagious, and while it is found predominantly among black Caribbeans, it negatively impacts black Africans too. Hence Modood's failure to distinguish between black Africans and black Caribbeans. His statements also indicate a theoretical conceptualization of blackness that, just like in the U.S. literature, connotes a disadvantaged class experience.

Taken together, it is presumed that just like in the United States different ethnic minority groups in Britain exhibit different modes of cultural assimilation due to competing cultural values. The high levels of university enrollment among South Asians and Chinese can be purportedly explained by their having a "better culture" than British blacks, a culture that passes on goal-oriented identities. Asians' high levels of educational attainment are reportedly explained by the social capital available in their ethnic communities, forms of social capital that promote high educational attainment, which are not found among the black British. In sum, British blacks eschew education, leading them to lower achievement, while South Asians and Chinese reject British working class culture—often racially depicted as black—and thus achieve socioeconomic success.

Segmented assimilation theory has been criticized for failing to recognize the existence of a black middle class. It has also been challenged for ignoring minority cultures of mobility among blacks that may foster assimilation. Minority cultures of mobility are "a set of cultural elements associated with a minority group . . . that provides strategies for managing economic mobility in the context of discrimination and group disadvantage."[37] Finally, it fails to recognize that being a member of a racialized minority offers not just disadvantages but access to certain programs, most notably affirmative action policies, that facilitate the black second generation's upward social mobility.[38]

Despite this particular view of blackness that informs key studies on the black second generation, we know very little about the identity formation process and ethnic identities of members of the black second generation in the United States or elsewhere.[39] Segmented assimilation theory's prediction that identity formation among the black second generation results in a reactive black ethnicity characterized by oppositional culture[40] was formulated at the turn of the twenty-first century when African immigrants and their children were not as significant a presence in both size and cultural impact in the United States and Britain.

In this book I take a different approach. First, I conceptualize the context of reception, a key dimension of segmented assimilation theory, to include additional factors affecting assimilation outcomes. In the course of my investigation, I discovered that each country's history, both general and specific to the immigrant group, is an extremely important aspect of the context of reception. Another set of important factors is a country's colonial history, national identity, and national myths. I found that Britain's colonial history was a critical element in understanding the racism Nigerians experience in Britain, as well as how the Nigerian second generation related to the nation and fashioned their ethnic identities. The Nigerian second generation in the United States were also affected by that country's history with black people and attempts to redress its racist past. The presence of a proximal host and interactions with this group are additional and important aspects of the context of reception for the black second generation. It is not just race that affects the identity formation process of the second generation. Interethnic relations between the groups, even as they all reside in countries that racialize them as black, is a key determinant of how the black second generation identifies.

Second, I extend segmented assimilation theory and the racialization framework by identifying several mechanisms that show how ethnicity and class matter in the assimilation outcomes of the black second generation, even in racialized societies such as the United States and Britain. The theory of segmented assimilation has been criticized for coming dangerously close to labeling some cultures as bad and others as good and for reproducing commonly held stereotypes that Asian culture is good and black and Hispanic cultures are bad.[41] But culture is not intrinsic to members of an ethnic group. Rather, culture develops out of structural arrangements within the ethnic community and in interaction with the wider society. Therefore, it is necessary to study different black immigrant communities to uncover whether, and in what ways, ethnicity is deployed as a resource and form of capital as it reportedly is by some Asian groups. In this book, I show how ethnic resources in Nigerian communities in the United States and Britain affect the identities and assimilation trajectories of the Nigerian second generation. In so doing, I extend the ethnicity-as-capital framework to the black second generation. Finally, as almost all the respondents in this book are middle-class professionals, their experiences add to our knowledge about the ethnic diversity of the black middle class.

THEORIES OF SECOND-GENERATION ASSIMILATION

The defining characteristic of contemporary migration to the United States, which began after the passage of the 1965 Immigration and Nationality Act abolishing the national origins quota system and replacing it with a preference system focusing on immigrants' skills and family relationships with citizens or U.S. residents, is that most immigrants are nonwhites from Latin America, Asia, the Caribbean, and Africa. A compelling question for immigration scholars is whether these immigrants will assimilate in the same manner as the earlier wave of white immigrants from Europe. For white immigrants who came into the United States between the eighteenth century and the early twentieth, assimilation occurred in generational steps, with subsequent generations becoming economically more successful and integrated into the American mainstream as they increasingly shed their ethnic cultures.

Immigration researchers doubt that nonwhite immigrants will have a similar assimilation experience. Some conclude that nonwhite immigrants, especially blacks and Hispanics, will be racialized and discriminated against because they are not white and thus will experience blocked mobility or downward trajectories.[42] The theory of racialization for the second generation developed from a study of second- and third-generation Mexican Americans and posits that "the strong force of assimilation in American society may be slowed or even halted by the counterforce of racialization." Further: "Today racial distinctions continue to be popularly accepted as natural divisions of humanity with an implicit racial hierarchy that largely defines one's place in society. The accumulation of racially discriminatory treatment disproportionately sorts those stigmatized into the bottom strata of class even as it privileges others."[43] Segmented assimilation theory, which sought to understand how race along with other factors complicated the pathway of assimilation—a pathway heretofore thought to be straightforward, at least for white immigrants, took a similar tack, arguing that children of black immigrants because of racial proximity to native American blacks, racial prejudice, and residing in places with high unemployment, were at risk of downwardly assimilating into a rainbow underclass.[44]

A large-scale study of second-generation adults—Russian Jews, South Americans (specifically from Colombia, Peru, and Ecuador), West Indians, and the Chinese—found no evidence of a second- generation decline, with the exception of Dominican men. The authors argue that there was in fact a second-generation advantage, which was facilitated by the key mechanism they term cultural creativity. The second generation are able to choose which aspects of a given cultural model to adopt—from their parents' culture or the cultures found in their new country—and their selective and creative combination of the two are highly conducive to success.[45] The study found that ethnic identities of second-generation adults are "situational, variable, and hybrid" and that "rigid census or survey questions" asking the second generation about their race and ethnicity are seriously flawed because they "clash with the multiple and complex origins and layers of meaning available to these young people when they think about racial and ethnic identity."[46]

Recent studies on second and subsequent generations of Mexican Americans find conflicting evidence on whether or not they are experiencing a downward decline. A large-scale study in California found that while there was no second-generation decline among Mexican Americans, there was a third-generation decline.[47] Another study concluded that the fears that second- and third-generation Mexican Americans would not experience progress across generations, as was the case among Europeans, are unwarranted. This study found that "second and third generation Hispanic men have made great strides in closing their economic gaps with native whites."[48] Other studies have found that some Mexican Americans are experiencing upward mobility and have assimilated into white mainstream America. However, despite their advances, they are becoming a racialized minority in the United States because of growing nativist sentiment among segments of the American population in response to increased Mexican, and specifically illegal, migration.[49]

Among Asian groups, many second generations have done very well academically and professionally. As a result, they are viewed as the model minority in the United States. The term *model minority* is used to refer to a minority group (racial, ethnic, or religious) that successfully adapts despite experiencing discrimination. A model minority is associated with high achievement on measures such as education and income or low crime rates. This concept has been critiqued because it homogenizes and racializes Asian Americans while obscuring the fact that not all Asian groups are doing better than the U.S. national average.[50] And despite their socioeconomic success, second- and subsequent generation Asian Americans are still racialized as distinct from whites and thus as perpetual foreigners.[51]

Various studies have looked at how race and class affect the assimilation outcomes of second generation Latinos and Asians, but not much is known about how the intersection of race, class (both parental and individual), and ethnicity affects the assimilation outcomes of the black second generation. And this is especially true for the adult African second generation. Racialization, the process and practice of it, still leave open the possibility that racial status will matter more than social class status for black people, and ethnicity for black immigrants and their children. The predictions of a second-generation decline for blacks and darker-skinned Hispanics, as well as statements that Mexican Americans' experiences are becoming analogous to that of African Americans,[52] assume the existence of only poor blacks. These influential theories in the field of immigration give short shrift to how social class intersects with race, how ethnicity can be a source of capital, and how the interactive effects of these factors have an impact on groups of the black second generation.

Thus what I argue in this book is that for black, especially African, immigrants and their children, of whom very little is known in the United States and Britain, it is necessary to examine how the resources black immigrants bring with them—human, social, and financial capital—might make a difference in their children's assimilation pathways and in how they navigate the ethnoracial contexts of American and British society. Furthermore, segmented assimilation theory does not adequately theorize the roles ethnicity and class play in the assimilation outcomes of the black second generation. It is not clear whether the theory's prediction that a reactive black ethnicity and black identity as the mode of identity formation is equally applicable to second-generation blacks of all social class backgrounds. The theory acknowledges that most nonwhite children with middle-class and entrepreneurial parents will be able to meet the challenges of the structural barriers of race with some equanimity.[53] But it is silent on how children of black immigrants will do this and also whether variations in class backgrounds among the black second generation will lead to different modes of identity formation. The question thus becomes, is the prediction of forging a reactive black ethnicity and black identity applicable to second-generation blacks from middle- and upper-class backgrounds? Some studies seem to suggest so.[54] Empirically we don't know much about the identity formation process for black immigrants and their children from a certain class background who are not Caribbean. My study addresses this void by looking at children of Nigerian immigrants, most of whom are well educated and /middle class. Examining the experiences of the Nigerian second generation will answer these questions and ultimately provide a more nuanced consideration of how race, ethnicity, immigration, and class intersect for black people in American and British society.

How Do the Black Second Generation Identify?

A number of studies have investigated the question of how the black second generation identify and proffer a number of answers. A seminal study on second-generation West Indian youths found three options: a black American racial identity, whereby they see themselves as being in the same situation as African Americans; an ethnic or hyphenated foreign national identity, based on their parents' foreign identities and which involves some distancing from African Americans; or an immigrant identity, which was viewed as temporary.[55] Those who identified as black Americans were more likely to believe that their opportunities were constrained because they are black, whereas those with an ethnic identity were more likely to believe that if one strove hard enough one would be successful. There was a class difference: the majority of youths from middle-class backgrounds, 57 percent, ethnically identified, whereas just 8 percent of youths from poor families and 20 percent of youths from working-class families ethnically identified. But even among youths from middle class families, over a third (36%) identified as black American and the plurality of the youths from poor and working-class families (46 and 45 percent, respectively) identified as black American.

The study linked ethnic identity to mobility, finding that youths who ethnically identified were more successful.[56] Youths who ethnically identified believed America had made some racial progress. They felt that the white people they came in contact with were aware of their ethnic distinction from black Americans, and they went out of their way to signal their difference from black Americans. For the large number of youths from all social class backgrounds who chose to identify as black Americans, the stance of opposition that was an integral component of this identity was "in part a socialized response to peer culture" but for the most part came about as "a reaction to the teens' life experiences, most specifically, their experience of racial discrimination." The author concludes that "the lives of these youngsters basically lead them to reject the immigrant dream of their parents of individual social mobility and to accept their peers' analysis of the United States as a place with blocked social mobility where they will not be able to move very far. This has the effect of leveling the aspirations of the teens downward."[57] A few studies argue that being American identified and/or choosing the black American identity is not linked to mobility.[58]

A key theme emerging from the study of second-generation ethnicity is the notion of "hybridity" that the second generation is creating new ethnic identities and new cultural content that are a mixture of their parents' homelands and cultures and the cultures found in their countries of birth or receiving countries.[59] Thus they are ethnic hybrids, whose ethnic content is a mixture of their parents' and their receiving country's cultures. Several studies argue that the black second generation (both African and Caribbean) are bicultural—identifying with both their parents' country of origin and their receiving country.[60] Most simultaneously hold both racial and ethnic identities.[61] Some others hold gendered identities.[62] A study of middle-class Haitians found that they had three ethnic identity options: (1) they could become American blacks, giving up their ethnic identity for a racial identity; (2) they could keep both racial and ethnic identities; or (3) they could adopt a "stance of racelessness."[63] The authors of this study argued that the three alternatives open to middle-class Haitian immigrants are indicative of the alternatives that other middle-class black immigrants (first and second generation) will face. A new concept, situational ethnicity, captures the complexities of second-generation ethnic identities and is used to explain how an individual possesses multiple ethnic identities and deploys them at different times based on his or her reading of what the situation demands.[64]

In Britain, all ethnic minorities are said to choose between four strategies of self-identification.[65] These are the dissociative strategy, where categorization is in terms of ethnic minority membership, not the majority group; the assimilative strategy, where self-categorization emphasizes the majority group and denies ethnic minority roots; the acculturative strategy, where the self is categorized approximately equally along both dimensions; and the marginal strategy, where neither dimension is salient to self-categorization but other social categories are used, such as student or squash player. Some people may consciously decide not to choose an ethnic or majority group identity.[66] Second-generation black Caribbeans are found to largely identify as British, black British, or a combination of black, British, and Caribbean.[67]

While these studies on ethnic identities of the second generation have increased our knowledge on the ethnic options and choices of the second generation, they overlook two important factors that affect identity formation among the black second generation: the importance of the relationships between the second generation and their proximal hosts for identity formation and the assimilation process; and how the class status of the second-generation individual affects how they identify. In this book I detail how social class affects the formation of racial and ethnic identities among the Nigerian second generation in the United States and Britain, paying particular attention to how class identities become entangled with the ethnicity and racial and ethnic identities formed.

I further extend what we know about the ethnic identities of the second generation, especially the black second generation, by showing that they have more ethnic choices available to them. First, for the black second generation, to be American identified does not mean only taking an oppositional stance that lowers aspiration and effort and signals disillusionment with America; it can mean espousing beliefs and holding attitudes that locate the individual in the mainstream. Second, a pan-African identity is emerging among the Nigerian second generation that is meaningful in both countries but especially in Britain. This is a made-in-the-receiving-country—made in the USA, made in Britain—identity that is different from or in addition to the black, African American, or black British pan-ethnic identities existing theories predicted for the black second generation. Last, I find that the Nigerian second generation have developed a multifaceted identity that combines multiple meaningful identities into one, which captures the full complexity of their lived realities and how these individuals see themselves and want others to see them.

It is important at this point in the book to clarify concepts of blackness and how I define and use *blackness* and *black identity*. Blackness and the rules that define who is black are socially constructed. In the United States, the "one-drop rule" was institutionalized to determine who was black. This is a rule of hypodescent that defines as black any person with an ancestor hailing from the African continent, no matter how distant the relation, who provided a single drop of black blood to all descendants.[68] Consequently, black people in the United States who have ties to the African continent—old ties like those of African Americans descended from enslaved African Americans and more recent ties among contemporary (post-1965) black immigrants from the Caribbean and Africa—are all regarded as black. In Britain, even though blacks were not enslaved in the motherland but in British colonies, a racial hierarchy, similar to that found in the United States, was established that places whites at the top and blacks at the bottom. However, in both countries, but especially in the United States, numerous studies point to the increasing diversity within the black racial category based on class,[69] sexual orientation,[70] ideology, and ethnic differences,[71] which is chipping away at the notion of a monolithic blackness or undifferentiated mass of black people.

I take the position that there is no monolithic blackness in these countries, if we are conflating race, ethnicity, and identity into a single matrix. I critique the prevalent view found in key studies in the field of second generation assimilation that black identity and blackness is characterized by a black culture that is reducible to an oppositional culture that devalues schooling and work and stresses attitudes and behaviors antithetical and often hostile to success in the mainstream economy.

My use of the term *black racial identity* is narrowly conceptualized to emphasize two key points: the power of assignment into the black racial category and the implications of said assignment. I view the black identity as a black racial identity, which means that an individual is assigned to the black racial category and understands the implications of this ascribed racial group membership and its low placement on the racial hierarchy on the life chances of black people. The black racial identity can and often does unite all blacks and mobilizes them in a fight against racism and racial inequality.[72] Because the color lines of both Britain and the United States are in flux largely because of continued large-scale migration from nonwhite parts of the world and increasing bi- and multiracial populations,[73] I argue that individuals and groups in the black racial category in both countries have space to construct their own meanings of blackness, that is, what being black means to them outside of, or in addition to, being assigned to the black racial category.

NIGERIANS AND AFRICANS IN THE U.S. AND BRITISH DIASPORAS

A Brief Note about Nigeria

Before describing the Nigerian, or generally the African, diasporas in the United States and Britain I want to turn to the nation of Nigeria itself, briefly sketching its demographics, culture, geography, and economy. Located in West Africa, Nigeria is the most populous nation in Africa and the seventh most populous nation in the world. Nigeria's population in 2015 was estimated at 181 million, which constitutes 15 percent of the total African population.[74] Nigeria gained independence from Britain in 1960 and has since gone through a mix of democratically elected and military governments. It is on its fourth successive civilian government, the longest period of civilian rule in Nigeria since independence. Ninety-five percent of Nigeria's revenue, is from oil and gas exports.[75]

The Federal Republic of Nigeria has an area of 923,769 square kilometers, which makes it slightly more than twice the size of the state of California. The country is bordered on the west by the republics of Benin and Niger, on the east by Cameroon, on the north by Niger and Chad, and on the south by the Gulf of Guinea. There are 250 ethnic groups in Nigeria, with the three largest being the Hausa/Fulani (29 percent), Yoruba (21 percent), and Ibo (18 percent). Together they comprise 68 percent of the total Nigerian population.[76] Five hundred twenty languages are spoken in Nigeria, but English is the nation's official language, a bequest from its British colonial roots.

Nigeria's ethnic divisions correlate with regional partitions. Northerners are predominantly Hausas and Fulanis, while southerners and easterners are predominantly Ibos, Yorubas, Edo, Ijaw, and Itsekiri. The northern groups are predominantly Muslim, while the ethnic groups in the South are predominantly Christian. The southern groups are significantly more educated than the Hausas and Fulanis, which has led to the southern part of Nigeria having significantly higher educational levels than the northern regions. The adult literacy rate among Nigerians in the north is 35 percent, while the adult literacy rate in the south and southeast is more than twice that, 74 percent.[77] This educational gap shows up in who emigrates. Nigerian immigrants in advanced, democratic, Western countries are predominantly southerners and easterners from the most educated regions. The national literacy rate as reported by the 2006 Nigerian census is 67 percent.[78] While only 7 percent of Nigerians over the age of 25 have at least a bachelor's degree,[79] 61.4 percent of first-generation Nigerians over the age of 25 in the United States have at least a bachelor's degree—an educational profile that is even more striking when compared to the U.S. national average of 29.3 percent.[80] In the United Kingdom, 61 percent of first-generation Nigerians over the age of 25 have at least a bachelor's degree, compared to the U.K. national average of 28 percent.[81]

Most Nigerian immigrants are social and economic migrants. Nigerians did not begin to migrate in large numbers outside the region until after independence in 1960. The stream of largely highly skilled migrants to the United Kingdom continued after Nigerian independence, and an increasing number soon began to migrate and settle in the United States. As a result, the Nigerian diaspora in the United Kingdom is on the whole older than that in the United States.[82] From the 1950s through the 1970s, emerging Nigerian elites moved mainly to the United Kingdom because of the colonial relationship. Most relocated to pursue further studies and, during the 1960s and 1970s, returned to Nigeria and took up middle-class jobs in the Nigerian civil service, the booming oil industry, and the growing private sector.

After a report reviewing the state of education in Britain's colonies in the 1920s found that Africans were poorly educated and the educational facilities inadequate, several U.S. foundations began to sponsor Africans to study in the United States.[83] Many Nigerians took advantage of this opportunity. One of the first to do so was Nnamdi Azikiwe, who entered the United States in 1925 and attended Storer College, Lincoln University, and Howard University. After graduating, Dr. Azikiwe returned to Nigeria and became the nation's first governor general and then its first president.

Observing the success of the returned migrants, other Nigerians realized that having a college degree was a direct path to having a good job, a middle- or upper-class standard of living, and, for some, shaping policy in government. Individuals began to seek out foundations and organizations that could give them scholarships for further studies overseas. Members of various ethnic groups came to believe that educating a few members of their group would help improve the lives of all members and lead to positive development; consequently, they began to tax themselves to send some of their young men to the United States and Britain.[84] During this period, a steady stream of Nigerian students to the United States and Britain was established.

The rate of migration to countries in the West, especially the United Kingdom, the United States, and Canada, spiked sharply in the 1980s and has remained high because of economic and political instability in Nigeria. The collapse of the petroleum boom in the early 1980s and the roll-out of austerity measures mandated by the International Monetary Fund to bail out Nigeria from its debt and budgetary crisis in the mid-1980s devastated the Nigerian economy. These factors, coupled with the opportunity for self-advancement, better jobs, and security (both economic and personal), pushed Nigerians in large numbers out of Nigeria to Europe, the United States, and several Arab states. This led to what is commonly called the "brain drain"—the loss of highly skilled professionals, among them doctors, nurses, and teachers. Current economic hardships, political unrest in northern and southern Nigeria, and worsening security has kept the rate of migration out of Nigeria high. In 2011, the unemployment rate was 23.9 percent, and over 70 percent of the Nigerian population lives below the poverty line.[85]

The highly restrictive immigration policies used to vet Nigerians seeking entry into Western advanced democracies, combined with the push and pull factors mentioned above, have created a culture of professional migration among the Nigerian middle and upper classes. For most educated Nigerians, the United States and the United Kingdom have been the top destinations. But even as these countries have tried to restrict entry to Nigerians and people from other developing nations, they have created policies that grant permanent resident status to well-educated and highly skilled migrants. The United States issues HI-B employment visas, which allow employers to obtain work permits for immigrants who fill a need that purportedly cannot be drawn from the domestic labor market. The federal government also runs the Diversity Visa Lottery program, which grants permanent residence (green) cards to educated individuals and skilled artisans. In 2011, the United Kingdom, under the conservative government of Prime Minister David Cameron, ended its highly skilled immigrant visa program, a point-based system very similar to the one operated by Canada. All of these programs have been used by educated Nigerians as a "get-out-of-Nigeria" card. It is not uncommon for Nigerians in the United Kingdom to have family members and friends scattered across the United Kingdom, the United States, and, less so, Canada.

Nigerian migrants have become an important source of development for Nigeria via remittances—whether financial, technological, skill based, or networks. One major benefit of out-migration is the large amount of money immigrants send back to their home countries, money that supports families and spurs economic growth.[86] From 2007 to 2012, Nigerian immigrants all over the world sent payments totaling $178 billion to people living in Nigeria.[87]

Since the return of democracy in 1999 with the election of President Oluwasegun Obasanjo, the Nigerian government has shifted from a hands-off to a hands-on policy toward its citizens in the advanced democratic countries in Europe and North America. They are now recognized as important to Nigeria's development goals, and the government is instituting policies to tap into their resources, with a special focus on Nigerians living in the United States and United Kingdom.

In September 2000, President Obasanjo met in Atlanta, Georgia, with Nigerians living in the Americas. Later that year, he held a similar meeting in London with Nigerians living in Europe. The purpose of these meetings was to engage Nigerians in the diaspora and create a mechanism through which they could effectively be mobilized and participate in Nigeria's development. The Nigerians in the Diaspora Organization (NIDO) was established in 2001, with the mission of being a stronger partner in Nigeria's economic development. The Nigerian National Volunteer Service (NNVS), as part of the office of the Secretary to the Government of the Federation, was established in 2002 to mobilize Nigerians at home and in the diaspora to participate in volunteer activities complementing the government's development efforts. Another outcome of government-diaspora interaction was the 2002 decision to allow Nigerians to hold dual citizenship.[88]

The Nigerian federal government also established the Department of Diaspora, with plans to upgrade the department to a Diaspora Commission in the Ministry of Foreign Affairs. Former President Goodluck Jonathan announced in April 2010 that the new commission would comprehensively harmonize the contributions of Nigerians abroad with a view to ensuring proper documentation of their input. As a commission, the organization will have more resources and powers, as well as a board of directors to oversee its affairs. The government has also established an 80 billion naira (about US$500 million) investment fund so that the diaspora can invest in the Nigerian economy. According to the proposal, any Nigerian citizen interested in furthering the country's industrialization but who lacks the means to do so can draw from the fund, which is part of the larger National Resource

Fund meant for local capacity building, technology transfer, and product standardization to boost the country's export of manufactured goods. July 25 has been designated Nigerian Diaspora Day, celebrating the individual and collective successes of Nigerians abroad and recognizing their contributions to nation building. All these initiatives are in the very early stages, and while their full impact is unknown, they seem to have resulted in getting some highly skilled Nigerians to return home.

The African Diaspora in the United States

Africans are the fastest growing black population in the United States, but the Caribbean population is larger and has been in the country about a generation longer. Together, the presence of these groups is increasing the ethnic, cultural, and socioeconomic diversity of blacks in the United States. According to the 2013 American Community Survey, Caribbeans comprise 9.3 percent (3.73 million) of the foreign-born population, compared to 4 percent for Africans. Of the approximately 1.9 million foreign-born Africans in the United States, 1.4 million are black Africans.[89] In 2000, there were 881,300 Africans in the United States, meaning the population grew at a rate of 82 percent in the first decade of the twenty-first century. According to the 2013 American Community Survey (ACS), the largest populations of first-generation African immigrants hail from Nigeria (228,000), Ethiopia (195,000), Egypt (183,000), Ghana (150,000), and Kenya (121,000).[90]

Putting these numbers in context, since the liberalization of U.S. immigration policy in 1965, the number of first-generation immigrants has climbed from 9.7 million, which was 5.4 percent of the total U.S. population in 1960, to 42.2 million in 2014, which is 13.2 percent of the total U.S. population. All nonwhite immigrant groups, and not just Africans, have grown significantly in population size since 1965. The number of immigrants from Asia has grown from 825,000 individuals in the United States in 1970, or 8.6 percent of the total immigrant population, to 12.75 million in 2014, or 30.1 percent of the total immigrant population. The number of immigrants from the Americas has increased from 2.6 million in 1970, or 27.1 percent of the total immigrant population, to 22.7 million in 2014, or 53.6 percent of the total immigrant population. The number of immigrants from Africa has grown from just 80,000 individuals in 1970, or 0.8 percent of the total immigrant population, to 1.93 million in 2014, or 4.6 percent of the total immigrant population.[91] The number of immigrants from Europe fell from 59.7 percent of the total immigrant population (5.74 million) in 1970 to just 11.2 percent of the total immigrant population (4.76 million) in 2014.[92]

Nigerians in the United States

Nigerians are the largest national group from Africa in the United States. They comprise 19 percent of all first-generation black Africans in the United States, a significant size given that forty-eight countries make up sub-Saharan (black) Africa.[93] A report on the Nigerian diaspora by the Migration Policy Institute calculates that there are 376,000 first- and second-generation Nigerians in the United States. They estimate that there are 163,000 U.S.-born (second-generation) Nigerians with at least one Nigerian-born parent in the United States.[94]

Nigerians are the most educated group of all immigrants in the United States.[95] According to the 2014 American Community Survey, 63 percent of Nigerians have at least a bachelor's degree, compared to the national average of 29 percent, 32 percent for whites, 47 percent for Asians, 12 percent for Hispanics, and 19 percent for African Americans.[96] They are very well educated, due to the type of immigrants who migrate out of Nigeria and the highly restrictive immigration policies put in place by the U.S. government to control migration from (especially black) developing countries. Many who migrated to Britain between the 1960s and 1970s for further education returned to Nigeria. Yet most Nigerians who migrated to the United States came intending to remain permanently.[97] Since the 1990s, a significant number of Nigerians have come into the United States under the Diversity Visa Lottery system, which was passed by the U.S. Congress in the late 1980s to balance the racial mix of new immigrants.[98] A total of 50,000 permanent resident (green) cards are awarded each year, and Nigerians are frequently one of the top recipient groups. In 2010, for example, 6,006 Nigerians were successful in getting green cards through this program. Turkey, with 2,826 recipients, came in second, and Iran, with 2,773 recipients, rounded out the top three.[99]

The median household income for Nigerians living in the United States is $61,289, compared to the median household income of $53,482.[100] In 2010, Nigerian men who worked full-time earned a median income of $50,000, compared to $46,000 for all U.S.-born men. Almost 25 percent of Nigerian U.S. households make over $100,000 a year, compared to 10.6 percent of African American households; and over 5 percent of Nigerian households earn over $200,000 a year, compared to 1.3 percent of African Americans.[101]

The top three regions where Nigerians are located are New York City, Maryland-Washington, DC-Virginia, and Texas.

The majority of Nigerians in the United States live in urban areas. They tend to be found in low- to middle-income neighborhoods that are extremely diverse, composed of significant numbers of other African immigrants as well as Hispanic and Caribbean immigrants. I use data from Boston and New York, which provide information on immigrants' residential patterns by national origin, to illustrate Nigerians residential patterns in cities. In Boston, Nigerians are found in the diverse neighborhoods of Dorchester and Hyde Park, which are majority minority and home to large numbers of African Americans and other black and Latin American immigrant groups. In New York, Nigerians are found in extremely diverse neighborhoods that have significant numbers of immigrants and especially in neighborhoods with sizable Caribbean, other African, and African American populations.[102] A sizable community of Nigerians (approximately 28 percent of Nigerians in New York) live in the Bronx, along with other Africans (especially Ghanaians), Caribbeans, and immigrants from Latin America.[103] Another 28 percent of Nigerians in New York live in Brooklyn, in neighborhoods with large numbers of Caribbeans, even though, overall, Asians are the dominant foreign-born immigrant group in Brooklyn. A third of Nigerians live in Queens in Caribbean neighborhoods and about 10 percent live in Staten Island.[104]

The African Diaspora in Britain

The 2011 U.K. Census revealed a major shift in the origins of the majority black group in Britain. In 2001, Afro-Caribbeans were the largest black group, but Africans soon became the larger group. From 2001 to 2011, the number of black people from Africa rose from 0.9 percent (484,783) to 1.7 percent (989,628) of the general U.K. population. During the same ten-year period, the black Caribbean population remained steady at 1.1 percent, increasing by only 29,204 people (a 3.3 percent increase). The black African population has doubled because of refugees and new migration patterns from many former colonies of Britain, where push-pull factors of political and economic stability have interacted with the perception of better opportunities and safety in Britain. The growth in the black African population is also due to those who settled and started having children. It is unclear whether the face of black Britain will change from black Caribbean to black African now that the latter are the larger group. In the same time period, 2001 to 2011, the Indian population grew from 1.05 million to 1.45 million, a growth rate of 37.82 percent; Pakistanis grew from 747,285 to 1.17 million, a population increase of 57 percent. Bangladeshis grew from 283,063 to 451,529, a growth rate of 59.5 percent; and the Chinese grew from a population of 247,403 to 433,150, a growth rate of 75 percent.[105] In short, Britain is becoming increasingly diverse ethnically and racially. Between 1993 and 2014, the foreign-born population in the United Kingdom doubled from 3.8 million to around 8.3 million. And in 2014, 13.1 percent of the U.K. population was foreign born, up from 7 percent in 1993.[106]

Nigerians in Britain

Nigerians are the largest national group from Africa in Britain. In 2001, there were 88,105 first-generation Nigerians living in the United Kingdom. By 2011, that number had risen to 191,000. Roughly one of every five black Africans in Britain is Nigerian. The number would be even greater if we added second-generation Nigerians, which we cannot do because it is impossible to identify them from the census data. Nigerians are the most educated immigrant group in the United Kingdom, and their educational advantage has carried over to the second generation.[107] Nigerians in Britain earn more than the national average income.[108]

The majority of Nigerians, three quarters of them, live in London. They are dispersed across the city, but most reside in the South London boroughs of Southwark and Lambeth and the London boroughs of Hackney and Camden. Most African immigrants live in neighborhoods with high concentrations of other African immigrants, but they are not trapped in these neighborhoods; many every year move into neighborhoods in London and Britain generally that have a lower concentration of Africans.[109] Thus, unlike in the United States, Nigerians as well as other Africans are not living in highly segregated neighborhoods in Britain.

Peckham in South London is home to the highest concentrations of Nigerians. It has become known within the community as the Yoruba heartland or mini-Lagos, and many of its businesses—hair salons, radio stations, butcher shops, newspaper vendors, real estate offices, and boutiques—are owned and run by Nigerians. Peckham is a low- to middle-income neighborhood. It is a majority minority neighborhood: whites are 29.2 percent of the neighborhood population, compared to 9.1 percent Asians, 7.1 percent mixed ethnic groups, and 50.4 percent blacks/Africans/Caribbeans. Among individuals of working age in Peckham, 34.5 percent are economically inactive and 19.7 percent receive welfare. Just 22 percent of Peckham residents own their own homes, which is 33 points lower than the national average. Fifty-nine percent of residents live in social housing, compared to the national average of 18 percent.[110] The borough of Southwark, which includes Peckham, falls in the bottom half of all thirty-two London boroughs on indices of poverty and neighborhood disadvantage.[111] And Peckham is more disadvantaged in terms of home ownership rates, proportion of welfare recipients, and proportion living in social housing than the borough as a whole. It is also more residentially segregated, with 40 percent fewer whites than in England generally.[112]

With the majority of Nigerians in the country living in close proximity, these London neighborhoods contain many ethnic Nigerian shops and businesses. Diners can choose from among more than three hundred Nigerian restaurants in London. There are numerous Nigerian shops that sell Nigerian goods such as clothing like *adire* (tie-dye) and *aso-oke* (a woven cloth indigenous to the Yoruba) and groceries.[113] Boroughs such as Lewisham and Southwark have a flourishing trade in "Nollywood" films. Nigerians in London practice a wide range of religions: an array of Christian Pentecostal churches—including the Eternal Sacred Order of Cherubim and Seraphim and the Celestial Church of Christ (so-called white garment churches), the Redeemed Christian Church of God (RCCG), and Christ Embassy—in addition to many Catholic, Anglican, Methodist, and Baptist churches and Islamic mosques.

The interracial marriage rate between Africans and whites in Britain is much lower than the intermarriage rate between black Caribbeans and whites. For black Africans, it stands at 13.6 percent for males and 8.4 percent for females. For black Caribbeans the black-white intermarriage rate is 35.9 percent for males and 22.5 percent for females.[114] A possible explanation for this is that over half the black Caribbean population in Britain is British born, whereas the great majority of the African population in Britain is still first generation. By the 1990s over half of all black Caribbeans were British born, and these individuals have increased the overall intermarriage rate of the group. Indeed, we see the influence of assimilation: both second-generation black Africans and black Caribbeans intermarry at much higher rates than their first-generation coethnics.[115]

Nigerians in Britain are the most educated immigrant group, with over 61 percent of the first generation over the age of 25 having at least a bachelor's

TABLE 1 Educational Qualifications of Major Ethnic/Racial Groups in the United Kingdom

	Whites	Chinese	Bangladeshis	Indians	Pakistanis	Caribbeans	Africans (without Nigerians)	Nigerians
High school diploma or less	60.9%	41%	74.4%	40.3%	64.7%	69.8%	56%	29.8%
Associate's degree or less	7.3%	4.6%	5.7%	5.4%	5.1%	8.5%	10.5%	0.7%
Bachelor's degree and higher	31.8%	54.4%	19.9%	54.4%	30.2%	21.8%	33.5%	61.1%
Total	100	100	100	100	100	100	100	100

NOTE: All columns are for first-generation immigrants over the age of 25. Data computed from the 2014 British Labor Force Survey.

degree.[116] See table 1 for the educational profile of the main racial and ethnic groups in the United Kingdom using the 2014 Labor Force Survey. Using a pooled sample of the 2005–6 General Household Survey, which was discontinued in 2007 and which was the only national British data set that allows identification of Nigerians by generational status, 65.4 percent of second-generation Nigerians over the age of 18 had at least a bachelor's degree.[117]

In summary, Africans in the United States and Britain are transforming the economic, cultural, and ethnic landscapes of these countries. In addition to starting a variety of businesses, they have established a niche in the health industry—working as doctors, nurses, certified nursing assistants, and lab technicians—in both countries. They are a significant presence on college and university campuses in both countries. In the United States, many Africans are entering the military.[118] Most maintain transnational ties with their home countries and send significant remittances to their home countries, to the point where monetary remittances in most African countries have surpassed foreign direct investment. And as they maintain these transnational ties, alongside strong national and ethnic identities, and introduce their diverse cultures into their new countries, Africans are diversifying and enriching black spaces and black communities, expanding the range of black identities that can be and are being formed and transforming wider British and American society.

THE RESPONDENTS

Education and Occupation Outcomes

As I mentioned in the introduction, the question that initially motivated me to do this study was how the children of well-educated African immigrants are doing compared to their parents. After narrowing my target population to the Nigerian second generation, I found that they are doing very well. Over 95 percent have at least a bachelor's degree, and almost all of them are professionals. These outcomes are consistent with social stratification and mobility literature. That is, a child whose father has a bachelor's degree is more likely to also have a bachelor's degree compared to a child whose father has minimal schooling.

In Britain, 78 percent of my respondents' fathers have at least a bachelor's degree (60.6 percent have a bachelor's degree, 14.1 percent have a professional degree, and 7 percent have a postgraduate degree). Seventy-one percent of their mothers have at least a bachelor's degree (55.6 percent have a bachelor's

	Education		Occupation	
	Britain	*U.S.*	*Britain*	*U.S.*
Maintained Father's Class (Stable)	27	17	52	36
Upward Mobility	29	15	10	15
Downward Mobility	6	17	3	5
Horizontal*	11	19	1	2

* In a different occupational class from father but in the same class stratum.

degree, 9.7 percent have a professional degree, and 6 percent have a post-graduate degree). These figures reveal that the majority of my respondents' parents are or were elites. Among the respondents, 91 percent have at least a bachelor's degree (48.6 percent have a bachelor's degree, 21.6 percent have a professional degree, and 21.6 percent have a postgraduate degree). The positive difference of 13 percentage points between fathers and children who have at least a bachelor's degree indicates that upward educational mobility has occurred. None of the 75 respondents in my study was illiterate; only 6 had less than a bachelor's degree, and of these 6, only 2 had less than some college. The educational attainment levels of my respondents and their parents are significantly higher than the average national educational attainment distribution for black Africans in Britain.

My respondents living in the United States are also extremely well educated. Eighty-four percent of their fathers and mothers have at least a bachelor's degree (of the fathers, 44.1 percent have postgraduate degrees, 8.8 percent have professional degrees, and 30.9 percent have bachelor's degrees; of the mothers, 32.9 percent have postgraduate degrees, 5.5 percent have professional degrees, and 45.2 percent have bachelor's degrees). That the parents of my U.S. respondents are highly educated is typical of highly skilled migration streams. Ninety-three percent of my respondents have at least a bachelor's degree (18.7 percent have postgraduate degrees, 21.3 percent have professional degrees, and 53.3 percent have bachelor's degrees). Table 2 summarizes how well the second generation in my study did educationally and occupationally compared to their fathers. Most were either stable, meaning that they replicated their fathers' class positions, or upwardly mobile, meaning that they improved upon those positions. A minority did worse than their fathers;

for all but three cases this was because of the class typology used.[119] There is a great deal of pressure on the second generation in Nigerian communities in the United States and Britain to do very well in school because being successful is increasingly defined as part of their ethnicity (see chapters 2 through 4 for a more detailed discussion). In both countries, Nigerian immigrants have had significant educational advantages—advantages that they have successfully transmitted to their children.

Neighborhood Context

Most respondents in the United States grew up in racially mixed or predominantly black neighborhoods. Studies on residential segregation in the United States find that black immigrants tend to live in close proximity to African Americans, either in the same neighborhoods or in neighborhoods surrounding poorer African American neighborhoods.[120] In Britain, the older second generation grew up in predominantly white neighborhoods because there were not many Africans or Caribbeans in Britain, especially outside of London, in the 1960s and 1970s. However, the younger second generation, those who grew up in the 1990s and 2000s, said they lived in racially mixed neighborhoods. Because Britain is not as residentially segregated as the United States, respondents who grew up in London and its suburbs were more likely to have had some racial mixture in their neighborhoods. Those who grew up in the northern cities of Liverpool and Manchester grew up in mostly white neighborhoods and in them had significant racial conflict with their white peers.

The majority of respondents in the United States and Britain went to neighborhood public schools that were predominantly black or racially mixed, although some older respondents, who grew up during the 1960s and 1970s, attended predominantly white schools. In the United States, some of the second generation went to magnet or public charter schools. Their parents wanted them to attend good schools but could not afford private schools; they viewed magnet schools as an excellent alternative. A few respondents who grew up in Britain went to posh private schools.

Family Life

Research shows that growing up with two parents is an advantage because it increases the number of adults who are available to provide support, both material and nonmaterial, to the child. Studies show that children who grow up in single-parent households or with absent fathers are disadvantaged in numerous ways. These children are more likely to drop out of high school, less likely to attend college, and less likely to graduate from college than children raised by both biological parents. Girls whose fathers are absent are more likely to become sexually active at a younger age and to have a child outside of marriage. Boys who grow up without their fathers are more likely to have trouble finding (and keeping) a job in young adulthood.[121]

Data from national surveys show that second-generation Africans are more likely to grow up in two-parent households than their African American and Caribbean peers.[122] Most of the second generation in this study grew up in two-parent households. For some, it took a while for one parent to join the family in the United States or Britain. Some (20 percent) had divorced parents, but I was unable to determine if there is a higher rate of divorce among first-generation immigrants compared to nonmigrants in Nigeria because the data are unavailable.

Transnational Social Fields

Immigration researchers define *transnationalism* as the "processes by which immigrants forge and sustain multi-stranded social relations that link together their societies of origin and settlement."[123] These relations are maintained through economic contributions, such as sending money back home or starting businesses; engaging in social activities, often sponsored by ethnic organizations; or political participation. Most parents of the second generation in this study engaged in transnational activities. Over 70 percent of these parents belonged to ethnic associations, and they often took their children along to the social gatherings sponsored by them. The parents saw doing so as a way to expose their children to their ethnic cultures and traditions. Most parents traveled frequently back to Nigeria but usually did not take their children with them. However, many of the second generation did visit Nigeria at least once. Despite minimally engaging in transnational activities themselves (see appendix B), the second generation is embedded in transnational social fields because of their parents' transnational activities and concerted efforts to expose and immerse their children in their ethnic cultures.

I asked respondents if their parents had shared stories with them about their reactions to life in Britain and the United States on arrival. Some parents had done so, and most of their stories shared themes of how unprepared they were for the cold winters and their experiences of racial discrimination. Most parents had come to pursue further education. Some of them found it difficult to secure jobs and housing in Britain. Those who came to the country in the 1950s and 1960s told their children about seeing signs in windows declaring, "No Irish, No Dogs, and No Coloreds Allowed." Many respondents' mothers in the United States had to retrain as nurses because they could not get good jobs using the skills and educational qualifications they obtained in Nigeria.[124]

CONCLUSION: THE IMPORTANCE OF CONTEXT

For the second generation of Nigerian ancestry, the racism of British and American societies is an important aspect of their contexts of reception. While the racialization processes in these countries differ significantly, there are a few striking similarities. We see the similarities in the settlement and treatment of racialized immigrants and in terms of the discrimination, racism, and hostility directed at them. We see it in how the state manages the entrance of racialized ethnic minorities as well as the resistance and resilience of racialized minorities in their efforts to survive and succeed. But even within these largely similar ethnoracial systems that have placed black people on one side of the color line, their demographic profiles differ, as do the broader historical and current political contexts. Thus the way race is framed in the two countries differs and is reflected in how the Nigerian second generation form their racial and ethnic identities.

The contexts of reception consist of other elements. The Nigerian second generation belong to diasporic communities that are the largest of all African groups in both the United States and Britain. The Nigerian migration into both countries is characterized by the movement of elites. This has created diasporic Nigerian communities in which the majority of first generation immigrants are well educated. The second generation of Nigerian ancestry in both countries had early family experiences that existing research tells us will give them some advantages into adulthood. They were more likely to grow up in two-parent households, and with parents who were highly educated. As adults, almost all have replicated or improved on their fathers' educational level. However, despite acknowledging the advantages possessed by these adults because of their parents' class location and high levels of human capital, not all came from affluent backgrounds, which was more common in Britain than in the United States.

The influential studies of the black second generation employing the racialization framework have posited blackness as disadvantaged. Yet these studies pay scant attention to how social class intersects with race and ethnicity and how these intersections for the black second generation lead to different social outcomes than predicted. Also, the framework of racialization elides the theoretical and empirical point of interest: how ethnic diversity among black people is playing out on the ground in British and American society. Three main research questions are asked in this book: *How does the national context of the United States and Britain affect ethnic and racial identity formation among the Nigerian second generation? How do the proximal hosts in each country influence ethnic and racial identity formation among the Nigerian second generation? How does the ethnicity of the Nigerian second generation interact with their racial status, and how does the interaction, along with social class, affect their identity choices?* In seeking answers, I hope to increase our theoretical insight into the complexities of racial framings and the intersections of race, class, and ethnicity for black people in British and American society.

TWO

"You Are Not Like Me!"

THE IMPACT OF INTRARACIAL DISTINCTIONS
AND INTERETHNIC RELATIONS
ON IDENTITY FORMATION

Kemi Oluto is a twenty-seven-year-old lawyer with her own small law practice. She lives in Texas. Both her parents have postgraduate degrees and are teachers. During her time in middle school, from her parents' and her personal interaction with some African Americans, Kemi learned that she was ethnically different. During middle school, Kemi said, "I had a lot of African Americans giving me a hard time for not doing what they were doing." They made fun of her "because of the way that [she] talked." They told her, "'You talk like a white girl.' But we did not grow up talking in slang. I had a lot of that." Kemi told me that her fraught relations with her proximal host peers "made me not like African American kids because they abused me a lot."

Kemi was viewed as an African by many of her African American peers. They told her Africans were people who were "smelly and less attractive" and did not conform culturally to the African American style of speech. But at the same time, many of her teachers viewed African students as better academically than African American students. Kemi also actively educated her teachers on the difference. As she put it, "I would educate them about it." At her school the widely held perception of Nigerians and Africans in general was that "Africans were so studious, that there are so many of us that were trying to go to college and they [some of her African American teachers] wished they could see that in their younger ones."

In college Kemi was again confronted with the social distance between Africans and African Americans when a student organization tried to encourage dialogue between the two groups. She recalled, "African Americans wanted to know why Africans don't like them." It was a very emotional meeting that "broke a lot of Africans down because they had to talk about when they were young. They said that African Americans teased us, that you said that we looked a certain way. That we smelled . . . and the African Americans said, 'You all like to hang out with white people,' and the African students said, 'But the white kids did not tease us the way you did.' I had to explain that the funny thing is it that it hurts more when it's coming from someone of your own color because you think—you already know the white man is going to act racist against you . . . but it hurts more that the person of your same color is also not your brother or your sister."

The question addressed in this chapter is how the children of first-generation Nigerian immigrants first came to learn that they are black but different. I discuss the first factor in beyond racialization theory: the extremely influential role relations with proximal hosts play in shaping ethnic identity. I consider how they identify as simultaneously black, holding a black racial identity, and ethnically different from their proximal hosts, African Americans in the United States and Caribbeans in Britain. As I show, for many the process began during childhood. Because the United States and Britain racialize ethnic minorities, especially black people, and puts them on one side of a stark racial divide opposite white people, little attention is paid to how children of black immigrants from Africa and the Caribbean relate to the more established black groups in these countries. Despite scholars' conclusion that ethnicity ultimately does not matter for black immigrants and their children because of racialization, we still need to know if different black groups, especially the black second generation, accept being indistinguishable from their proximal hosts without contestation. As I show in this chapter, the responses to racialization among the Nigerian second generation are more complex than previous scholarship has discussed.

The research questions addressed in this chapter are the following:

1. How, according to my respondents, did proximal hosts respond to the second generation during childhood to early adulthood?

2. Were their reactions welcoming, hostile, or indifferent or a combination of any of the three? If relations were rife with tension, what was the source of friction?

3. How does national context matter? Are there national differences in relations between the proximal host and the second generation of similar ancestry?

To understand how their interactions with proximal hosts influenced respondents' identities, I utilize the framework provided by the migrant ethnogenesis theory on identity formation. This theory seeks to combine the micro and macro approaches to ethnicity, stressing "the point at which the structural conditions that shape the overall categories of ethnicity and the cognitive conditions which operate on the individual level to shape immigrant behaviors and identities converge."[1] According to the theory, a new immigrant's identity is shaped by three social actors. The first actor is the individual immigrant, who "uses elements of his or her own cognitive map to determine his or her own identity and attaches a positive or negative valence to that identity."[2] The second is "society at large, which uses elements (race, religion, etc.) to determine the immigrant's identity as well as to attach a positive or negative valence to that identity." The third actor is the *proximal host* and their response to the new immigrant. The proximal host is "the waiting category in the minds of the individuals in the receiving society" to which they would assign the immigrant.[3] By identifying the pivotal role in identity formation played by the proximal host, the theory incorporates how structural conditions and power dynamics inform categorization and illuminate immigrants' responses to being absorbed into the proximal host category. As black immigrants and their children settle in the United States and Britain, two societies with different racial framings and racial hierarchies from their home countries, how does the black second generation navigate these racial contexts? Given the relatively demeaned group status of their proximal hosts, how do we assess the ambivalent reaction the second generation and their parents have to being absorbed into these categories?

I expand the ethnogenesis model by addressing its underdeveloped aspects. In addition to these three actors, I show that other key social actors shape the second generation's identities. One of these is the parents, who play a pivotal role in how children navigate the racial contexts of American and British society. They help their offspring make sense of their tense relations with their proximal hosts and actively seek to provide an alternative option that balances their racial status (being black) while demarcating ethnic boundaries. In the next chapter, I discuss how teachers and other authority figures in the educational system are another set of actors that influence identity formation. In this case, from their interactions with teachers and other school administrators, students began to identify educational aspirations as an ethnic boundary distinguishing them from proximal hosts. Last, my findings show how schools are a major site of interaction with proximal hosts for the second generation.

BOUNDARIES BASED ON ORIGIN

"African Booty Scratchers" and "African Bubus"

Every respondent from the United States said they experienced discrimination from African Americans. The region or state in which they grew up made no difference. Nor did the neighborhoods where they grew up or whether they attended public or private schools. Fraught relations largely took the form of being on the receiving end of teasing, ridicule, and social ostracism. In Britain, most but not all respondents reported experiencing discrimination from Caribbeans. For some, this discrimination was very severe. In school and in her neighborhood, Michelle, who was introduced at the beginning of the book, had a "rough time" getting along with most of her black Caribbean peers. She recalled:

> I had a run-in with a girl who was a notorious bully and paradoxically was of Guyanan extraction herself but pretended that she was from Jamaica or wherever. She and I had a falling out, we weren't friends, but we had a little row during a class . . . sports, a PE lesson, and thereafter, really big bullying, really, really big; really bad. My best friend at the time, who is still one of my best friends, she is originally from Jamaica, it just became a case of she and I really. We went through a whole school year where other Caribbeans and the few Africans in the school were either part of the bullying group or they were too scared to be associated with us for fear of being bullied themselves. So we stuck together like glue. The bullying went up a level in the sense that we would come out of school and there would be a whole group of girls waiting for us. Somebody would say that they wanted to have a fight with me or with Nicole. It was a really horrendous time. We were frightened at times to go to school. She lived across the road from the school, but she had a stepfather, and he would say, "Look, you're gonna walk in there every day with your head held high," and he would come and meet us after school, and if anyone wanted to fight you, he would say, "Look, you have to do it 'cause otherwise it will never end."

However, she had close friends among the proximal host, even as other members of the proximal host were giving her a tough time in school. So the boundaries were not always clear-cut. For others, the discrimination played out as verbal abuse, teasing, and ridicule.

Some might be tempted to dismiss teasing as part of the normal scene of growing up, but for the Nigerian second generation teasing from proximal hosts had a more deleterious meaning: it marked them as different. Temitayo, a twenty-eight-year-old physician who came to the United States when she was two, explained, "Many of us have horror stories as children—the whole experience of being called 'African booty scratcher.' We were not beaten or hit, but these are emotional words—and words do break your bones. They always say only sticks and stones hurt, but words do hurt. They hurt more than violence sometimes." There is evidence of this cost carrying over into adulthood. Temitayo shared the experiences of one of her Nigerian friends who, she said, "told me, 'I cannot stand that I was called African booty scratcher, and because of that there is no way I can be friends with these people. They don't like me. They don't want me to be their friend. Why would they call me something like that?' And she is a grown woman telling me this. This was in college, and she still holds on to those hurts."

Kemi agreed that these fraught relations influence her perceptions of African Americans now as an adult. She said, "I still have that mentality that I don't understand African Americans. They comment that 'I don't like any of you [Africans]. You are mean to us.' And I have to explain to them that here is the deal, when some of us came here when we were younger you teased us in school." And "even till today, I do not have a lot of African American friends." An outgrowth of the tense relations is the social distance existing between many of the second generation and members of their proximal hosts as adults.

Respondents report that tense relations between the Nigerian second generation and members of their proximal hosts in both countries has resulted in unfamiliarity with each other. This was the experience of Linda, a twenty-four-year-old nurse in the United States.

> I grew up in a neighborhood with a lot of African Americans. And at some point I really did not enjoy it because I was made fun of by African Americans, and I figured they would be the people I would speak with or become close to, but they ended up making fun of me. So I found myself hanging out with Caucasians, Asians, Indians, and Hispanics. I did not fit in with the African Americans. Most of the African Americans that I dealt with always put the African stereotype on me. They kind of ostracized me. They called me "African booty scratcher." They didn't really understand my culture, and in a way, I did not understand their culture, and so that is where the bridge was broken when I was growing up.

When I asked her what the African stereotype was, she said, "That we were all as black as night; that we all had an odor; that we did not know how to speak English well. One good stereotype was that we were all smart." Most of the second generation report that they grew up hanging out with people from other ethnic and racial groups who they deemed friendlier.

Although second-generation Nigerians were discriminated against by both white and black peers, they experienced most of the ridicule from their proximal hosts. Tunji, a thirty-two-year-old management consultant in America who immigrated from Scotland at the age of seven, recalled, "African Americans were probably the worst group that called me names. It was always based on my African heritage, living in trees, monkey, African booty scratcher, stuff like that. It was a hundred percent black. In fact, I would say I didn't have a negative experience with white people until well into my twenties." It was the same for Gbenga, a thirty-two-year-old lawyer who came to the United States when he was seven. "I never had any issue with white kids. I was able to make friends with white kids. It was African American kids who gave me a tough time." According to Chinedum, a thirty-year-old manager who was born and raised in the United States, "white Americans weren't stupid enough to call me African booty scratcher. Whites did not make fun of my name. They would not dare come to my face and say 'African booty scratcher' like the African Americans." In America, respondents said white peers were not as hostile to Africans as African Americans were. Antiblack discrimination exists in the United States, of course, but at this stage in the lives of second-generation Nigerians, African Americans were the main antagonists. They were the ones who told the Nigerian second generation that they were uncivilized people from the deep jungle who were inferior to them. It is also possible that their white peers were more wary of antagonizing second-generation Africans because they were not sure how they would respond.

Respondents from Britain reported slightly different experiences. The Nigerian second generation living in Britain, especially those who grew up in the 1970s and 1980s and are in (or beyond) their late thirties, had frequent run-ins with white people. Magda, a British-born paralegal secretary who grew up in London, did not "have a very good experience" with white people and reported having very "racist experiences." She said, "When I was seven I was stoned. When I was ten, I was spat on. Every day in school I had people taunting my name." Respondents who grew up in the north of England, in towns like Liverpool and Manchester, had similar experiences. Michael, a forty-one-year-old financial analyst who was born and raised in Britain, shared his experience: "Primary school was rough because we lived in a predominantly white area. And that was pretty much what it was in the seventies because there were fewer blacks. England then is not like now. You hadn't all these political correctness and equal opportunities and so on. So for people to verbally and physically attack you wasn't uncommon. We used to defend ourselves. My parents physically fought people. We as kids physically fought people, and you also had the experiences of not being able to go out. Some groups like the National Front were marching and those kind of things."

White people in these times and in these cities wanted all black people gone from Britain. It did not make a difference whether they were Caribbean black or African black. This hostility in Britain was inflamed in the late 1960s with the rise of the British National Party, whose platform included the expulsion of all black immigrants. The conservative parliamentarian Enoch Powell's 1968 "rivers of blood" speech about the dangers of unrestricted immigration, which he said was compounded by immigrants' refusal to assimilate into British society, was well received by the nonblack British populace. That such racist and antiblack sentiments came from the lips of a high-ranking political figure gave the vitriol the sheen of respectability.[4] Once the British government and both parties, Conservative and Labor, saw how popular these anti-immigration calls were, they began an era of restrictive immigration policy that continues to this day.[5]

The Nigerian second generation in Britain were embattled on both sides—by their black proximal hosts and by their white neighbors. But respondents reported more problems with Jamaicans than any other Caribbean national group, primarily because Jamaicans are the largest Caribbean group in Britain, with some respondents perceiving Jamaicans to be the most aggressive of all Caribbeans. As in the United States, black Africans in Britain were also called "African booty scratcher" by proximal hosts. But the term most common in Britain was "African bubus," which is the equivalent of being called a monkey. They were also called "bush babies" and "slave babies." "Slave babies" is an interesting slur because the African second generation do not have a history of being enslaved by the West, a fact that they cite often to distinguish themselves from proximal hosts. Respondents who grew up in Britain in the 1960s to the 1980s had it worse than respondents who grew up in Britain in the 1990s and 2000s. The former group, who were in their thirties and forties at the time of my interviews, experienced much more verbal abuse. Some physically fought with Caribbeans. In some cases, knives and stones were used. But just as with the second generation in America, most of the conflict was expressed through demeaning racial/ethnic jokes.

The reasons for the interethnic conflicts varied, but the time period in which a respondent's childhood occurred is determinative. For those who were preteens and teenagers in the 1960s to 1980s, conflict with Caribbeans arose because they said the latter felt superior to Nigerians. During this period, Africans were seen as uncivilized people living in jungles. Respondents believe that from around the 1990s Caribbeans came to perceive Nigerians as arrogant because of their higher level of education. The history of slavery also was a factor. For example, a reason respondents, regardless of age, emphasized Jamaicans resenting Nigerians is that their ancestors sold Jamaicans into slavery. They told me that racial incidents between the two groups peaked in the mid-1990s and have since fallen.

Pejoratives such as "African booty scratcher" and "African bubu" were used to draw a boundary between the proximal host and the African second generation. Proximal hosts used these words because, according to respondents, they saw themselves as more civilized and as superior to Africans. Michelle remembered being surprised: "I realized all of a sudden, it was a big shock to me, coming from a school where I was totally accepted by *white people* to not be accepted by what I thought was my own kind and actually to be called 'African.' If someone called you 'African' it was an insult in my school."

The general response of the proximal host to the Nigerian second generation was surprising to respondents because they all originated from Africa, even if they had left the continent at different times.[6] Respondents said they believed African Americans felt that the centuries they had spent in the United States, even if a significant portion of it had been as slaves, had a civilizing influence. In comparison, Africans who recently arrived from the continent were perceived as coming from the bushes and closer to monkeys than human beings. Many of these views are drawn from the mass media's portrayal of Africa and its people. This seeped into one of the frequent comments made to the Nigerian second generation in both countries: "Go back to your jungle."

This negative view of Africans has changed significantly since the turn of the twenty-first century. Now most respondents concede that the reputation of most Africans, and in particular Nigerians, has improved in both countries.[7] One reason is the increasing numerical strength of Nigerians. More of them are now living in Britain and America, and it is more rare for an African and his or her siblings to be the only black students in a school. Another factor they cite is the increased African cultural presence. There are now numerous African restaurants and shops in many British and American cities. As Funke, a physician who lives in Texas, said, "Back in the day, you had to go to the Indian or Hispanic food store to buy African food. Now you can go to an African food store. There are tons of them. Before, if I wanted to buy lace, I would have to beg an aunt in Nigeria to please buy and send me ten yards of lace. Now I just go to a lace store or I go to a head tie store. There are just so many Africans around that they make living in America as an African very easy; just like how the Hispanics live in America because there are so many of them."

The same thing is happening in Britain. More Africans have migrated and are migrating to Britain. Moni, a twenty-three-year-old nurse who grew up in London in the late 1990s and 2000s, nicely summarized the period effect: "There was conflict between Nigerians and Jamaicans, calling us 'African bush babies,' cursing African people. Now Africans are recognized. They are doing well. Now I can say that I am Nigerian. Those who were afraid of being Nigerian or saying that they were Nigerian, now say, 'Yes, I am Nigerian.' There is pride now because we are doing well."

BOUNDARIES BASED ON PHYSICAL DIFFERENCES: "HER LIPS ARE SO BIG"

Black communities are far from immune to the widely accepted idealized white standards of beauty. Proximal hosts in both countries extended their belittlement of the sub-Saharan African second generation to appraisal of physical features. Nigerians were associated with darker skin, coarser hair, stronger facial features, and thicker bodies. In other words, while the proximal hosts may have been black, the Nigerian second generation was considered blacker. Boundaries were drawn based on perceived physical differences.

Desola, a solicitor who was born and raised in Britain, was told by a Caribbean man that she was too beautiful to be African because she was very light skinned. "He told me that he would never have thought of me as an African black." Laura, a twenty-five-year-old financial analyst who was born and raised in the United States, was able to gain acceptance as an African American when she was younger because she, too, is light skinned. She now strongly identifies as Nigerian. Growing up, though, she wanted to be African American. She said, "I didn't like the way the Africans looked. I didn't look African. No one would suspect. Most Africans have strong features. I didn't have that. No one really could tell I was African. I just couldn't stand it, being from a jungle. I had those ignorant stereotypes in my head. I did not want to associate myself *at all* with Africa. I just distanced myself from the whole African part of me. I didn't want to be associated with it at all."

Darker-skinned second-generation Nigerians could rarely do what Laura did. This was the case with Sade, a thirty-three-year-old professor who was born and raised in the United States. She described herself as having "strong features" and a "hulking physique." Boys did not find her attractive, and she did not really date in high school. She remembered that for her in particular it was a taboo to "crush on anybody," especially white guys in her school:

> You don't put yourself out there to be vulnerable that way, but I always felt that there was an underlay of race going on there. You feel the racial vibe out on the sport field when there is a display of physicality or a display of yourself, the body. And there are issues around people looking or people observing you in the way that is not the most flattering. I remember at some point there was an older girl I remember going to the bathroom, and she was there with her boyfriend, and she said something like, "My God, her lips are so big!" Something like that in a pretty loud whisper that was obviously meant to be heard.

Sade admitted to internalizing this view of her body as different and unattractive: "I remember it now, so obviously it was impactful."

But despite judgments about lighter skin versus darker skin expressed by black girls, few girls of any shade succeeded in dating across racial lines. Thus, in the arena of dating, Nigerian and African American girls were all in the same boat because they were black.[8] It was different for boys. Black boys could and did date across the color line, mixing romantically with girls who were white, Hispanic, and Asian.

An outside observer might think that the boundaries drawn between Nigerians and native U.S. blacks and between Caribbeans and Nigerians in Britain do not make sense because all three groups originate from the African continent and are assigned to the black racial category. Yet these differences were interpreted as symbolically important, which has consequences. They contribute to the tense relations respondents say exist between the groups, which translates into a degree of social reservations between the groups in adulthood. These events, according to Linda, helped to "break the bridge" for close intergroup relations.

The legacy of slavery, colonialism, and legal color segregation around the world, maintained by an ideology of white superiority and black inferiority informs these incidents. Black people with light skin, aquiline features, and fine hair texture enjoy relatively higher social status in both black and white communities because they are seen as coming close to the widely accepted definition of beauty, according to a white standard. Many black people have internalized this definition of beauty, and this was manifested in some of the interactions between the Nigerian second generation and their proximal hosts in both countries.[9]

BOUNDARIES BASED ON STYLE:
"YOU HAVE SPIDERS ON YOUR HEAD"

The process of styling hair in threads is straightforward: the hair is divided into sections, and black woolen or cotton thread is used to gather the hair together. Threading was a popular hairstyle for Nigerian mothers to give their second-generation daughters because it was easy to do. Mothers saw it as an age-appropriate hairstyle—one that made their daughters look presentable. But for the second-generation girls, having their hair in threads meant open season for teasing and ridicule: "You have snakes in your hair," "You have spiders in your hair," and "Medusa" were the taunts thrown at them. Threading made many outcasts in school. As a matter of fact, all women in the study recalled the problems dressing their hair in threads caused them. According to Amara, a twenty-three-year-old physical therapist in the United States, "My hair was a big thing. I mean hair is always a big thing for any woman, especially an African American woman, African woman. And I will have my hair—she [her mother] will tie it with thread. So of course you have Medusa at school because they don't understand what's going on . . . so I was a social outcast."

In Greek mythology, Medusa was a beautiful maiden until Athena transformed her beautiful hair into serpents and made her face so terrible to behold that the mere sight of it turned onlookers to stone. It is this aspect of Medusa—the one with serpents for hair and a horrifyingly ugly visage—that African American peers of Nigerian immigrants were alluding to when they called girls who went to school with threads "Medusa." They were saying sub-Saharan African girls were ugly.

Second-generation boys were not always exempt from the teasing over grooming and style choices. For boys, style of hair and frequency of haircuts were as much a marker of difference as threads was for girls. Seun told me that his hair was a cultural marker that made him different from African

Americans. He says they made "fun of my hair" because "I didn't really get the same kinds of haircuts that the other guys got in school. Everybody else was coming to school with fades, you know, with designs in their hair. Meanwhile, my hair was, you know, regular, there was nothing to it, just groomed normally." Among black people, a lighter skin tone often correlates with having finer-textured hair. Seun was dealing with being too dark skinned and having bad hair. And to compound these problems, he did not have acceptable grooming standards according to his African American peers. Even though he went to the barber once a month, his black American classmates seemed to go once a week. They latched onto these cultural practices to claim that he was not black like them. As Seun's experience illustrates, white-based definitions of beauty were sometimes extended to black males.[10]

Threads and other hairstyles that marked the second generation as different were a problem, but tribal marks were a bigger problem. Tribal marks are a cultural practice of some ethnic groups in Africa in which skin on the face and body is cut with a sharp instrument. Facial tribal marks can be long or short slashes. They can be very visible marks, occupying the entire side of the face, or tiny slashes placed at the sides of the eyes.[11] Bose, a twenty-five-year-old secretary in the United States, has tiny ones alongside her eyes. She recalled, "When I was younger, a lot of kids used to ask me why did I have that, 'What is it for?' 'Was it a lion that did that?' 'What kind of animal slashed your face?'" She got these comments from both her African American and her white peers.

ERASING MARKERS OF DIFFERENCE: "CALL ME LU INSTEAD OF ADEOLU"

Respondents in both the United States and Britain attempted where and when possible to erase the cultural markers that signaled their difference from their proximal hosts. These attempts took several forms.

Ethnic names were an immediate marker of difference. In school, ethnic names conferred alien status on the second generation and made it difficult for them to fit in, which was their desire at the time. Eche, a twenty-six-year-old nurse practitioner in the United States, recalled that having an ethnic name was a "headache" when she was in school. She said, "Growing up as a little child I felt that it was like a curse in a way because nobody could pronounce it. The teachers could never pronounce it. My first name was hard, and my last name was even worse, so I think it was the combination of both. I always knew when they were looking to call my name because the teacher will be reading the paper and looking up and looking down; and so I would just raise my hand because I knew that it was mine. For my own children, I know that I will also give them American names, one of each."

Eche told this story now with humor, but at the time she, like many others, wished she could go by a different name. She shortened her name. So did many others. In elementary school, Sade told everybody to call her Erica. "So I was Erica," she told me. Adebowale shortened his name to Bo, and Seun, a respondent in Britain, anglicized his to Shawn. Their experiences give them unique insight into the challenges of integrating as a black immigrant in these countries. Kike, a physician in the United States, said, "I ruled out certain names for my kids because of the connotations when turned to English. For example, I didn't want them to go around with a name like Bimbo [a shortened form of *Abimbola,* a Yoruba name that means someone who is born into wealth]. I was particular about giving names that I felt are easily pronounceable."

Some respondents denied being Nigerian or African in elementary and middle school. They identified with the predominant black group (except if it was Haitian, because Haitians were seen as poor people and ranked the lowest of all black ethnics) in their schools or neighborhoods. Denying one's Nigerian or African heritage most often occurred when the heat was turned up on being a foreign black, either because people from one's parents' home country had a poor reputation, such as Nigerians being notorious fraudsters, or because they were part of a very tiny minority in their schools. But some respondents viewed their Nigerianness as a source of strength. They believed, as Ike did, "that if values were well set at home" the second generation would be less likely to deny their ethnic heritage when challenged about it in school or in the neighborhood. They felt that although one might not shout from the rooftops that one was Nigerian, one would not deny it.

Girls took control of their fashion choices as soon as possible so as to change what Wunmi, a thirty-three-year-old paralegal in the United States, described as "the aesthetic part of it." Natural hair was permed (chemically relaxed) to remove the curl and achieve hairstyles judged by their peers more fashionable and appropriate. Clothes were upgraded to more fashionable styles. Accents were quickly adjusted to sound more American or British.

Despite attempts to erase cultural markers of difference, the young second generation never lost the feeling that they were black but different. Oyinkan, a twenty-six-year-old nurse in the United States, summarized this feeling of difference from kindergarten to the twelfth grade:

> Throughout my years, like in preschool, you were different, so nobody wanted to have anything to do with you. In elementary school, you were different. You had some people that hung out with you and others that did not, but you were still different, and for the most part, for me, it was useless having an American friend. There was no point because there wasn't anything to build the relationship upon. No trust, no similarities per se. Middle school was kind of the same way because you weren't really in the same neighborhood and you didn't really have the same upbringing and you weren't allowed to do the same things. You grow up feeling like an outsider. You were only around Nigerians on Saturday and Sundays. Whether someone is in church on Sunday or there is a birthday party on Saturday. But on Monday through Friday your name isn't Becky. Your name isn't Sarah. It is not Benjamin. Your skin isn't light. Like I remember preschool, people made fun of me for being dark, but it's one of those things.

Oyinkan listed the main challenges the Nigerian second generation faced in school that kept them constantly aware that they were different. Their names were often not easy to pronounce, and as children they did not feel the pride their parents felt when giving them these names; now, as adults, they see these names as testaments to alienness. They found refuge when hanging out with coethnics in their homes, at social events, and places of worship if these were predominantly Nigerian. But this sense of comfort ended once Monday came around and they headed back to school. Their cultural backgrounds and the ways their parents raised them were quite dissimilar from their peers, a point I discuss in the next chapter. In the words of one respondent, parents told their children, "Outside this home you are in Britain [or America], but once you come in and close the door, you are in Nigeria. Get that clear!" In short, intrablack physical and cultural differences created social distance between the Nigerian second generation and their proximal hosts.

The school experiences of the second generation in both countries were a mixed bag. Having a good, bad, or indifferent school experience depended on several factors: the racial composition of schools; whether they attended affluent suburban schools, city schools, magnet schools, or private schools; and whether they attended schools with large Nigerian and sub-Saharan (black) African populations. Those who attended affluent suburban schools had less fraught relations with their proximal hosts, regardless of the racial or ethnic composition. Respondents who attended private boarding schools in

Britain gained acceptance from their peers by excelling in sports. Some male respondents in the United States also achieved acceptance through sports, but the flipside of this was that some felt teachers and school administrators did not expect them to perform well academically. While several female respondents in Britain talked about participating in sports as a means to gain acceptance and become popular, none of the female respondents in the United States linked participation in sports with acceptance from or popularity among their peers.

A bad time in school often became better once accents sounded more American or British, when greater familiarity with how things were done in these countries was gained, when they jettisoned parents' old-fashioned styles and became more hip, and when classmates got to know them better. In sad contrast to what most had innocently expected, that their proximal hosts would be their natural allies, the respondents learned that in the United States they were not, according to their peers, African American. And in Britain they were definitely not perceived as similar to black Caribbeans.

These childhood experiences of respondents revealed that the proximal hosts assigned meanings and attached symbolic significance to certain physical traits and cultural elements that nonblack and/or other black groups of different ethnicities in different contexts and places do not. And the cross-national similarities in the proximal hosts' response are rooted in the legacies of the ethnoracial traumas of black people—slavery, colonialism, legal color segregation, and global antiblack sentiments.[12] It also became obvious that the similar history of slavery that unites the two proximal host groups, African Americans in the United States and Caribbeans in Britain, in part caused the similarities in their responses to the presence of the Nigerian second generation.

That the childhood experiences of the Nigerian second generation with members of their proximal host have left a lasting impression is contrary to the claim that name-calling incidents are impersonal encounters that though "hurtful were not overly dramatic" and "in contrast to bad encounters with the police, did not generally leave lasting scars or deep anger."[13] It is argued that who discriminates and the type of discrimination that occurs have an impact on how the victim reacts. When the perpetrators of discrimination are seen as representatives of the state, for example, they may be viewed as representing negative treatment by the larger society. For people in already marginalized groups, discrimination from representatives of the state or larger society can reinforce already held feelings of exclusion and stigmatization.[14] I agree that experiences of discrimination can have differential effects on the discriminated because of the power dynamics at play and the degree of agency to fight back that victims of discrimination believe they have.

But what I show in this chapter is that the intraracial and interethnic conflicts between the second generation of Nigerian ancestry and their proximal hosts did leave lasting impressions on the second generation. Their proximal host peers were not representatives of the state but simply people of similar race and age. Some respondents did acknowledge that ignorance was a factor and that things became better once they acculturated a bit more, especially if they lost their foreign accents and picked up American or British accents. For the Nigerian second generation, the name calling during childhood was a site where the interplay of race and ethnicity was enacted. The nature of their interethnic relations with proximal hosts during their school years is an important reason their racial status did not overwhelm their ethnicity and make them "just black," as predicted by theories influenced by the racialization perspective.

CONCLUSION: MY BLACK IS DIFFERENT

The childhood experiences of respondents in both the United States and Britain had a lasting impact on the identities they hold as adults. In both countries, respondents reported that when they were younger, relations with proximal hosts were tense and fraught with conflict and that it was constantly communicated to them that they were different. I made a key point in this chapter: the Nigerian second generation as part of the African second generation have not assimilated seamlessly into their assigned category because their presence was contested by their proximal hosts. The tense interactions between the Nigerian second generation and their proximal host peers made the former realize that they were black but different, and this realization set them on the path to forming distinct ethnic identities that they say differentiate them from their proximal host peers.

I show that in addition to structural barriers of race being a part of their context of reception, the presence of and interaction with their proximal hosts is key. Segmented assimilation theory argues that identity formation for the black second generation results in a reactive "black" ethnicity because of racial propinquity, residential proximity to lower-class blacks in poor neighborhoods characterized by limited economic opportunities and high unemployment rates, and racial prejudice and discrimination, all of which will make them develop a conflated racial and ethnic identity characterized by an oppositional culture.[15] This did not happen to the Nigerian second generation in either the United States or Britain. Interaction with their proximal hosts during their school years led them to develop a reactive ethnicity—in response to their tense relations with their proximal hosts—that was not a black reactive ethnicity but a diasporic Nigerian ethnicity, a point I expand on in detail in chapter 4. Such developments within different black communities, how they define blackness alongside ethnic diversity, have not gotten much sociological attention. The childhood experiences of the Nigerian second generation showcase the interplay of race and ethnicity and the contestation of a monolithic blackness by both the Nigerian second generation and, as they report, their proximal hosts even when people with black phenotype are racialized and placed in a separate position in the racial hierarchy.

There were significant national differences in the Nigerian second generation's, as part of the African second generation, interaction with their proximal hosts. Sharper ethnic boundaries between proximal hosts and the second generation were reported by respondents in the United States than in Britain. Triggers of intraracial conflict were more extensive in the United States than in Britain. The second generation in the former country commonly experienced intraracial conflict between themselves and African Americans. The most common form, largely from schoolmates, was teasing and ridicule about having un-American accents, physical differences such as darker skin and "nappy" hair, and cultural differences. In Britain, the second generation also reported intraracial conflict between themselves and Caribbeans, particularly Jamaicans. However, the ethnic boundaries between themselves and Caribbeans were not as rigid because black groups were banding together to challenge institutionalized racism from white people. Differing ethnoracial systems is one explanatory factor for observed differences. So too is the fight for black civil rights in both countries.

Respondents' accounts of interethnic tensions with proximal hosts during their school years reveal the diversity of blackness across nation of origin and ethnic lines. Several studies address class diversity among black people.[16] Their stories show that the school experiences of the black second generation affect their identity formation and perceptions of proximal hosts. This is noteworthy because many members of the black second generation may be perceived as, and are, by definition, native blacks since they were born in their parents' country of settlement. Their accounts reveal that among black people, meaningful distinctions and social prestige rankings exist among different African and Caribbean national and ethnic groups within the black racial category, even as processes of racialization unfold in the national contexts.

THREE

"It's Un-Nigerian Not to Go to College"

EDUCATION AS AN ETHNIC BOUNDARY

Adaora is a twenty-eight-year-old physician doing her residency program in ophthalmology. Her mother had very high educational aspirations for her. She was expected to go to college. She recalls her mother asking her, "What are we celebrating because you graduated from high school? You are supposed to graduate from high school! I will celebrate when you do something even beyond college." Adaora interprets this expectation in ethnic terms. She believes that educational aspiration distinguishes her and other second-generation Nigerians as ethnically distinct from African Americans: "There is a true difference between first- and second-generation Africans versus those that came here in 1619 [African Americans]. I don't care what anyone says. There is a difference in the attitude. There is a difference in your determination, the belief. First of all, education was always something that you knew you had to do. It wasn't an option. Education is really big in our culture." Parents' messaging was part of the process by which the educational experience and achievement of the Nigerian second generation in the United States was ethnicized; they came to view the importance of education in their communities as something inherently Nigerian.

This chapter examines how the intersection of race, class, and ethnicity explains the educational outcomes of the Nigerian second generation, how they interpret their school experiences in relation to their proximal hosts, and how they have ethnicized much of their experiences to delineate ethnic boundaries between themselves and their proximal hosts. It discusses how ethnicity is capital for the Nigerian second generation. It fleshes out the second key factor in beyond racialization theory: the way ethnicity-as-capital shapes how the Nigerian second generation identify and facilitates their positive socioeconomic outcomes in both the United States and Britain. In addition, I address how another critical factor shaping respondents' identity formation process is their interpretation of educational experiences as indicative of distinct cultural values between themselves and their proximal hosts. Formative to their demarcation of ethnic boundaries between themselves and their proximal hosts are negative interactions, discussed in the preceding chapter, and educational experiences, a process that was reinforced by the messages they received from their parents. Their parents continually told them that they were not allowed to become too Americanized or too British. That ethnicity might be a source of capital or a driver of good educational and occupational outcomes for the black second generation has rarely been considered. The position of segmented assimilation theory and its variants that ethnicity is not a source of progress but a mark of subordination for the black second generation is an example of the view of black culture as monolithic and deficient.[1] This study shows how ethnicity is a source of progress for the black second generation as it interacts with social class and race, a discussion that has heretofore been largely limited to a discussion of certain Asian groups in both countries.[2]

Studies of the varying educational outcomes among youths, including second generations, have yielded several explanations. The most powerful predictor of a child's educational attainment or socioeconomic status is its parents' educational attainment level or socioeconomic status.[3] According to the status attainment model, a child whose father earns a bachelor's degree is more likely to have a bachelor's degree than a child whose father does not earn a bachelor's degree.[4] Over 75 percent of the second generation in my study have parents with at least a bachelor's degree. And in line with the status attainment model, over 90 percent of this group have at least a bachelor's degree.

There are other attempts in sociology to explain positive social outcomes among children. The view that ethnicity serves as social capital is the most applicable to the Nigerian second generation. In his discussion of ethnicity as a form of capital, James Coleman argues that human capital among the younger generation can be created from the social capital contained in the networks of parents and communities.[5] Examples of ethnicity becoming capital are the exchange and dissemination of information among group members that assist their children to enroll in the best schools and organizing out-of-school lessons to prepare their children for important exams. The immigration policies of the United States and Britain have created a highly selected population of first-generation Nigerian immigrants. They possess very high levels of ethnic capital, which they then transmit to their children, the second generation.[6] Ethnic capital is defined as "the average human capital stock of the ethnic group" and also as "the quality of the ethnic environment in which a person is raised."[7] It is linked to intergenerational mobility because "persons who grow up in high-quality ethnic environments will, on average, be exposed to social, cultural, and economic factors that increase their productivity when they grow up, and the larger or more frequent the amount of this exposure, the higher the resulting quality of the worker."[8]

Ethnicity also becomes capital via effective social norms holding children of the ethnic group to high educational standards. This was the case for the second generation of Nigerian ancestry in both the United States and Britain. I found that an effective social norm existed in the diasporic Nigerian communities as children came to accept it was "un-Nigerian not to go to college." Parents and other family members and the community were all committed to ensuring that Nigerian children graduate from college.

It must be stressed that respondents saw educational aspiration in distinctly Nigerian terms that distinguished them from their proximal hosts as well as other ethnic groups, despite research showing that all parents, including immigrant parents, have high educational aspirations for their children.[9] The critical point here is that while less educated parents might not have the opportunity to ensure these aspirations are actualized for their children, the Nigerian second generation for the most part had parents who were college graduates and who had the resources to support their children's educational careers. They are also members of communities characterized by high levels of human capital that collectively instituted the social norm that their children must be college graduates. The Nigerian second generation did not point to selective immigration policies that shaped the high level of human capital among their parents but instead employed cultural narratives to explain why they did well in school. This interpretation pushed to the background the structural advantages many of the second generation enjoyed from having highly educated parents and from the operation of their ethnicity as capital.

THE ETHNICIZATION OF EDUCATIONAL EXPERIENCES

The educational experiences of respondents in both the United States and Britain influenced the construction of their ethnic identities. To understand how this happened, it is necessary to discuss how academic performance among black and white students, as well as among other ethnic minority students, is analyzed in the United States and Britain.

Explaining the Educational Performance
of Youths and Immigrants

Cultural Explanations: The Acting White Thesis. In the United States and Britain academic performance is often analyzed through a racial lens. When it is viewed in this way, instead of through the lens of factors such as social class background, school quality, and neighborhood quality, we find that significant racial gaps in academic performance exist, especially between black and white students. On average, same-aged white students outperform black students on a variety of academic measures.[10] In the United States, the academic achievement gap is not limited to black versus white students but extends to Native Americans and Hispanics, who also perform lower than same-aged white peers.[11] In the United States, Asian Americans on average perform better than their white and other ethnic minority counterparts, which has given rise to Asian Americans being viewed as a model minority, so called because their performance on several social indices such as education and occupation outperform the national U.S. average. However, critics have argued that the pan-ethnic Asian American label obscures the fact that this racial group comprises many national groups and that some, such as Laotians and Hmongs, are not doing as well as other Asian groups, such as Indian Americans, Korean Americans, and Chinese Americans. In Britain, on average, whites perform better than black Caribbeans, but Africans on average perform better than whites and so also do several other ethnic minorities, including Indian and Chinese Britons.[12]

Investigations into why academic performance among these countries' youths are differentiated by racial or ethnic group membership have developed multiple theories, some of which emphasize structural factors while others emphasize cultural explanations. In addition to this, several influential theories in the field of education and immigration link the educational performance of ethnic minority youths to the racial/ethnic identities they hold.[13]

Starting with cultural explanations for the black-white gap in academic achievement, the most influential theory in this school of thought, the cultural ecology theory proposed by John Ogbu, posits that many African

Americans reject academic excellence because they reject the dominant achievement ideology that sees education (getting at least a college degree) as the tried and true pathway to middle-class status. The theory argues that voluntary minorities will do better in schools than involuntary minorities because they have positive attitudes to education and trust in the school system and are willing to learn useful traits. Involuntary minorities, specifically African Americans, develop an oppositional culture that sees the learning of useful traits as a threat to their (black) identity and thus view behaviors that will be rewarded in school and facilitate good academic outcomes as "acting white." To avoid acting white, they "creat[e] identities in opposition to whiteness by refusing to speak standard English, do one's homework, get good grades, and/or fully engage in school."[14] Ogbu and his colleagues argued that African American students in the United States do not strive to do well academically because they see doing well in school as betraying their racial and ethnic identity.[15] Ogbu and Simons argue that this was what explained in part the differences in academic performance between African Americans who do poorly and voluntary minorities such as Asians who get better grades.[16]

The thesis of acting white has influenced the study of second-generation minorities—their educational and occupational attainment, their cultural assimilation, and identity formation—in both the United States and Britain. As Natasha Warikoo notes, "Segmented assimilation theory employs the oppositional culture frame to explain school failure among minority children of immigrants who live near African Americans in urban areas." There is said to be a "contamination effect," which leads certain groups such as Haitian Americans and other black immigrant groups to downward mobility.[17] The thesis of acting white is also used to explain the educational performance of young first- and second-generation Latinos.[18] The theory has also crossed over to explain the black-white educational gap among British students. Many studies explain the poor educational performance of black Caribbeans compared to white and Chinese Britons by offering similar cultural explanations to those found in the United States. According to these explanations, black Caribbean students do not perform well academically because they do not do their homework, are disruptive in class, and come from dysfunctional single-parent households that do not support good academic performance.[19]

While extremely influential, the acting white thesis and its variations have been heavily criticized. Many scholars disagree with the notion that African American students do not value education: African Americans students have more positive attitudes to education than both white and Asian students, trust in the school system, and do not dis-identify with doing well in school.[20] Prudence Carter, in her study of low-income black and Latino students in New York, questioned the acting white thesis for its implicit assumption that students associate school achievement with whiteness.[21] She found that students had internalized the dominant achievement ideology—the belief that education is the main route to socioeconomic mobility. However, they differed in how they managed their identities, cultural styles, and educational beliefs to engage in school. She found three types of students: *noncompliant believers,* those who believe in education but do not always comply with the rules of educational attainment; *cultural mainstreamers,* who embrace the dominant cultural repertoire or body of cultural know-how and who, although expressing their own racial or ethnic background as a central part of their identity, portray most cultural behaviors as racially or ethnically neutral; and *cultural straddlers,* who deftly abide by the school's cultural rules while simultaneously creating meanings with their coethnic peers. Cultural straddlers are more successful socially among their African American and Latino peers than are cultural mainstreamers because they possess the resources to strategically navigate between multiple cultures, including their ethnic and peer groups, communities, and schools.[22] Carter concludes that all students, including low-income ones, embrace the normative values of academic achievement and success but are critical of and disadvantaged by an education system that values and endorses white middle-class attitudes and behaviors.

A study of black Caribbean and Indian children of immigrants in London and New York found no evidence that children rejected the dominant achievement ideology.[23] This study, along with Carter's, found that cultural markers such as wearing baggy pants, speaking nonstandard English, and listening to hip-hop and rap music, which Ogbu and colleagues interpreted as the attendant cultural signifiers of the embrace of an oppositional culture, were just forms of cultural expression. Both studies found that among ethnic minority youths black cultural styles were in vogue and conferred social status. Both studies suggest that the the acting white thesis does not explain the academic performance of second-generation ethnic minority youths in both America and Britain and that their academic performance should instead be found in structural explanations.

Finally, the theory has been criticized because its voluntary/involuntary minority dichotomy makes an implicit assumption that academic performance among students within each minority type is homogeneous.[24]

Consequently, the theory is not able to satisfactorily explain heterogeneity in students' academic performance within each minority group once they are disaggregated by national grouping, region, or school structure, and so on. Ogbu makes a problematic assumption by classifying children of recent African immigrants as involuntary migrants. He argues that the African second generation will become black Americans because of societal discrimination, residential segregation, and propinquity to and intermarriage with native blacks. He argues further that their academic achievement will be similar to that of African Americans and that they will be downwardly mobile because of the contamination effect of African Americans.

But this view, like that predicted by segmented assimilation theory and racialization theories, downplays the likelihood that the high educational qualifications of many parents of the African second generation will be correlated with good academic and occupational outcomes consistent with patterns predicted by the status attainment and social reproduction models. Indeed, several studies find that when black students are disaggregated into African Americans and first- and second-generation immigrant Africans and Caribbeans, first- and second-generation immigrant blacks outperform their African American peers.[25] In Britain, first- and second-generation immigrant Africans outperform their Caribbean counterparts.[26] These studies show that there is ethnic diversity in educational performance among blacks in both countries.

Structural Explanations: The Melding of Ethnicity-as-Capital with Structural Factors. An extension of cultural explanations for students' academic performance gave rise to the model minority thesis, which is used to explain the better educational performance of many second- generation Asians compared to both blacks and whites. The model minority thesis posits Asians have a family-mediated ethnic culture that fosters good academic performance. The popular narrative is that Asian American mothers drive their children to excel academically and that Asian Americans are very studious, are extremely respectful to their parents, and are respectful to teachers and therefore receive more opportunities to excel.[27] But a critical analysis of why many second-generation Asians do better in school than their black, white, and other ethnic minority counterparts reveals that what seem to be cultural explanations actually rest on structural factors.[28]

The model minority thesis has been criticized by scholars for several reasons. Some scholars argue that by emphasizing family cultures, the cultural argument shifts the emphasis away from powerful institutional and other factors outside the family that are crucial to understanding success.[29] As Vivian Louie notes, "It is indeed true that motivation and optimism, which are integral aspects of the cultural narrative about educational success, are definitely both important to becoming successful. However, researchers, educators, and policy makers have to think more critically about where this motivation and optimism actually come from, and how they are maintained or depressed by the opportunities and constraints immigrants and their children find in the United States."[30]

In her study on the children of Chinese, Colombian, and Dominican working-class immigrants, Louie found that a key factor in their paths to college was having access to resources that provided critical help at important times, like referrals to a gifted class, a better middle school, after-school programs, and quality college counseling. Her research also showed that residential segregation and ethnic community wealth played important roles in shaping different opportunities for the second generation.[31] The working-class Chinese were less residentially segregated and thus had access to better public schools. In addition, even when they lived in ethnic communities with substantial rates of poverty, these communities had a lot of transnational and ethnic wealth, which allowed for educational investments; they had access to institutions that helped with schooling and ties to middle- and upper-middle-class Chinese who provided key schooling information.[32] Both were key advantages that were not as readily available to the Dominicans and Colombians, despite the fact that they were also highly motivated to help their children with schooling in America. And these differences in resources by ethnic group led to varying academic success of each groups' second generation.

The theory of cultural frames—"ways of understanding how the world works"[33]—and particularly the success frame developed by Jennifer Lee and Min Zhou is also helpful for explaining why educational achievement among the second generation differs by ethnic group membership.[34] They argue that that while all immigrant parents and their children value education, the frame through which they define a "good education" differs across ethnic groups. According to them, "some members of the second generation frame a 'good education' as graduating from high school, attending a local community college, and earning an occupational certificate that allows them to work as a laboratory technician or dental assistant. Others frame a 'good education' as graduating as the high school valedictorian, getting into a highly competitive university, and then going to law or medical school in order to work in a high status profession."[35] Consequently, they argue, members of different second-generation groups "construct remarkably different notions of what a good education and academic success mean depending on the frame that is accessible to them and which they adopt." And for these "frames to be effective, they need support and reinforcement mechanisms[,] . . . which is where ethnicity comes in."[36] In short, groups define success in different ways and whether success for the second generation is achieved is contingent on the ethnic resources marshaled in the immigrant community.

I found Lee and Zhou's formulation of a success frame, in conjunction with Coleman's consideration of ethnicity as capital, very useful in analyzing the educational experiences of the Nigerian second generation in both countries and how they came to ethnicize these experiences to draw ethnic boundaries between themselves and their proximal hosts. For the Nigerian second generation in both countries, the question becomes how their incorporation into the racial hierarchies of the United States and Britain with interact with having, for many of them, highly educated middle-class parents and how will these interactions affect their educational experiences. In other words, would race matter more than social class or vice versa? Will their experiences mirror those expected of the children of middle-class parents as predicted by the status attainment and social reproduction models? Or would the link be disrupted because of their race? Does being racialized as black affect how teachers relate to them, especially considering the negative stereotype of blacks as a low achieving minority? If teachers have lower expectations for their school performance compared to white students in the same class, will they receive a different quality of education from nonblack immigrants and natives? The intersection of race and class can also work in the opposite direction. Is it possible that teachers recognize that many of the Nigerian second generation and other African second generation have highly educated parents and as a result treat them differently from how they treat members of their proximal hosts? These are questions that I answer below.[37]

THE RELATIONSHIP BETWEEN ETHNICITY AND EDUCATION AMONG THE NIGERIAN SECOND GENERATION

I found that among the diasporic Nigerian communities in the United States and Britain, the expectation was that children, the second generation, had to complete college. One form of social capital that fosters high levels of human capital among the second generation is effective social norms.[38] In the Nigerian communities in both countries, the effective social norm is that it is, in the words of Jibola, a twenty-six-year-old hotelier in the United States, "un-Nigerian not to go to college." Ike, another U.S respondent, agrees: "Education was the thing if you are a Nigerian, because not to get an education is almost a shameful thing. If you are not doing well in school or if you are not graduating from college, it is a shameful thing, and even now it's still there. It's expected in our culture that we do well and succeed." Ike's explanation of the social norm makes clear the criteria for membership in the Nigerian community. The norm is succinctly expressed by Kemi: "You know, pretty much nothing less than getting a college degree will do. Definitely, if you are a Nigerian, that is just the norm." An ethnic group can be defined as "a collectivity within a larger society having real or putative common ancestry, memories of a shared historical past, and a cultural focus on one or more symbolic elements defined as the epitome of their peoplehood."[39] For Nigerians in the United States and Britain, that children, the second generation, graduate from college with a bachelor's degree is an epitome of their peoplehood.

This highly effective social norm has emerged largely as a result of the high levels of ethnic capital found in the communities, which is related to the highly selective nature of Nigerian immigration to the United States and Britain. As previously noted, the immigration policies of both countries have shaped their Nigerian populations such that approximately six of every ten first-generation Nigerian immigrants have at least a bachelor's degree, which is an educational profile in the American and British diasporas that far outpaces the national average in these countries as well as in Nigeria. Sociological literature tells us that one way highly educated parents transmit their advantage to the next generation is by having high educational aspirations for their children. Highly educated parents are also likely to have the resources, information, and know-how needed to ensure their children do well in school. Over 75 percent of my respondents' parents had at least a bachelor's degree, and their high educational attainment translated into high educational aspirations for their children. They expected their children to do well in school and to go to college and beyond. As Ike said, "My parents worked hard, and they expected us to do well academically. So there were high expectations. My father was the type of father that if you brought home 92 percent he'll ask you where the other 8 percentage points were. So we were expected to do well.

The expectation was just to do well." Here we can recall Adaora's mother telling her that she will only begin celebrating her daughter's achievements when she did "something beyond college." Adaora met this expectation by becoming a physician.

Another way parents' high rate of education influenced the second generation is that the latter grew up in households in which they were expected to attend college. This is an example of what Pierre Bourdieu calls habitus, the dispositions, aspirations, and likes and dislikes we are socialized to have.[40] Adaora took it for granted growing up that she would complete college. She was socialized to have this aspiration because of her habitus and was surprised to discover that it was not the same for her African American peers in her elementary school. She said, "From the time I was in kindergarten, I was already discussing with my mum what college I was going to. And I remember when I was in third grade and was like, 'I want to go to IU like my mummy.' And they, my African American classmates, were like, 'IU, what is that?' I am like, 'How do you not know what IU is? How do you not know what Indiana University is? It is a college. Don't you know what college is?' And so it was such differences like that that I noticed." It is possible that her African American classmates' parents had not attended college and hence were not having such discussions with their children at home. But Adaora interpreted this interaction with her African American peers as one that showed ethnic differences between the two groups rather than potential class differences.

In Britain, the second generation also has the success frame that they must attend university, specifically a good university, and then get a good job. Bimpe, a twenty-seven-year-old management consultant whose father is an architect and whose mother has a bachelor's degree and works in the legal sector, discussed how the Nigerian second generation are told, "You go to school, the best school, and get the best career." According to Rukhe, a solicitor in Britain with a sister who is a physician and a brother who is a barrister, the educational and occupational success of the three siblings was due to their father. He was a successful entrepreneur, and because of him she "was able to afford the best kind of education." "He instilled the self-esteem I have in me," Rukhe continued. "My dad would regularly tell us that we can achieve anything we put our minds to education-wise. He told us that education is the key, and he was really strict about exam results and all of that kind of stuff. He had very high expectations of us." Folarin, a twenty-eight-year-old respondent, told me, "[It's] education first. You are expected to go to college, and then after that you are expected to get a higher degree, whether a master's degree or a doctorate, most likely a doctorate. You are expected to be the top in your class."

The high academic expectations of parents were reinforced by members of the Nigerian community, all of whom expected their children—in a communal sense—to do well, and in fact not only graduate from college but pursue professional degrees like medicine, law, engineering, and pharmacy. Accounting will do in a pinch. According to Chinedum:

> For Nigerians, my parents, there was just one thing you needed to do: succeed in school. *You have to, you have to graduate.* Honestly, I can remember that one of my aunts gave me a call right before I was about to drive down to go to college, and she told me that there is no one in our family that has gone to school and not graduated. So, when some of the black Americans you see say like, "Okay, well if you make it, you make it," or "You are probably the first in that family that has gone to college," that is not part of our culture. . . . All our family who had been to school were either out of school working or still in school and working on another degree. There are so many freaking degrees that everybody is getting that it is ridiculous. When you're growing up with your Nigerian parents, all you know is education. Education is the key. Education, education, education. You want money? You'll need to get an education.

Note Chinedum's use of the word *culture* when discussing educational aspirations and community expectations. Like the other respondents in the United States and Britain, he has come to see pursuing education as an intrinsic part of what it means to be Nigerian. But this definition of what it means to be Nigerian, I argue, refers only to the elite, found largely in diasporas in Western advanced countries and among the middle and upper classes in Nigeria.

Since completing college is part of how Nigerians demarcate an ethnic boundary, there is tremendous pressure on the second generation to go to college, to pursue professional degrees, and when possible—which for parents was always—to obtain postgraduate degrees. A British respondent spoke for many other respondents when he said, "Nigerians are overrepresented in the universities in Britain. Nigerians are there all doing their accountancy, and law, and medicine, and whatever it is they are doing." Nat, a solicitor, mentioned he wanted to be an actor, but his parents dissuaded him. He explained, "They told me that I had to choose between law and medicine. That I needed to choose a degree that will give me security in the future." He chose law.

In the United States, Ezigbe, a twenty-three-year-old social worker who was searching for a job when I interviewed him, recalled, "As a kid I remember if I wasn't doing too well I would be compared to another Nigerian's son or daughter. I guess that's their way of motivating you to do as well or even better than the next kid. So it is a competition." He found the constant comparisons upsetting, "because I just wanted to be judged off of what I was doing." He wanted his parents to tell him what they wanted him to do better and not make it a "battle between families." "I feel that that is a problem with the Nigerian community," he said. He feels there "is too much of a competition to the point where" parents just want their kids to succeed so they can "show off," which "turns me off." Onyinye, a twenty-two-year-old hospital tech who came to the United States when she was two, agrees. Laughing, she said, "Nigerians in Queens, New York, you could just as well get a town crier to let them know my daughter got a scholarship, has entered this school, has got this job, is traveling all over the world."

Some respondents reported that parents brought in reinforcements drawn from their friends and friends' children to emphasize to their children the need to do well in school, stay the course, graduate from high school, and then choose a good university and obtain a good degree. Their parents often got other successful second-generation coethnics to talk to them about aspirations and the need to strive harder in school. But some respondents felt that such role models put a lot of pressure on the second generation, which for some was a bad thing. Temitayo, a physician, lamented about what is going on in the Nigerian community in her midwestern city. In regard to the strong sense of competition among parents of the second generation, she replied, "Oh my God!"

> Nigerians are about competition and who has what and who has this. Everyone wants to be a doctor or a pharmacist. If I had a dime for every person that says that my parents made me to go to medical school I will be rich. It is just a status thing that I think is funny. There is competition among parents on whose child or daughter can get into these top schools in the state. The competition is, "Oh my child wants to pursue engineering," "Oh my child is applying to an Ivy League university." When I talk to the younger generation, because their parents send them to talk to me because they think I did well in school, they all basically vent for about two hours about the pressure they are under to perform.

The effectiveness of the norm of educational aspiration is strengthened by social support, status, honor, and other rewards Nigerian parents enjoy when their children do well, win scholarships, and go to good colleges. Status is built into the boasting done by parents and the accolades they receive for having raised their children "right." The second generation also enjoy accolades but also face significant pressure to conform to this norm. While some, like Ezigbe, resented the pressure, others, looking back, said they are grateful for it. They credit that pressure with making them highly educated professionals. As Onyinye put it, that pressure is "one of the reasons why we do so well compared to other blacks, especially African Americans."

Respondents also mentioned that parents shared information among each other about the best charter or magnet schools in the United States and the best grammar schools in Britain and how to successfully apply for admission. Although not all respondents attended these schools, many reported that such information was shared in their homes. Some respondents, especially the ones in Boston, said they attended after-school exam preparatory classes organized by ethnic associations their parents attended. This was one way the Nigerian community in Boston supplement what their children are taught in school.

It is clear, then, that the success frame of respondents in both the United States and Britain was that they must graduate from college and preferably obtain professional degrees. This success frame was supported and reinforced by the effective social norm in diasporic Nigerian communities of both countries. I use the term *diasporic* to emphasize the selective nature of these communities. The high level of educational attainment among parents boosts the ethnic capital in Nigerian communities, which in turn fosters high levels of educational attainment among their children. The Nigerian second generation in both countries have success frames similar to those held by many second-generation Asians in both countries.[41] These frames, and the support and reinforcement provided by their ethnic group membership, help explain why these second-generation groups are high achieving in both countries.

National Differences in Institutional Support from Educators

In the United States, Mostly Supportive but Sometimes Antipodal. Success frames that are informed and supported by effective social norms in the ethnic community require other forms of support. One is institutional support from teachers and school administrators. I found a marked national difference in the institutional support respondents thought they received. The majority of respondents in the United States said they had received support from their teachers in school and that their teachers did not disparage their high academic aspirations. In contrast, the great majority of British respondents reported that they received no support from their teachers and school administrators and in fact their academic aspirations were often disparaged.

In general, U.S. respondents reported they received good to great support from their teachers. They said that their teachers (both black and white) had high expectations of them. Some, like Tabira, said teachers had high expectations for them because they were children of recent African immigrants. According to Tabira, teachers had different expectations for her because they knew she was Nigerian or African: "If I started messing up or something like that, they would kind of be a little disappointed and they would kind of be, 'Tabira, we know you know better than that.'" Kemi recounted, "I had very wonderful teachers. I was in honors classes, and when I was in regular classes they forced me to go to honors. I had teachers who wanted 'too much.'" However, like Titi, she also experienced racism from her white teachers when she was younger. In many respondents' experiences, including that of Kemi, moving from a working-class, predominantly black neighborhood and a pre-dominantly black public school to a more affluent neighborhood, whether predominantly black or white or mixed, resulted in having better relations with teachers and African American peers. It was in her mixed high school in the more affluent neighborhood that Kemi had "wonderful teachers" who supported her. Kemi's relations with her proximal hosts also became much easier: "When we moved and we moved to a more affluent neighborhood, they all talked white. They all talked the way that I talked even though they were black. And this was new because I thought all African Americans talked slang but then realized we were the same."

Kemi's experience shows how social class matters. Relocating to schools with students of all racial and ethnic groups from middle-class backgrounds eliminated a source of tension, especially from members of the proximal host. For some respondents, who attended predominantly black schools in poor to middle-income neighborhoods being in advanced placement (AP) classes reduced their interaction with students, reportedly mostly African American, who gave them a tough time for "speaking very, very white" and being too engaged in class. For those accepted by magnet and charter schools, the institutions served the same function as being in AP classes. Both, which admit only the best students, created a protective zone from African American peers who gave them a tough time for "acting white." Simisola, a thirty-year-old teacher, told me she was not pressured to "act dumb" in her AP classes: "We [she and two second-generation Nigerian friends] never had the mentality that 'I am going to act dumb or ghetto.'" Simisola is making a class distinction when talking about her proximal hosts and also about her class status—that she will not be "ghetto," which my respondents used to pejoratively refer to African Americans who they felt were from poor, dysfunctional families.

A few respondents said their teachers did not treat them any differently from African Americans and in fact expected them not to do well because they racially associated them with black people and thus as underachieving. Adamu, a twenty-eight-year-old IT specialist, mentioned that his teacher told him he was not going to amount to anything, and he felt that she said this because he was black. He told me he went back to his high school "the summer after my freshman year [in college] to show her my admission letter." But most respondents felt that the institutional support offered them came and went at different stages of their educational career.

Titi is a great example of the antipodal nature of the second generation's experiences with teachers and school administrators. She began her educational career in middle school because she came to the United States at the age of twelve. She told me that her teachers "*loved*" her because "they knew I was different," and they put a lot of pressure on her to do well academically. She recalled:

> I remember a teacher found out that I was African. She was like, "Oh my gosh, you'll probably find this school very easy." She was telling me, "If you ever find yourself finding your class, your studies, hard, then that means you've conformed to being an American." And I don't think I quite understood what she was saying at the time, but she was saying that things are easy for you because you do have a bit of an African mentality. You are used to being challenged. If you ever think things get hard and you are not getting challenged, that means you've Americanized yourself. That means you have conformed and you are slacking. And I was just like . . . I would never forget that. And I think about that, like okay am I challenging myself given the opportunities around me or am I complaining? I think about that.

Titi was already enjoying the advantages of having highly educated and wealthy parents. Her parents made it clear to her that loafing around was not permitted. It "was not a choice because I come from a family where education is *really* important." She continued, "I have a lot of cousins who are physicians, architects, and engineers; so my whole thing was to hide that I was a good student [because of the teasing she got from her African American peers], not to stop it." Having many coethnic role models is another way the high levels of ethnic capital in the Nigerian diasporic communities in the United States and Britain boost the academic and occupational achievements of the Nigerian second generation; they do not look to white or proximal host peers as the frame of reference for comparing and charting their progress. Titi also had duties at home that made her "very responsible." In summarizing her experience growing up in the United States, she said, "When I got home, it was very much like you left the United States at the door and entered into Nigeria."

But Titi found out that although she had been her teachers' pet in middle and high school, with some emphasizing her as ethnically different from African Americans, she was nevertheless lumped in with all the other black students when she attended an Ivy League university. Like African Americans, she was seen as not good enough. She thought her professors and other colleagues believed she had only been admitted because of affirmative action. She recalled being asked by a friend of a friend what college she attended. When Titi told her, she said that the person expressed surprise: "'Oh, how? I didn't know you can go to Princeton.' And I was like, 'What does that mean? Why are you so surprised?' Little things like that broke me down." She started "getting a lot of smack from white people," which made her realize that though she was a foreign black, in some situations she was "just seen as black." She recalled that as her doctoral cohort prepared for an important comprehensive exam "a lot of my white counterparts got a lot of help from professors. We [black students] didn't go to professors because they believed we could not pass the exam. My white friends would go see everybody in the department. I would only go see the black professor, a Caribbean immigrant. He was like, 'You can do it. I know you can do it.'"

Being seen as "just black" caused colleagues, professors, and undergraduate students she taught in graduate school to doubt her competence. She said:

> They just question you. If I say something, they go check up behind me like this is what she says, but I'm not sure if she is right. Even when I'm teaching, I was teaching a class in summer, teaching an introductory class for society health, which is my department, my track. So when you talk about anything, they will say, "Are you sure? I'm not sure. I'll go check the textbook." In class, when you answer a question like 1 +1 is 2, the professor would say, "Yes, not really," and ask another white student, who would give the same answer and the professor would accept the answer and tell the student "Oh, bravo, you're

smart." And I was like, "I just said the same thing!" People would come to me after class and say, "You just said that." I would be like, maybe I didn't say it in the language they understand.

In Britain, Little to No Support. Respondents' experiences suggest that in Britain it was very different. Respondents were lumped together in the school system with all other black students, Caribbeans and other Africans, and they faced what Pauline called the "bigotry of low expectations." They felt that teachers held racist assumptions that they could not do better. Because teachers expected them to be poor students because they were black, they did not demand they do better. In fact, many respondents said that teachers were quick to tell them to lower their academic aspirations. In Chuka's experience, "If you told a teacher that you wanted to be a doctor or a lawyer or some kind of professional type of job, they will outright come out and tell you, 'Oh, I don't think you will be able to do that. Have you thought about ... ?,' and then you will get a long list of menial laborer type tasks. They will just outrightly dismiss your academic abilities and whatever aspirations you had, just like knock it on the head or deride it."

The bigotry of low expectations was also expressed in the notion that the second generation would be good athletes and entertainers because they were black. In particular, black males were targeted with this stereotype. Oye told me, "When you speak to teachers and ask them genuinely what is the best thing for their black students, and they ask, 'Can they play football [soccer]? Can you play football? Can you run? Can you sing?' None of these academic things." He recalled that some of his teachers made comments that were racist, yet obscure enough to hide their true sentiments—although one of Oye's teachers got suspended for making a racist comment about him. Often, Oye said, you could tell from "their body language, but you couldn't pin them down on it. They would say something like, 'We don't need people like you in this school'—that kind of thing. And you were like, 'What do you mean, people like me? People like me as in naughty, or do you mean people like me as in black?' And obviously you knew what they meant, but because it could mean naughty, they kind of ducked the issue and said they meant naughty."

Naughty is a loaded term. It meets at the intersection of race and gender. It is more often used to refer to black students than students from any of the other minority groups, and then more often to refer to black boys than black girls. This was the racial undertone that made Oye ask his teacher what he or she meant by "naughty" because the teacher did not use the same term when talking about his white and South Asian classmates. Oye's experience is consistent with research in Britain showing that teachers widely perceive black boys as more troublesome than all their other students. Some researchers assert that this perception biases teachers against black male students and makes them less supportive, which in turn works to depress the students' academic performance.[42]

Chuka attributes becoming a lawyer, in spite of his teachers' brutal dismissal of his academic aspirations, to his mother, who told him, "You can be what you want to be; it is not what other people tell you to be," and to having role models, some drawn from his family and others, like Nelson Mandela, who were successful black people. Without strong support and reaffirmation from parents and from the many highly skilled coethnics in their transnational kin and social networks, the second generation would not have done well in school. Only a few respondents, such as Adex, had a handful of teachers who encouraged him to study once they knew he was African and was working full-time.

Sam Echekoba's case illustrates the barriers the Nigerian second generation had to overcome in school and how the support of parents and the resources marshaled in their ethnic communities helped them succeed academically. Sam was born in Britain to middle-class parents. He is the first of eight children. His father is a physician and his mother is a midwife. Sam is a physician, married to a Caribbean woman. He is one of only two respondents in Britain with a Caribbean partner. He lives in a white neighborhood in London. In school, he and his siblings were the only black students. Sam found life in Britain in the 1980s difficult: "I lived the life of an ethnic minority. By this I mean, I was sidelined and I did not feel 'mainstream.'"

Growing up, he and his siblings had very low self-esteem. They were "not doing well at all in Britain" because they did not expect much from themselves. They developed these low expectations through interaction with their white peers and teachers in school. Sam said:

In primary school, like many institutions, people stratify people according to those that are in the in-group and those that are not. For the [stratification] to have any value, there needs to be subjects. It was easy to classify the black people and the Indian people as the lowest of the low, the underclass. And this ranking was reinforced by the teachers. I remember the time when I did a test and scored 30 percent and the teacher said to me, "Well done," as if to say I was meeting my expectation, whereas another student scored 70 percent and the same teacher said [to the student], "How could you miss all these questions?" It was almost like a negative reinforced cycle where all the black people, yes, they all came from my family, yet we were all doing badly and so we just presumed that we were crap. [Laughing] Socially, we were hanging out with people that had learning disabilities in retrospect. We used to do country dancing and nobody will want to dance with my sister, you know, saying that she is black, etc. We were dealing with all this in school, so our interest wasn't really academic. We were just trying to get through the experience in one piece, really.

His parents finally intervened and sent them to boarding school in Nigeria. He reports that they realized racism and racial discrimination were hurting their children's academic performance and emotional well-being, and they knew they could not afford to remove all eight children from public schools and put them into private schools. In Nigeria, Sam experienced severe culture shock. He was accused of being an *ajebutter,* which means "soft," and an *oyinbo,* "a white foreigner." But after a while he adjusted to a life without running water and other amenities one takes for granted in Britain. Looking back, he said that Nigeria "saved" him and gave him a chance because it made him a stronger person.

Upon his return to England at the age of seventeen after six years in Nigeria, he found the British school system was still discriminatory. Sam's teachers still had low expectations for him. He would not have become a physician doctor if he and his parents had not fought against his biology teacher's discrimination. She told him that he was not good enough to get into medical school. Sam recalled:

[She was just] pissing on my aspirations. In Britain, you have a predictive grade system, where when you apply for university you have to apply before you get to the final exam. The school has to write on your forms that, well, we think this student can get an A or we think this person can't get an A. On that basis, people are selected. Because I was doing biology, chemistry, and physics, I needed to get an A in all three to get into medical school. And my biology teacher told me straightaway, "Look, I don't think you can get an A. So I am not going to be predicting you an A."

Because of this, Sam wanted to switch from biology to math and jettison his goal of becoming a doctor, but his father refused to simply accept that decision and went with him to meet with the school administrator. They reported what the teacher had said, and the administrator told Sam to take a wait-and-see approach. "Do the mock exam," he was told, "and then based on your performance the teacher will predict your biology grade." He got the highest score of all students in the mock exam, and "so whether she liked it or not she had to predict me an A because if she didn't predict me an A she could not predict anyone else an A."

The ability to send children back to the home country is an example of a resource immigrants can access even in the face of constrained financial circumstances.[43] Even though Sam's parents did not have a lot of disposable income, they were well educated and middle class, and their social location greatly influenced who and where Sam is today. They were hands-on parents who were invested in their children doing well academically. Despite being financially fragile they possessed middle-class cultural capital that made them forbid Sam from dropping out of school or not attend the university because of poor performance and lowered ambitions. They were fortunate to have the option of sending Sam and his siblings back to Nigeria. And time in the home country, as they hoped, was able to repair the damage done by life in Britain. The time Sam spent in Nigeria strengthened his Nigerian ethnic identity, and this strong sense of self enabled him to reject the subordinate position his peers back in Britain thought all black people should be in.

On the whole, my respondents' teachers did not recognize the possibility that young Africans who had well-educated parents and who were raised in immigrant communities that could generate ethnic resources that would in turn boost their academic performance could be good students. Sam's story, the critical role played by his parents, the resources they marshaled—not always financial but mostly social and cultural—to weaken the effects of racial discrimination for being black, was a common story among the Nigerian second generation in Britain.

Ethnicizing the Educational Experience

Respondents came to ethnicize their educational experiences and used it to delineate ethnic boundaries between themselves and their proximal hosts. Their reaction is similar to that of the second generation from different Asian groups who have come to racialize their high educational achievement as an Asian American phenomenon.[44] A key difference between the two is that while Asian Americans have racialized their performance to delineate racial boundaries between them and other racial and ethnic groups, the Nigerian second generation have ethnicized their good educational experiences as something causally linked to their Nigerian culture and identity as Nigerians and use this frame to delineate ethnic distinctions within the black category. This distinction is part of their identity formation process, which in addition to the fraught relations they had with their proximal host peers set them on the path to forming distinct identities that differentiate them from African Americans in the United States and Caribbeans in Britain even as they simultaneously accept their racial status as black.

For some respondents, using education as an ethnic boundary between themselves and their proximal hosts was a response to being accused of acting white by some of their proximal host peers. Even though studies have shown that black youths have high educational aspirations and embrace the dominant achievement ideology,[45] some of my respondents were accused of acting white because they were studious. They also, as part of the acting white charge, were accused of "speaking very, very white" or "speaking standard English" or "not talking with Ebonics" and not "acting black at all." Amara, a twenty-three-year-old respondent in the United States, said that she, like some of the other U.S. respondents, felt pressured to conform to an expectation of what black people were supposed to be like.

> Oh yes. I was supposed to be like them. . . . I was supposed to conform to them, but I never did. And that was one of the things that did separate me when I was little. [It] was the fact that I did not act like a typical stereotypical African American. . . I do not conform to a typical—if you see me, I do not look like the typical African American woman or stereotypical woman. I do not have on the heels with the hair and the nails and the makeup and the things like that and because I'm like that . . . I don't speak that way [mimics Ebonics]; so, in college people were like, "She don't act black at all," and I'm like, "How do you act a color?"

Indeed, it has been pointed out that "acting white" has more to do with cultural styles and not on students' attitudes to schooling and failure to embrace the dominant achievement ideology, and the experiences of these respondents in the United States seem to confirm this argument.[46] Using Carter's typology of students, from their recollection of their school experiences, most respondents would be classified as cultural mainstreamers—students who embrace the dominant cultural repertoire or body of cultural know-how and who, although they express their own racial or ethnic background as a central part of their identity, portray most cultural behaviors as racially or ethnically neutral.

However, some of my respondents in both the United States and Britain said that being accused of acting white by some of their African American peers was also due to their high performance in school. Titi had to stop raising her hand in class in response to teachers' questions because it got her into trouble with her African American peers. She said they made comments like, "She knows everything. She's always raising her hand." In response, she "started sneaking around and studying at home. I didn't want to be educated because I will be an easy target for my peers. So, everything I did, I did it at home, I wouldn't pay attention at school, but it was hard." She then alluded to cultural differences between herself and her African American peers: "We [Nigerians] respect teachers. You don't even talk back to your teacher. So even though I didn't do my work I found it hard to talk back to a teacher like they [African Americans] did." She extended the critique of African Americans and their approach to education compared to Nigerians and their children, concluding "being smart or being educated wasn't valued" by them.

Gbenga, a thirty-two-year-old lawyer, is another example of a respondent who was accused of acting white. He too used this experience to draw an ethnic boundary between Nigerians and African Americans. He said, "The pressure was there, but I never conformed to it. In fact, I would look at them [African Americans] and—this is the bad part—I knew that they wouldn't really amount to anything, whereas I knew I would. As a kid, it's the way I got through it, by realizing that their ways were destructive." Because the respondents who were accused of acting white were accused of this by African American peers, it allowed them to interpret the charge in a way that strengthened their view that they were a different kind of black and in fact that they were ethnically and culturally different.

The charge of acting white was also made in Britain. Michelle is one such example. She told me that she was under pressure from her proximal host, her Caribbean peers, to slack off in school. She attended the local comprehensive, which "was probably 90 percent black." She lived in an area in London that "was mixed in terms of wealth," and in school she experienced a lot of bullying. Before her father divorced her mother and took his money with him, she had attended a private school with a lot of white kids, so she and her older sister did not speak with "cockney accents," which, she said, "are in this country associated with the lower classes. So you had two black girls with African parents and they speak funny. So we were classic candidates for bullying." As in the United States, cultural styles such as language were markers that elicited the charge of acting white from their black Caribbean peers. Michelle went on to say:

The other constant battle, apart from not being encouraged by some of the white teachers, was with my own peers. I was going to school with kids who didn't have a lot of hope, who didn't have people at home who cared and encouraged them. So they didn't understand why I wanted to work. Some of them would ask me, "Why do you want to do law? Why do you want to be somebody?" And it was a constant battle not to succumb to people who wanted you to start smoking and go out with boys, which was a big no-no as far as my mom was concerned, you know, and all that sort of things, and lead you astray basically. So that in itself was a battle because, as I say, they didn't have a lot of hope. There was a very, very strong feeling that you really should fall into the majority and not be doing what you were doing.

In discussing her fraught relations with her black Caribbean peers, Michelle drew several moral and cultural boundaries between them and Nigerians: black Caribbeans did not have parents and family members who encouraged them and supported them to do well in school; they engaged in behaviors such as smoking and being sexually active at a young age that were forbidden by her mother and by Nigerians generally.

Also, Michelle's account is another example of the lack of institutional support that respondents never received from educators.

A lot of teachers and school administrators were quick to tell me that I could not achieve my high academic aspirations because I was black. In terms of the career guidance that you got . . . there was a very stupid careers teacher, when I told her I wanted to do law and at the time for some crazy reason she said to me "It's extremely hard. I'm sure you're going to find it very hard to get into law, particularly anything company, commercial, or anything like that." She was very discouraging. She did not really assist me in finding anything more about it. And so I was really very much on my own in terms of finding out which law courses would be the best to do.

We also see that her mother was a hands-on parent whose high educational aspirations for her children drove them to do well in school. She too viewed her mother's expectation and support as something uniquely Nigerian: "I did feel limited in that sense [having a racist careers teacher], I definitely did. But then at home I was Nigerian. And as you know with Nigerian parents, there's nothing that you cannot do. And so my mother, my parents had separated by then, my mother, wasn't going to stand for anything less than us being ambitious and wanting to do something." Today Michelle is a barrister.

The experience of the Nigerian second generation in school in both the United States and Britain strongly echoed the message they were getting at home, that though they had black skin that placed them in the black racial category, they were different from their proximal hosts. An unintended consequence of the intraracial conflict between the Nigerian second generation and their proximal hosts was that it made the former less likely to succumb to the peer pressure to develop attitudes and behaviors that would silence the charge of their "acting white." They came to view doing well in school as something they could hold on to—something that would give them a better basis for differentiation from their proximal host peers and that would give them a positive sense of self. In short, they felt that being smart, being one of the best students in class, was an achievement that made them feel that even if they were not popular, even if their schoolmates didn't want to date them, even if they were miserable in school, at least they had this one thing: they were going to be successful. The mantra "you are not like me" that characterized the relations between the second generation and their proximal hosts in school gave them the space to construct their own version of blackness, one that acknowledged their black racial identity but that placed greater meaning on their being ethnically Nigerian.

The social norm that it is un-Nigerian not to go to college along with the other ethnic resources marshaled in their communities and their parents' high human capital and middle-class cultural capital were all mechanisms that helped the Nigerian second generation in both countries achieve academic success and put them on the path of forming ethnic identities that differentiated them from their proximal hosts.

CONCLUSION: THE ETHNICIZATION OF THE EDUCATIONAL EXPERIENCE

An important part of my argument in beyond racialization theory is that the childhood experiences of respondents in both the United States and Britain had a lasting impact on the identities they hold as adults. I showed in the preceding chapter that fraught relations with their proximal hosts prevented the Nigerian second generation from assimilating seamlessly into their assigned category. This chapter continued the investigation into the impact of childhood experiences on identity formation. From the findings in this chapter and the previous one, I show that parents and educators are key social actors that affect identity formation. And that school, particularly in regards to interaction with proximal hosts, is an important site where identities of the new immigrant are impacted.

Two main points were made in this chapter: ethnicity can be an engine that drives socioeconomic success for the black second generation; and the Nigerian second generation in both countries ethnicized their educational experiences. Despite being racialized as black, they ethnicize their exceptional academic achievements as something "Nigerian" and use it to delineate ethnic boundaries between themselves and proximal hosts. They ethnicize education and being high achievers as something that flows out of Nigerian culture despite noncultural explanations being part of the process.

Most parents, whether natives or immigrants, have high aspirations for their children. The difference in their children's school performance lies in the ability to actualize ethnic capital to enable these aspirations. It has been established that the socioeconomic status of parents is the strongest predictor of a child's socioeconomic status. Children from affluent backgrounds have parents who have the resources and the middle-class cultural capital that transmits the attitudes and behavior that are valued and rewarded in educational institutions.[47] Many of the Nigerian second generation enjoyed the advantages of being children of elite parents. Parents' exercised cultural capital to create a home environment where education was the priority, channeled their children into professional occupations, steered them away from nonconservative ways to achieve success, talked to them about university choices, and went to school to fight for their children when they felt they were being discriminated against. Parents' human and cultural capital was bolstered by the social capital found in the Nigerian communities. Extended family members and coethnic friends served as human capital–boosting role models for the second generation. These are all examples of a minority culture of mobility deployed by Nigerian parents to ensure their children become college graduates and obtain jobs placing them in the middle class. While some respondents complained that the pressure to do well academically was an onerous burden, most attributed their success as adults to it.

The stories of the Nigerian second generation are very similar to those reported in studies of the second generation of many other immigrant communities, especially some Asian groups in the United States and Britain.[48] But on a key point, the Nigerian second generation have a competitive advantage over some Asian groups because they have higher levels of ethnic capital in their communities compared to, for example, the Vietnamese in the United States. However, there is little evidence of ethnic group or community-wide organization or coordination of strategies to the extent found in certain Asian communities. Among the Vietnamese and Chinese, for example, parents buy or rent a home based on the school district, work to have their children placed in honors and advanced placement classes, and enroll children in supplementary education classes and programs.[49] These tangible ethnic resources are widely used by almost all families and involve purposive institutional investment and community-wide organization in the ethnic community. These strategies are buttressed by the intangible resource of "the effort mind-set" that claims performance and achievement may be improved with sustained effort.[50] While my respondents associate being Nigerian with graduating from college, they did not report strategies as well organized and community-wide as those reported in sociological research on some Asian communities.

Strategies promoting high educational and occupational attainment among the Nigerian second generation in this sample remain primarily at the level of individual efforts among parents. Many of the strategies utilized by parents are rooted in being educated elites who expect their children to follow their footsteps and graduate from college, and marshal resources at the family level to meet this goal. Only in Boston did respondents report that after-school and exam preparatory classes are organized through ethnic associations. Nigerian communities in both countries, then, are not maximizing the available public and ethnic resources to the same extent that some Asian communities do.

Still both communities share a commonality, though it sometimes operates differently, in that their ethnicity has become capital that boosts the socioeconomic outcomes of their second generation. Consequently, academic success is not a racialized phenomenon, or a black and white phenomenon, or something that should be ethnicized, even though many of the second generation, like those in my study, are inclined to interpret it as such.

FOUR

Forging a Diasporic Nigerian Ethnicity
in the United States and Britain

Linda Okpara, a twenty-four-year-old nurse, was born in New York, went
back to Nigeria when she was a baby, and then returned to the United States
when she was eight years old. I met Linda on a warm summer day at the
annual picnic of an association for Nigerian youths in Boston. Linda ada-
mantly states that she is not African American. She wants people to know
that there is a difference between the three main black groups in the United
States:

> Honestly, I would love it if there was some kind of a distinction between us
> and African Americans because whenever I walk down the street everybody
> just automatically assumes that I am African American, and I don't know
> why, but it just rubs me the wrong way. They automatically assume that my
> first name is Kesha or LaTesha and basically assume that my last name is
> Williams or Jenkins, not knowing that I do have a Nigerian culture, that I
> have a Nigerian side. It may sound rude, but I don't want to be associated with
> the African American past or culture. That is why I want to have the
> distinction.

She continued, "Here in America, but not lately with Obama being president and stuff, but whenever someone who is not African American, when
they think of an African American person, they automatically think of, okay,
somebody who is ghetto; somebody who is uneducated; somebody who is
unmarried, who has five kids by different partners; somebody who doesn't
amount to anything; somebody who gets welfare. And if you do happen to
be African American and successful, they automatically assume that you did
it on the white man's back or something like that." Linda rerepeats the negative stereotypes of African Americans held by many people in the United
States. She takes it a step further by using these negative stereotypes to

inform the cultural and moral boundaries she employs to distinguish ethnically between Nigerians and African Americans.

Because she does not want to be seen as an African American, Linda takes many steps to signal her difference from them. She expresses her ethnic difference vigorously:

> People pick up on it, and *they kind of find it deranged.* Whenever I introduce myself, you know, I don't introduce myself with just my first name. I always introduce myself with my first name and my last name. On my car I have a Nigerian flag hanging on my rearview mirror. What else? Just little things, I have a T-shirt that has "Naija [Nigerian] girl" written on it, and I wear it around all the time. Just little things, and it has gotten to a stage, you know … My older brother is living in Nigeria. When he came over, I'll ask my father how come he has those three marks on his face, and my father would say, "It was a traditional thing we did to him when he was a baby." Then I'll get mad at parents and say, "Why didn't you do this to me?," because whenever they see this on my brother's face they would automatically and rightly assume that he is African, and I wanted that for myself. So, you know, those little things right there.

In Britain, respondents also drew boundaries between themselves and their proximal hosts, and they used moral and cultural boundaries to delineate the ethnic lines between Nigerians and Caribbeans. Lamide is a twenty-six-year-old engineer who was born and raised in Britain. Like Linda, Lamide does not want to be lumped in, in terms of ethnicity, with her proximal host. She was taught by her parents and now emphatically states that she is ethnically different from her proximal hosts. She told me, "At home, your parents always tell you that you're Nigerian, so, you know, don't get it confused. Even though I was born here [in Britain], I was still disciplined as a Nigerian. At home, me and my sister we would talk about respect, you know, how to respect your elders, and my parents would sometimes say, "Jamaicans don't respect their parents. But you're not Jamaican, you're Nigerian."

"When anyone ever asks me, 'Where are you from?,' I would say, 'I'm Nigerian.' But they would say, 'So where did you grow up?' They could tell from my accent that I don't have a strong Nigerian accent, so I say I grew up in the United Kingdom." I then asked how she expressed her Nigerianness, and she replied, "I would say there are certain things that I wouldn't do because I know that's not right in terms of going against my upbringing. I would never swear to an adult, I would never get drunk; I would never get pregnant without being married. I would never be irresponsible. I will also do well in my education. I also try and do well in my career. I'll be very respectful to my elders."

This chapter looks at the ethnic organization of second-generation adults of Nigerian ancestry in the United States and Britain and how a diasporic Nigerian ethnicity is forged among the second generation. Linda's and Lamide's stories reveal that the Nigerian second generation in both the United States and Britain believe that they have an ethnicity differentiating them from proximal hosts. This ethnicity has been formed in relation to and in the shadows of their proximal host and thus necessitates the use of symbolic boundaries between themselves and their proximal hosts.

According to segmented assimilation theory, the mode of identity formation for the black second generation will be a reactive ethnicity, which highlights "the role of a hostile context of reception in accounting for the rise rather than the erosion of ethnicity."[1] Portes and Rumbaut gave several examples of how ethnicities, ethnic identities, and ethnic group-consciousness are strengthened in the wake of ethnic conflicts: Korean Americanness was strengthened among second-generation Korean Americans in Los Angeles in the wake of the 1992 ethnic riots that saw over 2,500 Korean businesses burned down. The Mexican identity of second-generation Mexicans was thickened during the campaign against and then passage of Proposition 187 in California.[2] Thus the process of forging a reactive ethnicity in the face of perceived threats, persecution, and exclusion will cause the children of black immigrants to embrace a black identity as they become aware of racial disparities and navigate racism in the United States. Portes and Rumbaut see the pan-ethnic black label as an ethnic identity and thus conflate racial status, ethnicity, and identity into a single status for all black people, both native and second generation, characterized by an oppositional culture.

This chapter examines the process of forging what I call a diasporic Nigerian ethnicity among the second generation of Nigerian ancestry in both the United States and Britain. It is diasporic because Nigerian as an ethnicity has gained salience only in the diaspora; principal organizing lines in Nigeria are usually based on ethnic group membership, religion, and sometimes social class. It is also diasporic because ethnicity is formed as members of the ethnic group adapt to each country's local ecology. I discuss the third key factor in beyond racialization theory—the impact of transnational linkages and perspectives on the identities formed by the second generation of

Nigerian ancestry. I discuss the transnational mechanism of "cultural embedding" that transmitted a diasporic Nigerian ethnicity to the second generation. I discuss the symbolic boundaries respondents use to delineate the ethnic boundaries between themselves and their proximal hosts. A key national difference is that U.S. respondents drew much brighter boundaries between themselves and African Americans than British respondents drew between themselves and black Caribbeans. The examination of the symbolic boundaries used to delineate the ethnic lines reveal the cultural elements members of Nigerian communities in the United States and Britain have selected as the most symbolically important ones that make them an ethnic group.

FORGING A DIASPORIC NIGERIAN ETHNICITY

Transnational Cultural Embedding: Learning to Be Nigerian

Respondents underwent a process of cultural embedding, and this process transmitted to them from their parents and other first-generation members of the community the symbolically significant elements that had been selected as what distinguished them as an ethnic group from their proximal hosts. My concept of cultural embedding utilizes insights from Pierre Bourdieu's discussion of one form of cultural capital–the embodied state. Bourdieu sees cultural capital as existing in three forms: "in the embodied state, i.e. in the form of long-lasting dispositions of the mind and body; in the objectified state, in the form of cultural goods such as pictures, books, dictionaries, machines; and in the institutionalized state, a form of objectification such as through educational qualifications.[3] According to Bourdieu, "The accumulation of cultural capital in the embodied state, that is, in the form of what is called culture, cultivation, *Bildung,* presupposes a process of embodiment, incorporation, which insofar as it implies a labor of inculcation and assimilation, costs time, which must be invested personally by the investor."[4] In the same vein, most respondents were exposed over time to the cultural values deemed as symbolically and critically important through their parents' strictures and home life.

Respondents in both countries were raised not to become like their proximal hosts. In both countries, the proximal host served as the main group against which their identities were formed. This is due largely to the low status of these groups. In the United States, many respondents were told by their parents not to become *akatas*. Nigerian immigrants in the United States and Britain use the term *akata* to refer to African Americans in the United States and black Caribbeans in Britain. It means "foreigner" or "strange black person." Kemi described not being akata thus:

> You respect your elders, you go to school, you do what you have to do. We have boundaries where some of my American friends don't. Some of them can talk anyhow to their parents. At the same token, some of them don't. So, I don't like to stereotype everybody, but more of my friends, more than those who do not, act in that stereotypical American way. I was always taught that that is not right. We don't act like that, we are much more . . . our culture doesn't show us that or things like that. Not that we are elevated to a different level, but we just have a code of conduct that we kind of go by.

Kemi's parents raised her with a "Naija" mentality, which she said is "more of an action thing than stuff that I can put it into words." Naija is the pidgin, or broken English term, for Nigeria or Nigerian mentality. I asked Kemi to tell me her understanding of what the "Naija mentality" is. She told me, "Basically don't act like an 'akata.'" Laughing, she said that she really should include herself in that group—African American / akata since she is an American-born black. Nevertheless, she concluded, "I actually get offended if I am put into it." Looking back, she told me that her parents "saved my life by raising me the way they did because otherwise I don't know where I would have been without their guidance." Her parents, family, and friends used the term *akata* to drive home a key message: Don't become a foreigner. Don't become unfamiliar with our culture and values. Don't eschew education. Don't become disaffected with schooling but rather stay focused and do well.[5] Ike concurs with the principal message preached by parents and members of Nigerian communities to the second generation when they were growing up. He told me that growing up akata always had a negative connotation and referred to African Americans. I asked him to list some of the things African Americans did that distinguished them from Nigerians. He replied, "As far as education, they don't go as far as the education might go. The women, sometimes they have teen pregnancies. Maybe they smoke weed; they hang out; they do things that I guess a regular person shouldn't do, someone that has good home training wouldn't do. They are out late at night instead of being in their houses; instead of being at home with their families. Things like that."

The same message was preached in Britain. The bottom line for parents, which was clearly communicated to their children, was that they would not be allowed to become *ajerekes* under their watch. This term is a close cousin to the more frequently used *akata* in America. The literal translation of *ajereke* is "someone who eats sugarcane"; it refers to Caribbeans and alludes to their slave history when their ancestors toiled on sugar plantations, the major industry on Caribbean islands during slavery. Both *ajereke* and *akata* are used by Nigerians to call attention to and reinforce the idea of historical, ethnic, cultural, and behavioral differences between themselves and the proximal host black group they meet upon their arrival.

Respondents believed that they were raised differently from their peers. At home, many felt they were not living in America or Britain. They were caught in two worlds. Their parents were very strict, much stricter than the parents of their peers, and often told them they were not American or British and "should get that straight."[6] The ways they were raised reinforced their foreign origins and cultural difference. The second generation who grew up in America talked more about wanting to participate in the same activities as their American peers but not being allowed to do so by their parents. For example, quite a number of Nigerian families in America did not celebrate Halloween because they associate it with demonic practices and the occult. When they were younger, most wanted to be just like their American friends; they wanted to eat American foods, not traditional Nigerian foods; they wanted to accept sleepover invitations; they wanted to stay out later at night. But they had much less freedom than their proximal hosts to do these things. As Oyinkan put it, "A lot of the time I just felt that for females in particular that the African American females had a lot less rules that they had to follow, to me. They were allowed to do a lot more outlandish things." The second generation wanted to fit in, but their parents made doing so very difficult.

Many also felt their manners were quite different from those of their peers in Britain and America. According to Adaora:

> In high school, when they asked me to do things, and I'm like my mother will probably say no, and they are, "Why don't you just ask her," and I'm like, "Trust me, I know she'll say no." And they keep on, "I don't see why you don't ask her?" And I am like, because you just don't step over that line with them [my parents]. My mother always told me, "I am not your mate." And that is when it comes out that, look, you know, how you guys run your home is a lot different from how my parents run their home. When my mother says no I can't start asking why. Once she says no, it's no. I've learned that she cannot always offer me explanations. She doesn't have to. She is the mum.

In Adaora's home, as in most homes of the second generation who lived with their parents, parents were revered and even feared. There wasn't much room to negotiate with a parent once a decision was made. This is quite different from how most children of middle-class parents are raised.[7] For the second generation, even though most of them came from middle-class backgrounds, talking back to or pestering a parent to reconsider a decision was considered being cheeky and resulted in discipline.

Almost all respondents in both the United States and Britain, except for those who did not reside under their parents' roof when they were growing up and a few whose parents had deliberately isolated themselves from the Nigerian communities in these countries, remember being taken along to uncountable Nigerian social events or gatherings when they were growing up. Respondents used words like "steeped" and "entrenched" to describe their exposure to Nigerian culture. They spoke of "being taken" to Nigerian events "whether they really wanted to go or not." They said they were often "tired" of being "dragged along" to these events. Some parents, as their children got older, told them to "look around" and use the opportunity to find "potential marriage partners."

For many of these respondents, attending Nigerian events with their parents was a "large" or "significant" part of their lives. Mary, a physician in Britain, recalled:

> When we came to the United Kingdom, very early 1990, 1991, my parents met up with other eastern Nigerians, the Ibos. They realized that there were a whole bunch of them from the same village living in the United Kingdom so they formed a townspeople meeting and to this day we go every fortnight. We have annual gatherings and fund-raisers. So I will say to an extent that that gave me a strong sense of identity. And those are the people that have formed my extended networks. Some of the people in their twenties that I am friends with now, their parents are my parents' friends.

She still attends "when she has time" and knows that is "where I can meet my aunts." Chinelo, a twenty-two-year-old female respondent who was born in the United States but moved back to Nigeria for four years to attend high school before coming back for college told me:

> If I see a grown lady who is a Nigerian and I have never seen her before, I will call her auntie even if she is not my aunt. We will speak and I will give her respect even if it is just because she's from Nigeria, the same country you're

from. You don't just wave your hands; you go to them and hug them even if you don't know the person. Half the time because I know my parents might know the person, just because of that, I'll go and greet you.

The social ties of having friends whose parents know your parents, as in the case of Mary, and having to show respect to elders, the Nigerian way, to Nigerians of your parents' generation, peradventure they know your parents, are an example of how intergenerational closure helped engender a form of capital that transmits a strong diasporic Nigerian ethnicity to the second generation and generates a strong awareness of group consciousness.[8]

Adesuwa, a twenty-six-year-old actress in Britain, said, "When people ask me where I am from, I always say I am Nigerian, even though I have to get a visa to go to my own country. I still say Nigerian because that is where I come from, even though I was born and bred here. That is still home. I have parents who have always drummed it into me and my brother from when we were small that you know you come from Nigeria. Nigeria is home. They took us home. So we know where we come from."

One way parents keep Nigerian ethnicity strong and vibrant in their children is to send them to live in Nigeria, where they are exposed to their roots and home culture. Some parents view such a sojourn as an opportunity for the second generation to learn Nigerian values that will act as a bulwark against corrupting U.S. and British influences. Some respondents were like Sam, who said that Nigeria saved him because the experience gave him high self-esteem. Some like Funke had ambiguous identities, but exposure to Nigerian coethnics and Nigerian culture revitalized their identities. She told me that when she was growing up, she felt African American until she went to Nigeria.

And then I experienced that and then I was proud to be a Nigerian. You know growing up, the African American kids will tease me and call me "African booty scratcher" and stuff like that. So growing up, African was like the worst thing you could be until I got into high school, and then I went to Nigeria and saw it for what it was and how fabulous Nigeria could be. And so, I was proud to be Nigerian. As soon as I came back, I told everyone I was Nigerian and everything about me was Nigerian. I was no longer African American.

Ike told me that being sent to live in Nigeria for two years when he was ten "definitely had a major impact on my life and upbringing."

When they told me I was leaving, I cried. I screamed. I felt like I was going to jail or something. I thought all my friends were going to forget about me, it was so hard, but I went there; I lived there. I experienced life in a boarding school, and that experience, I mean, you can't even pay for that experience. It was invaluable. I grew up so much. I learnt to become independent. I did well academically there and you just had to develop your sense. I really grew up a lot from that experience and it changed me. I know Nigeria has changed, and I haven't been back since then because of school and everything, but that experience definitely changed me. Before, my brothers and I were really a handful for my parents, but when we came back we were better behaved, less wasteful, less wasteful of food, definitely. We ate all of our food. We were more appreciative of what we had. We were more disciplined and more respectful to elders. We were more respectful of elder people.

Parents also sent their children back to Nigeria to get them away from bad influences that derailed them from performing well in school. This was the experience of Yetunde, a twenty-eight-year-old female pharmacologist: "I tried to rebel against the way my parents tried to raise me up. I ran away twice. She [my mother] sent me to Nigeria because I was going down a bad path. The people I was moving with had no future. That is the thing about living in the Bronx. So I moved around with a lot of friends from low-income families. They don't think about college. They just think about work and getting into trouble and stuff like that; so my mom wanted to remove me from that." I asked Yetunde why she ran away from home, and she said she was "being young and stupid." She recalls her two years in Nigeria from the age of seventeen to nineteen as the best years of her life. She told me that she learned morals and Nigerian culture. She was not aware that she was being sent back to Nigeria. Her mother told her that she was going back for a holiday and then told her she was staying once she got to Nigeria and confiscated her passport. I asked her if she knew the outcomes of her friends; she told me that none of them had gone to college.

Being able to send their children back to Nigeria was a resource for Nigerian parents, a form of social capital that existed in their ethnic communities. Other immigrant communities have this resource also. This strategy of removing children from bad company, or as a way to toughen them up or make them more fluent in the ethnic culture, worked to culturally embed their children in an environment where their Nigerian ethnicity was strengthened. All respondents who spent some years in Nigeria during their formative years (between the ages of seven and eighteen) agreed that it was a beneficial experience. They learned much about Nigerian culture, grew tougher and more independent but at the same time remained respectful of their elders and became more appreciative of the resources and opportunities available in the United States and Britain compared to Nigeria. Also, as mentioned earlier, before migrating to the United States and Britain, parents, most of whom were well- educated, sent their children to live with siblings, close relatives, or close family friends who were similarly educated, lived in urban areas, and were equipped (materially and domestically) to take good care of their children. Their children were enrolled in good schools and were prepared for gaining admission to college or university either in Nigeria or when they returned to the United States or Britain. Consequently, my respondents did not suffer an academic deficit upon their return to the United States and Britain.

In the United States, most parents believed very strongly in negative stereotypes about African Americans, and they told their children not to befriend or hang out with them. According to Uju, a twenty-two-year-old female, "Nigerians can be racist. They think every African American is doing bad. They would rather you hang out with whites and not African Americans because they feel that whites are more quiet and are less likely to get into trouble." Parents who did not explicitly forbid their children to hang out with African Americans specified the African Americans they did not want their children to associate with. Lola's parents "only dissuaded me from hanging out with African American women who were pregnant. If my mum knew this person and she became pregnant, that would be the last time I would hang out with that person. My mum entertained the stereotypes like 'their women don't respect their elders, they don't take education seriously, they have sex and have babies, and I don't want you to be like that.'" According to Ehi, "My parents never wanted us to hang out with those from the 'hood."

Some respondents were unhappy about what they felt was a very discriminatory view. They often ignored their parents' strictures but knew that if their behavior changed significantly, such that they were becoming akatas, their parents would come down hard on them. The messages of Nigerian parents are similar to the messages elite and stable middle-class African Americans gave their children. Those parents also worried that their children would, through friendships, pick up bad habits from lower-class blacks.[9]

In Britain, respondents were told not to hang out with Caribbeans. Parents draw much sharper boundaries against Caribbeans than did the second generation. Many parents feared close association with Caribbeans led children to have bad outcomes. Emem, a twenty-two-year-old female, remarked, "I have some Caribbean friends, but they are not very close. I live with my parents, and if I tell them that I am friends with Afro-Caribbeans, they will use stereotypes against them. They will say, 'Caribbeans! They do drugs! They party! They do not like education.' So I cannot bring them home to my parents because of the discrimination." This distrust is also expressed in parents' strictures against marrying Caribbeans. Bode's father told him that he would be disowned if he married a Caribbean girl. Muyiwa, who is a thirty-five-year-old electrician, recounted, "When I was younger, I used to go out with a Jamaican girl, and my mom went absolutely nuts." Emem described the situation many of the second generation face on the issue of dating and marrying Caribbeans: "Parents will give you the evil eye if you tell them you want to marry a Caribbean person." Translated, this means that parents would radiate unambiguous and strong disapproval, expressed with the expectation that the child will abandon such nonsensical ideas and immediately conform to the parents' position. This strong deterring pressure worked among the Nigerian second generation interviewed in this book: of the thirty-one married respondents only two had Caribbean partners: Sam Echekoba, who had a Caribbean wife, and Maggie, who has a Caribbean male partner with whom she has a young child.

What became clear from talking to respondents in both the United States and Britain about how they were raised by their parents and within Nigerian communities is that very negative stereotypes of the proximal host are widely disseminated in these communities and are used in the process of forging the second generation's ethnic identities. Furthermore, as I show later in the chapter, these views were used to both delineate the differences between the two groups and establish the cultural elements that unified Nigerians. The negative stereotypes they hold of African Americans and Caribbeans are largely drawn from the media's portrayal of them and their experience with some members of the proximal host in their schools and lower- to middle-class neighborhoods. Of course, many African Americans and Caribbeans are successful members of the middle and upper classes. There are many who disconfirm these negative stereotypes. But as social psychology studies have found, while the bad behavior of the in-group (here, Nigerians) is attributed to situational or environmental factors and seen as the exception, the same bad behavior among the out-group (here, the proximal host) is attributed to disposition and deep character flaws. As a result, disconfirming evidence does not overturn the negative stereotypes.[10]

In both countries, ambiguous identities and the identities held as teenagers became concretized when the second generation were attending college or in early adulthood. A growing Nigerian and African population, coupled with more opportunities to interact with first- and second-generation coethnics of similar age, was the main reason most cited for why they ended up with Nigerian-centric identities. In college, they met a mix of first- and second-generation Nigerians, which afforded them the opportunity to meet same-age peers who were rich in things Nigerian and who were viewed as culturally authentic Nigerians. Many of these people could speak Nigerian languages, Nigerian pidgin (broken English similar to Caribbean patois), and knew the country, its history, and its current events. This exposure to fellow Nigerians came at a time when many were being accused of being inauthentic Nigerians by first-generation Nigerians in the United States and Britain and by Nigerians back home when they visited. For those who were interested in learning more about their roots and all things Nigerian, these individuals were a good resource. Nena, a twenty-four-year-old financial analyst, is a good example of how identities were concretized in college. She was born and raised in Britain and went from identifying as British and black British to identifying simultaneously as Nigerian and Ibo (a Nigerian ethnic identity) and African (a diasporic pan-ethnic identity) in college. She said:

> When I was much younger it used to be drummed into your head, "Okay, you are black, but you are British. You were born here, you schooled here, you are British. First and foremost, you are black British." There was this whole black British togetherness, but when I started growing up and going to Nigeria more, I began to realize really and truly, "You are not British. You are African. You are black African." As I became older, as I started leaving school and went into college and now started meeting other girls similar to me and who were more openly Nigerian and African, who hadn't schooled here like I had and came in much older they were just African—just their whole style, their whole flavor, I related to them more. I then adopted and realized the importance of calling myself an African or a Nigerian.

Most enjoyed meeting their coethnics in larger and more diverse groupings and tended to gravitate to them, citing higher comfort levels. They lived the adage birds of a feather flock together. Pamela is a twenty-four-year-old lawyer in Britain, and she remembered associating with Nigerians and other Africans "because you have similar backgrounds, you have similar experiences, so you just get on. We have more in common. You do so just because you kind of take comfort with people similar to yourself." Jibola said, "You draw comfort from one another commiserating about how strict your parents were growing up. This is something all second-generation Nigerians in the United States understand. We often send jokes around in email chains that talk about this, and you can only understand it if you are one of us." Other unifying topics are unpleasant experiences they had with their proximal hosts and the pressures put on them by parents and friends in the diasporic and transnational Nigerian communities to do very well academically and live true to Nigerian values.

Some of the second generation reported that there were tense relations between some African immigrants (both first- and second-generation) and African Americans in college. Being brought up differently by their parents made them realize that there were real cultural differences, not just physical differences, between the groups. This knowledge, along with their fraught relations with their proximal hosts, made them choose more Nigerian- and African-centric identities after arriving at college and into adulthood. It was in college that most attained a place of being comfortable with who they are. As Monica said, "[Forming an ethnic identity] is a process. When you go to college then you find out that you are Nigerian, and you are proud of who you are. You become proud of your body identity. I am proud that I have the nose. I am proud that I have the hips, and that I have the skin." Ultimately, in America, most of the Nigerian second generation became comfortable with being black but not African American. Similarly, in Britain, most became comfortable with being black but not Caribbean or black British.

DELINEATING ETHNIC BOUNDARIES

After the cultural embedding the second generation lived through growing up, I was interested in investigating what being Nigerian meant to them. What was the content of their Nigerian ethnicity? Based on the fact that ethnic identification requires two simultaneous processes, signaling difference and establishing similarity,[11] what cultural differences did they see as existing between themselves and their proximal hosts? This question about dissimilarities is significant because it is impossible to successfully be a member of an ethnic group without establishing what makes your group different from another group (an "us vs. them" dynamic). But you must also agree on what you and other members of your group have in common. So the question about similarities is also important. Both processes are important because they generate feelings of membership in and attachment to the group.[12]

I found that the second generation of Nigerian ancestry in the United States and Britain hold very meaningful identities that are based on what I call a *constructed diasporic Nigerian ethnicity*. It is diasporic because it has increased salience away from Nigeria. Within Nigeria, groups are mobilized generally on the basis of ethnic group; for example, being Yoruba, Hausa, Ibo, or Ijaw; or being Muslim or Christian; or being a southerner or a northerner. It is only outside the country that the Nigerian national ethnicity has become an ethnic identity that Nigerians from different ethnic groups are happy to claim. As an ethnicity created in the diaspora, "Nigerian" is quite different from what it is back in Nigeria. The second generation—whether they call themselves fully or partly Nigerian, or hyphenated Nigerian-American, or American, African, or black—are influenced by Nigerian values. Yet the "Nigerianness" my respondents talked about does not describe the entire universe of Nigerians but just a segment and an elite segment at that. When they talk about Nigerians valuing education to the extent that it is "un-Nigerian not to go to college," they are referencing a "Nigeria" made up only of people with high human and financial capital and significant intangibles that promote high achievement.

Nigerian ethnicity is thus diasporic because this is not the truest picture of Nigeria. As a country with 181 million people, Nigeria is ranked 121st in terms of gross domestic product (GDP) per capita, at $2,688. It has an illiteracy rate of 68 percent and an average of eight years of education for the entire population.[13] In Nigeria, only 7 percent of the adult population has at least a bachelor's degree, compared to approximately six of every ten first-generation Nigerian immigrants in the United States and Britain. This huge gap shows that the immigration policies of both countries, combined with the selectivity of Nigerian migrants, has created a diasporic Nigerianness that differs greatly from what exists in Nigeria itself. The Nigerian ethnicity in both countries is also diasporic because its cultural content is hybridized. Even though respondents say that they are ethnically and culturally different from their proximal hosts, they cannot avoid exposure to and interaction with them, so the two cultures have intermingled.

Here I present evidence on respondents' views of the cultural elements that make up the diasporic Nigerian ethnicity. I examine the symbolic boundaries they are using to delineate the ethnic boundaries between themselves and other groups within the black racial category. Scholars who study boundaries divide them into two types: social boundaries, which are objectified differences like class and race, and symbolic boundaries, which are defined as "the types of lines that individuals draw when they categorize people.... They are evaluative distinctions—different ways of believing that 'we' are better than 'them.'" There are three main types of symbolic boundaries: moral, socioeconomic, and cultural: "Moral boundaries are drawn on the basis of moral character. They are centered around such qualities as honesty, work ethic, personal integrity, and consideration for others. Socioeconomic boundaries are drawn on the basis of judgments concerning people's social position as indicated by their wealth, power, or professional success. Cultural boundaries are drawn of the basis of education, intelligence, manners, tastes, and command of high culture."[14]

The adult second generation of Nigerian ancestry in the United States and Britain drew numerous cultural, moral, and socioeconomic boundaries to differentiate themselves from their proximal hosts. In the United States, the primary criteria respondents used to draw the boundaries of their ethnic difference were having roots, having a culture, having a mind-set that values education, and having values such as respect for elders and hard work. The secondary criteria included having more stable families and being socially conservative. Like the second generation in the United States, the Nigerian second generation in Britain see themselves as different from their proximal hosts. The primary criteria respondents used to draw the ethnic boundaries between themselves and Caribbeans were having a mind-set that values education, having values such as respect for elders and hard work, and having stable families.

However, there is one key difference between the two sets of respondents: those in the United States drew much more rigid boundaries between themselves and African Americans than did those in Britain between themselves and Caribbeans. In Britain, while respondents also used symbolic boundaries, they were not as bright as the ones drawn by their U.S. counterparts. The difference in the salience of the boundaries rests on two facts. First, Nigerians in Britain recognize that they are in the same situation as Caribbeans: both are unwelcome immigrants from Britain's former colonies, and as black people both face significant discrimination from white Britons. Second, there are signs that social class segregation is stronger than in the United States. My British respondents' reports on their friendship networks reveal that they and Caribbeans live in what I call segregated class worlds, because they had few close friendships with Caribbeans. Thus the Nigerian second generation in Britain did not need to police the boundaries between themselves and their proximal hosts as frequently as did their counterparts in the United States. Several studies in the United States suggest that black immigrants have the added motivation to do so because of the perception in many quarters of American society that black immigrants are the "good" blacks,[15] whereas because all black people are viewed with suspicion in Britain there was no added motivation for Nigerians to distance themselves from Caribbeans. Rather they felt that all ethnic minorities are made to feel like outsiders.[16]

The Symbolic Boundaries Used to Erect Ethnic Boundaries against the Proximal Host in the United States

"We Have Roots." Most second-generation adults of Nigerian ancestry consider themselves intrinsically different from African Americans because they have "roots." In contrast, almost no African Americans, except the few who can afford DNA testing to trace their ancestry, can trace their lineage to a particular village in a particular country in Africa. Having no roots is seen by many of the second generation as one of two fundamental ethnic differences between the two groups and is linked to a wider critique of the basic value orientations and culture of African Americans. "Having no roots" means many things to first- and second-generation Nigerians in the U.S. diaspora. Ibidun, a physician whose parents are both physicians, came to the United States when he was four years old. In his interview he revealed several symbolic boundaries that he uses to distance himself from African Americans, although he expressed discomfort about expressing them: "I'm not African American in the sense that my ancestry, my direct genetic lineage, is Nigerian from Africa. I hate to put it this way, but I don't have any blood of slaves in me. That might sound bad, and I don't mean it to sound bad, but I'm not an African American in that sense. I'm a Nigerian American."

For some, like Ibidun, African Americans' lack of roots is a result of their forced removal from Africa and subjugation in America, which does not apply to Nigerians, a conclusion that forgets slavery also occurred on the African continent during this period. For others, like Ike, having no roots means that African Americans have a problematic culture. Ike said, "They don't have a culture like us. They are searching for their roots, especially the ones that are descendants of slaves. Their ancestors came from or were brought over from Africa. They don't have as strong a cultural identity. They cannot say, 'Oh, this is exactly where I come from.' They cannot trace their lineage back, which we can do." It must be said, of course, that African Americans have a rich culture that influences many aspects of American life and in some areas is in fact the dominant cultural influence.

"Those Chains That Weigh Them Down Don't Weigh Me Down." Most respondents felt that African Americans are too consumed with the injustices done to them in the past and in society today and have allowed the social relationships of race to constrain their ambitions and provide excuses for why they have not achieved more. Many respondents felt that slavery, the collective memory of it, the racial subordination of blacks that went with it, legal segregation, and the many racial injustices throughout America's history have made African Americans different from second-generation Nigerians and first-generation Nigerians also. Idowu, who was introduced at the beginning of the book, summarized many respondents' opinions as to why. He acknowledged that African Americans have experienced significant racial injustice but still believes that the fact that many are not doing well in this country is partly their fault. He believes that the experience of slavery and legal segregation produced a mentality among African Americans that manifests in "their predilection or taste for flashy clothing, which they regard as important and necessary." He, like many African Americans in the public sphere, wants them to prioritize education over these "frivolous pursuits." As an individual of Nigerian ancestry, Idowu said, he stands "very unequivocally on the side of education is the path to success. You have got to do it. It is very important. But in the African American community it is not so clearcut." He says there is some racial bias at play because "if you walk down Madison Avenue, you will see plenty Asians, whites, and many others totally engaged in what might be seen as frivolous pursuits" too, but for them, it is not regarded as such.

Idowu commented that because of slavery and government-supported segregation, African Americans feel that the system is rigged against them:

> They were slaves two hundred years ago, and immediately after slavery for a hundred years there were Jim Crow laws. And even though they left the South and moved to the North, they were repacked into housing projects and weren't afforded decent education and had to use separate and unequal facilities. And I think the chain, maybe the weight of all of that over generations and generations, is what maybe makes a lot of new members in their com-

munity disenfranchised from the system or makes them think we have to operate outside of it. So they are afraid or unwilling to kind of operate in the larger white society.

This mentality, according to Idowu, makes African Americans culturally different from Africans. Idowu concluded, "It might not necessarily be their fault when you take a cultural or social historical look, but I am just not associated with that—those chains that are weighing them down don't weigh me down."

This view of having a different way of interpreting racial incidents compared to African Americans was attributed by some respondents to having a frame of reference that draws heavily from their immigrant background. Titi told me that she wants outsiders to recognize the difference between Nigerians and other black groups: "I do think that my values and my thoughts are different from African Americans' and I want that known. It is important to me that my children know this. I feel that I'm holding on to a lot of Nigerian values because I want to pass them on to my children." She described the foreign values that differentiate her from African Americans as not letting racial discrimination and injustice from whites get her down:

There are a lot of things in this country that are not fair. We are not on the same plane education-wise and I'm talking racially. Blacks and whites and Hispanics and Asians, we don't go to the same schools, we have different rates of college graduation and even high school graduation rates. We know that it is not equal. So, I think for me, some of my values is to understand that life is not equal, and I don't let that get to me. I always say I choose my battles because life is a battle. There are a lot of things that are not equal but it is not my job. I have to pick my battles. I can't fight every battle because I'm not going to win many of them. I have to pick the battle I want to fight. So I think when I compare myself to a lot of my African American friends, there is this thought that this is not fair or anything will happen to me today. Just constant battling that I feel that they have and for me, I have learnt to not fight every fight. I think about what's the most proper for me. When I was doing my PhD, I had a lot of smack from the pilgrims. I call the white people pilgrims. I got a lot of smacks from them, but if I spend my time attending to every smack I get, every battle, every negative comment I get, I won't even want to come to class. I would not be able to complete one class. So I just decided to grow a tough skin and pick my battles. So that is one of the values that I think differentiates us Nigerians from African Americans where they just feel like [heavy sigh], "I just can't get ahead. Everybody is just trying to keep me down." And for me, I come with the thought that of course I can get ahead. I already know that everybody is trying to keep me down. So when you come to me with a negative comment, you are not surprising me. I expect that from you. So I feel that I am ahead of the battle because I already know I'm in a battle. I don't have to keep reacting every time somebody says something. And so that is just one of the things I think that is different. For me, when I go back home, when I go back to Nigeria, I just think about people who don't have the same opportunity that I have. So I'm always thankful for these opportunities that I have. I think about those who don't have the opportunity and that gets me forward. I think for African Americans, they think, men, "Look at all the opportunities that the white people have and I don't have." For me, it's a different comparison. I compare myself with the people behind me who wish they were where I was, while I think African Americans compare themselves to people ahead of them. And I feel like it's a whole different perspective. When you look behind you, it pushes you forward. When you look at the people ahead of you, you are so mentally fatigued by the space between you and the person ahead of you that you can't get there.

Titi is not naive about the racial inequalities that exist in the United States. As a black person, she has experienced racial discrimination, but she believes that Nigerians' emotional response to discrimination is what differentiates them from African Americans. Because she lived in Nigeria until she was twelve, Titi's frame of reference draws on her own experiences living in Nigeria. She explains her "foreign" values or the "values" that make her different from African Americans as having a cultural frame of reference that allows her to be very thankful of the opportunities she has in America compared to Nigeria. This cultural frame of reference stopped her from assimilating according to the pathway predicted for the black and Hispanic second generation in segmented assimilation and racialization theories. She did not become disillusioned by her experiences of racial discrimination; they did not cause her to lower her aspirations and develop a reactive ethnicity with the end result that she fell into the black underclass. On the contrary, the frame of reference made her embrace the opportunities available in the United States and interpret her experiences of racial discrimination as part of the lived realities and struggle of living in the United States.

Respondents' family and kin social networks also helped develop their frame of reference. Idowu and Mohammed, who were born and raised in the United States, developed their frames of reference from their parents and family members and friends. Mohammed said, "I have a lot of family that come from Nigeria to the United States and they influence us [he and his siblings] a lot. They tell us of the hardship. I also see my parents. They came to the United States for schooling. I do not want to not take advantage of being born in the United States." The frame of reference informed by personal experience or from their parents and family and friends stories is an important mechanism that fostered the motivation to achieve among respondents. The stories these respondents tell reveal how ethnicity can become capital via the social networks and relations that exist in their Nigerian communities. But even though we as sociologists can analyze it to see how their ethnicity and immigrant background has become a resource for the second generation, and how the racial experiences of black immigrants and their children are considerably different from that of African Americans, the second generation themselves understand and discuss this advantage in the language of ethnicity and as cultural values that are part of what make them ethnically different from their proximal hosts.

Furthermore, the racial socialization of the Nigerian second generation is different from the racial socialization of African Americans. The Nigerian second generation have acquired a unique understanding of race from their parents. Their view is that being black is not synonymous with being African American, and by this I mean being ethnically the same as African Americans. They believe that the call for racial unity can and should be denied if it is not aligned with one's best interests.

Consequently, though most of my respondents, like almost all other black people living in America, have experienced antiblack discrimination,[17] their common response is similar to Deola's: "We don't have a chip on our shoulder because of slavery. We don't think 'the man' is keeping us down. Racism does not faze me like it does African Americans."

"Pretty Much Nothing Less than Getting a College Degree Will Do." Just like when they were children, as adults respondents view attitudes to education and educational performance through a racial frame and use it as a vehicle to make claims about ethnic difference between themselves and African Americans. I have discussed that "it is un-Nigerian not to go to college" is an effective social norm in the Nigerian communities in the United States and Britain and so will just briefly reiterate that this is one of the most important symbolic boundaries used to draw the ethnic lines between themselves and African Americans.

Respondents also mentioned that this emphasis on education is being noticed by outsiders.[18] Oyinkan said, "I have one friend who is from Dominican Republic, and she asked me one day, 'Do Nigerians do anything else besides law, medicine? Are they anything else but doctors, nurses, physical therapists, lawyers, accountants?' And I was like, 'I don't know what to tell you.'" Oyinkan, of course, was saying that she could not dispute what her friend said. While some respondents resented the pressure put on them by their parents and members of the community, others, looking back, say they are grateful for it.

"We Have Values." The widely held view among the second generation of Nigerian ancestry in the United States is that Nigerians "have values." *Values* was the word most frequently used when describing the differences between themselves and African Americans.

In the eyes of most of the Nigerian second generation, African Americans have different values because they "do not show respect." They talk back to their parents. They do not value family, evidenced by the high prevalence of absentee fathers and single-female-headed households. They don't value the institution of marriage, evidenced by the high incidence of out-of-wedlock children and teenage pregnancies in their community. They are not hard-working. And they exploit the welfare system. However, many studies show that African Americans do value education just as much as other groups, and there are many African Americans who are successful, not in jail, not on welfare, and so on. However, most respondents tended to use the negative stereotypes of African Americans and not their positive achievements to inform the cultural and moral symbolic boundaries they drew to delineate the ethnic boundaries between Nigerians in the U.S. diaspora and African Americans.

This was especially true for respondents' parents, but the second generation were more open to judging African Americans on an individual basis. When asked to describe his relationship with African Americans, Ndubusi, a twenty-five-year-old male who works in a biomedical firm and has a college degree, said, "I have no problems with them. I think you have to judge them on an individual basis. You have to judge each individual. I don't judge based on group membership."

Almost all my respondents told me that Nigerians strongly value respect for elders. There are rituals of respect many of the second generation have to observe. Some find this onerous and alien growing up in America, which is more casual about such things. Shubby is an example of someone who finds Nigerian rituals of respect irritating. He said, "Nigerians say you cannot shake hands with your left, or that you must greet one another when you come in. I just don't buy into these things at all and they irritate me." Some parents were very strict, wanting their children to observe these rituals of respect in all situations, including in the home. Others expected their children to observe these rituals of respect in traditional and public social settings but not in the home. However, the minimum expectation was respect. Sometimes these rituals of respect were incomprehensible to Americans, as Bose, a twenty-five-year-old female secretary, reported: "Like, in the Yoruba culture, if you see adults, you have to prostrate [lay down flat on the ground] to them. African Americans don't understand that. They see that as you are worshiping the person. They don't understand that we do that as a sign of respect. They call their elders by their first names, but in our culture we have to say 'auntie' even if she is not our real auntie."

Respondents believe that Nigerians value hard work. Ike said, "I think Nigerians are very highly motivated, are a very intelligent people. When they come over here, they quickly take advantage of whatever opportunity they can because they have no one to fall back on. Especially if they are the first person coming over here from Nigeria, they have to make ends meet. They can't call up daddy and say, 'Oh, please give me some money.' They have to start working, and they work hard." He feels that his uncle's immigrant experience in the United States showcases what it means to be Nigerian. "My uncle is not yet a permanent resident. He came to the United States about eight or nine years ago. When he came, he started doing odd jobs. He worked at one point in a factory bottling coke. From there he became a nurse with an associate degree. Then he got his bachelor's in nursing. From there he applied to medical school, and is in medical school now." Ike said that his uncle is paying for medical school from his earnings as a nurse since he is not a citizen and thus "doesn't qualify for financial aid." He concluded by saying, "This is just the kind of drive we have. We just have no other option. We have to make it."

Not all respondents had this glowing view of Nigerians. A few, like Skin, were very critical of Nigerians living in the United States. Skin is twenty-six years old and has lived all his life in America. He grew up in the projects in Brooklyn before moving to Long Island, New York. His neighborhood and high school in Long Island were predominantly made up of Jews. He played football and obtained a football scholarship to attend college. He said, "I went back to Nigeria when I was eight years old, and I hated it. It was too hot. I have never been back since, and I don't want to go back. I don't like the way Nigerians act or behave." When asked how he identified, Skin said, "I am 100 percent American. America means everything to me. It is the best. It is the best in culture, in people. It is the best in the world. The only way I am Nigerian is through my parents. My roots are Nigerian. I see myself as American. In fact, I look at my mother and her relatives and they all act and live as if they are in Nigeria. I don't understand it or like it." "Nigerians are too cautious about things," he continued. "Nigerians are just so rigid. They want things done in a certain way. They act and revere things I cannot stand, the opposite of the way I behave. I don't know how to explain it. Nigerians like to judge people a lot, and they judge them from the appearance. For example, my friend's parents judge me because I wear an earring, but they don't know me. When I was growing up, there were a lot of Africans and Nigerians that came to hang out in my house. But I did not like them at all. I did not like the way they behaved, so I got my own circle of friends."

I asked respondents to describe their relations with Caribbeans, another sizable black group in the United States, to investigate whether they also drew ethnic boundaries between themselves and Caribbeans or whether they blurred these boundaries because they both have immigrant backgrounds. I also asked respondents this question to investigate whether they were consistent in claiming that members of the black racial category in the United States could have different ethnicities even given the country's history with black people and its tendency to take a monolithic view of blackness or whether they were defining a distinct ethnicity as an attempt to distance themselves only from African Americans, the group that over the course of U.S. history many other immigrants have distanced themselves from and, as some put it, the group on whose backs immigrants have stepped in order to assimilate.[19]

What I found is that the Nigerian second generation believe in diverse ethnicities within the black racial category in the United States. Almost all respondents agreed that the three main black groups, Africans, Caribbeans, and African Americans, are culturally different. However, while respondents demarcated bright boundaries between Nigerians and African Americans, the ethnic boundaries they draw against U.S. Caribbeans are not as bright. They see Caribbeans in the United States as similar to them. Many respondents described Caribbeans as their "cousins." All respondents who had interacted with Caribbeans viewed them as having similar cultural norms regarding education, ambition, and drive, despite differences in terms of food, language, and style, According to Habibat, "They have similar spiritual, educational, and family beliefs like we have." Gbenga agreed: "I find a lot of similarities between the Nigerians and Caribbeans. They are conservative also. There is an emphasis on education, emphasis on family." He is comfortable enough with them that he dated a Caribbean woman. He was single when I interviewed him. When asked what he meant by "conservative," Gbenga said, "[It] means socially conservative, as in we believe in family first, we believe in God, we worship God, we are Christians. We don't pierce our, whatever body part you can think of, we don't pierce it. If you are not a woman, you don't wear an earring. We don't do dreadlocks, that kind of thing."[20] On the whole, the second generation who had interactions with both African Americans and Caribbeans said they had warmer relations with the latter. This is in part because Caribbeans are also immigrant blacks, which carries more weight than the fact that Caribbeans, like African Americans, have a history of slavery.

The views expressed by the Nigerian second generation, especially about African Americans, must be contextualized in the history of U.S. race relations and racial politics that have uniquely shaped the African American experience. The Nigerian second generation and their parents, part of a group that is highly selected, came to the United States with significant advantages that their proximal hosts, African Americans, did not have. And black immigrants and their children, as individuals who are racially black, are able to benefit from institutions and programs established through the Civil Rights movement to advance the upward mobility of minorities in the United States.

Throughout U.S. history, new immigrants have sought, as part of their strategy to gain full social inclusion and assimilate into American society, to distance themselves from African Americans. White immigrants from southern and eastern Europe gained entry into an enlarged white category in part by distancing themselves from African Americans.[21] Asians advanced their sociopolitical interests and expanded citizenship rights by contrapositioning themselves against African Americans.[22] The sociologist Nancy Foner points out "that the civil rights movement in putting black-white issues on center stage in the national agenda, helped blur, what were then considered racial boundaries among European groups, allowing Jews and Italians to 'vanish into whiteness.'"[23] And while this was happening, Asian Americans' success in presenting themselves as model minorities also helped brighten the boundaries between blacks and whites. The end result of all this was a new racial order that enlarged the white category, incorporating the different European groups that prior to that time were not seen as white; brought Asian Americans closer to whites and further from blacks; and kept blacks at the bottom of the racial hierarchy.[24] And history shows that these immigrant groups sometimes borrowed the strategies and languages of struggle being used by African Americans during the Civil Rights movement to advance their fight for social inclusion.[25] But the Nigerian second generation are aware that they cannot fully distance themselves from African Americans, and most do not seek to do so. Neither do any contest that they are racially black. I show in the next chapter that all hold a black racial identity in which they identify with their proximal hosts, recognize the economic, social, and political implications of being black in the United States, and are mobilized in the fight against antiblack racism.

Even though black immigrants and their children from the Caribbean and Africa are sometimes portrayed as a success story in the United States, with their success framed against African Americans, their racial status makes them vulnerable to racial discrimination. A close look at the data reveals that despite higher levels of education, black immigrants are not receiving a commensurate return to their education.[26] A study of Caribbean immigrants that tested the different reasons given for their success—immigrant selectivity, having a superior culture, and being favored by white employers over African Americans—found that it could only be attributed to immigrant selectivity. Thus white employers' favoritism does not seem to lead to higher wages for black immigrants in the labor market.[27] Furthermore, as black people, black immigrants and their children have the racial body that is being surveilled, policed, and often incapacitated by the punitive state, which makes them vulnerable to future racial incidents that can derail their success. Thus the monikers "better blacks," "good blacks," and "preferred blacks" when used to describe black immigrants and their children ignore that much of their success is owed to the higher levels of human, financial, and social capital many black immigrants and their children from the Caribbean and Africa possess, along with other considerable intangibles, and not to a more equitable playing field. Such monikers also obscure the fact that these immigrants are being discriminated against in the labor market and in the public space. Questions that need to be investigated are how successful the third generation of these highly selective populations will be and how first- and second-generation black immigrants from lower-class backgrounds, such as African refugees and their children, are faring in the United States.

Finally, the role of the state in maintaining racial categories and racial inequality must be mentioned. As the sociologists Michael Omi and Howard Winant point out, "The racial system is managed by the state—encoded in law, organized through policy making, and enforced by a repressive apparatus. Under a law and order ideology, the racial state after the civil rights era promulgated new laws and adapted new technologies of violence and oppression that reestablished racial stratification and inequality."[28] A process of criminalization where the state intrudes into their everyday lives in order to regulate deviant behavior and maintain social order is enveloping black and Latino youths, primarily men, in unprecedented numbers.[29] The sociologist Victor Rios describes this ubiquitous process of criminalization as the "youth control complex," which "is the combined effect of the web of institutions, schools, families, businesses, residents, media, community centers, and the criminal justice system that collectively punish, stigmatize, monitor, and criminalize young people in an attempt to control them."[30] Some schools, especially those in marginalized communities, are now a pipeline introducing youths of color to the criminal justice system, for school administrators and teachers, "whenever any student misbehaved[,] . . . would threaten either to call the police, to send them to jail, or to call a probation officer."[31] Community centers that are supposed to be sites for rehabilitating youths and helping them integrate into society are often staffed by officers from the criminal justice system who put pressure on them to snitch on their friends, which has terrible consequences for them if they are found out. Thus the rise of a punitive state is rolling back the gains won during the Civils Rights movement even as it is reinstituting practices that are destroying the life chances of many black and brown individuals and blocking their mobility into the middle class. And all this is happening alongside the "containment of movement demands for equality and a racial democracy under the ideology of colorblindness."[32]

The Symbolic Boundaries Used to Erect Ethnic Boundaries against the Proximal Host in Britain

Like their U.S. counterparts, the most common boundaries British respondents draw are cultural and moral ones. They stressed having positive values and prioritizing education as the two key differences between the groups. But unlike U.S. respondents in regard to African Americans, British respondents did not claim ethnic distinctions based on Caribbeans' having no roots. Instead, they view Caribbeans as people who do not value education as highly as Nigerians do. They largely make this charge against Jamaicans, the largest Caribbean island group in Britain. Take, for example, Oye, a thirty-two-year-old sales representative, who said, "One thing Africans don't like is that they do not like to be classified as Jamaican, because in Britain white people like to say the black population is too relaxed, but it is the Jamaicans that are relaxed." Oye then switched to the term *Afro-Caribbean*, even though he is still referring to Jamaicans: "Afro-Caribbeans don't like studying. White people say blacks are more relaxed, but that is not true for Nigerians. They have three or four degrees."

Oye's response raises the question of whether respondents think that white people see a difference between Africans and Caribbeans. Most respondents said it depends on the region of Britain and people's educational level. People in London and other places that have a sizable population of ethnic minorities are more likely to see the difference between the black groups. But white Britons in remote, rural places tend not to see a distinction between black groups. Most respondents felt that educated people are also more likely to be aware of the ethnic diversity among Britain's black population than are less educated people.

While respondents said that they enjoy some elements of Caribbean culture, such as food and music, they believe that Caribbeans are less ambitious and less driven than Nigerians. Adetayo, a twenty-three-year-old female engineer, said, "I love their food. But I personally don't have them as friends. Jamaicans are not on the same level. They are not going the same way. I have where I am going to. They want to make money but not to strive academically or try to get somewhere. I don't think they like school anyway." This view is very similar to that held by the second generation in the United States about their own proximal hosts, African Americans. But the second generation in Britain refer more explicitly to class.

The second generation in Britain, like their U.S. counterparts, draw interwoven cultural and moral boundaries against the proximal host. When I asked Bukola to characterize relations between the groups, she exclaimed:

Oh, my God! There is such a conflict. I think it has not been dealt with on such a large scale. People see the black-white conflict as more prominent, so everything else gets brushed under the rug. I don't have many Caribbean friends. The attitudes are different. There is some bitterness there. Africans are always studying. We don't get on very well. They have a preconceived idea of us, and the reason for the conflict is the slave trade thing, how we sold them. They don't want to say they are African; they want to distance themselves from it. They feel that we think we are better than them, we are more educated. I don't want to generalize, but there are very many single-parent families among Caribbeans, and they have this mentality about that, that they can have kids outside marriage, which is a mentality different from ours. We Nigerians want to marry and then have kids. Also, we have a strong culture, but they don't.

Chuka picked up where Bukola left off:

> When I was growing up, the Nigerians that I met, their parents kind of pushed the kids academically, career-wise, job-wise. A lot of Jamaicans did not have that. So now, a lot of them still have social issues, as in, maybe their parents are not together or they have got other siblings, half brothers and half sisters. They have not got that nuclear family kind of setup and also not having that kind of academic push, some of them. So they have kind of mirrored [become] what they grew up with. So they have got kids out of wedlock, and they have got menial jobs.

The belief that the Caribbean community is rife with family dysfunction is prevalent among Nigerians. Many respondents described Caribbeans as not valuing the institution of marriage, which is purportedly why they have so many teenage and out-of-wedlock pregnancies. Many respondents mentioned and disapproved of the practice of cohabiting before marriage, having children with multiple partners, and being dependent on welfare, which they said were common practices among Caribbeans in Britain. They described Caribbeans as having different attitudes from Nigerians and Africans in many areas, such as disciplining children, valuing education, staying married and being willing to work at it, and taking care of one's family. Caribbeans were described by some respondents as lazy. But, as is the case with their U.S. counterparts, these views of Caribbeans do not accurately represent Caribbeans in Britain. Caribbeans as a whole value education and the institution of marriage. Many are middle class. They discipline their children just as Nigerian parents disciplined the second generation, they have high educational aspirations for their children, and they advocate for them with teachers and administrators.[33]

Some respondents said there was distrust between the two groups, and most respondents did not have close friends who were Caribbean. A few said Caribbeans dislike Nigerians and that they would rather kick a Nigerian when he was down than come to his aid. Dapo believes this very strongly. He was born in Britain but lived in Nigeria for several years as a teenager. He had had bitter experiences with Caribbeans, especially Jamaicans, and told me:

Let me tell you the truth here. We blacks, we don't love each other, and we're not willing to help each other. I have a lot of friends from Jamaica, but we just say hi to each other: "Hello, how are you, blah, blah." Like that. There's no solid entire relationship that I would go to their house to visit them, because when they know that you are making it or have something in your mind that you want to do, they can come stab you or come shoot you because they're jealous. So those are the kind of things I'm trying to avoid from them. They can borrow money from you. You want to collect the money back? You got to go aggressive, and it's going to cause problems. So maybe they can call the police on you or they can stab you to kill you or to do something like that. My brother was stabbed to death in 1994 in front of my house. This was a Nigerian guy, and a Jamaican killed him because of ten pounds. So since then, I try to avoid them.

Like their U.S. counterparts, the second generation in Britain are engaged in a simultaneous process of delineating who their proximal hosts are and delineating the boundaries of their own ethnicity and describing its ethnic content. They are describing, like the second generation in the United States, a diasporic ethnicity created by an elite segment of Nigerians in the diaspora. The diasporic Nigerian ethnicity in Britain is one in which members claim to be Nigerian on the basis of being well educated, being ambitious, and having conservative family values. They also agree that they as a group have a higher class position than Caribbeans.

A few respondents were critical of Nigerians and some of the content of Nigerian ethnicity in Britain. Dayo, a thirty-two-year-old male, said:

They expect kids to grow up quickly in Nigeria, and then when they grow up quickly they still want to keep them under their thumb. For instance, you're not allowed to move out of the house until you get married, and then when you get married they want to raise your children for you, they tell you what to do all the time. I think the respect in Nigeria, as much as I appreciate it, sometimes goes overboard and some people do abuse it. People come into your home and they know your mom and dad but they act like they are your mom and dad and they give you command tones like go and do this, I want to eat this, go and cook this, and you look at them and you say no you don't have that right, my mom and dad have that right but you don't have the right to do that. I think that the power is abused when it shouldn't be and that's probably the culture that I still can't get along with and my mom knows that. When her friends come in I just ask to leave the room because I don't like the way they try to talk down to you.

The second generation also engage notions of blackness differently from Caribbeans. They do not primarily identify as black, which distinguishes them from second-generation Caribbeans, who identify as black and British.[34] Bello, a forty-three-year-old lecturer who was born and raised in Britain, explained, "A Nigerian never emphasizes being black. We just talk about being Nigerian or being African. It is only West Indians who emphasize the word *black*. That is what I have noticed. Black is important to them. I think this has to do with the fact that they are disconnected from their culture, so they associate with black, but Nigerians associate their culture with Nigerian, Edo, Yoruba, etc." Bello's point about Caribbeans being disconnected from their culture is very similar to what many of the U.S. respondents said about African Americans. Indeed, the differences in identification patterns of the Nigerian and the Caribbean second generations can be explained by the different histories these groups have with the British.

Finally, the ethnic boundaries drawn between the second generation of Nigerian ancestry in Britain and their proximal hosts are made more complex by the dominance of British street culture, also known as British youth culture, which draws its cultural content largely from Caribbean culture. A growing development, particularly in London, among preteens and teenagers, irrespective of race, ethnicity, or socioeconomic background, is the consumption of urban minority culture. They talk alike, using similar slang; they have similar accents; they dress in the same way, with baggy jeans belted at the hips and exposing their underwear, and name-brand sneakers; and they exhibit similar loud and sometimes aggressive behavior on the streets and at times belong to gangs that frequently engage in knife fights. This is consistent with several studies of youth in Britain that have found that many nonblack youths have appropriated black urban culture, finding it cool.[35] According to Michelle:

> The street culture, which originated from the Caribbeans, really, has now become unified—loads and loads of different cultural and social groups. And so that's why you might see a middle-class child who goes to a private school and a child who has left school because he got thrown out walking around the street doing bad stuff both dressed the same. Because there is one culture, and it's really originated from the Caribbean street culture. And so everyone wants to be black now, sound like a black person. I always say, if you close your eyes on the bus and listen to a group of schoolchildren, you would not be able to tell who's black, who's white, who's Chinese, Asian. They all sound the same. And it's because there's been this sort of assimilation, everyone is blending together, everyone wants to be cool, and what's cool at the moment is all the black things, rap music, all of that stuff.

Respondents mentioned that before the mid-2000s it was extremely rare to hear of a Nigerian kid being on the street, joining gangs, and engaging in criminal activities but that such occurrences are quite common now. The rash of gang knife fights in London in 2008 saw a number of the aggressors and victims coming from the Nigerian community. As a result, it is no longer possible to draw bright and sharp boundaries between Nigerians and Caribbeans when talking about the teenage second generation.

According to respondents, there is a growing fear within the Nigerian community in Britain that the teenage second generation, because of cultural diffusion, which really cannot be halted, are becoming less Nigerian and more "street." At the same time, some acknowledge that Nigerians and Africans are gradually introducing their own influence into the black culture in Britain. Considering that Africans have become the largest black group in Britain, their influence on black culture in Britain should only grow.

Explaining the Differing Views of Caribbeans

The symbolic boundaries the second generation of Nigerian ancestry in Britain and the second generation of Nigerian ancestry in the United States draw against their respective proximal hosts are virtually indistinguishable, even though the proximal hosts are two different ethnic groups residing in two different countries. What is distinctly different are the ways the second generation in the United States and in Britain treat the Caribbeans in their respective countries. In Britain, they distance themselves from the Caribbeans, while in the United States they align with them. In fact, while some of the second generation in the United States view U.S. Caribbeans as their cousins, none in Britain viewed British Caribbeans in this light. This differential treatment reveals that the fact that Caribbeans have a history of white-owner slavery while diasporic Nigerians do not is not the key that explains the difference. Rather, the difference is sourced in several other factors.

The first explanation for why Caribbeans in Britain are viewed negatively while those in the United States are viewed somewhat positively or neutrally is that Caribbeans in the United States have a higher group position on the educational and income hierarchy than Caribbeans in Britain relative to other groups. British Caribbeans rank just above Bangladeshis and Pakistanis, who are at the bottom. Thus, it is not beneficial for Nigerians, who are the most educated immigrant group in Britain and rank even higher than white Britons on the education scale to be assimilated into the Caribbean group because for many of them this would mean downward mobility. This holds true even as studies show that Africans including Nigerians are not receiving a commensurate return to their education levels in the British labor market, something that has also been found true about Africans in the U.S. labor market.[36]

One reason Caribbeans in Britain have a lower income and educational rank than Caribbeans in the United States is that the two groups arrived in different migratory streams, as noted by Foner. The major wave of Caribbeans to Britain started earlier. Many of them were soldiers who had fought for Britain during the Second World War and after the war decided to settle in Britain. Another large group of Caribbeans migrated to Britain beginning in the 1950s to fill labor shortages in the National Health Service (many as nurses) and in industry, such as the rail system. The free movement of people from all British colonies to Britain until 1962, when Britain changed her immigration policies to require entry visas from citizens of former black colonies, allowed many unskilled migrants who could come up with the price of a ticket to migrate and settle in Britain. Although there were also many skilled workers, only about 10 percent were classified as white collar. In contrast, West Indians who migrated to the United States between 1962 and 1971 were better educated, largely because U.S. immigration policy required an entry visa, which resulted in a highly select population of legal Caribbean immigrants. Among them, 15 percent were professionals and another 12 percent worked in other white-collar occupations.

Another reason Caribbeans in the United States are more successful than those in Britain is that Caribbeans in New York, where many are concentrated, benefit from the presence of a preexisting black community that needs services and patronizes their businesses. This allows West Indians to occupy an intermediary position between African Americans and white Americans.[37]

Finally, because U.S. Caribbeans are recent migrants, they, like African immigrants, are seen as part of the U.S. immigrant story. They too are regarded as hardworking immigrants pursuing the American Dream. Caribbean and African immigrants have been described as "elevated minorities" compared to African Americans and as such "are able, at times, to distinguish themselves from their native-born black counterparts and move closer to in-group status," which is defined as a social unit with boundaries that are collectively generated and maintained in order to mark the differences between insiders and outsiders.[38] Thus both groups of black immigrants and their children can sometimes move into the position of "preferred blacks" over African Americans in the United States. This development gives members of both groups room to adopt the dominant discourse of drawing boundaries against African Americans and distancing themselves especially from the African American poor, as almost all other immigrants groups to America have historically done.

CONCLUSION: FORGING A DIASPORIC NIGERIAN ETHNICITY WHILE CAUGHT IN THE RACIAL BIND

This chapter examined several transnational mechanisms within Nigerian communities in the United States and Britain that have shaped the ethnicity and ethnic identities held by the Nigerian second generation in both countries. I showed in the preceding chapter that a large part of the cultural distinctiveness of Nigerians in the American and British diaspora is based on key forms in which their ethnicity is capital, and that these forms of capital are solidly rooted in the highly selective nature of the immigrant streams from Nigeria into these countries. I introduced an additional mechanism—cultural embedding—that helped transmit a diasporic Nigerian ethnicity to the second generation. This process strengthened the ethnicity and increased the ethnic-group consciousness of the second generation.

The distinct ethnicity the Nigerian second generation hold which differentiate them from their proximal hosts show that black people in both countries are not a homogenous group with a set of behaviors and attitudes that are self-defeating and self-perpetuating. Several studies have discussed the distinct ethnicities and identities held by first generation black immigrants in the United States. My findings show that it is not just a first generation phenomenon; having distinct ethnicities and self-given ethnic identities that differentiate from their proximal hosts exists in the second generation. However, the Nigerian second generation draw symbolic cultural, moral, and socioeconomic boundaries that echo much of the negative stereotypes held about African Americans in the United States and Caribbeans in Britain. Several prominent scholars who have studied black immigrant ethnic identity processes have been accused of propagating in mainstream scholarship a view that denigrates African Americans and their culture, using "immigrants purported ethnic identification to further a subtle yet insidious, racialist discourse about United States-born black cultural inferiority."[39] Their narratives reveal that many of the second generation and their parents have uncritically internalized the racist discourse and explanations for persistent disadvantage among some segments of the black population. In addition, because of their differential racial socialization and the advantages enjoyed from their parents' resources and the different forms in which their ethnicity has become capital and despite their experiencing racial discrimination and being aware of the racial disparities that exist in these two countries, they are not fully convinced that the structural explanations for persistent black poverty among segments of the black population fully explain the state of the black poor. All these factors also explain why they did not develop a reactive ethnicity and why their racial status has not overwhelmed their ethnicity.

One question that emerges from this discussion of the diasporic Nigerian ethnicity in the United States and Britain is can the Nigerian second generation be viewed as a model minority? To some, they are.[40] News articles abound about U.S. black immigrants, and Nigerians in particular, being higher achieving blacks than African Americans. A recent book named Nigerian Americans as one of the most successful groups in the United States (along with Mormons, Jews, Iranian and Lebanese Americans, Cuban Americans, and Indian Americans), and the authors argued that the successes of these groups could be explained by their cultures.[41] But even as Nigerians are seen as a high achieving group in the United States, other less flattering views of Nigerians are widely held in American society. Nigerians have a reputation for being fraud artists and scammers. They are known for sending emails that peddle fraudulent business opportunities or requests for financial assistance from individuals in dire straits. In 2014, Ted Cruz, a U.S. senator from the state of Texas, who ran for the 2016 Republican nomination for president, alluded to this view of Nigerians as email scammers in his criticism of the Affordable Care Act. His statement offended many Nigerians in the American diaspora. Many in the Nigerian community, in addition to the Nigerian ambassador to the United States, requested an apology from the senator, but he did not give one.[42] His spokesman said he was joking. This incident illustrates the widespread nature of this poor view of Nigerians in America. Similarly in Britain, Nigerians, although associated with high educational attainment, are also viewed as, in the words of David Cameron, former prime minister, to Queen Elizabeth II, "fantastically corrupt."[43] So while their educational and occupational attainment levels show that they are a successful black group, there are less flattering views of them circulating in both British and American society.

Furthermore, despite the respondents' portrayal of ethnic difference hinging on cultural distinctiveness or particularity, I show how Nigerian success cannot be fully attributed to culture. Indeed, ambition and self-motivation are important parts of what it means to them to be Nigerian and are contributory factors to their success. But the mechanisms that have made them successful and upon which they have constructed the Nigerian ethnicity found in the British and American diaspora have their genesis in the extreme selectivity of the Nigerian first generation and the social capital generated from the ethnic resources within their communities that have helped create human capital and ethnic-group consciousness in the second generation. This means there is nothing intrinsically or inherently Nigerian about the cultural elements the Nigerian second generation use to delineate the ethnic boundaries between themselves and their proximal hosts. I have shown in this chapter and the preceding one that Nigerians in the United States and British diaspora value high education attainment and career success highly but that they are not unique in this regard. Most other groups, both native and immigrant, in both countries prioritize education and the success that comes with it.

In both countries, what is unique among Nigerians is the integration of being well educated and being successful into the definition of Nigerianness. Put another way, they have ethnicized significant aspects of their experience. This development reflects what scholars note about ethnicity—that claims of what makes a group an ethnic group do not have to be based on objective factors.[44] Claims can be subjective. After all, an ethnic group is "a collectivity within a larger society having real or putative common ancestry, memories of a shared historical past, and a cultural focus on one or more symbolic elements defined as the epitome of their peoplehood."[45] The key phrase here is "a cultural focus on one or more symbolic elements defined as the epitome of their peoplehood." Consequently, researchers need to "pay more attention to the subjective elements in ethnic survival such as ethnic memories, values, symbols, myths and tradition." Members of an ethnic community must be made to feel not only that they form a single "super family," but that their historic community is unique, that they possess "irreplaceable culture values," and that their heritage must be preserved against inner corruption and external control.[46] The myth of election, an advanced formulation of the subjective and cultural origin of the ethnic group, serves to mobilize members of the ethnic group and community and is what ensures its long-term ethnic survival. My respondents' narratives of what makes them Nigerian and distinct from their proximal hosts reveal that in addition to having parents who come from Nigeria, they have selected educational achievement and the value of respect as core elements of their ethnicity.

And this is why identity is a label with impact. As Frederik Barth notes, "Claiming an ethnic identity implies being a certain kind of person. . . . [I]t also implies a claim to be judged, and to judge oneself, by those standards that are relevant to that identity."[47] Respondents in both the United States and Britain acknowledge that the definition of Nigerian ethnicity has imposed expectations that have influenced many of their decisions and lifestyle choices. We see, based on their experiences and narratives, that ethnic identity has consequential impact on members of the group.

Furthermore, their definition of what makes them Nigerian is an adaptation to the local ecologies, the social and historical environments of the United States and Britain. The findings in this chapter show the continued relevance of the presence of the proximal host in how the Nigerian second generation construct their ethnicity and identities. Along with the varying salience of Nigerian ethnicity outside of Nigeria and in the diaspora, the Nigerian second generation must negotiate being racialized as black and assigned as coethnics to the status of their proximal hosts. And respondents expressed ambivalence about this assignment because of the overall low social status their proximal hosts have in American and British society. This means that the formation of their ethnicity and self-given ethnic identities cannot be external to their race.

Consequently, despite evidence of Nigerians' success, they cannot, like Asians in both countries, become honorary whites, or become white, if the boundary between whites and nonwhite ethnic minorities outside of blacks blurs to make the color line a black/nonblack one. In short, because of their race, the Nigerian second generation do not have the right bodies to pass out of the black category and into the white or honorary white category, which is theorized by Eduardo Bonilla-Silva as the category that buffers white people from the collective black category. The honorary white category comprises well-off Mexicans and Hispanics, certain Asian groups such as Koreans and the Chinese, and American Indians who do not live on reservations.[48] Last, race complicates the process of identity formation and the lived experiences of the Nigerian second generation in ways that cannot be equated with the Asian and Hispanic second generation.

An example of the differential ways race impacts identity formation of the black second generation is that even as the Nigerian second generation celebrate and interpret their successes in regard to their presumed cultural distinctiveness, they are racialized. They are embedded in the global racialization process of black people that continues to propagate "dehumanizing and racist representations of Africa and the people of African descent."[49] Africans, particularly sub-Saharans, are seen to be part of a continent that is the face of poverty, starvation, corruption, and failed states.[50] The overreaction to the Ebola outbreak in 2014 and the fear that the disease would migrate to the West, instead of remaining contained in Africa, is another example of the former's power in the world. Thus what is clear is that even as this group of the black/African second generation articulates their ethnic distinction, they cannot remove themselves from being affected by their assignment in the black racial category.

FIVE

On the Horns of Racialization

MIDDLE CLASS, ETHNIC, AND BLACK

Every day, Temitayo Tella, a physician who came to the United States when she was two, deals with being middle class, black, Nigerian American, and African. She has discovered that being a child of African immigrants means different things at different times in the United States, but it means more positive things when her middle-class status is obvious. She was born to middle-class parents. Her father holds a PhD and is a lecturer in a tertiary institution. Her mother has a master's degree and is an accountant. Sometimes, being black overshadows her identity as a Nigerian American. She is aware, as many others have pointed out, that in public spaces, where the most visible aspect of oneself is race, other characteristics are often over-shadowed.[1] Sounding very much like a sociologist, she said, "There is this identity factor that we [black people] share because sometimes our discriminations are the same. I mean, a lot of white people are people who are racist, and they see us as one. They don't see a distinction between an African and an African American. So, for instance, if I'm scared of black people or I don't like black people, even before the black person talks, even with an accent or without an accent, I would always say, 'I don't like black people, so I'm going to treat them all in a certain way,' and this is more about the white person."

At other times, and this has been happening to her more frequently now that she is an adult, her ethnic difference from African Americans is recognized. People are surprised at how well she has done, and their surprise offends her. She finds that they become less surprised when they learn she is the child of African immigrants, not a native American black, even though she came to the United States when she was two. She said, "We Africans keep on surprising them. I am the black person that is always surprising them. My sister and other Africans I know are always surprising them because they expected something else and they are not seeing that. And I've always felt that was happening. I don't have any proof, but as I got higher and higher, people are shocked when you do well or you win something or get something. I have felt that shock out there. I guess we can't really call it a form of discrimination." She went on to say:

> We get that all the time, like, "Wow, you are so smart." I am, "Why are you so surprised?" I went to school. I went to college. It is okay to be shocked. It is okay to be impressed by somebody's intelligence, whatever. But I don't want you to be impressed by my intelligence because of my race or because of my ethnicity. I want you to be impressed by intelligence because you are impressed by intelligence. But Obama was the best example of what most of us have been going through. A lot of us are successful, and now I would even include myself as a successful black person who has made it in life. Like Oprah Winfrey. It doesn't have to be just Oprah. It could be a doctor who is black. We are anomalies, it seems. "Oh, they don't fit the typical description of what I was expecting." Like wow, okay. Ben Carson.[2] You can name anybody—you [referring to me, the interviewer], like all the black people in your school.[3] They are anomalies according to this society.

Temitayo Tella's story shows how race affects the identities and lived realities of the Nigerian second generation interviewed in this book and reveals the endpoints of their ethnic identification journey. The negative stereotypical view of African Americans envelop her, a daughter of Nigerian immigrants, even as she identifies as Nigerian American and African. And she has come to identify with other black people in the United States largely because she is aware that her black skin puts her in the same boat with them. The end point for the Nigerian second generation is that even as they maintain their ethnic distinction from their proximal hosts and police the boundaries, they, because they are racially black, are assimilating into the black middle class in the United States and Britain. Temitayo has come to realize that successful black people in the United States are united by their success. The people she named as successful include African immigrants, second-generation Africans like herself and President Barack Obama, who identifies as African American, and African Americans like Oprah Winfrey and Ben Carson. As they assimilate into the black middle class, the adult Nigerian second generation acknowledge that they share things in common with other middle-class blacks. It is leading to an emerging loose coalition of all middle-class blacks. This coalition, while it blurs the ethnic boundaries between the groups, does not erase the cultural differences; it only reduces the urgency to signal difference. I found this to be true in both the United States and Britain.

In this chapter, I examine how respondents' racial status as black affects their daily lives, how social class influences how they identify with black people, and how their interactions with white people in professional settings also shape their identities. The questions addressed in this chapter include, Do outsiders notice an ethnic difference between the Nigerian second generation and their proximal hosts? What stories did respondents tell about experiencing or not experiencing racial discrimination? Were there occasions when being a black ethnic made a difference? To investigate these questions, I discuss the workplace experiences of respondents to see what can be gleaned from the interplay of race and ethnicity in this arena and examine how their treatment by white people shapes their sense of themselves as simultaneously Nigerian, African, and black. I also address the extent to which notions of linked fate—the belief that the fates of individual blacks are linked to that of the group[4]—affected how respondents viewed issues of race, racial solidarity, and ethnic diversity among black people. What I argue here is the Nigerian second generation are not downwardly assimilating into a "rainbow underclass" as predicted by segmented assimilation theory but are integrating into the middle class as black people. And the factors identified in beyond racialization theory (see chapters 2–4), explain how and why they have maintained an ethnic distinctiveness from their proximal hosts and why most have attained positive socioeconomic outcomes.

And as they enter the black middle class, they are redrawing it along ethnic and, as other studies have shown, class lines.[5] Most of the Nigerian second generation whom I interviewed, as middle-class professionals, are using several strategies—minority cultures of mobility strategies—in their daily lives. Minority cultures of mobility are cultural elements that provide "strategies for economic mobility in the context of discrimination and group disadvantage." They are used to handle problems that arise from contact with the white majority in professional settings and interclass contact with their minority community. And they provide "interpretations of and strategies for managing these problems."[6]

For respondents, interclass conflicts with members of their minority community were not with Nigerian coethnics but with the proximal host. I discovered that respondents in both countries are redrawing the black category along class lines by making class judgments about their proximal hosts and based on these judgments deciding which member of the proximal host to befriend and which to shun. They used a class schema to make these judgments. Schemas are a cognitive process that "guides perception and recall, interprets experience, generates inferences and expectations, and organizes action."[7] Examples of schemas are "being stopped by the police for DWB [driving while black]" or "being-watched-in-the-store-as-if-one-were-considered-a-potential-shoplifter."[8] The class schema they use is "This-black-person-is-not-like-me-unless-he/she-is-middle-class-and-well-mannered."

The class schema is used to draw socioeconomic boundaries between themselves and their proximal hosts. It builds on the cultural and moral boundaries they draw between themselves and their proximal hosts. It allows them to draw more fine-grained distinctions between classes of members in the proximal host and themselves. They are uncomfortable with blacks who they feel embody negative black stereotypes even if they have money and belong to the middle and upper classes. They are comfortable with members of the proximal host they see as similar to themselves: respectful, college-educated professionals, and like-minded. Their relations with members of the proximal hosts are based on these class judgments, which are being made constantly. Thus they see commonality among all middle-class blacks, as Temitayo made clear, and also draw very bright boundaries between themselves and the black poor.

This class schema was used more often by U.S. respondents than British respondents. U.S. respondents commonly used bifurcating phrases such as "ghetto blacks and blacks," "poorly behaved blacks and well-mannered blacks," "professional blacks and stereotypical blacks," "educated blacks and ignorant blacks" when describing their relations with their proximal hosts. While respondents in Britain used social class to organize their social interactions with their proximal hosts, for many of them the class boundary they drew remained largely academic because of the limited interaction and number of close friendships they had with black Caribbeans as adults.

To negotiate racial discrimination in the workplace, U.S. respondents, believing that working harder would resolve the problem, use the strategy of "stepping up their game." Another strategy is "minimizing ethnic difference" to make white colleagues more comfortable with them and increase their organizational fit. They also learn middle-class consumption patterns and activities such as eating sushi and playing golf. As attempts to ensure success in middle-class workplaces, the strategies of second-generation Nigerians are very similar to those employed by African Americans in middle-class jobs and work settings.[9] Respondents in Britain used similar strategies to negotiate the social dynamics of their workplaces but on the whole either ignored incidents of racial discrimination or sought refuge and support in their ethnic and faith communities.

IN THE UNITED STATES: BEING BLACK AND ETHNIC

Do white people notice ethnic differences within the black category? The answer is yes and no. There is evidence that white employers prefer hiring black immigrants over African Americans because they view them as more hardworking and less confrontational.[10] Later in this chapter, as I discuss the workplace experiences of my U.S. respondents, I show that this employer preference is being extended to some members of the second generation. But some of the second generation have experienced workplace discrimination that, in the words of one of my U.S. respondents, is "analogous to the African American experience."

A good example of how ethnic diversity among blacks is both recognized and not recognized can be found in university admissions data. Black immigrants and their children are disproportionately represented in elite American universities.[11] Administrators keep track of the ethnicities of the black students enrolled but don't seem to be overly troubled about the overrepresentation of black immigrants and their children in their enrollment figures. The initial objective of affirmative action policies was to redress cumulative generational disadvantage in African American communities, but it has since evolved to achieving diversity. In this evolution, while intrablack differentiation is noticed, it is not taken seriously enough to disqualify black immigrants (both first and second generation) who might be from middle- and upper-class backgrounds.

Several studies have shown that black immigrants and their children have some leeway to become the "preferred blacks" in the United States over African Americans.[12] Other studies have suggested that class plays a role in determining whether whites treat black immigrants differently from African Americans. In one study, poor inner-city youths had no experience of whites treating West Indians differently from African Americans, whereas middle-class suburban youths felt that whites did.[13] But another ethnographic study—this one of Jamaica-born adult men in New York—found the opposite. The longer these men had lived in the United States and the higher their social class, the less they believed that whites favored West Indians over

African Americans. The author attributed the change to the men being victims of racism.[14] Most of the research in this area has concerned West Indians, and researchers have rarely asked the view of white people. But there are some surveys that measured white people's attitudes to other racial and ethnic groups. Results of one recent survey looking at prejudice against African Americans, Africans, Jamaicans, and Haitians suggest that whites were most prejudiced against Haitians and least prejudiced against African Americans.[15] The case of Barack Obama, the first black president of the United States, also suggests that noticing intrablack differentiation can go hand in hand with still seeing all black people as members of a single race.

While a few ethnographic studies found evidence that whites seem to prefer West Indian and African immigrants over African Americans, they were based mainly on interviews with black immigrants and a few with white employers.[16] Quantitative studies, however, have not found any evidence that white people's preference for immigrant blacks over African Americans gives those immigrants an economic benefit in the labor market. A study on West Indian immigrants tested the white favoritism thesis and found no evidence to explain why West Indians have been more successful than African Americans and even Africans in the U.S. labor market. The conclusion was that the more plausible reason for West Indians' success is that they are positively selected—they have more tangible (e.g., education) and intangible qualities (e.g., ambition) than their compatriots who did not migrate.[17]

Studies on contemporary African immigrants in the United States have found that African immigrants, despite their higher levels of education, do not receive commensurate returns on their education in the labor market.[18] Many are doing well but have taken a long and winding journey to get there. It appears that West Indians are more successful than Africans in the labor market because they get better returns on their education than do African Americans and Africans, once other variables, especially years of schooling, are controlled. But in raw figures, Africans have higher incomes than both African Americans and Caribbeans. Many Africans have retrained upon migrating to the United States in order to get high-paying jobs that give them a middle-class standard of living. A possible explanation why Africans get a lower return on their education is that Africans experience more discrimination than West Indians, either because some Africans have less facility with the English language or because they tend to be darker skinned than either African Americans or West Indians, which triggers more severe racial discrimination; as a result of this discrimination, they are stuck in poor-paying jobs and ethnic niches.

That the evidence cuts both ways reflects two things. First, whether white people take intrablack differentiation seriously depends on the situation, issue, or institution being observed and the actors involved. The answer also likely varies by region, racial and ethnic composition of neighborhood, individuals' own backgrounds, degree of exposure to black people of different ethnicities, the qualitative experience of these interactions, and a whole host of other factors that can only be ascertained with further research. Second, significant shifts are occurring in the U.S. racial and ethnic classificatory system. The increasing multiracial populations in the United States are complicating old racial classifications. New groups are entering the country—Asians and Hispanics—that do not neatly fall into either the black or white racial category. New ethnic groups within the black category are chipping away at the notion of monolithic blackness. All these changes are creating some space for middle- and upper-class blacks—both immigrant and native—to occupy a place where other identities such as class status along with race determine their experiences. Putting it another way, there is an opportunity for these black groups to thread a middle path—one where race is not always a racial stigma or determinative of their socioeconomic outcomes. And even when blacks are victims of discrimination, it does not mean they have no other choice than to develop a reactive black ethnicity with the theorized set of self-defeating and self-perpetuating behaviors that will lead them into enduring poverty. Neither will it erase their ethnicity, which as I have shown in the preceding chapters has cultural elements that promote good social outcomes, something that is found as well in many nonblack immigrant and native communities.

The Complicated Life of Being Black and Ethnic in the United States

Many respondents told me that they had experienced racial discrimination in the United States. Some said they had "been followed around while shopping" to make sure "they did not steal anything." Others said they had been discriminated against when they were growing up. One respondent remembered she and her siblings "being told they could not swim in the swimming pool" in their neighborhood in Texas. They were actually told to "get out" of the pool by a white male janitor. Others had been discriminated against by educators in their schools and universities. Almost all agreed with Temitayo "that a lot of white people see us as one" and with Titi, who said, "At the end of the day, we are just black. They don't see the green-white-green colors of the Nigerian flag on your forehead or the Jamaican flag. We just see black."

Perceptions of Racial Discrimination in the Workplace

An important site for the Nigerian second generation when discussing anti-black discrimination was the workplace. Respondents' reports on their workplace experiences were varied. A bit less than half (43 percent) felt they had not been discriminated against because of their race. The majority (57 percent) felt they had been discriminated against because of their race. Some respondents who felt that they had been discriminated against at work thought that their experiences were analogous to those of African Americans. Others seem to have experienced a combination of being racially discriminated against by bosses and some colleagues while at the same time enjoying support for being a minority.

Respondents who said they had been discriminated against at work felt the discrimination occurred at certain key points in their careers: evaluations and promotions, mentorship, and organizational support. This correlates with the points of workplace discrimination experienced by African Americans.[19]

Respondents in jobs with a lot of face-to-face client interaction reported that they often felt that clients did not want them to attend to them because they were black. Respondents who were nurses told me of occasions when white patients refused their services or expressed a preference for a white nurse to the nursing supervisor. If the patients could not get a white nurse, they were hostile and uncooperative. Linda spoke of her experience: "In my nursing clinical when I go there and perform my duties, every once in a while older Caucasian patients may not want me to touch them for any reason. Just little things like that. They don't outright say, 'I don't want your care,' but whenever I enter their rooms, they are like, why do I have to get this one? They look at me weird to see if I'm not taking anything from their room."

A few respondents mentioned that they had been discriminated against by African Americans working in contract and grant offices, often in the public sector, because they felt that black ethnics did not qualify for the same opportunities as African Americans. Wole, a self-employed contractor in Maryland, frequently finds that his company is removed from consideration for some contracts by African American state workers because he is "not really African American," even though he is an American citizen. His experience reveals that the recognition of different ethnicities among black people is also happening among black people themselves, and this interplay of race and ethnicity and recognition of his ethnic difference was not to his benefit.

A few respondents narrated incidents they had originally perceived as black-on-black discrimination but later came to learn were attempts by African Americans to assist fellow blacks through tough love. Such was the case with Adaora, a doctor, who said that when she started her residency program, "two of my chiefs were African Americans and they were really hard on me, and they said the reason why they were harder on me than the other interns was because they want me to be better because they didn't want anyone to doubt my knowledge."

Many respondents believed that black people are discriminated against with regard to promotions. In their experience, being a black ethnic did not matter; the discrimination was against all black people. Laura, a banker for over fifteen years in New York, felt that she was not given the same opportunities as her white colleagues, even though she was more qualified.

> In a corporate setting racism manifests itself in the opportunities that are given or that are made available. As a minority person, it is typical to have to do pretty much double or triple the effort. I find myself, as a college graduate with a master's degree and a very difficult certification to come by, having to compete with people of different races but who have just a college degree. So I think in that respect, and this is just speaking frankly, that the opportunities are less available in terms of moving up. I have worked in three big companies, and it seems that the rule of engagement is quite the same, in the sense that opportunities are less available for black people. And my edge is usually that I have all these qualifications but in certain instances they don't seem to make a huge difference.

Respondents' stories of being disadvantaged during promotions were tied to their perceptions that they are poorly mentored in their organizations. Many respondents complained that their white colleagues had much better mentoring and company support than they did. They felt that their superiors gave their white colleagues many more opportunities to prove themselves and hence make their case for promotion. This feeling was especially pronounced among respondents who were lawyers. They said they could not get partners to take them on as protégés and either formally or, more important, informally mentor them. For this reason, many of them struggled with feelings of not belonging. Ima is a good example of how this lack of mentoring and organizational support becomes internalized, giving rise to a sense of inferiority.

> At my workplace, or should I say for lawyers, it is difficult for us to succeed. We have less support. It is something that just manifests itself very quietly. You just don't get mentored. You don't make the connections you see other people making with the partners and senior lawyers. And you get to thinking: Is it me? Is it something I did? Am I not good enough? I find it very frustrating always having to question myself and whether I belong. I don't think my nonblack peers are troubled about these issues. We are disadvantaged in the patronage system.

This creeping sense of self-doubt was widespread among respondents who felt they were being discriminated against at work for being black. They reinterpreted this experience as a personal fault, whereas in fact discrimination is a product of historical and contemporary formations of race in the United States.[20]

Unprompted by the interviewer, Gbenga, a lawyer in his mid-thirties, commented on similarities he saw between his experience and that of African Americans.

> My experience more closely mirrors the African American experience in the professional setting. I think you have to be better, you have to work harder, and I feel like that more than my white counterparts. I feel that my work product has to be better and I can never make a mistake, that kind of thing. I also feel that I have to create more of my own opportunities. I feel, professionally, that my white counterparts, they have opportunities carved out for them, and I may have to make more of my own opportunities. So what does that look like for me in the law firm? I think one of my white peers may from the senior partner be given a small client for him to develop and groom in a relationship over time. For me, I don't see anybody doing that for me. I have to bring in my own clients, create my own clients. So in a sentence, I think my experience at this law firm more closely mirrors that of the experience of African Americans in general. When I am at work, I think I'm going through the same things that African Americans are going through.

For respondents who said they had experienced racial discrimination in the workplace, racial status overrode their ethnicity and influenced some critical social relationships they had in the workplace. Despite these experiences, none of them had developed a reactive ethnicity.[21]

Do Outsiders Notice the Ethnic Difference?
Enjoying Nigerian Ethnic Capital

I asked my respondents if they thought outsiders noticed their ethnic difference from their proximal hosts. Or in other words, do outsiders see differences between the black groups? Among blacks, there exists recognition of difference among the groups. A recent study of the three main black groups in New York, African Americans, Caribbeans, and Africans, found significant attitudinal and behavioral differences among them. For example, the study found that African immigrants are the most optimistic about life in America and the possibility of achieving the American Dream, Caribbeans are the least optimistic, and African Americans are in the middle. African immigrants are viewed by all three groups as the most hardworking, while African Americans are viewed as the least hardworking (although African Americans view themselves as the least hardworking, they do so to a lesser degree than do Caribbean and Africans).[22] Caribbeans are less optimistic about the possibility of forming intraracial coalitions, while African Americans are the most open to forming such coalitions.[23]

The consensus among respondents is that whites and Asians are becoming more cognizant of such differences among blacks, even though ignorance of these differences remains. In the United States, institutional recognition of black group heterogeneity is lagging behind the demographic reality, as the U.S. census form does not disaggregate the black racial category like it does the Asian category; the single racial option available to all black groups on the census form is "Black, African-American, or Negro." However, changes in the race question that will go into effect in the 2020 census allow those who tick the "Black, African American, Negro" box to write in their national origin or ancestry, if they choose. Many respondents told me that outsiders are noticing the difference between them and African Americans. They have observed that when outsiders notice the difference between them and other blacks, their interaction with them noticeably improves. Having ethnic names helps cue this difference. It is immediately clear that they are not native American blacks (although there are some native blacks who have adopted African names). They say it makes white people more comfortable with them. They want to know more about their country, where their parents are from, their immigrant story, and so on. Onyinye said, "I used to think no before, but now I say yes. Many whites like blacks with culture. They are more open, want to ask you questions. So when I introduce myself as Nigerian, they are always interested and want to know more." African Americans have a rich culture that is extremely influential in shaping both American and a global culture, but Onyinye's statement that "whites like blacks with culture" alluded to the fact that white Americans see recent African and Caribbean immigrants and their children as the preferred or better blacks than America's native blacks—African Americans.

They say there is growing realization that Africans, and especially Nigerians, are well educated. Many, like Kemi, have had white people tell them, "Africans: you are hardworking, you all go to school, you are all not like the typical black people from here." She finds this uncomfortable because in praising Africans, they are denigrating African Americans. She thinks this is racist, especially when it is said by white people, even though she has these same discussions of ethnic difference with her Caribbean friends. Deji, a twenty-seven-year-old engineer who is currently a teacher, is also uncomfortable when white people denigrate native U.S. blacks as they praise Africans. He said, "People look at black Americans as a lower group, as lower class, and Nigerian Americans as more educated and a hardworking people." Though he is uncomfortable with this intraracial ranking, he said, "In this type of situation, I will say I am Nigerian. Hey, look at me! I am a good one! I will totally milk it." He thinks that Nigerians have a higher status that African Americans in American society. "When I tell people I am Nigerian, people look at me and see me at a higher level. I have an Asian friend, and he tells me stuff like, 'If I have a company, I will just hire Nigerians because Nigerians are so smart and hardworking.' Another friend from around Rutgers and Princeton says Nigerians are so smart. When I told him I was Nigerian, it elevated me in his eyes. So I would be a total sucker not to milk it, not to leverage it. But, at the same time, I don't really like it at the cost of African Americans."

Kemi's and Deji's statements reveal the presence of some racial solidarity among the Nigerian second generation when they hear these comments from white people. Many privately think these things and say them among friends, and they are happy to enjoy the advantages that comes from being children of black immigrants and being perceived as immigrant blacks despite having been born in the United States. Deji's experience also shows that nonblacks are aware of Nigerians' distinctiveness. This unique position of Nigerians in the United States and Britain is tied to the distinctive class status (most are highly educated) of Nigerians, which has been shaped to be highly selective by these countries immigration policies and their relatively large population size when compared to other national African groups.

Similar situations in the workplace lead me to argue that some respondents enjoy Nigerian ethnic capital in the workplace. I define Nigerian ethnic capital as the advantage Nigerian ethnics in different contexts, such as in the workplace or education sector, enjoy that results in their having differential experiences and outcomes when compared to African Americans. I define Nigerian ethnics as first- and second-generation Nigerian immigrants. Obinna, a twenty-seven-year-old pharmacist born and raised in the United States, said:

> Now that I'm working, I kind of see having an ethnic name as an advantage. There is a big generalization, I think, when it comes to African Americans in this country. So a lot of times when I am like working, yeah, and I come across a manager who is from a different race and he sees my name is different, he usually then asks me where I am from. And you can see the difference in tone, in terms of like having a conversation with me, and finding out that I am from a different country and I have such a unique name. Usually, when people hear my name I usually get positive responses.

Other respondents felt that having an ethnic name could be a disadvantage in the labor market, and a few said it made no difference. In situations where employers want to hire someone whose name they can pronounce, the resumes of applicants with difficult-to-pronounce names are put aside. Some of the second generation shortened their ethnic names or changed their English second names to their first names to improve their chances of success when searching for jobs. Such was the case with Uloma, a twenty-six-year-old female contract lawyer who came to the United States at eleven. She told me:

> If you see the card that I gave you, I used my middle name because I definitely noticed that. Actually one of my friends straight up told me that. After I graduated, I went off and I worked for a law firm in Japan, and then I decided to come back. And I came back right when the recession set in, and so it was difficult to get jobs at that time, and I was putting out my resume, but I was surprised that I wasn't even getting called for interviews. It is a different thing if you get called and there are maybe two or three people that you think are better than you. But I wasn't even getting called for interviews, and I was like, that's strange. So I had one of my friends, who is also an attorney and had been working already—she graduated before me—look at my resume. She is Asian. She has an Asian first name, but she had started using her middle name of Elizabeth. And that was the first thing she told me, "You know, maybe you should just use your middle name and just initialize the first one

in case they have to look you up they can still find your information, but just for them." She said it just makes them feel more comfortable if they can pronounce your name. She told me that the initial reaction if they look at your name and they cannot pronounce your name is that they just don't want to bother. And it worked! I was so amazed, because it was the exact same resume. It wasn't like anything changed except the name, and it worked! It worked! It is crazy, but it just let me know that is how it is.

When asked if they tried to signal to outsiders' difference from other blacks, especially African Americans, respondents split three ways. Some said no because "we are all blacks." Others said that they did not actively engage in trying to signal difference. The rest said yes and, like Linda Okpara (see chapter 4), tried to signal their difference especially by making finer-grained class distinctions between middle-class African Americans, who they identify with, and lower-class African Americans, who they do not identify with.

Perceiving Discrimination While Enjoying Nigerian Ethnic Capital: The Case of Idowu. Sometimes incidences of antiblack discrimination overlap with experiences of enjoying Nigerian ethnic capital in the same organization. Idowu's story is a case in point. He is a twenty-four-year-old stockbroker on Wall Street. He felt that he had been discriminated against by some white colleagues. He got his internship with a financial organization on Wall Street through a nonprofit organization that seeks to place young male minorities (blacks and Hispanics) in companies on Wall Street and in the Banking District in London. During his first few weeks as an intern, he was given a poor evaluation that would have destroyed his chances of getting a job in the company:

> I remember early on in the internship, they sent a report back to my sponsoring organization that said, "We are not sure that he has the right quantitative ability." And to me, I felt that was a joke. I will do calculus around your head, you know. And these people said I did not have any quantitative ability. I think what was even more upsetting about that was that they had not given me any quantitative work to do. And my sponsors came back and said, "We are very confident in this guy's quantitative ability. We think you need to look harder." And then they did. And then during the internship I worked on different projects and I demonstrated that I had the requisite skills.

At the same time, he had some ethnic minority colleagues who mentored him. They made it possible for him to get his present job in the same company where he did his internship.

During my internship I worked with a lot of junior people, and it was much more diverse at that level. There was actually a Nigerian guy, an analyst, who I kind of latched myself onto. I hung out with him, and you know, it was probably because of him and a few of the others that I was able to get the job offer. It was easier to connect with those guys because a lot of them were immigrants from Pakistan, India, etc. I just connected with those folks. I and other immigrants just have a kind of connection.

Even as Idowu enjoyed the advantage of being a black ethnic among his non-white immigrant colleagues, he benefited from being categorized as racially black, as his racial status was what allowed him to enter the program that placed him in the internship. Affirmative action has worked exceptionally well as an integration policy for the black second generation.[24] Idowu's experience provides support for the argument that middle-class occupations will become more racially and ethnically diverse as more ethnic minorities get opportunities to ascend into them.[25] And as Idowu's case shows, ethnic minorities in such positions can then in turn help other ethnic minorities get similar jobs. His experience shows how coalitions can be built among ethnic minorities in mainstream middle-class jobs. Without his ethnic minority colleagues the white bosses who discriminated against him might have succeeded in barring his entry.

Responses to Workplace Discrimination

It is theorized that different sources of discrimination lead to different responses and consequences.[26] Discrimination from white people in public spaces is more likely to be experienced by blacks and Hispanics, and their reactions will be discouragement, anger, and/or reactive ethnicity. Discrimination from whites in jobs and schools is more likely to be experienced by the Chinese and upwardly mobile blacks and Hispanics, and their response is to try harder. Discrimination from minorities in public spaces and institutions is more likely to be experienced by the Chinese, Russians, blacks, and Hispanics, and their response will be distancing and stereotyping.[27]

Respondents felt that they had to work harder than their white peers so no one would question whether they belonged in their jobs or might have gotten their positions through affirmative action mistakes. Dara, an events manager, said, "I feel that we [blacks], not African descent only, even black Americans, any minority, really have to work harder, and I still feel the same way now because I'm not white." They needed to be the first in and the last out of work. They needed to dress professionally. They needed to work very hard and do a lot of networking to ensure they were considered by their superiors for promotions and other opportunities. A few respondents had quit their jobs in corporate America to start their own businesses because of what they saw as an unequal playing field that was tilted against black people. These respondents' response more closely aligns with discouragement according to the typology of Kasinitz and colleagues.[28]

An important theme that emerged among respondents who felt they experienced discrimination in the workplace was the need to minimize the ethnic difference between themselves and their colleagues, especially white colleagues. Respondents said this made white colleagues and bosses more comfortable with them, which would in turn ensure that they received better evaluations, were admitted into those social networks important for promotion, and were considered for promotion when the time arose. According to Idowu:

> One of the things they stressed was that they [the staff at the placement organization] said, "Look, a lot of you guys are in this organization because your skin color is different. You are different. You cannot afford to accentuate those differences in any other way. So do not go to the bank and dress differently or dress loudly or try to dress spectacularly. That would make you look even more different, and that is alarming to people." They don't want that, etc. So, in my dressing, when I go to work, I wear either a white or blue shirt with dark blue or black suit. No pinstripes. No checkered prints, nothing. I wear black shoes. I make sure they are laced up. Don't ever wear loafers. Make sure your hair is cut. Make sure you don't have facial hair. You cannot join them with facial hair. You will look too different.

Many respondents see the wisdom of learning new cultural practices in order to fit in with their colleagues. These are lighthearted but important cultural practices such as golfing and eating sushi. Others mentioned taking care to speak proper English at work, not slipping into slang or speaking with strong Nigerian accents or in pidgin. Many respondents had discovered that to earn promotion to management they needed to become socially adaptable and learn those social skills that have been given symbolic significance by their white peers and superiors.

But the problem of trying to fit in by minimizing ethnic difference is not a problem confined only to black immigrants. It is a problem that all black people face in the corporate world. As Feagin and Sikes note, black people "in corporate America are under constant pressure to adapt unidirectionallyto the values and ways of the white world."[29] Many white people perceive black cultural styles as "inappropriate for occupational tasks involving responsibility or authority."[30] The onus is on the black executive to learn the social skills considered appropriate to the position by white superiors because black cultural styles and ways of doing things are largely devalued in the corporate world. So even though many of the Nigerian second generation said they do not exhibit an African American cultural style, they are still caught in the expectation that they learn the white way of doing things.

Racial Solidarity and the Black Second Generation

In the face of racial discrimination, whether personally experienced or witnessing other black people being discriminated against, respondents took on a black racial identity and exhibited racial solidarity with all other black people.[31] Dara told me, "I have noticed with Africans that the only time we can consider ourselves one with African Americans is really when we are talking about racism and stuff. We all stand eye to eye on that. We would never understand the whole four hundred years of craziness, but there is this unspoken kinship because anything we experience today is just because of our skin color. And it kind of breaks down the wall a little."

Dara's statement raises the notion of linked fate and respondents' views about racial solidarity. The concept of linked fate was developed to explain why African Americans have remained a politically homogeneous group, despite widening economic inequality within the group. However, other scholars point out that belief in a linked fate among black people is threatened or weakened by differences in class location[32] and diversity in sexual orientation.[33] As Dara noted, recent African immigrants and their children do not share the history of slavery with African Americans, but they still have a sense of kinship because African blacks all experience antiblack discrimination,[34] even though the different historical experiences strain the moments of common understanding. Cultural differences still exist, and ethnic boundaries are still drawn between the groups. Dara also said, "We have never held hands and sang 'Kumbayah,'" but at "certain times you could tell that the walls come down because we finally get each other, just for a moment."

Many respondents said they have been racially discriminated against, and these experiences reminded them that they were black in the United States.

Seeing the often-racist representations of black people in the mass media, reading and hearing about multiple incidents of antiblack discrimination, and seeing evidence of racial inequalities—from residential segregation to deteriorating inner cities to racial imbalance in mass incarceration—also remind them that they are black. To many, the social relationships associated with being black and the many racial injustices that flow out of these relationships are in the air breathed in the United States.

The Nigerian second generation stand alongside African Americans in other contexts as well. All of the respondents felt strongly that African immigrants and their children should enjoy the benefits of affirmative action policies. Their political party memberships and voting patterns also mirror those of African Americans. Among those who are interested in U.S. politics and who vote, all but one respondent (who is a Republican) are members of the Democratic Party or are Democratic Party–leaning independents. The election of Barack Obama as president of the United States in November 2008 was one of those moments Dara talked about when the ethnic divisions within the black category were forgotten. All blacks shared in the pride that a black man had attained this heretofore inconceivable goal.

The Nigerian second-generation respondents generally did not fight their racial identity as black and did not seek to pass out of the black category. One respondent, Funke, told me that she does not go "crazy" or "try to look for another identity": "As I got higher I appreciated the fact that sometimes it makes sense for people to think that we are on the same page, because if it's anything you have to do it together as black people in this country." But for all respondents, recognizing and accepting a black racial identity did not mean they were ready to jettison their ethnic difference from African Americans. Funke's statement is an example, as she went on to say, "However, I am African, and this is why I want them to understand that I'm not African American. But at the same time, I want things to go well for African Americans as well." Tunji Mills, who attended a historically black college and whose preferred identification is "I am," stated, "I don't think of myself as African or African American. I'm just black." Moyo nicely summarized this position: "We are the same skin color. We are black like them." But despite their having a black racial identity as one component of their multifaceted identity, the notion of linked fate with other black people in the United States was weakened along ethnic lines, discussed in chapter 4, and along class lines, which I turn to below.

When I coded respondents' descriptions of their relations with African Americans, it was very clear that they made distinctions between African Americans on the basis of social class. But the distinctions did not end with class membership. Respondents prioritized behavior and similarity in mindset alongside class status. The Nigerian second generation have incorporated several elements of African American culture into their hybridized ethnic content. Most of them did not seek to completely distance themselves from their proximal hosts, with many not seeing this as possible. Many were born in the United States, have American friends, and are aware of the racial disparities in society and the ongoing racial prejudice and discrimination that black people, including them, face. What they all seek to dissociate themselves from, as shown in chapter 4, are the negative stereotypical cultural and behavioral traits associated with African Americans, which I would say are frequently ascribed to all black people. This sentiment came out clearly in Monica's discussion of the kind of neighborhood in which she would like to live.

> If I want to describe a kind of community I would like to live in, I wouldn't put stereotypical black Americans in it. That's a blunt statement. That's what it is. I would not want to live in a neighborhood with stereotypical black people. I mean the way they're seen on TV, like P. Diddy.[35] I don't care he has much money. I wouldn't want to live next to him. I don't like flashiness. I like being low key, and [I like] people if they are up to something, I like people who if they are doing something they will want to be better at that thing. They are respectful. So what I do like are young black professionals, who are about something; they want to be better at something, not reap where they haven't sown. That's a community of people I want to be with. We want our community to grow, and if that excludes the stereotypical black Americans, then I don't care.

"Reap where they haven't sown" is code for those who are welfare dependent, those who are criminals, and those who pursue illegal gain. Here Monica emphasized behavior, what she does and does not consider acceptable. She is comfortable with African Americans she sees as similar to her: those who are respectful like she is, who are college-educated professionals like she is, and who are serious minded like she is. These characteristics are the "me" in the statement "you are not like 'me.'"

U.S. respondents were particular about behavior, and they attached class-specific subcultures to individuals in certain social classes. They do not want to associate with those blacks who exhibit behaviors such as talking loudly, hard partying, and so on that they associate with lower-class blacks, the underclass, and ghettos (the latter term was used only by U.S. respondents). According to one respondent, "African Americans and Africans have different cultures. Upper classes are stricter in terms of education than lower-class groups. So you have to separate the groups out." Sade, another respondent, told me that she has "a complicated relationship with African Americans. It depends on class. The lower class exhibit the stereotypes of laziness. I have a libertarian streak and think you should help yourself before you expect help. They also feel that Africans think they are better than them. Middle-class blacks, there is this thing, a competition between the two groups." These two quotes show the disaggregation of African Americans into different class groups with different behaviors in the minds of second-generation Nigerians.

Most respondents saw religious faith and religiosity as a guarantor of acceptable behavior. The majority of my U.S. respondents are Christians. For those who are religious, a religious African American is more likely to have the behaviors that they find acceptable because, in their experience, Christians, especially committed Christians, tend to be more socially conservative. They are less likely to engage in hard partying, drinking, immoral behavior, and so on. Consequently, they said they were more comfortable associating with African Americans who shared similar Christian beliefs and values. Even those who were not serious Christians knew Christian African Americans would be a better and more comfortable fit for them. Thus having similar religious beliefs and corresponding high religiosity is a supplementary source of membership in the new middle-class-based category/group.[36]

Many respondents felt that educated African Americans are more welcoming to them and are more willing to accept their cultural differences and even celebrate them. They reported that poor and lower-class members of the proximal host were much more hostile to them and often made fun of them because of their cultural differences. Seun described his experience with African Americans as "all over the map." "This goes back to the way they perceive African immigrants," he told me. "Some want to put me down because of my heritage. Others are excited about my difference. It goes by class. People of higher income bracket tend to be more open and willing to recognize difference in a positive light, but people of a lower class—they lack exposure to people of different cultures. They are more closed minded. They tend to think of us as a little strange." Another respondent, Jide, discovered that warmer relations with African Americans were dependent on being similarly educated and having similar goals. He said, "I think I have a great relationship with African Americans—not all African Americans, but African Americans with something in common with me. I think my friends are all successful African Americans, successful Nigerians, and we all know the value of education and we have future aspirations."

These differential experiences reinforced the class distinctions and class-specific cultures and behavior respondents made about African Americans. It makes sense that if one is more comfortable with well-educated blacks, it is this group of blacks that one will associate with and see as having multiple things in common with. This is the central premise of the contact theory, which holds that increased contact and social interaction will lead to reduced prejudice. And I found that this was happening among the Nigerian second generation as they are finding out that they have things in common with similarly educated African Americans and with African Americans from similar social backgrounds.

In Seun's description of his relationship with African Americans, we can see the explicit use of class as a sorting mechanism: "I love African Americans. I went to school with them. I like their music. I am the person who does not necessarily categorize based on race. I categorize based on class. I relate to both class groups differently. I put myself in that category of blacks who have the same social class as me."

The experience of the second generation of Nigerian ancestry, as expressed by Sade, Jide, and Seun, corresponds to the class divisions within the black population that other studies have found. Several studies, for example, found that elite middle-class African Americans use class-based identities to distance themselves from poor African Americans.[37] Elite middle-class African Americans were also fearful that their children would learn bad habits from these poor blacks, something I also found among Nigerian parents, as discussed in chapter 4. Many middle-class African American families live in close proximity to poor blacks, and the parents—like the parents of my U.S. respondents—feel that their children are constantly in danger of going down the wrong path, toward criminality or downward mobility.[38] A 2007 report from the Pew Center concluded from their survey of black people that "African Americans see a widening gulf between the values of middle class blacks and poor blacks." Sixty-one percent of blacks felt that the values of middle-class blacks had become more different from the values of poor blacks. Only 23 percent of blacks felt that middle-class and poor blacks had a lot of shared values.[39] These findings of class divisions and racial attitude differences based on class divisions within the black category have led some to note that "although black may appear to be a monolithic category to non-blacks, it is indeed a diverse one."[40]

IN BRITAIN: A LIFETIME OF DISCRIMINATION

A major difference between the Nigerian second generation in America and the Nigerian second generation in Britain is that even though respondents in both countries report that they have experienced racial prejudice and racial discrimination, the second generation in Britain talked about it far more. While the primary story their counterparts in the United States told concerned their differences from African Americans, the primary story the second generation of Nigerian ancestry in Britain told was one of racial discrimination in their everyday lives from childhood up to the present day. These experiences of discrimination at different stages of their lives and in different institutions and sectors of British society have strongly affected their views of their country and how they identify. This cross-national difference between the U.S. and British respondents reveals an interaction between national context and the identities that immigrants form. The next chapter continues the examination of this interaction as it focuses on the second generation's identificational assimilation—their development of a sense of peoplehood based exclusively on the host society. In the remainder of this chapter, I discuss how race influences identity formation and the lived realities of the Nigerian second generation in Britain.

According to respondents, in Britain it is difficult to forget that one is black. They say the black second generation are made aware that they are black at an early age. And they are reminded that they are black as they go about their daily lives. According to one respondent, to forget that one is black for one day in Britain "is not realistic." Another said, "In this country as a black person . . . if I woke up tomorrow morning and I forgot that I was black, people will remind me." In an innocent moment, a female respondent, recalled being told by a white British male colleague that she "got some ghetto friends coming to Aberdeen" when she told him and other colleagues that she was expecting visitors. She felt that her colleague basically assumed that "because I'm black, they must be ghetto." As adults, the Nigerian second generation continue to face many irritating events that constantly remind them that they are black and therefore different and foreign. These include being mistaken for the janitor or nursing assistant instead of the doctor in hospitals, being mistaken for the secretary instead of the lawyer in courtrooms and law offices, and shopkeepers, especially Asian ones, placing your change on the counter instead of in the palm of your hand. Several of the common contexts for and aspects of discrimination mentioned by respondents are discussed below.

Discrimination in Public Spaces

Unlike the United States, where an element of U.S. national identity is that America is a land of immigrants, Britain does not have a national myth that welcomes immigrants, especially immigrants from former nonwhite colonies. This hostility against immigrants is particularly aimed at black immigrants. The rise but now waning popularity of the British National Party, whose platform calls for the expulsion of all black immigrants in order to reclaim an essential Britishness, affirms this view and extends this hostility to other nonwhite immigrants as well.

Michelle, like many other respondents, got a taste of this antiblack racism from white nationalist groups when she was in primary school.

> Outside of school, there was another aspect, dimension, which you had to deal with in the 1970s and 1980s which was really, really, terrible racism, overt racism, from the National Front, who were very prevalent in those days. The National Front is an organization which actually still exists today but is called something else, which is the British National Party. And in those days they were called the National Front, and they were very racist, overtly. They were against anything nonwhite, anybody. And it was something that a lot of teenage boys and older men would join. They fashioned themselves as a version of the Nazis—they used swastikas and the British flag as symbols in those days. They would dress in a certain way. They would wear big black boots. In fact they were not that dissimilar to the white supremacists in America. I think there is a particular group that dress like this. They wear very, very tight jeans, big black boots, and a particular kind of jacket, which was an old army jacket, and a shaved head, a skinhead, which sometimes would have a swastika engraved or etched on it. And they would run around the street chasing black people, black boys particularly. And it's funny, as I say, we always lived in this area and funny we ended up buying here.
>
> When I was . . . six, we moved to a house on this main road right at the other end. And towards that bottom part of the road there are a couple of

very big council estates [government housing] in which primarily white working-class people lived in, and there were very big groups of people who supported the National Front or were members of it. And so I remember as a child about eight or nine when things were much freer, much safer, [this was the mid-1970s] my mom would send me to the store for some bread or whatever, and I might see a group of them standing on the corner, and yelling at an eight-year-old girl, "nigger," "blackie," "wart," all the names they used to insult black people, and sometimes they would say they were going to chase me. But I've grown up and gotten to know black guys who lived in East London, which is another area that had real problems with racism, and they were literally being chased. They might come off the bus and be walking home and hear someone shout "NIGGER" and then see a whole group of them chasing them down the road. And if you weren't careful, that's what they'll do. Knives weren't so big then as they are now, but generally what they would do is beat you to death. They might get you down on the ground and stamp you. That is the whole point of the boots. They would use them to kick your head, and all the rest of it. There were some fatalities, but generally they would beat you up . . . so quite bad. That was the other sort of dimension that you were dealing with as a child of African or West Indian parents.

Then people started fighting back, I would say it was the Caribbeans, the Jamaican people. Jamaicans had a reputation for being tough, carrying knives, that sort of thing. They started fighting back, a lot of incidents of gangs fighting each other, and then it started to calm down. What then happened, the National Front and British National Party started focusing on other cultural groups that were more vulnerable, and by this time it was the Asians. There had been an influx of people from India, Pakistan, Bangladesh, and they were much more vulnerable, tended not to fight, and so they then started focusing on them. They literally would go on what they called "Paki bashing." They had a song that they would sing, and that was an evening out; they would go out, see if they could find some Asian people, and beat them up. So it was a hard time to be in England.

According to Michelle, in Britain today, antiblack racism still exists, but now there are class differences in how it operates, and it is generally more covert.

Now it is very different. It's a strange country, actually, because of course there is still a lot of racism. The difference between the working class and middle class and upwards is that the working-class people are overtly racist and they will tell you to your face you're a nigger or whatever, you know where you are with them. But the middle-class people, they don't do that: that is vulgar. But what they will do is prevent you from progressing in the workplace. They might give you a job, but a lowly job, and you'll never get higher than that. And so that's the kind of thing you would experience now. But in terms of the overt people targeting you on the street and beating you up, you don't hear about that anymore. So in terms of racism, to get back to your question, as a black person in this country, you really don't get overt racism in the same way.

Oye, like Michelle and most others, agrees that things have changed significantly for black people in Britain. In the past, racial incidents were much more overt. Oye is a thirty-two-year-old medical representative who was born in Britain. He went to Nigeria when he was two and came back when he was eleven. He remembers walking down the street and hearing mature Britons calling him "the N word." What he calls a "perfect example" of this kind of treatment occurred when he went on a road trip with his football club, and "there was a little young boy standing beside his dad just shouting 'black b, black b, black b,' and his dad was patting him on the head. It happened all the time." But things have changed a bit now that there are more black people and other ethnic minorities in Britain. "When we arrived, there were very few, but now, almost every corner you turn, there is a person of color, either black or Asian, Chinese. And because of that, I think that the ignorance has gone down a bit, because people are aware that if they use racial epithets anyone can turn around and defend that person."

Respondents say that racial discrimination still exists and is still quite rampant, but it is more subtle in its operation. The majority of white Britons who are still antiblack or anti-immigrant are "keeping quiet." Michael, a forty-one-year-old finance analyst who is British born and raised, concurred: "People are still racist. People are still unfriendly. However, the rules of engagement have changed. Before, you could go into work and say 'I don't like blacks' or you say 'I don't like homosexuals.' You do that now in Britain and you are likely to get dismissed. So a very dumb racist would say that and lose their job. But a smart one would not say that or even befriend you or whatever the case may be. But they will still hold those views."

Gender Dynamics in the Experience of Racial Discrimination

More men than women reported experiencing racial discrimination in Britain. According to respondents, white Britons tend to view black men more suspiciously than black women. Alex described elderly white ladies crossing to the other side of the road when they saw him coming down the street, and he said it always irritates him. According to Demola, the bias against black men is so great that "if you get excited as a black man in Britain, you are described as being aggressive." Many of the male second generation felt there was a double standard for black men. According to Dimeji, a twenty-seven-year-old salesman:

> White people are afraid of blacks. You raise your voice and they get intimidated. You might get into a conversation with them and the conversation gets a little bit heated and you raise your voice, the volume of your voice goes up, and they get afraid. And they try to get you into trouble for it, saying, "Oh, he is being aggressive." That is one thing black people are accused of. It doesn't matter if you are African or Jamaican or what. White people behave lousy and do their own stupid things like binge drinking and having fights and stuff, and the way they describe it is being "laddish." He is being a lad. But when you are black and you do it, you are aggressive and violent.

Many of the male respondents had gotten into trouble with the authorities despite their best efforts to avoid confrontations. Chuka remembers this happening to him frequently as a teenager in the 1970s and 1980s: "Back in those days, if you were black, you would be routinely stopped and searched for any arbitrary reason. And depending on which police officer stopped you, you could not just be stopped and searched on the street, you could end up being taken back to the station, taken into the van, and beaten up." When this happened, he explained, the police would commonly say that the black youth was "resisting arrest" or had "assaulted a police officer." Consequently, black men "could quite easily get a criminal record for no apparent reason." To him, a reason the 1981 race riots in England occurred was because "black people had had enough." But they were constrained in their fight against racism because "at the same time, if the law, the police, were racist, how do you report it, yeah? Who do you report it to?"

Among the men I interviewed, some expressed a quiet distrust of the British judicial system. They saw unequal treatment of all black people but especially black men, and Caribbeans and Africans were in the same boat in this regard. Their response was in keeping with what Kasinitz and colleagues found: the impact of racial discrimination is more damaging when it comes from representatives of the state because these events can be interpreted to mean that the individual is being marginalized and not accepted by society.[41] However, contrary to what was feared by the authors of segmented assimilation theory, my male respondents did not lower their aspirations. Rather, their experiences of racial discrimination caused them not to identify with Britain.

The female second generation of Nigerian ancestry I interviewed did not experience such rampant antiblack discrimination, especially in public spaces and by officers of the judicial system. Like the men, they felt they were discriminated against at work, but for the most part they agreed that they had it easy compared to their male counterparts. While many of the men had to constantly modify their behavior so as not to seem "aggressive," the women did not have to do this. They modified their behavior in other ways—to fit in easily with white Britons. Emem, a twenty-two-year-old university graduate born and raised in Britain, said, "I can get on with all the different groups. I just slide along. I know what I have to say, how to talk with the white people. I know what they like and what they will not like. I also know what to say to Indian, Asian people."

Ibinabo, a forty-two-year-old British born and raised lawyer, calls this adaptability "social education." She believes that many first-generation Africans don't have it and that many second-generation African males don't possess it because of the racial discrimination targeted at them. None of the men I interviewed talked about adaptability, which I define as knowing how to behave with members of other social and racial groups to ensure trouble-free interaction and to achieve your objective. For example, if one learns that white people like it when people are polite when interacting with them, one says please and thank you as often as needed. It means following the rules and not butting up against the system and its conventions. The women were much more able to do this than the men, for all the reasons discussed above.

Perceptions of Racial Discrimination in the Workplace

Over half of the respondents (56 percent) in Britain said they had experienced antiblack discrimination in the workplace. Some respondents felt that this discrimination manifested or increased as a black person climbed up the career ladder. Some commented that all black people are completely blocked from reaching the top. According to Tami, a British-born forty-year-old human resource manager, "It gets much, much, much harder, and as you climb up the corporate ladder people become much, much, more aware of your color. I know that up until a certain point in my career I found it easier to get promoted, but as I climbed up the corporate ladder it got much more difficult. And that has to do with the fact that one, you are female, and two, that you are an ethnic minority regardless of whatever people in power say, that they don't take these things into consideration. They are *lying*."

The women I interviewed were aware of the double strike against them for being both female and black. But the men were worse off. Similarly, multiple studies of black workers in the British labor market find that Caribbean women are doing better than Caribbean men, while highly educated first-generation African men suffered the worst ethnic penalties among all ethnic minorities in the workplace—both visible (Indian, Pakistani, Bangladeshi, African and Caribbean) and white (Irish and Western Europeans). Those with university degrees were eight times more likely to be unemployed than their white British male counterparts.[42]

Michelle narrated an incident concerning two black female friends of hers.

> A friend of mine had an experience recently that she was telling me about at work. She works for a newspaper, gets along very well with her boss, and has deputized [filled in] for him. She had been told she was excellent and all the rest of it. When it came down to it, he didn't tell her there was a vacancy for a deputy, and he brought someone in over her head completely and installed him and literally told on her on Friday, "You're getting a new boss on Monday." "What new boss?" "My new deputy," her boss told her. And she said to me, "Look, at the end of the day, this particular newspaper just isn't ready for a black person in that particular role, so they will use me to do all the work, but they won't give me that title."

Michelle and many others felt that for both black men and women the glass ceiling was still very much present.

Racial discrimination in the workplace took three major forms: being passed over for promotions, being given the worst jobs, and being discriminated against by clients. The second generation strongly believe that black people are often blocked from entering management or certain specialties that are more highly remunerated than others in the same occupation or are given less attractive assignments. One study, which did not include second-generation Africans, found that second-generation Caribbeans and Indians were less likely to get a job in occupations that required at least a bachelor's degree, compared to white Britons of the same age and with the same qualifications. This finding supports the second generation of Nigerian ancestry's reports of being blocked out of certain jobs. The study also found that once second-generation Caribbeans and Indians managed to access high-level jobs, they got the same kinds of jobs as people of British ancestry with the same qualifications and appeared to earn similar wages.[43] My respondents, however, reported a different experience. Some were in similar jobs held by white Britons but had been, or had heard of other black people being, blocked from entering upper management positions. Others felt they had been passed over for promotions, given poorer job assignments than their white colleagues in similar positions, or prevented from entering the better remunerated specializations. Some, like Tami, believed that this discrimination was not limited to black people only but affected all ethnic minorities in Britain, a belief that is confirmed by multiple studies, which find that all ethnic minorities in Britain suffer an ethnic penalty in the workplace compared to the charter population. The charter population is whites of British ancestry who are the same age and have the same educational qualifications and marital status as the ethnic minority.[44]

Magda, a British born and raised paralegal, is very bitter about her experiences in the British labor market. She felt she had been passed over for a promotion and a salary increase because of her race: "I have experienced discrimination every day at work. I work in a city law firm. It is as clear as day, the institutional racism in the city. You have people making up things to complain to your boss about you, or people will talk to you like you are an animal, like we are back in the old days of slavery. I have had that."

Magda is particularly aggrieved because she believes less qualified white women have been promoted over her.

Recently, opportunities to expand on my income were thwarted while the other girls who have fewer skills than me and are so obviously less qualified than me get the opportunities. They get as much overtime as they want. Very subtly, there are different ways they hold you back. But these things are not things you can really take legal action against because they are not calling you a nigger. So what can you do? That is how it is today. That is what gives the false perception that racism is no longer is with us, especially when I have spent so many years in the city and everywhere I go I meet the same thing.

Some respondents felt that black people are given the more difficult or less attractive jobs while white people are given the cushier ones. According to Sam, "In mental health, if you look at psychiatric nurses, the psychiatric nurses that are in the community are mostly white. The psychiatric nurses chasing around criminals, who have criminals as their patients, are black." And this is happening even when blacks and whites have the same educational qualifications and experience, and even when the black person has more experience than his or her white colleague.

Other respondents said that black people are discriminated against in certain specializations. Highly compensated specializations in such fields as law and medicine are very difficult for black people to enter. This was Michelle's experience.

> Where there is money—for example, in law, that would be commercial law, intellectual property, media, criminal law, and patent law, all of the things that involve money and business and people making lots of money—that is hard to penetrate as a black person. There's still a lot of racism; it's very much a closed shop. It's not impenetrable, but it is much, much more difficult. The demands in terms of your academic background are very high. They want people who've master's from Cambridge, Oxford, Harvard, that sort of thing. They set the bar very high, and that will by definition exclude a lot of black people who were born over here who might have had a state education which wasn't really all that great.

Those in jobs with a lot of face-to-face client interaction said they were often discriminated against by employers and clients alike. They said employers were aware that some clients were less willing to receive attention from black people and consequently took race into consideration in making hiring decisions. Respondents who were nurses, doctors, and certified nursing assistants frequently had clients who refused their services, asked superiors to give them other (white) personnel, or thought black medical practitioners were incompetent or dishonest. I interviewed two individuals who had switched from law and retrained, one as an IT professional and the other as an accountant. They felt that since these occupations involved less face-to-face interaction, they would experience fewer incidents of discrimination than if they continued practicing law.

When promoted to management, a few respondents said they had to be careful not to give management the feeling that they were overly fraternizing with subordinate black coworkers. Bidemi, an electrician, wondered to himself why all his managers were white and why all the managers who were black were trying to be white. He said, "I think they do that so that they can be accepted by their colleagues, their white colleagues. They are given better jobs when they act white." He found that before his black managers were promoted to management, they were friendlier to their black coworkers. This changed once they got promoted. They began to speak and act differently to their black subordinates. "Now that you are lower than them," he explained, "they sort of distance themselves a little bit from you, maybe to not make themselves look bad to the management staff that might say, 'Look at this guy, we bring one black person into management and look at how he is behaving.' So I think black managers feel that they have to tone it down a little bit.

You can see it in the way they carry on. The way they behave is just discriminatory. They take it to the next extreme."

Some respondents believed that black cultural capital is devalued in the workplace. A study in the United States found that many white people perceive black cultural styles as "inappropriate for occupational tasks involving responsibility or authority," and it seems that this is happening in Britain too.[45] I met Pauline, a thirty-one-year-old university administrator with a master's degree, at the Nigerian embassy in London. She had come in with her two sisters to get a Nigerian entry visa to attend her first cousin's wedding. She and her sisters were dressed in chic and very trendy professional outfits. They were well coifed and fully made-up. They had not visited Nigeria in over fifteen years and had brought their first-generation Nigerian cousin to help them navigate the visa application process. Despite being born and raised in Britain and identifying as more British than Nigerian, Pauline felt she had been passed over for promotion because she was black. She said, "I know at least five times that this has happened to me and it is 100 percent because of my color."

> You have to code-switch, because if you don't have that diversity as a black person, you are not going to survive because you have got the British white European culture as the dominant one. So you cannot just relate in a black or African sense. You need to put on different hats, and the black people who have not learnt that are not very successful because they are taking a black culture into the corporate world and so they don't get anywhere, they don't get interviews, they don't get jobs. To be a successful black person, you have to be aware of all the cultures and be able to slot into the different segments. That is what I feel.

When I asked Pauline how she has responded to being passed over for promotion, she told me that she just puts her head down and works harder and keeps the faith that her hard work will pay off in the future.

One constant refrain among the second generation was the subtlety with which racial discrimination against black people occurs in Britain today. The subtlety of it, however, did not make its effects less severe in terms of occupational satisfaction, economic well-being, and emotional and psychological discomfort. Many said a lot of it came through as a "vibe," in body language. It could be a look: a look of boredom when a black person is speaking, or not paying attention to the person, or treating the person as invisible. One of the barristers said, "Every time you go to speak [before the judge] there's some kind of irritation, a rubbishing of your arguments . . . yeah." It came through in the form of being blocked from reaching the pinnacle of one's profession with no one saying a word or explaining why. Sometimes a white colleague who is a friend might pull back the curtain and let the black person know that it is time to move on or that he or she would not get the promotion to become upper management because of being black.

Respondents agreed that suspecting that they did not get upper management jobs because of their race sometimes made them feel paranoid. But as one of them said—and it is a sentiment all agreed with—"In the climate of Britain right now, nobody wants to be deemed to be racist. Black people are very much more accepted, ostensibly, within society. I mean, don't get me wrong, English people are fantastic at covert racism. You would never know unless you've grown up here why things keep happening, why you can't make any progress with some things. They'll be smiling at you every day and saying good morning to you." Yet the subterranean and subtle quality of workplace discrimination makes it very difficult to confront and/or successfully prosecute.

The general attitude of the adult Nigerian second generation toward discrimination is cynicism and resignation. Respondents reported more experiences of discrimination from white people than their U.S. counterparts. Those who have experienced workplace discrimination see it as part and parcel of the discrimination they experience in Britain, and the totality of these experiences reinforces their belief that they are not British but Nigerians who happen to have British citizenship. Most have slim to no hope that things will improve, primarily because they feel that these discriminatory episodes are too covert to be confronted.

For some females, experiences of discrimination are complicated by ageism and sexism in the workplace. Some, like Pauline, had decided simply to focus on their work. They hoped that if they work hard, the situation will improve. Others, like Michelle, looked for self-validation outside work. They drew on their religious faith to see them through the tough times and counted themselves fortunate to have good jobs that helped provide for their families. However, for women and men alike, refusing to acknowledge workplace discrimination was the most common response strategy. Oye said, "I probably don't notice it that much, because sometimes when you go down that path and a job comes up and you don't get that job, you think, 'Well, is it because I wasn't good enough for that or I didn't do good in the interview? Or is it because of the color of my skin?' But then again, you can't be that cynical every time, so you just take it on the chin as the person who got the job is better, and you move on."

The consensus among respondents was that taking notice of racial discrimination, and of workplace discrimination in particular, was not to one's advantage. It was self-defeating and only made one bitter. According to Shawn, a thirty-four-year-old investment broker:

> There are some people who don't like me, and I don't like them, and who knows for what reason? But I don't immediately go to, "You don't like me because I am black, that is why you have this problem" or "You don't like me because I am competitive or I am loud." So I very rarely experience any kind of racism in my view in my workplace. And if I did, I probably wouldn't care about it too much because it just holds you back and changes you and the way you think, thinking, "Are they all racist?" I don't have time for that. It doesn't add any value. I have done pretty well. I am quite happy with my career. Everywhere I have wanted to go, I have gotten there in the end.

Many respondents said that people who discriminated against them for being black didn't know better. Having this attitude helped them keep a strong sense of self, prevented them from developing a sense of victimhood, and let them remain happy and/or content. And their religious faith helped them maintain this attitude.

Respondents' experiences of consistent and continuous discrimination in Britain drove higher levels of transnationalism, compared to respondents in the United States, because these experiences engendered feelings of unbelonging in Britain. Many attended transnational churches with headquarters in Nigeria, such as the Redeemed Christian Church of God (RCCG). These churches have predominantly Nigerian congregations that are a mix of generational and age cohorts. Consequently, they are sites for replenishing and strengthening Nigerian ethnicity and ethnic identities. More of them engaged in significant transnational activities such as regularly sending money to dependent relatives and doing business in Nigeria. In contrast, in the United States, the transnational activities of the few who were transnational were mostly taking money gifts, clothing, and other small personal items to family and friends during infrequent visits to Nigeria (see table in appendix B). Requests from Nigeria for money were often passed on to parents. Respondents in Britain found it easier to be more transnational than their U.S. counterparts for additional reasons. Britain is geographically closer to Nigeria, making it cheaper to travel back and forth. Also, Nigerians in Britain are not as geographically dispersed. Most Nigerians in Britain live in London, and the Nigerian community in London has stronger and denser ties to Nigeria than do the Nigerian communities in America, creating denser transnational fields for the second generation in Britain compared to the second generation in the United States.

Racial Solidarity and the Black Second Generation

The second generation of Nigerian ancestry did not draw as sharp boundaries against their proximal hosts, Caribbeans, as did their U.S. counterparts against African Americans, and this is primarily attributable to their experiences of racial discrimination. Racial discrimination unites all black people in Britain and even other ethnic minorities like those from South Asia since they all experience it. Gilroy explains entrenched institutional racism in Britain as being a result of the country's failure to deal with its racist past. Because its colonies were far away, Britain has not had to directly and comprehensively confront the underpinning ideologies of white superiority and hostility to immigrants, especially those from its black former colonies, that supported slavery and colonialism and today keep institutional racism against black people entrenched in British society.[46] The serious race riots of 1981 that occurred in four main cities in England, London, Birmingham, Leeds, and Liverpool, are a critical event for respondents who were teenagers and adults at that time because they realized that all blacks, and not just Caribbeans who took the lead in the riots, were in a fight together against unequal treatment, limited opportunities, economic marginalization, and racial discrimination.

Black immigrants, both Caribbeans and Africans, are largely unwelcome in Britain, and the Nigerian second generation are aware of the largely unwelcoming reception extended to black and other nonwhite ethnic minorities in Britain. Even though Caribbeans are thought of as the nation's *native* black population,[47] they have not resided in the British homeland, in significant numbers, for as long as African Americans have resided in the United States. This, in conjunction with the fact that all immigrants from Britain's nonwhite former colonies are unwelcome, recent (postcolonial) Africans and their children do not have a similar space as do their counterparts in the United States to be viewed as the "preferred" or "better blacks." Also, some respondents mentioned that the colonial experience of Caribbeans and many of the Africans living in Britain and the widely held view that the colonial experience was an exploitative one on the part of Britain helps unify the groups. The colonial history the groups share allows members of both groups to answer the taunt of "go back to your countries" with the retort "we are here because you were there."[48] But seeing themselves as racially black and sharing sentiments of racial solidarity with black Caribbeans did not in any way mute the cultural differences the Nigerian second generation believe exist between the two black groups.

Respondents' political party memberships and voting patterns mirror those of black Caribbeans. Of those interested in U.K. politics and who vote, all but one respondent (who is a Conservative) are members of the Labor Party or vote Labor. Respondents also showed a black racial group consciousness with blacks in the United States. Almost all were excited about the election of Barack Obama as president of the United States in November 2008 and shared in the pride that a black man had attained this heretofore inconceivable goal. A respondent told me that while he had "never followed the U.S. presidential election ever, ever. I just had no interest in it. This one I was glued to, I actually stayed up till 4 or 5 o'clock in the morning to hear them announce that the president of America is a black man. We stayed up and we listened and afterwards that's all we could talk about. It was a happy moment because I think it just shows that black people paid the price being enslaved and one of them is now the most powerful man in the world. So we have come from slavery to equality with the whites. "

Some of them spoke of the "Obama effect," a rising belief that anything is possible for a black person. But almost all respondents were skeptical that a black man would be elected prime minister in the near future. One respondent felt that the British masses were amazed that Barack Obama could be elected president: "You could tell in the British media and all the other pundits the shock that they had, the disbelief. They felt that he was never going to make it, that he was a long shot. And there was shock and reluctant acceptance when he won." Even though he could imagine British people voting for a black prime minister, he told me, "The establishment, the system won't allow a black person to get to that position." Another respondent, Bayo, in response to my question about whether he thought there could be a black prime minister, told me, laughing, "I think hell would freeze over before that happened." He went on to say, "As much as they [white Britons] think they're not a racist country, as much as they think they are diverse, higher up in the hierarchy there's a lot more racism going on. In the United Kingdom, they don't even have a Member of Parliament (MP) in the front bench who is black, and for you to actually go further in any party you have to be in the front bench and there is none of them in the front bench that is black."

Last, the ethnic boundaries drawn between the Nigerian second genera- tion and their proximal hosts are made more complex by the widespread dominance of British street culture, which draws its cultural content pre- dominantly from Caribbean culture but attracts all racial and ethnic groups and all social class backgrounds. As a result, it is no longer possible to draw very bright and sharp boundaries between Nigerians and Caribbeans when talking about the teenage second generation because British street culture paints in some gray.

Using Social Class as a Sorting Mechanism to Order Black-on-Black Relations

Like their U.S. counterparts, the second-generation Nigerians in Britain use a class schema to make class and behavioral distinctions and judgments of similarity or difference between themselves and members of their proximal host. They use the same class schema, This-Black-Person-Is-Not-Like-Me- Unless-He/She-Is-Middle-Class-and-Well-Mannered. As discussed in chap- ter 2, when they were growing up, they were the ones being told "you are not like me" by the proximal host, but now they are the ones telling members of the proximal host "you are not like me"—unless the proximal host member mirrors "me," as described in this phrase.

An example of this class schema in operation is Sam's discussion of being a middle-class black man and choosing to live in a white neighborhood so that he would not be seen as black and poor. He struggles with the fact that black people in Britain have been made the face of criminality and poverty.[49] The widespread view in Britain that blackness connotes poverty, criminality, or a disadvantaged class experience is why Sam said, "When a black person is driving a nice car they get stopped by police."

The way in which black people are perceived in Britain has made Sam iden- tify by class. He said, "I think part of the problem that I have as a second- generation person is that if I was to entirely accept or feel British in the land- scape at present, to some degree that would be to accept being part of the underclass. And at present, I don't accept the way things are. I feel that I should be in the middle class and that is where I fit, but society generally feels that I shouldn't be. Society generally feels that I should be part of the underclass; a large section of society feels that way." In fact, Sam's refusal to live in a black neighborhood shows that he has accepted it as the way things are in Britain. He signals his middle-class status by telling people who mistake him for a janitor that he is a doctor and by choosing to live in a predominantly white neighborhood. I asked him how that worked, and he said, "You have to define where you are going to live. You have to define who you are going to hang out with. As a black person, you have to decide: do you want to live with black people or do you want to live with middle-class people, because the two are not necessarily the same. So if you live with black people, you are exposing yourself and your family to underclass people. Unfortunately, in Britain, ethnic minorities have some values that you do not share such as lower aspirations and generally poor resources. If you decide you are going to be middle class, then, yes, you will be in a more affluent area with probably less crime."

Sam himself had come to believe that living with black people means living among the black underclass. This is actually erroneous. Studies show that racial discrimination against black people in housing—from realtors to banks and mortgage lenders redlining territories to white flight—has led middle-class black people to live in close proximity to working-class and poor blacks.[50]

Respondents see a basis of commonality among all blacks that are similarly well educated and like-minded—people who are ambitious, are well mannered, and have similar values. Maggie, a forty-one-year-old lawyer who was born and raised in Britain, one of two respondents with a Caribbean significant other, said: "My parents had some sort of prejudice against Caribbeans. To some degree, they were looked at as people who did not like us, who were not as ambitious. As an adult my relationship with them is fantastic. I have a Caribbean partner and have a baby with him. It is a bonus for black people to get together. Full stop! As long as you have the same vision and are like-minded." The second generation are creating their own relations with their proximal hosts, choosing to befriend those with similar educational levels, who are professionals, who are middle class, and who have the right behaviors.

The boundaries of "us' and "them" are constantly being redrawn, depending on the circumstances the second generation face. One example of the complexity of this boundary work is when there are quarreling factions. According to Rufiat, a twenty-three-year-old, "We are all Africans, but we do not have the same nationality. We are still rivals. If I see a Ghanaian and a Jamaican quarreling, I will take the side of the Ghanaian. If I see a Ghanaian and a Nigerian quarreling, I will take the side of the Nigerian. It will go deeper. If I see a Jamaican and an Englishman quarreling, I have to think twice about whether I support the Jamaican. If he is quiet, I will support him. If he is rude and loud, I will not support him."

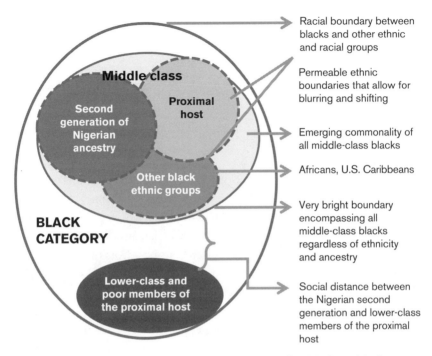

FIGURE 1. Class schema and its consequences for black-on-black group relations.

In confrontational situations, Nigerian coethnics come first with no questions asked, and Africans come second. That a proximal host is also racially black does not guarantee that he or she will be supported over a white person or someone of another race. "Rude and loud" is code for non–degree holders and nonprofessional workers who like partying and drinking. "Quiet" is code for middle class or for someone who does not exhibit urban street culture. Similarity in class status was often viewed as connoting similar interests and goals that guaranteed racial solidarity with the proximal host in tense situations. But respondents were not unmindful of the fact that having money enough to belong to the middle or upper classes does not necessarily mean that an individual has a similar mind-set.

Figure 1 summarizes the multiple and crosscutting boundaries that the second generation draw as a result of simultaneously holding ethnic, racial, and middle-class identities while grappling with the identificational consequences of having less than ideal proximal hosts (as racially framed by wider society). The boundary processes are basically similar in the United States and Britain. The second generation use the class schema This-Black-Person-Is-

Not-Like-Me-Unless-He/She-Is-Middle-Class-and-Well-Mannered to expand their ethnic boundaries to include other blacks of similar middle class status, and concurrently contract their boundaries to exclude lower class and poor blacks while holding their ethnicity distinct from other black ethnicities but still accepting membership within the unifying black racial group.

CONCLUSION: A MULTIETHNIC OR VARIEGATED BLACK MIDDLE CLASS

An unchanging fact in the story of the black second generation, of which the Nigerian second generation are a part, is that they cannot form their identities or live their lives in the United States and Britain without grappling with the issue of race and how it affects their lives. This chapter sheds some light on several ways in which the adult Nigerian second generation confront the impact of race even as they hold very salient multiple identities combined into a multifaceted one. Most respondents are college-educated professionals who accept that they are part of the black middle class and as such have things in common with other similarly educated and similarly minded blacks, be they African Americans or Caribbeans. As a result, as the Nigerian second generation, as part of the black/African second generation, integrate into American and British society, they, along with the first generation, are creating a more diverse black category on both ethnic and class lines.

Many studies in both countries have assumed a poor or working-class black person as emblematic of blackness. My findings, however, reveal a more complex picture of how class background shapes identity formation. I found that a form of class-based pan-ethnicity is occurring. On the one hand, respondents are disassociating from blacks of a certain class or are concerned about being associated with them. On the other hand, it is their shared class or professional status with other blacks that shapes their sense of themselves as being discriminated against in the workplace and their sense of identification as simultaneously Nigerian, African, and black. The adult Nigerian second generation draw cultural and moral boundaries to make distinctions within class. Even when African Americans or black Caribbeans in Britain might be middle class or wealthy, my respondents still identified differences within the black middle class based on presumed behavioral, cultural, and moral differences. The significance of this means that black identity or black pan-ethnicity might still be at times fragmented or not as cohesive just because one controls for class or identifies a shared economic class status. It also means that for my respondents, "Nigerianness" or "Africanness" is not simply associated with a class background or only class markers.

There are some notable national differences in the experiences of the Nigerian second generation. British respondents were very aware that all black people are unwelcome and face racial discrimination, which is usually covert. I found no evidence that they enjoyed specifically Nigerian ethnic capital for being children of Nigerian immigrants in the workplace. Those who felt they had been discriminated against all spoke of being discriminated against on account of being black, and though they had very few Caribbean contemporaries as they climbed higher on the career/organizational ladder, they were of the opinion that the existence of an "ebony ceiling" would affect black Caribbeans and other blacks too. In contrast, some respondents in the United States enjoyed Nigerian ethnic capital in the workplace for being children of Nigerian immigrants.

In Britain, the colonial experience that Nigerians and many Caribbeans share is a point of unity for the two groups. This unifying historical and contemporary experience of racialization and exploitation, even though the Caribbean experience of slavery sometimes strains the understanding, makes the Nigerian second generation speak in terms of an overall environment of hostility and discrimination against all black people in Britain as well as against ethnic minorities from Britain's other nonwhite former colonies in Asia. For this reason, the primary story my British respondents told about their lives in Britain was that of discrimination. In contrast, largely because they are finding room to be seen as the preferred or better blacks, the primary occupation of my U.S. respondents was detailing how, why, and in what ways they are different from African Americans.

Last, the blurring of boundaries between middle-class first- and second-generation immigrant blacks and middle-class members of the proximal host has potentially serious implications. The main black group the Nigerian second generation are distancing themselves from are the poor of the proximal host. In this they are similar to the middle-class members of the proximal host, who also distance themselves from poor blacks, although other scholars point out that this is quite difficult for them to do because they live in close proximity to them either in familial relationships or in their neighborhoods.[51] A future where black people become increasingly divided by ethnicity and class could lead to the black poor being left further and further behind. It would no longer be that only white America or white Britain does not care about the black poor; all middle-class people, including the black middle class, would be abandoning the black poor. The attitude of the black middle class would become one of increasing exasperation that the black poor are not helping themselves, as is presently the attitude of many respondents in both the United States and Britain. In a 2007 Pew Center survey, we see this shift in attitudes already occurring, with over 53 percent of African Americans saying that blacks who don't get ahead are mainly responsible for their situation. And 71 percent of whites and 59 percent of Hispanics agree. Just three in ten blacks say discrimination is the main reason blacks don't get ahead, even as most blacks believe that antiblack discrimination remains a pervasive fact of life.[52] To prevent a widening of the gulf between middle-class and poor blacks and prevent further abandonment of the black poor, more attempts have to be made to create and nurture ties between new blacks and their proximal hosts and then between middle-class and poor blacks.

In summary, the experiences of the Nigerian second generation in both countries reveal that race still plays a significant role in their lives, even though most of them are college-educated professionals with very strong and meaningful ethnic identities held in conjunction with a racial identity. However, the nuances of race and the degree of racial solidarity with the proximal hosts vary by national context, a variation largely due to each country's history and sociopolitical context.

SIX

Feeling American in America,
Not Feeling British in Britain

Chuka Eke has very strong feelings about Britain, few of which are positive.
His voice dripped with disgust and disillusionment as he answered questions
about his experiences in Britain, what being British meant to him, and
whether he identified as British. Chuka has lived his entire thirty-nine years
in England and has experienced upward social mobility. His father was an
uneducated ship's cook, his mother was an uneducated domestic worker, and
he is a barrister. He stopped practicing law because of the antiblack discrimination he faced from clients, judges, court staff, and colleagues and bosses in
his law firm. He felt this discrimination was preventing him from reaching
the apex of his law career and that it would be better for him to change
careers. He chose accounting because it does not always require in-person
interaction with white Britons.

When asked how he identifies, Chuka said he is African and Nigerian. He
does not identify as British. He told me that he could not understand how
black people, even if they were born and raised in Britain of immigrant parents like he was, could identify as British. He was amazed that any black
person could be so proud to be British as to die for it. "I don't really buy into
the Black British concept. You meet a lot of black people in Britain who are
proud to be British, who are prepared to die for queen and country—me,
never." Britain, he said, has over the centuries, especially during the era of the
British Empire, exploited black people and other nonwhite peoples in its
colonies and is still doing so today.

> I don't believe in Britain. The system of Britain, they call it empire of coloni-
> alism, is to me just barely a form of terrorism. You [Britain] go into other
> people's countries not invited, you control them by force. Maybe a hundred

and fifty years later, it is then called an ex-colony. You invite these people to Britain to build the country up when you needed them, in the early 1950s, 1960s, whatever the case may be. As soon as the country is prosperous then you want to limit immigration. You want them to apply first, get stays. These are all historical facts. So, for me, I don't buy into it.

Chuka links Britain's exploitative relations with its black and Asian immigrants to what he sees as a double standard, where nonwhite immigrants are told they should want to, and should, become British, while emigrant Britons, because of national pride in being British, do not take up the national identities of their new countries: "England was in India for about three hundred years, but you don't see the English people using Indian names or saying, 'I am Indian because I was born in India,' that 'My father and grandfather were born in India, so I am Indian.' They always class themselves as British wherever they are in the world, and they are proud of the fact." He applies the same logic to his own case: "I originated from Nigeria, and I am proud of that fact."

None of Britain's national myths are meaningful to him. In response to the question, "What does being British mean to you?," he answered, "It means that I have got a passport. I have got a British passport with all the rights and privileges that it allows me to have. But as for loving the country, loving the culture, the queen, the history—not interested."

In sharp contrast to Chuka Eke in Britain, Sade Bankole in the United States waxes lyrical about what being American means to her and why she feels American. She was born in the United States and is thirty-three years old. Like Chuka Eke, she holds a professional degree, a PhD from an Ivy League university. Unlike him, she has replicated her parents' middle-class status, as her father is a physician and her mother is a part-time high school teacher and homemaker with a master's degree in business administration. "I get teased especially by my foreign friends because I am very moved by the American story. I am moved by it as a child of an immigrant, that it's a great nation, or it has the potential to be a great nation, the greatest ever. I think there's something beautiful in founding a nation on an idea. I think that there is something I really like about being part of that kind of story or narrative, especially as a second-generation immigrant whose parents came looking for a better life or who came looking for that sort of opportunity and made the move."

Sade said that in America people have the freedom to be what they want to be.

I remember that I was sort of a tomboy, and I remember going to Nigeria and being told, "Oh you cannot wear pants," and I was like, "What?" "You can only wear skirts," and I was like, "What? This is crazy." And so I appreciate that freedom, the social freedom. There is vast opportunity here. There is an ability for people to at least think that they can attain the American Dream. The whole social mobility thing, the freedom to move up I think is nice. I like that. I also like the vastness of the country. I have seen most of it, and it is something. I guess I buy into the myth of America. That is the best I can say.

Unlike Chuka Eke, she does not think identifying with the nation where she was born is a betrayal of her Nigerian heritage. "First and foremost, I am American, and I don't think that diminishes my heritage or where I come from because 'American' to me always means 'American-plus.' There is no such thing as American in any sense because everybody has come from somewhere. I identify as American. I sound American. I dress American. My taste has been shaped by being here. You know, I have lived in Nigeria for three years total of my life, it is part of me, but I am American."

Throughout the preceding chapters, I have been making the case that national context matters with regard to how new immigrants form their identities. The first part of this chapter fleshes out this argument. It examines why two immigrant groups of the same ethnicity have very different views of their respective countries and have made very different ethnic identity choices. The two countries, though very similar—both are advanced Western democracies with diverse populations—have different preoccupations and idiosyncrasies that affect their new citizens in very different ways. The United States, despite nativist sentiment and exclusionist policies at different periods, generally imagines itself as a land of immigrants that gives new immigrants room to settle and flourish if they work hard and play by the rules. Black immigrants (Caribbeans and Africans) and their children feel that, despite ongoing racial discrimination, they too can live the rags-to-riches story popularized by Horatio Alger in the late nineteenth century—the story of the American Dream. They have come into a country that has made significant racial progress since the time of slavery, and they are not burdened by the cumulative generational disadvantages of African Americans. In contrast, in Britain, all ethnic minorities are seen as foreigners and as alien to the imagining of what it means to be British. The civilizing mission of Britain was supposed to happen away from Britain and not in the British motherland. For these reasons, ethnic minorities in Britain find it difficult to access the identities "English" and "British," though many try.[1]

In the second part of this chapter, I discuss the ethnic identities the adult second generation of Nigerian ancestry have chosen. Identity involves "knowing who we are, knowing who others are, them knowing who we are, us knowing who they think we are, and so on."[2] It is "a multi-dimensional classification or mapping of the human world and our places in it, as individuals and as members of collectivities."[3] I find that the adult second generation of Nigerian ancestry in the United States and Britain hold multiple identities that combine to form what I term a multifaceted identity that captures who they really are, how they see themselves, and how they want others to see them.

IDENTIFICATIONAL ASSIMILATION AMONG THE NIGERIAN SECOND GENERATION

Both Britain and the United States, along with other countries in the West with sizable immigrant populations, have had to establish multicultural policies to accommodate their ethnically and culturally diverse immigrant populations.[4] Multiculturalism as a policy and in practice allows, and in some cases supports, ethnic groups to maintain a certain degree of ethnic identity and culture. It also encourages governments to instruct public institutions to modify their rules, practices, and symbols to accommodate the beliefs and practices of immigrant groups.[5] One theoretical underpinning of multiculturalism is that celebrating each group's racial or ethnic identity and giving it room to flourish promotes better integrated citizens. The United States and Britain have taken different approaches to multiculturalism. Multiculturalism is Britain's official policy at the federal level, and the country has invested in multicultural education in school curricula and debated and called for citizenship education—teaching immigrants that they have commonalities with their host country's population underpinned by the human rights convention and a common language. The United States has taken a more hands-off approach, expecting immigrant groups to assimilate and find their place in American society as they go about their daily lives.[6]

Today the efficacy of multicultural policies is questioned. Critics argue that multiculturalism has led to reification and the essentializing of cultural differences, that is, an ethnic group "balkanization," that undermines social cohesion and a common national identity and that by undermining cohesive national collectivity makes the nation vulnerable to security threats.[7]

What I find is that multicultural policies by themselves cannot deliver better-integrated immigrants. These policies must be undertaken in conjunction with other government projects and policies to integrate immigrants and make them welcome. How these efforts align with national identity, how they influence immigrant experiences, and how they engage with the nation's history with regard to ethnic immigrants are what influence what being British or American means to the second-generation adults of Nigerian ancestry.

When one talks about identifying with a nation, one has to discuss nationalism and national identity. Nationalism is the tenacity with which ethnonational groups have fought to maintain their distinct national identity, institutions, and desire for self-government.[8] Contrary to some scholars' expectations, postmodernism has not brought about the decline of nationalism. It has also not given way to cosmopolitanism, where individuals have supranational identities. The primary reason for the strength of nationalism in this era of globalization is the realization that strong nation-states are necessary to guarantee individual rights. Another reason is the fact that individuals derive some cultural meaning from national identity.[9] National identity is an imaginary yet powerful construct. Nation-states are defined as imagined communities because "the members of even the smallest nation will never know most of their fellow members, meet them, or even hear of them, yet in the mind of each lives the image of their communion."[10] Members of a nation-state need to have some sense of commonality or shared identity in order to sustain a deliberative and participatory democracy.[11] Common language, public holidays, and self-government can affirm national identities. National myths are crucial building blocks of a national identity. Thus every nation needs myths that define and inspire the people. These myths are not chosen arbitrarily but are selected from the people's common history, culture, and ancestry.[12]

To analyze what being British or American means to immigrants, one also has to pay attention to notions of belonging. Notions of belonging bring together the sociology of emotions and the sociology of power. Belonging is a thicker concept than citizenship. It is not just about membership, rights, and duties; it is also about the emotions that membership evokes. Belonging is about emotional attachment, about feeling at home and feeling safe. And belonging tends to be naturalized; it becomes articulated and politicized only when it is threatened in some way.[13]

The U.S. National Identity: Clear and Widely Disseminated

The national identity of the United States comprises well-known national myths. The nation's core origin myth is that it is a country of immigrants, which is related to another central myth, the American Dream.[14] America is a country that welcomes all hardworking immigrants, and these immigrants, in turn, see America as a land full of opportunities. The American Dream is the promise that all who live in the United States have a reasonable opportunity to achieve success as they define it (material or otherwise) through their own efforts and resources.[15] This ideology is widely held by Americans.

The flipside of this belief in the American Dream, also held by many Americans, is that if one does not succeed it is one's own fault: one did not strive hard enough. Of course, certain individuals face severe structural disadvantages that reduce the probability of their achieving the American Dream. For example, social class plays a large role. Individuals who come from affluent backgrounds are more likely to succeed than individuals from the lower or under classes, holding level of personal effort constant. This is what we know as class reproduction. There are also racial and ethnic obstacles to achieving the American Dream, such as the black-white income gap and even larger black-white wealth gap. These gaps cannot be attributed solely to differential effort; they are also due to accumulated generational disadvantage and discrimination.[16] The ideology of the American Dream is inculcated in children via the public school system, which teaches them the skills needed to attempt achievement of the American Dream.

The other central trope in American national identity is the belief in freedom. A lot of the language of freedom is drawn from the Declaration of Independence and the Constitution. Of course, there are contradictions in the talk about freedom in American society. Some Founding Fathers were slave owners even as they wrote in the Declaration of Independence, "We hold these truths to be self-evident, that all men are created equal." But the prevailing consensus is that the United States has made great progress in race relations even while acknowledging that racial disparities still exist in education, income, wealth, and health and that more still needs to be done.

Social science research has shown that notions of freedom vary by racial group. Orlando Patterson found that whites rank the ability to move freely, security, and citizenship as their most important freedoms, while for African Americans the three highest-ranked freedoms—no doubt reflecting the nature of black experience in the United States—are security, negative freedom (being free from racial discrimination), and inner freedom. Patterson hypothesizes that security and citizenship would be the most important categories mentioned by immigrants and children of immigrants—a hypothesis that would be interesting to test among second-generation Nigerians at some future date.[17]

These elements of U.S. national identity—a country of immigrants, belief in the American Dream, and freedom—are clearly articulated and widely disseminated in the public space.

Britain's National Identity: An Identity in Crisis

While the U.S. national identity remains rooted in the nation's conceptual origins, British national identity has undergone major changes over the past century. Before the Second World War, Britain identified as the British Empire and saw itself as a conquering people called to civilize other nations and populations.[18] Within two decades after the war, Britain's colonies gained independence. The British social historian and broadcaster Richard Weight states that as "the Empire disappeared the raison d'être of Britain disappeared because it was primarily established to further the quest for Empire."[19] With the fall of the empire, the crown was no longer the focal point of national identity, the Church of England did not have the power to unify the British people, and the British Broadcasting Company (BBC) lost its monopoly, allowing myriad other television and radio stations to contribute to the shaping of national culture. Postwar Britain also saw the rise of devolution programs, with Scotland, Wales, and Northern Ireland fighting for minority rights—self-governance and independence. Devolution further undermined what was once understood as Britishness.[20]

It is claimed that the core of Britain's identity in the twentieth century was founded on the Second World War, that Britain was able to resist and stop the Nazis, but in the twenty-first century that war has lost its "patriotic allure"; it is no longer a source of pride for the British Isles as a whole.[21] The presence of the European Union has further undermined Britain's national identity as Britons adopt continental habits and patterns of consumption, despite Britain's resistance to becoming Europhile. In 2016, the British people voted to exit the European Union. In sum, one can say that Britain is experiencing an identity crisis. It is argued that colonial and postcolonial politics influence Britain's current national identity—that Britain suffers from "postcolonial melancholia": an "inability to mourn its loss of Empire and accommodate the Empire's consequences." Furthermore, he says, several legacies of Britain's imperialist era are still influencing present-day sociopolitical contexts. For example, the legacy of white supremacy works alongside the legacy that understands immigration "as being akin to war and invasion."[22] Consequently, immigrants, especially black immigrants, are blamed for destroying a once-homogeneous British culture, and many individuals as well as organizations such as the British Nationalist Party (BNP) believe that the expulsion of black immigrants will contribute to Britain being great again.

Because of this attitude about race, Britain maintains differential relations with its former colonies, depending on whether their populations are predominantly black or white. This differential treatment is played out on many stages. For example, citizens of Australia and Canada do not require entry visas to visit Britain, but citizens from black former colonies in Africa and the Caribbean do, even though all are members of the Commonwealth of Nations, which was created with the promise that citizens of all member-states would not need visas to enter fellow member-states' territories. Elements of colonial legacy are also evident in the institutional racism found in Britain today. Blacks and other ethnic minorities are disadvantaged in the British judicial system.[23] Ethnic minorities also suffer an ethnic penalty in the labor market, as evidenced by their lower wages.[24] And black people are seen as having a culture that is inimical to success. Black immigrants in Britain are treated quite differently from white and nonblack immigrants such that "melancholic Britain can concede that it does not like Blacks and wants to get rid of them but then becomes uncomfortable because it does not like the things it learns about itself when it gives vent to feelings of hostility and hatred."[25]

Officially, Britain's national identity is based on the English language and adherence to European human rights conventions.[26] Both scholars and British politicians frequently allude to core British moral values, such as "individual liberty, equality of respect and rights, tolerance, mutual respect, a sense of fair play, and the spirit of moderation," alongside other components of British identity such as democracy, cultural diversity, and having a

European, Atlantic, and global orientation.[27] Which of these are emphasized or revised as components of the national identity is in constant flux. However, no matter how it is constructed, Britain's national identity in the twenty-first century has two fundamental problems, particularly with respect to how immigrants and their children identify. First, its components are not sufficiently defining. Second, they lack emotive appeal. If they cannot elicit positive emotions, they will not be widely disseminated and accepted by new immigrants. These problems are further compounded by the exclusionary aspect of Britain's national identity.

WHAT DOES BEING BRITISH/AMERICAN MEAN TO YOU?

Wanting to tap into immigrants' identity, national identity, sense of citizenship, and notions of belonging, I asked all the respondents what being British or American meant to them and whether they thought of themselves as British or American. I expected to hear similar tropes from respondents in both countries; I expected respondents, regardless of country, to articulate shared sentiments or national myths unique to their country, based on the theory that some sense of commonality or shared identity is required to sustain a deliberative and participatory democracy.[28] Instead, the different responses among interviewees in the two countries revealed how these national factors interact with the experiences of the Nigerian second generation on the ground and affect how they interpret those experiences. This interaction has led to striking differences in identificational assimilation—defined as the development of a sense of peoplehood based exclusively on the host society—of the second generation in the two countries.[29]

In the United States, most of the Nigerian second generation articulated shared national myths and sentiments, whereas in Britain, most of the Nigerian second generation had narratives that, though widely shared among them, were not the national myths. U.S. respondents had a strong sense of peoplehood with America. They believed in the American Dream; saw America as the land of immigrants, opportunities, and freedom; and identified as American.[30] In contrast, the second generation in Britain did not have a strong sense of peoplehood with Britain. They were emotionally detached from Britain, did not have a strong sense of belonging to Britain, and did not see themselves as British. Only a few espoused awareness of and belief in Britain's national myths.

"I Don't Identify with Britain"

The initial response of many respondents in Britain to the question, "What does being British mean to you?," was a long pause and a laugh or "I don't know." I grouped the respondents' answers into three main categories: an instrumental view, "nothing in particular," and a multicultural narrative. Over 80 percent of their responses fell into the instrumental and nothing in particular categories. A few respondents felt that the question was abstract and that there is no consensus on what it means to be British.

"It Means Having a British/Red Passport." The largest number of respondents held an instrumental view of what it means to be British: it was about the advantages that accrued to them by being citizens. It was not about emotional attachment to Britain. Hope is a twenty-nine-year-old brokerage officer born and raised in Britain. Hers is a classic example of this response: "It means having a very flexible passport, being able to travel without much restriction. It is, honestly, the citizenship. I don't feel British in any other way, other than when you travel your accent is British and you get to use a British passport, but beyond that I just—I am Nigerian through and through." Enitan concurred: "I don't know. It just means that I have got—It means nothing in particular. I think African means a lot more to me. Being British is the fact. It is the way the world is. It can open some doors to me. That is the only thing for me. It opens some doors. Having a British passport makes it easy to travel around. Then it is easier to get jobs around the West."

Respondents mentioned other benefits of holding a British passport: it is a source of protection—they cannot be deported—and it gives them legal grounds to fight for resources. They also mentioned that being British helps in the workplace because foreign-born immigrants are often discriminated against and non-British immigrants are less likely to be promoted when there is an opening. So, for those with the instrumental view, the majority, being British confers a sense of security against deportation and workplace discrimination, and it confers rights to access resources.

"Being British Means Nothing to Me." Respondents' low identification with Britain came into sharper focus with the respondents' second most common response: being British means "nothing in particular" to them. Shawn migrated from Nigeria to Britain when he was nine years old. Both of

his parents have bachelor's degrees and are businesspeople. His father is wealthy and sent him to an exclusive all-boys' private boarding school in Britain while his parents stayed back in Nigeria. Shawn earned his bachelor's and doctorate degrees from Cambridge. I interviewed him in one of London's trendy bars. When I asked him what being British meant to him, he said, "I don't know. I don't feel it is my homeland. Their symbols and celebrations don't move me. I do not support their sport teams. I am not emotionally touched by their remembrances. I do feel that I belong. I have been here for twenty-five years. That is it, really."

If we go by Norman Tebbit's famous "cricket test," Shawn, according to his statement that he doesn't support British sports teams, does not belong (even though Nigeria does not field a cricket team). Tebbit, a secretary in Margaret Thatcher's Conservative government, proposed that proof of whether an immigrant has allegiance to Britain is if he cheers for the British national cricket team in a game against the team from his home country. Yet despite Shawn's lack of emotional identification with British cultural and national symbols, he feels he does belong. By the cricket test definition, Dapo is not British either. He said, "Being British means nothing to me. If it comes to a war between Nigeria and Britain, I will fight against the British."

Some respondents articulated a British identity that they then rejected. They saw being British as "getting drunk, not respecting your elders, not doing well in school, taking it easy, not really caring about the future" and a "British culture that means drinking, drugs, sex, parties, and fish and chips."

The majority of respondents expressed a combination of these two main responses: having no nationalistic pride and holding an instrumental view of British citizenship. Being born and raised in Britain with no experience of living outside Britain did not guarantee that someone would identify as British or have strong feelings of allegiance to Britain. He or she was equally as likely to not identify with Britain as those who had arrived as children. Respondents who voiced both of the most common views often made a distinction between legal status—holding a British passport—and having a subjective and/or emotional attachment to Britain. Many of them expressed an instrumental view of what it means to be British and then added something like, "I am only British because I am born here." Many agreed with Rabi, who said, "Being British to me is really something that denotes where I am born—born in Britain, born and raised in Britain. Being British acknowledges my birthplace. That is probably the extent of it."

"Tolerant, Respectful, and Accommodating." A few respondents (five) used a multicultural narrative to describe what being British meant to them. Britain is a country of laws, a multicultural society, and a country and people who are, as one of them said, "tolerant, respectful, and accommodating" toward immigrants. They saw Britain as a country that accommodates ethnocultural diversity even as it grapples with racial and ethnic inequality. These were the only respondents who used British national myths when talking about what it meant to be British. Pauline was one of the few who did this, as well as one of the few who identified primarily as British. To her, "being British is being able to look at everything around you and being able to incorporate, put your own flavor. Britain and what being British means is always changing. It is more dynamic in its identity than most other countries. Being British is redefining yourself all the time."

What is interesting about the responses of the second generation of Nigerian ancestry in Britain in this study is that none of these interviewees is economically marginalized. Almost all have at least a bachelor's degree and hold a professional white-collar job. Whether their life story has been like Chuka Eke's, whose parents were uneducated and lower class and who is now a lawyer turned accountant, or Shawn's, who has maintained his parents' middle-class status, in terms of intergenerational social mobility Britain has been good to them. So why don't they feel British?

"Why Should I Feel British? They Don't Think of Me as British"

Britain's colonial history is particularly important in explaining the identificational assimilation outcomes of the adult Nigerian second generation. Many see Britain as a country that historically and to date has established exploitative relationships with less developed countries and their people.[31] When I asked Goke, a twenty-seven-year-old graphic designer born and raised in Britain who owns a small business, why he does not feel British, he said that Britain "historically has not welcomed people from other nations openly, except they have a particular service in mind. If Britain wants a particular service from you, then they would welcome you with open arms. As long as you do that particular service, as long as you stay within that particular remit, within that particular box, then you are fine because, basically, from my understanding, that is how the British Empire was so strong."

Goke linked Britain's relations with its immigrants to its colonial and postcolonial politics.

They [Britain] went into our country and dominated. So they put you in little boxes: you do this and we do this. This is your place, and this is our place. And so, from that, that is what they have carried on. For example, when they went on recruitment drives in the West Indies—they did that after the Second World War—that is the reason why they [black Caribbeans] came over in the first place, and if not for that, they would not have been welcomed. And they were not welcomed by the people. They were welcomed by the government, who needed them at the time. And when they no longer needed them, when the government felt that they could do without them, then the situation changed. The British state and its institutions have put certain blockades in the way for a particular progression for people that they have previously dominated. So, once you have come over, [they say,] "Okay, this is your job, this is the job that we want you to do. So, if you stay here and do your job, everything will be okay." But that job—there is no opportunity there for growth and development unless you break out of that box. But to break out of that box means that you will be isolated, and then you will be seen as a troublemaker. So that is my answer to that.

For Goke, Chuka Eke, and others, the fact that Britain exploited its colonial citizens and is currently exploiting its black citizens as well as ethnic minorities from its nonwhite former colonies, such as Indians, Pakistanis, and Bangladeshis, affects how they view Britain. The second generation of Nigerian ancestry see black immigrants commonly filling poor to middling occupations but not good or professional occupations. As discussed in chapter 5, many believe or have seen that barriers are in place to prevent blacks and South Asians from progressing beyond a certain point in the British workplace. A study based on census data found that, compared to their white peers, second-generation ethnic minorities are less likely to be found in the British "salariat," which consists of salaried employees such as managers, administrators, or professionals that have relatively secure employment, an incremental salary scale, fringe benefits (e.g., pension plans), and significant promotion chances.[32] A legacy of Britain's colonial history in the British labor market is "the proliferation of service work and the reappearance of a caste of servile, insecure, and underpaid domestic laborers, carers, cleaners, deliveries, messengers, attendants, and guards."[33]

From their experiences, respondents have concluded that black people are not truly welcome in Britain. Sam said he does not see himself as British because he is not given the space to feel British: "Well, I know that I am

[British], but I don't have the strong feeling of affiliation to either Britain or Nigeria as I think that I have the right to have. Part of the reason for this is that you can't go through a system dealing with prejudice, dealing with various challenges, feeling defined by your color, feeling that acceptance is just that, acceptance, it is not love, just acceptance, and then embrace that as feeling British. For instance, people often ask me, 'Where are you from?' And I say that I am from Manchester. And they say, 'No, no, no, no, no, you are from Nigeria.'" He said further, "In order to feel something, to some degree, you need other people to reflect that back to you. But that is not reflected back."

Bolade, like Sam, will not allow herself to feel British when she knows she is not welcome. She asked me, "Why should I feel British? They don't think of me as British. I see some people who have lost their identity, and I look at them and go, 'why?' You don't belong here. They don't see you as one of them." Hope was more direct, claiming that blackness places you on the outside looking in on British society: "I am not British because Britain is not for black people. It is seen as a country of opportunities, but the opportunities are not universal." Many respondents said that they were "more Nigerian than British." Chimkamtu, a twenty-five-year-old physician who was born and raised in Britain, added, "Racism does exist, and Nigeria is the one place that I can go where they cannot discriminate against me, and so that is where I choose to make my home. If the British National Party comes into power, we are all going out. They don't want non-Caucasians."

Increasingly restrictive immigration policies, alongside the increasing popularity of the British National Party, only confirm respondents' feelings of being unwelcome in Britain. The British government in 2011 ended several immigration policies that allowed entrepreneurs, investors, and highly skilled migrants to migrate and settle in Britain. As it makes immigration policy more restrictive the British government is also instituting stricter hiring laws that dictate that a job can only be offered to a non-British and non–European Union citizen upon conclusive evidence from the hiring organization that the position cannot be filled by a Briton or European Union citizen. The effect of this hiring law is increasing job discrimination against African and Asian immigrants, including foreign physicians in the National Health Service, who are well qualified and in many cases more qualified than their British and European Union peers.

British respondents made a clear distinction between having a British passport and feeling British. There was a high correlation between answering

"No" to the question, "Do you think of yourself as British?," and not having a British or hyphenated British identity. Of course identities are fluid and not mutually exclusive, and some of the second generation whose primary identifications were not British or hyphenated British still thought of themselves as British. Because a significant number of the second generation believed that Britain does not fully accept blacks, I decided to ask them if they felt that they were English, since over 95 percent of those born in Great Britain were born in England. This question elicited laughter and statements such as "You have to be white to be English" but not one affirmative response. So most were not British and all were definitely not English.

But their experiences of discrimination and Britain's colonial and postcolonial history are not the only reasons that very few of the second generation articulated British national myths. It is clear from their responses that these national myths do not provoke an emotional response from them. Over 80 percent of them did not articulate the national identity and narrative that is debated at the macro level by most British scholars and politicians: that is, that Britain's national identity revolves around the English language, human rights, and key British moral values. Contrasting this to the responses of the Nigerian second generation in the United States drives home the importance of immigrant inclusive national identities and national myths that provoke an emotional response and can inspire members of the nation.

"I Buy into the Myth of America"

In response to the question, "What does being American mean to you?," almost all of the U.S. respondents' answers were similar to Sade Bankole's. They expressed strong belief in America's national myths. They believe in the American Dream and see America as a land of opportunity and freedom. I grouped respondents' answers into three main categories: opportunities, freedom, and not really being American, which I discuss below. Over 70 percent of respondents fell into the first two categories.

"Being an American Means That You Have Opportunities." The most common response to the question, "What does being American mean to you?," was, "It means opportunities." Thirty-seven respondents mentioned the word *opportunities* in response to this question. Their responses narrate a belief in the American Dream—that they can be successful in the United States if they work hard. According to Adaze, a thirty-eight-year-old female accountant:

Being an American to me means that you have opportunities. In spite of everything, you can still get to wherever you want to. You might come across different obstacles in the world, but after a while you will get to your goal, you will still get there. The opportunities that I have here, I doubt if I will have it if I were in Nigeria without the financing and knowing a lot of influential people. Being an American also means you are exposed to a whole lot of information, not that people outside of America don't have this information, but things move very fast. You can be a professional, or you can be anything you want. This is America. If you want to be a plumber, you can be a very successful plumber, and if you want to be an accountant, you can be a successful accountant too. The opportunities are there. They might not be easily accessible, but if you work hard, certain things will come to you. I wouldn't want to be anywhere else.

Wole confirmed that being American means belief in the American Dream: "It is a state of mind. It is almost defined by the American Dream. I can do anything. It is more about individualism than collectivism. I am 70 percent individualism. We believe in freedom. We believe in rights for everybody, that you can do anything you want to do if you work hard for it."

When talking about opportunities, some meant educational opportunities. Chiamaka, a twenty-two-year-old female born and raised in the United States, said, "I see [opportunities] in educational terms. In America, you can get an education anywhere you want. There will always be funding for you. I see it as being able to advance academically." Many felt that America's being a land of opportunities obligated one to take advantage of these opportunities. Most respondents who had spent some of their formative years in Nigeria held this view. Etim said, "I have a lot of opportunities compared to Nigeria to do what I want to do. That's the key thing. In Nigeria, you have opportunities, but they are not that great. A million people may be fighting for the same position." Nnamdi agreed and linked the opportunities present in America to what it means to be a Nigerian ethnic in America: "Being an American, to me, is to have a lot of opportunities, freedom of opportunities. And so being a Nigerian American is that I should be able to make use of these opportunities."

"America Means Freedom." Respondents' second most common response to the question referred to the national myth of the United States as a land of freedom. This meant freedom to succeed, freedom of speech, freedom from discrimination, freedom of movement, freedom of the press, freedom of choice, freedom to pursue opportunities and self-advancement. According

to Daniel, being an American is "based on the Constitution. A free man who has the liberty to speak his views and not be discriminated against, be who you want to be without any prejudice. It is a freedom I am more sensitive to. It is a blessed thing, the fact that I can travel out of the country without thinking about a visa. It is a great gift." Like many of his British counterparts, Daniel mentioned the value of holding a passport from a major Western country because it facilitated international travel, but his response differed because he also exhibited positive emotions about his country.

The word *freedom* covered a lot of ground for the second generation. Gbenga, in response to the question, said, "There is a lot to that. The first thing that comes to mind is the way of life. It means a higher standard of living. It means greater freedom than the majority of the world. It means great freedom of the press, great freedom to go to shops and live where you want to live. Lots of freedom. And it means a lot of opportunities, more opportunities than other folks in the rest of the world get."

All of the respondents who spoke of being American as meaning both having opportunities and having freedom thought of themselves as American even when it was not their primary identity. Much of their freedom narrative was influenced by the Declaration of Independence and the Constitution. Unlike African Americans, for whom negative freedom and inner freedom were two of the three most common responses to the same question in Patterson's study, the freedom the second generation speak of is freedom to pursue opportunities and to achieve self-actualization.[34] African Americans were describing lived experiences of freedom, while the Nigerian second generation named freedoms of opportunities. Highlighting this difference supports the discussion that second-generation Nigerians identify with the immigrant American story, not with the African American history of slavery story.

"Can't Say; I Am Not Really American." Some respondents found it difficult to answer the question because they did not see themselves as American or fully American. For example, one woman who was born and raised in the United States said, "I don't think I am a hundred percent American, so it is hard to answer this question." To others, being American meant denying their Nigerian heritage, something they were not willing to do. As one put it, "It is weird. For me it is mostly about—I never see myself as an American. I see myself as a Nigerian living in America. When I see some people as American, I always feel they do not have a cultural background like we have." She was referring to African Americans.

A few respondents used the word *citizenship* when answering this question, in a manner similar to their counterparts in Britain: to distinguish the legal status of citizenship from emotional attachment to their country. Some made a cultural difference claim to make the same distinction. For example, Abiade, a twenty-seven-year-old female consultant, said, "That is a tough question. I think it is just a nationality. I don't think it is my citizenship. It is where I . . . I have spent a significant amount of my life, but it is not my foundation. I don't think my culture says American. When I talk of citizenship, I mean culture. Many Nigerians that grew up here and say American, I still say that they are Nigerian because they are not being brought up as American. Their cultures are still part of them." Another respondent told me being American means "nothing really. I think it is just a place where you live. Your identity does not come from here." Both of these respondents are arguing that cultural meaning, their cultural identity, comes from outside of the United States—their parents' country of origin.

A few who felt neither American nor fully American nevertheless knew the tropes used to describe America and produced them. For example, Monica, said, "It means freedom, but I am not the right person to ask." She did not think of herself as American but could give the appropriate response. Tunji laughed, then said, "It is a question. I don't know because I am not American. I know what I am supposed to say. I am not from here, I am not from there. I don't define myself by any of these characteristics. I don't understand what these terms mean."

Both Nigerian and American. The majority of the U.S. second-generation Nigerian respondents thought of themselves as American because they felt that in America they could be themselves, be individuals who happily straddle two worlds—their parents' ethnic culture and immigrant community and the wider American society—and create syncretic cultural content and transnational identities. They formed their narratives of what it means to be American between kindergarten and the twelfth grade—from their parents' stories of the United States presenting expected and unexpected opportunities; from common usage of U.S. national identity tropes in the mass media; and from U.S. politicians, whose use of national identity rhetoric is commonplace, especially during election campaigns.

The presence of affirmative action policies and the respondents' view that they should be beneficiaries of those policies also colored their responses. The election of President Barack Obama was also a seminal moment in their conception of and belief in what it means to be American and what being American meant to them. His election opened up previously unimaginable possibilities and gave them a strong sense of acceptance and belonging, especially because many saw him as a second-generation African immigrant, like them.

Comparing U.S. and British Respondents'
Ethnic Identification Patterns

In this section, I discuss the self-selected primary ethnic identity of the Nigerian second generation in the United States and Britain. Figure 2 shows that more U.S. respondents identified primarily as American or Nigerian American compared to the number of British respondents who identified primarily as British or Nigerian British. The majority (N = 48) of respondents in Britain identified primarily as Nigerian, while a little over a third (N = 29) of U.S. respondents did so. Among U.S. respondents, there was significant overlap between those in the Nigerian and Nigerian American categories, as many who identified primarily as Nigerian American were equally happy to identify as Nigerian, and vice versa. It did not make a difference to them because they felt they were a combination of the two cultures. In contrast, among British respondents, those who identified as Nigerian identified solely as such. They saw Britain as the place where they happened to live, not a place or an ideal that commanded their allegiance and/or emotional attachment. Fewer respondents in Britain had hyphenated identities (i.e., Nigerian-British) compared to U.S. respondents because of their lower levels of identification with Britain and the fact that hyphenated American identities are a more common convention in the United States than in Britain. Furthermore, more respondents in Britain identified as Nigerian compared to their U.S. counterparts because they live in denser transnational social fields that replenish and strengthen their Nigerian ethnicity.

Britain has denser transnational fields than the United States for a number of reasons. First, Britain has a long historical link with Nigeria, a former British colony that won its independence in 1960. Historically, Britain was the preferred destination for migrants from Nigeria because of the similarity of language and educational systems, and before Britain changed its immigration policies in 1962 to require an entry visa from members of their black former colonies, migration to Britain was easy. During this time, most

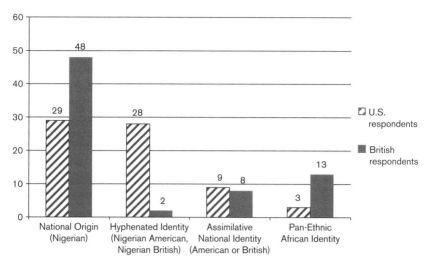

FIGURE 2. Comparison of the primary ethnic identity of respondents in the United States and Britain (self-identification).

Nigerians migrated for educational purposes, and many of them returned to Nigeria with their young families upon finishing their studies. This return migration created a significant population of the second generation who, though born in Britain, lived in Nigeria until young adulthood, when worsening political and economic conditions in Nigeria, from around the mid-1980s, drove them back to Britain for college and university and permanent settlement. Such children are called "Tokunbos" among the Yoruba. And most of those who returned to Britain are very Nigerian in their orientation, ethnic identity, and cultural practice. Such two-way return migration is not as common in the United States, as large-scale migration from Nigeria to the United States did not begin until after the mid-1980s, when conditions in Nigeria worsened. These migrants did not expect to return to Nigeria until their old age, if then.

Second, because more of the second generation in Britain has lived in Nigeria compared to the U.S. second generation, they have stronger Nigerian-centric identities and more robust Nigerian ethnic content. I found sending teenage children back to Nigeria to toughen them up and give them a greater appreciation for Nigerian culture was more common in Britain than the United States. As in Sam Echekoba's case, it was perceived as a way to remove children from antiblack environments that depressed academic performance and self-esteem. These returned second generation can by themselves keep Nigerian culture and ethnicity vibrant, while many of the U.S. second generation need the help of first-generation Nigerians to do so.

Third, Nigerian immigrants are not as geographically dispersed in Britain as they are in the United States. It is common to hear Nigerian languages being spoken on buses and trains in and around London. Also, Nigerian-headquartered pentecostal Christian churches, such as the Redeemed Christian Church of God and Christ Embassy network, are politically more recognized in Britain. London politicians, including London's former mayor, Boris Johnson, and former prime minister, David Cameron, have spoken to RCCG's congregation of between 10,000 and 30,000 believers at its all-night prayer vigils held every three months in London's Excel Centre. These strongly transnational churches are the preferred destination for many new Nigerian immigrants looking for a home church and for Nigerian visitors looking for a doctrinally sound church at which to worship.. These churches have a large number of mixed-age and generational cohorts. For all these reasons, they serve as repositories of Nigerian culture and as sites where Nigerian culture and Nigerian identities are replenished and strengthened. Such churches and church networks exist in the United States, but their presence in terms of both congregation size and political presence is not yet as significant.

The ethnic identification choices of the Nigerian second generation in Britain in this study differ quite markedly from that of British Caribbeans. According to the Fourth National Survey of Ethnic Minorities, 57 percent of Caribbeans chose the acculturative strategy—identifying with both their ethnicity and British society in what researchers termed "adding on" rather than an either/or approach. And 32 percent chose the dissociative strategy— that is, they did not think of themselves as British—and one in six chose the marginal strategy—they did not think of themselves as being part of a black Caribbean ethnic group.[35] Another study found that among African and Caribbean youths in Britain (ages fourteen to sixteen), Africans identified with Britain much less than did their Caribbean peers.[36] So while the overall ethnic identification pattern of the second generation of Nigerian ancestry differed markedly from that of Caribbeans, the overall self-selected ethnic identification pattern of the Nigerian second generation in Britain is similar to the pattern observed among the Nigerian second generation in the United States.

All the second-generation adults of Nigerian ancestry in this study, regardless of how they identified, are ethnic hybrids. Despite their clear understanding of what it means to be a Nigerian in the U.S. and British diasporas, that they have lived all or almost all their lives in these countries has made them ethnic hybrids. All ethnic groups adapt to the environment they find themselves in. And for the second generation of Nigerian ancestry, the identities they hold and their ethnic content have been influenced by local, foreign, and global factors. Their cultural content is hybridized. They cannot avoid exposure to and interaction with their proximal hosts, so the two cultures have intermingled. This has occurred especially in the arts and entertainment, primarily music. A recent example is the Broadway production "Fela," about the Nigerian music icon Fela Anikulapo Kuti, originator of the Nigerian Afro-Beat sound. American hip-hop and rap star Jay-Z and Will Smith and Jada Pinkett-Smith, well-known U.S. actors, are coproducers of the play. Jay-Z is of the opinion that Fela's music was influenced by James Brown.[37]

For the second generation as a whole, there has been a loss of Nigerian languages, especially among the British born and raised. Only a minority in both the United States and Britain can speak their native ethnic languages (see table in appendix B). The majority told me they can understand but not speak a Nigerian language, and most of those who speak it are not fluent. Some of their parents were dissuaded from teaching their ethnic language to their children because of warnings from teachers and school administrators that doing so was likely to confuse children, retard their fluency in English, and set them back academically. Approximately 10 percent of respondents are active members of Nigerian national or ethnic associations, compared to over 70 percent of their parents. This number excludes those who attend the organizations' social events but do not attend regular meetings.

Respondents in both countries combined the cultural elements they see as the best from various cultures to create their ethnic content. Jide, a twenty-six-year-old U.S. respondent explained:

I say I'm more American than Nigerian because I have been here for the most part of my life. I have experienced the African American culture more than I have experienced the Nigerian culture, even though my parents are Nigerian. A simple example: if you talk about the sport I like to play, I play baseball.

Nigerians don't know much about baseball. I play this American type of football which Nigerians don't really know anything about—well, they know, but they are not interested in it. Whereas somebody who is really Nigerian knows soccer, but that type of football, I don't really care for that. So the difference is there. When it comes to food, I eat Nigerian food and I love Nigerian food, but I can easily eat American food for a long time too. When it came to women, before I married, I could easily date a Nigerian and I could easily date an African American.

But he ended up marrying a Nigerian woman. This hybridized content is another reason I describe the Nigerian ethnicity found in the United States as diasporic.

Like the second generation of other nonwhite immigrant groups in both the United States and Britain, the Nigerian second generation embrace some aspects of American and British culture and reject others. This process is described as "selective acculturation" and is seen as the typical mode of incorporation for Asians in the United States and Britain.[38] Respondents "like the music" of their proximal hosts. They "like their food." However, they do not like that they, in their opinion, do not value education to the same extent. In the words of one respondent, "I like the music. I like rap music. That is what I listen to. But still I want to strive for better. I want to go to my highest, get a degree. I want to get a master's. I'm not going to be somebody that is going to be on the street all my life or somebody that will just stop at a high school diploma." He sees the critical difference as one of values and drive but still likes their "style." He continued: "I still like their culture, I think it is funny. I think it is a great culture and it has a lot of spirit in it and there is a lot of humor to it, but I still want to aspire. I don't want to be just a statistic, just be African American." This respondent, Ezigbe, had accepted as true the negative stereotypes of African Americans and despite being black, sees himself as culturally superior. But as previously discussed, African Americans value education just as much as other groups, and they have created strategies to combat institutional racism.[39] Thus what Ezigbe's statement shows is that different individuals within the black category have competing views of what it means to black and very clearly engage in an us/them narrative.

In Britain, while respondents also drew symbolic moral, cultural, and socioeconomic boundaries between themselves and their proximal hosts, Caribbeans, they were more outspoken about rejecting cultural elements found in wider British society, especially among white Britons, such as "drinking too much alcohol" and "pub crawling." They reject a particular

British identity or way of being British, which was, according to Anna, "getting drunk, not respecting your elders, not doing well in school, taking it easy, not really caring about the future." It is specifically a rejection of British working-class culture. What is striking here is that the Nigerian second generation, though racially black, are rejecting the culture that many associate with British blacks, revealing the different definitions of blackness that are emerging from within the black community in Britain.

In both the United States and Britain, respondents have drifted from their parents' culture, some more than others, as is to be expected in the process of intergenerational assimilation. Even though most of them are embedded in transnational social fields, only a few engage in transnational activities. They exhibit significant differences from most first-generation Nigerians and Nigerians back in Nigeria, and they are very aware that they are ethnically slightly different. They are less traditional; they hold more egalitarian views on gender and women's roles. They chafe at the male chauvinism and paternalism they see as rife among older first-generation Nigerians. According to Obiageli, a respondent in the United States:

> The upbringing of the kids is just the wife's work. I think this mentality is mostly African in nature. In America, they are more modernized. Dad stays at home in some instances and mum goes to work. I don't think that would really be heard of in Nigeria—the dad will stay at home and not go to work taking care of the kid while the wife is at work. I don't think Nigerians would be comfortable doing that. Here I've seen it happen. Here women work and share home responsibility with the spouse. For example, my parents have been married for over twenty years; there are very few memories of my father taking us to the park or whatever; they are very few.

Their practice of Nigerian cultural rituals is diluted. For example, in the respect rituals that call for kneeling down to greet elders, the kneel is not as deep, the girls' knees no longer touch the floor, the boys no longer prostrate flat on the ground but simply gesture to indicate that they will get around to it sometime. Even this level of observation is infrequent; most respondents have simply abandoned such observances. They are cultural hybrids who are increasingly comfortable with being so.

In sum, despite being ethnically hybrid and distinct from the first generation, most of the second generation feel strongly that they are still Nigerian, even if they do not choose "Nigerian" as their primary identity. Respondents are what I call Nigerians *with a twist*. For them, what makes one Nigerian is not necessarily wearing Nigerian clothes or eating Nigerian foods, which some of them do and some of them don't. While speaking a Nigerian language matters, as it is a tried and tested way of passing on an ethnic identity and culture, for them it is not a marker of being Nigerian. According to my respondents, what makes them Nigerian is the values, the attitudes, the way of seeing things. To be a true Nigerian one has to be well educated, have the desire to be successful, with education as the primary pathway, and one has to understand respect—the thinking and the performance of it, with frames of reference including people, experiences, and stories and events in Nigeria. I asked Chinelo how she expressed her Nigerianness as a second-generation Nigerian in the United States, and her response nicely summarizes the feelings of almost all of the Nigerian second generation interviewed for this study.

> For me, a lot of it is through my beliefs, clothes, and language, foods I cook, what I choose to eat, but that is not the most important part. The most important part is the values and beliefs, the upbringing. I mean, I don't have any kids, I am not married, but those types of things are the things I take away—the cultural stuff, the respect that you show for your elders, the importance of education. I am not saying that I would not have gotten those same beliefs if my parents were American, but to me that is something that was instilled in them back in their childhood in Nigeria, those are the things that they have taught me that I know came from our culture, and those are the type of things I would want to do for my own family when I have one.

This is also the view in Britain. Respondents stated that values matter more than rituals or cultural practices. My British respondents also argued that being an authentic Nigerian does not require one to be fluent in a Nigerian language, eat Nigerian food, or wear Nigerian traditional attire. As Adex said:

> Because of my way of life they [the first generation] tend to think that you're not Nigerian. I just ask them what does "fully Nigerian" mean? Is it that you speak your native tongue anywhere to anybody? Does it mean dressing in your African attire, because if that's what Nigerian means they are way wrong. Being Nigerian is showing the strong part, showing that we are a very studious people and we learn very well, better than most people, in this country anyway, and also that we are educated. I believe that most Nigerians are very educated people and I think that's what being Nigerian is. We are brought up with a value and we stick to that value.

A MULTIFACETED IDENTITY: COMBINING MULTIPLE IDENTITIES INTO ONE

Scholarship on the ethnic identities of the second generation in both the United States and Britain is discovering that single ethnic labels are increasingly incapable of capturing the complexities of identity formation.[40] Some of the reasons for this increasing complexity are burgeoning biracial and multiracial populations; the predominance of ethnic hybrids due to meshing of local, foreign, and global influences among the second generation; situational ethnicity, where the identity chosen is contingent on the situation or goals that need to be accomplished at a particular time; and transnationalism.

In talking to my respondents about their lives in the United States and Britain and their choice of ethnic identity, I realized that their selected primary ethnic identity did not successfully capture and express how they saw themselves and how they wanted others to see them. It did not satisfactorily encapsulate the complexities of their lived realities, particularly the ways race and the ethnoracial contexts of the United States and Britain influenced their process of identity formation. Respondents had multiple meaningful identities they used to navigate their daily lives and interact with members of the different racial and ethnic groups in their countries, and I found that it was only when these identities were merged into a single multifaceted identity did one fully capture who these second generation adults of Nigerian ancestry know themselves to be and how they want to be viewed.

Their multifaceted identity encompasses a black racial identity that reflects their acknowledgment of the economic, social, and psychological implications of being assigned to the black racial category; a Nigerian identity that is tightly linked to the diasporic Nigerian ethnicity; a middle-class identity that is intertwined with their Nigerian identity; and a pan-ethnic African identity that is still in the nascent stages in both the United States and Britain but more so in the former.

With this multifaceted identity, the Nigerian second generation are able to expand or restrict boundaries depending on the circumstance. When experiencing or witnessing antiblack racial discrimination, respondents say they identify as and with black people. At other times boundaries are constricted to include only sub-Saharan Africans or only Nigerians. The contingent nature of these parameters and the overlapping ethnic and class identities illustrate how in their daily lives respondents grapple with ethnic pride, transnational cultural frames of reference, racial discrimination, and an awareness that their middle-class status is a buffer against some of the injuries of race. All respondents had this multifaceted identity, no matter how they identified and no matter what nation they lived in. It is not situational ethnicity, because they are not deploying a particular identity based on their reading of what the situation demands. I find that they use all their multiple identities *together* to navigate the ethnoracial contexts and social milieus they reside in. The constituent elements of their multifaceted identity are discussed below.

A Nigerian Identity

All respondents, regardless of whether they self-identified primarily as Nigerian, British, American, Nigerian British, Nigerian American, or African, said that Nigerian values were the foundation of who they were ethnically. The internal weight given to these Nigerian values varied by individual, but their influence was never completely absent. Thus being shaped by and living by Nigerian values created the sense of shared group membership that all of them have.

The key Nigerian values are hard work, respecting elders, education, and honoring and taking care of family. Other important values, which are not as widely held, included not dating as teenagers, not staying out late at night, not drinking or partying too hard, not being promiscuous, and not having children out of wedlock. Respondents indicated that most of their life decisions are shaped by these values and said they would pass them on to their children. For respondents, as mentioned earlier in the discussion of being accused of being inauthentic Nigerians, it is not the performance of cultural rituals or the consumption of tangible Nigerian goods that are important; it is the values and mind-set acquired through socialization that are important. The centrality of Nigerian values to the second generation of Nigerian ancestry in both countries was captured by Yetunde's succinct statement, "Nigerian values are the principles I live by."

Because the second generation spoke of living by Nigerian values whether or not they self-identified as Nigerian, I see the Nigerian identity as a composite part of the multifaceted identity. Take Daniel, a thirty-one-year-old computer programmer, for example. He was unsure of his identity: "I don't know what my identity is. I am my mother's son. They raised me with Nigerian values, so I recognize it and respect it and it influences the goals I have. My ma did not have time to teach me the culture, and I did not grow up with Nigerians. I have lived my life as an African American here." He ended up marrying a first-generation Nigerian woman. Oye, a British respondent, said, "I am African first and Scottish second. The fact is that I love Nigerian culture; there's a certain part of the culture that I don't agree with and I don't like, and there is a part that I feel has made me the person I am today and without it I would have maybe turned out for the worse."

An African Identity

The term *African* was used constantly by respondents in conversation as a short-cut way of referring to recent (post-1965) African immigrants and their children. With the influx of black immigrants from many nations in Africa, it is quite exhausting to keep the different African nationalities straight, not to speak of trying to keep track of the different ethnic groups and their cultures. So "African" has become a convenient self- and group-referencing identity. The caveat, though, is that this pan-ethnic identity in its current employment refers to the postcolonial wave of the African diaspora. While there are historical links between the older waves of the African diaspora (those that saw the forcible migration and resettlement of Africans as slaves to the Caribbean and the Americas), the link between the older and recent waves and a remembrance of common continental origin is downplayed in the current usage of the pan-ethnic identity "African" in the United States and Britain.

There is also increasing institutional support for being African in the United States and Britain. Funke used African and Nigerian identity interchangeably, but she also used it in a pan-ethnic way when talking about businesses that have been established to cater to Nigerians and other African immigrants. The way she used the African identity is consistent with the way all respondents used it. She said, "The new Africans are living in America as if they're still in Nigeria. They still do their thing. The whole profile of us in Houston has changed. Back in the day, you have to go the Indian or Hispanic food store to buy African foods; now you go to an African food store. There are tons of them."

When asked why and how they were using the term, many respondents did not have a clear answer. Kunle, a forty-three-year-old who is a partner in a law firm in London, gave me one of the clearest responses as to how and why: "I use the term *African* very loosely. If a white person said to me, 'You are an African,' I wouldn't mind. But if they went further and tried to define an African characteristic, then I would object." Analysis of how the respondents in this study used the term *African* revealed that it was often used in association with several cultural elements. These include high educational achievement, a focus on education, strong religious beliefs, and stricter parental upbringing compared to black Caribbeans and whites in Britain and compared to African Americans and whites in the United States. In Britain, where the identity "African" is more commonly used, a movement to create a political-cultural group of all sub-Saharan African immigrants and their children to fight for resources has not occurred, though it might yet.

A Black Racial Identity

None of the respondents in this study contested that they were racially black, and they understood that the position of blacks at or near the bottom of the racial hierarchy in the United States and Britain has serious economic, social, and psychological implications. As I showed in the preceding chapter, their boundaries expanded to include all blacks in the face of antiblack discrimination. Respondents did not desire to pass out of the black racial category; instead they did not see themselves solely through the prism of race. The reality that race cannot be external to their identity formation process is illustrated by what a British respondent told me: "In Britain, I am not allowed to forget that I am a black man. If I do, I will be reminded."

A Middle-Class Identity

It is the Nigerian second generation's middle-class identity that reinforces their ethnic identities.[41] Put another way, their middle-class identity is ethnicized and intertwined with their diasporic Nigerian ethnicity. Feeding and reinforcing each other, they sharpen the boundaries between the individual and the lower, working, and poor classes of the proximal host and blur the boundary between individual and proximal host blacks of similar middle-class status and mind-set. This is leading to a loose grouping of all middle-class blacks in each country, a loose grouping that blurs the ethnic boundaries among this stratum of group members but does not erase the perception of cultural differences among the groups. The role of class in their Nigerian second-generation identity formation process was discussed in great detail in the preceding chapter.

The Multifaceted Identity: An Adaptive Response
to Life in the United States and Britain

As black people in the United States and Britain, second-generation Nigerians' racial identity is not optional. The racialized context of British and American society is a structural factor assigning them, irrespective of their preferences, as black. Their multifaceted identity is created in response to both their parents' ethnic heritage and their ambivalent reaction to being viewed as coethnics of their proximal hosts, an ambivalence driven largely by the negative stereotypes of their proximal hosts. But as black people in countries that racialize black people as separate from all other groups, race is an important factor in their identity formation process.

However, the multifaceted identity the Nigerian second generation have shaped and selected does not follow the predictions that flow out of the racialization framework that they would form a black identity that is both racial and ethnic and that makes them culturally indistinguishable from their proximal hosts. The second generation of Nigerian ancestry vociferously reject the proposition that black is an ethnic identity. Their position is summarized by the words of a U.S. respondent: "I see myself as black, but I don't think 'black' and 'African American' are synonymous. When I think of black people I feel that it includes African Americans from the slave trade, it includes African immigrants, and it includes Afro-Caribbeans." In short, respondents consider "black" an umbrella category holding all people assigned as racially black.

Multiple studies on the assimilation of the second generation across races and ethnicities have found that the second generation tends to accept and use the racial/ethnic categories already present in the new country.[42] Thus second and subsequent generations of different Asian national groups have come to accept and identify as Asian American, and Latino and Hispanic are identities commonly used by immigrants from Mexico and Latin America. In Britain, people from Bangladesh, India, and Pakistan use the pan-ethnic identity South Asian. Africans and Caribbeans use the pan-ethnic category black or black British. But contrary to what has been theorized, among this group of the black second generation, African, rather than black, is their pan-ethnic identity of choice.

For African immigrants in the United States, African is an emerging pan-ethnic identity. It is not a strictly "made in the USA" identity because the main option available for people of African ancestry on U.S. census forms is

"Black, African-American, Negro," but it is an identity that emerges in response to being in the diaspora because back in Africa most individuals identify first by their ethnic group or nation-state or religion, not as "African." I argue that the African moniker and identity in the United States is still in the embryonic stage because it is not yet being used as a basis of mobilization to fight for resources.[43] I believe that as long as African immigrants and their children enjoy the benefits of affirmative action, they will not really push to be disaggregated from the black/African American/Negro category. This multifaceted identity allows the Nigerian second generation to manage the crisscrossing and intersecting boundaries that result from their racial, ethnic, and pan-ethnic group memberships.

However, the African identity, while an ethnic identity, is also a racialized one because most individuals who take on this identity fall within the black racial category (with the exception of many white Africans). As the British census forms show, "African" is not a separate racial category but is viewed as a subcategory or ethnic grouping under the larger black racial category that includes blacks of different ethnicities. But what the African identity does for recent immigrants and their children from sub-Saharan Africa is that it allows them to stress and signal ethnic diversity among blacks, that contrary to the widely held belief in American and British societies all blacks are not the same.

CONCLUSION: IDENTIFICATIONAL ASSIMILATION AND A MULTIFACETED IDENTITY

It is the emotive appeal of national identity—the relevance and unifying ability of national myths in the face of increasing racial and ethnocultural diversity—and the positioning of a nation's national identity with regard to including or excluding recent immigrants that shape the ethnic identities of the second generation. Thirty-seven respondents in the United States have an American or Nigerian American identity—and potentially many more in the Nigerian category would identify in these ways. But just ten respondents in Britain have a British or Nigerian British identity. This striking difference in ethnic identification patterns illustrates the importance of national identity in respondents' primary ethnic identity choices. And it provides support for my claim that a country's national identity is an additional explanation for why its new immigrants identify the way they do.

While the second generation of Nigerian ancestry are citizens of the United States and Britain in the formal definition of the word, citizenship itself is not enough. If identification and belonging are a matter of degree, the second generation in the United States have stronger degrees of identification and emotional attachment to their country than the second generation in Britain do to theirs. If we imagine an axial line, with the left end indicating passionate commitment to country and belief in one's country's myths and the right end indicating low identification with country, seeing few to no elements of the country's way of life in oneself and feeling at home in the country only enough to want to continue to live in it, the second generation in the United States will cluster around the left end to the middle, and the second generation in Britain will cluster toward the right end, a bit removed from the middle.[44]

It is apparent that in Britain, despite multicultural projects, multicultural education, and citizenship education, immigrants are not convinced that they are equal and valued citizens, irrespective of race and the identity they choose to prioritize. The fact that British national identity is in crisis and is hostile to immigrants, especially black immigrants, compounds the problem. On the one hand, institutional racism and what Gilroy calls "Britain's post-colonial melancholia" have made the second generation of Nigerian ancestry view and experience Britain as not quite welcoming. On the other hand, negative perceptions of Britain's colonial and postcolonial politics are wide-spread in Nigerian communities in Britain, and these views engender noni-dentification with British national identity. As a result, the greater majority of the second generation in Britain, when articulating what being British means to them, do not proffer shared sentiments or common identity or national myths of Britain.

The experiences of the second generation of Nigerian ancestry in both countries point out a disconnect between multiculturalism, as a debate and in implementation, and the sense of belonging that it is intended to help immigrants feel. On the one hand, the United States takes a laissez-faire approach to multiculturalism—and it sees results of widespread articulation of shared sentiments and myths among its immigrant population. On the other hand, Britain makes multiculturalism its official policy in dealing with diversity, but it has not seen widespread articulation of shared national senti-ments and national myths among its immigrant population. These differ-ences in both effort and outcomes indicate that indeed multiculturalism is not *the* solution but just one among a slate of projects that could foster immi-grant integration.

Furthermore, the politics of belonging operate differently in the two countries. In Britain, the presence of the British Nationalist Party, with its call for expulsion of immigrants, along with the constant boundary policing against second-generation ethnic minorities, threatens immigrants' sense of safety. A study of Asians and Black Caribbeans found that "through hurtful 'jokes,' harassment, discrimination, and violence . . . their claim to be British was all too often denied."[45] Alongside all this, the disconnect between the multiculturalist national rhetoric about inclusion and the national identity in Britain has made it more difficult for the second generation of Nigerian ancestry to identify as British, even as they are pushing back against being assimilated into the Caribbean group under the broader umbrella "black British." In contrast, straddling two cultures—the parents' ethnic culture and American culture—is the default position of the second generation in the United States. The comprehensiveness of the U.S. response to past ethnoracial traumas and having a national identity that welcomes immigrants in the broad non-group-specific and historical period sense has made it easier for the second generation of Nigerian ancestry to see a pathway to being ethnically distinct from African Americans while still being American.

The chapter also discusses the primary self-selected ethnic choices of the Nigerian second generation. Their ethnic choices were influenced by transnational linkages. Several mechanisms, such as spending lots of time with coethnics in the United States or Britain and or in Nigeria, having Nigerian-centric friendship networks, and being culturally embedded—a parental upbringing strategy that immersed the second generation in Nigerian culture during their childhood—increased the chances of identifying as Nigerian or hyphenated Nigerian. At the very minimum such exposure ensured that the second generation would have significant elements of Nigerian culture in their hybridized ethnic content. Across all generational cohorts and second-generation subsets, those with limited contact with Nigerians were more likely to have assimilative national identities.[46] Many of the second generation who spent no significant time in Nigeria or in communities with a sizable Nigerian population had ambiguous identities until they went to college, where exposure to and association with a mixed generational cohort of Nigerians strengthened their Nigerian ethnicity and led them to develop Nigerian and/or African identities.[47]

But these self-selected ethnic choices of respondents in both countries did not successfully capture how they see themselves, leading me to argue that their ethnic identities are best understood as multiple identities forming a multifaceted identity. It is cross-national because the multifaceted identity of the second generation in the United States and Britain have the exact same constituent elements. It distills from the diasporic Nigerian ethnicity the core values the Nigerian second generation view as central to who they are. It engenders a shared sense of group membership among the second generation of Nigerian ancestry and members of the Nigerian community in both countries. The multifaceted identity provides the complete picture of who they are and how they differ from others and was created in response to both their parents' ethnic heritage and their ambivalent reaction to being viewed as coethnics of their proximal hosts, an ambivalence driven largely by the negative stereotypes of their proximal hosts.

It allows them to grapple with and resolve the tensions arising from having ethnic pride and close ties to and identification with their parents' ethnic and national cultures, having transnational cultural frames of reference, experiencing racism and being constantly reminded of how being black affects social relationships, recognizing the structural constraints imposed by race on their desires and efforts to be distinct from their proximal hosts, and their awareness that middle-class status and the maintenance of this status acts as a buffer. By holding a multifaceted identity, the second-generation Nigerian adults demonstrate they are cognizant of the social and historical contexts in which they are forming their ethnic identities.

Conclusion

This book examines the identity formation processes of the adult second generation of Nigerian ancestry to understand what their experiences reveal about the intersection of race, ethnicity, immigration, and class in the United States and Britain. Race and racial categorization still hold great social and political power in contemporary British and American societies, and social scientists rightfully emphasize the multidimensional ways race structures the external categorization and life chances of black people. But less attention has been given to how imposed racial categorization intersects with other key factors and processes that shape identity formation among black people. Given the prediction that imposed racial categorization and discrimination will overwhelm the children of black immigrants and subsequently push them into the black underclass, the nuances of race and racial framings among the black second generation are often undertheorized. This book provides a more complex portrait of how the intersection of social class (both parental and individual) and ethnicity informs identity construction among the black second generation in two national contexts, the United States and Britain. I also show that the interactions of these factors with race are engendering new conceptualizations of blackness, which require us to move away from viewing blackness as monolithic. Also, as my findings demonstrate, we should no longer conflate blackness with a disadvantaged class experience or as lacking social capital.[1]

From the experiences of my respondents, I developed a new theory—*beyond racialization*—which identifies three key factors influencing identification patterns among the Nigerian second generation and which help explain why the Nigerian second generation did not forge a reactive black ethnicity and black identity and instead achieved more positive socioeconomic outcomes. The first is the presence and response of the proximal host to the new group. I stress that it is not just race, in this case, being black, that affects how the black second generation will identify, but the nature of interactions with the proximal host. The second factor is the importance of ethnic resources that foster high educational and occupational attainment among the Nigerian second generation and affect the construction of being Nigerian in the British and U.S. diasporas. The third factor is transnational linkages and perspectives. Transnationalism and its impact on the identity formation process of the black second generation has been undertheorized in the literature on the assimilation of the black second generation. Although studies have found that members of the black second generation have hyphenated identities or ethnic identities tied to their parents' country of origin, or are bicultural and/or ethnic hybrids, none has comprehensively spelled out how transnational processes operate in the lives of the second generation of different black groups. This is what I have taken up here.

For the Nigerian second generation, being culturally embedded in transnational social fields and taught the cultural elements selected as most important to what it means to be a Nigerian in the United States and Britain gave them dual frames of reference to identify beyond African American or black British. They were and continue to be exposed to first-generation Nigerians, which keeps their Nigerian ethnicity and identity vibrant. Most respondents belong to transnational churches with sizable congregations of mixed-age and mixed-generation Nigerian and African cohorts. These places of worship serve as repositories of Nigerian culture and as sites where Nigerian culture and Nigerian identities are strengthened. These transnational mechanisms help chart alternative assimilation pathways for the black second generation such that forging a reactive black ethnicity is not the sole identity option available to them.

CHOOSING ETHNICITY WHILE NEGOTIATING RACE

A key argument I make in this book is that ethnicity can be a source of social capital that fosters high levels of socioeconomic attainment and transmits ethnic distinctiveness, especially from the proximal host, for some black second-generation groups. And for Nigerians, the fact that their ethnicity can be capital is founded on the hyperselectivity of first-generation Nigerians in both countries. In chapter 4 I discuss how the Nigerian ethnicity being claimed by respondents is best described as a *diasporic Nigerian ethnicity:* an ethnicity forged by a largely elite segment of the Nigerian population. The experiences of the Nigerian second generation add to what was predicted for the black second generation in segmented assimilation theory. Despite its emphasis on how high levels of human capital in the parental generation, stable families, and a positive mode of incorporation help the second generation succeed educationally and economically,[2] the theory provides few details about how these factors facilitate success among the black second generation. As I show, ethnicity serves as a source of capital for the Nigerian second generation, with its different forms fostering upward social mobility. And for those from middle-class backgrounds, it helped maintain or improve on parents' middle-class position.

The experiences of the Nigerian second generation are quite similar to what is found among other second-generation groups in the United States and Britain. Like the Nigerian second generation, the parents of second-generation Asians in both Britain and the United States try to teach and enforce ethnic cultures. There are intergenerational dynamics among all of these groups where the children are not quite the same as their parents. For example, they do not observe their cultural practices as closely as do their parents. They have become ethnic hybrids whose ethnic content is a syncretic mix of local, foreign, and global cultures.[3] Many of the second generation, especially women, whether Asian, African, or Caribbean, are very critical of the patriarchal traditions practiced in their ethnic communities and cultures.[4]

Ethnicity is an engine that drives socioeconomic success among the Nigerian second generation. Several of the mechanisms operating among Nigerian communities in both the United States and Britain are valuable for the adult Nigerian second generation. Ethnicity provides social capital for the Nigerian second generation just as it does for several Asian groups in both the United States and Britain, even as the forms that capital takes differ across immigrant communities. In some Asian communities, organizing after-school preparatory classes within the community and the broad dissemination of information in ethnic newspapers about the best schools and strategies for admission, information that is collected from and disseminated to members of all social classes, are forms of capital enjoyed in these communities.[5] The Nigerian second generation also utilize success frames just like some Asian groups do, where success is defined as obtaining a degree from a reputable four-year college and getting a professional job.[6] However, I found minimal evidence of well-organized and community-wide support strategies like those found in many Asian communities, and this raises caution flags about the ability of Nigerians to sustain similar levels of socioeconomic attainment among third and subsequent generations and across all social classes.

However, even as ethnicity is a source of progress for some groups, including Nigerians, a key difference that cannot be overemphasized is that race affects the lives of black people in distinct ways when compared to other ethnic minorities in both countries. We see some evidence of this in the fact that black people are assimilating into the mainstream at a much slower rate as measured by their proportion in middle-class professional jobs, intermarriage rates with white people, and residential integration compared to Asians and Hispanics.[7] Even though nonwhites are assigned racial or ethnic identities distinguishing them from whites, who are still treated as the racial norm, there are signs that the racial/ethnic boundaries between whites and Asians as well as Hispanics are becoming increasingly blurred. The same cannot be said for the boundaries between blacks and whites. In short, despite class mobility among some, including many of my respondents, black people hold a distinct position where they are not able to fully and completely integrate into American and British society.[8]

THE ROLE OF NATIONAL CONTEXT

The role national context plays in the ethnic identities and identificational assimilation of the second generation is very important. In chapter 6 I discuss why the adult second generation of Nigerian ancestry feel American while those in Britain do not feel British. I found that in both countries national identity—its clarity and degree of dissemination to the populace, the emotive appeal of national myths, and the country's history of immigrant reception—influenced the ethnic identification process. In particular, colonialism played a significant role in influencing how the Nigerian second generation in Britain identified. Many of my British respondents see Britain as an exploitative power—it exploited its colonies in the past and is exploiting it ethnic minorities, especially its black citizens, today—and this perception fueled their low level of identification with Britain. They also felt that white Britons are hostile to immigrants from their nonwhite former colonie, and this perception made them draw less sharp boundaries against their proximal hosts, black Caribbeans, compared to the Nigerian second generation in the United States, since they saw themselves as being equally unwelcome. In contrast, as I discuss in chapter 4, the Nigerian second generation in the United States placed more weight on slavery—in that they did not share the history of slavery with African Americans—and used this distinction to draw sharp boundaries between themselves and African Americans.

These findings show the importance of considering the historical linkages between the sending country and the receiving country when analyzing how new immigrants identify. Consequently, when studying the ethnicity and ethnic identities of the second generation, in addition to analyzing structural factors, a historical perspective must be introduced. In order to strengthen participatory democracy, countries need to reconsider their myths of national identity to define and inspire increasingly diverse citizenries. On this point, Britain has a lot much work to do than the United States.

NEW DIVISIONS WITHIN BLACK

Blackness is defined in multiple ways even in racialized countries such as the United States and Britain. What Amara, one of my female respondents in the United States, told me in the course of her interview is quite revealing of how the Nigerian second generation approach the question of being black in the United States and Britain. In response to some of her African American peers in college accusing her of not "acting black" at all, she asked them, "How do you act a color?" In effect Amara was asking whether having black skin and the other physical attributes that are considered the physical markers of being a member of the black race meant all black people had to be the same. She disagreed, as did all the respondents I interviewed for this book. She said to me, "I was supposed to be like them [African Americans]." But she did not feel that she should and/or could be pressured to be like them.

The adult Nigerian second generation in both countries defined blackness in multiple ways. They hold a black racial identity that understands the economic and social implications of blacks' low position in the racial hierarchy and are mobilized in the fight against antiblack discrimination in their societies. However, despite this, they also emphasized ethnic distinctions within the black category. The Nigerian second generation in both countries stressed divisions within the black category based on class status and moral and other behavioral distinctions. They sometimes used the larger pan-ethnic identity

African. All use this pan-ethnic label conversationally, but it was chosen more often as the primary self-given identity among the Nigerian second generation in Britain, largely because it is as an ethnic option under the larger Black British category on Britain's census forms.

All the respondents held a multifaceted identity, which allows boundaries to expand so as to include and identify with all black people, especially when experiencing or witnessing racial discrimination. At other times boundaries are constricted to include only sub-Saharan Africans or only Nigerians. The contingent nature of these parameters and the overlapping ethnic and class identities illustrate how in their daily lives the second generation of Nigerian ancestry grapple with ethnic pride, transnational cultural frames of reference, racial discrimination, and the awareness that their middle-class status acts as a buffer against some of the injuries of race. Having a multifaceted identity enables the second generation to maintain their ethnic distinction even in the face of the forces each country's history and ethnoracial context brings to bear on black immigrants and their children to become "just black," forces that many scholars feared would override the ethnicities of new black immigrants and their children and racialize them into an undifferentiated single ethnic group characterized by an oppositional culture and a disadvantaged class experience.[9]

But despite their articulation of an ethnic distinction from their proximal hosts, I have shown that second-generation Nigerian adults are integrating into the black middle class. As more attention is being paid to the class diversity among black people, with many pointing out that not all black people are poor, from dysfunctional families, or welfare dependent and that middle- and upper-class blacks exist in both the United States and Britain, I argue that we also have to start talking about a multiethnic or variegated black middle class that is diverse both in terms of class and in terms of ethnicity. The key point that must be made here is that this ethnic diversity is coming not just from first-generation black immigrants in the United States and first-generation African immigrants in Britain; it is being maintained by the second generation also.

In the United States, there is increasing recognition that black people are a diverse group of people. In a 2007 poll conducted by the Pew Research Center, 37 percent of blacks felt that blacks could not still be thought of as a single race because of the diversity in the community. A bare majority (53 percent) felt it was appropriate to still think of blacks as a single race because black people have much in common. A 2008 CAAPS/ABC News

Black Politics Study poll found that 47 percent of blacks believe that African Americans should stop thinking of themselves as a racial group and instead view themselves as individuals.[10]

Furthermore, members of the black community have different attitudinal positions based on class status. The same 2007 Pew poll found that more people believe that the values that middle-class blacks hold are different from the values of lower-class and poor blacks. In a similar vein, a 2010 Pew poll found that most black people believe that blacks and whites have grown more alike in terms of their core values while the values of affluent blacks and poor blacks have become less alike.[11] Several studies on the black middle class show that even as middle-class blacks strive to distance themselves from poor blacks, in many cases they have no choice but to live in close proximity to them because of racial discrimination and residential segregation.[12] This close proximity to poor blacks, along with ongoing antiblack discrimination, helps explain the fragility of the black middle class and the peril many of their children face as they transition into adulthood.[13] Taken together, these studies and polls tell us that the black community is cleaving along class lines.

However, what I argue in this book is that even as black communities in the United States and Britain become more economically unequal and more diverse by class, they are becoming more diverse along ethnic lines too. The experiences of the Nigerian second generation in both countries show that blackness does not have to connote a disadvantaged class experience or that to be black is to be unfortunate.[14] Multiple mechanisms, such as transnationalism and ethnicity-as-capital, reveal how the intersection of national origin, ethnicity, and social class provides different and better assimilation pathways for the black second generation. In sum, the experiences of the Nigerian second generation in both countries show that even as racialization processes keep race an integral aspect of the identity formation process of the black second generation, ethnic distinctions are nevertheless maintained.

A promising research agenda would continue to study the intersection of race, ethnicity, and class among the second generation of other groups also viewed as at risk of downward mobility or of being racialized and possibly politicized in both countries. I see beyond racialization theory as potentially applicable to other nonwhite second-generation groups that have been theorized to be at risk of downward mobility because of race and the barriers imposed by their racial status. Researchers in future studies need to pay attention to the nature of relations between the second generation and their proximal hosts and how the overall social status position of both the proximal host and the immigrant group in society affects these relations. Investigating how transnational linkages and perspectives provide alternative cultural frames of reference, racial socialization, and alternative or additional ethnic options to the second generation that might help them maintain ethnic distinctiveness and/or forge unique multifaceted identities even in the face of processes of racialization is another promising line of inquiry. Researchers can investigate to identify forms of capital that exist in these immigrant communities that affect how their second generation form their identities and that foster other positive assimilation outcomes. As I showed, the key forms of capital operating within Nigerian communities that influenced their second generation's identities and fostered positive socioeconomic outcomes were the powerful social norm that "it is un-Nigerian not to go to college" and the multiplicity of highly educated professionals in their social networks that served as role models and benchmarks to measure success. There might exist in these immigrant communities similar or different forms of ethnicity-as-capital that help explain divergent assimilation trajectories and outcomes among their second generation. Finally, another promising line of investigation is to consider the roles religion and gender play singly or in combination with other factors in explaining the assimilation outcomes of the nonwhite second generation in the two countries studied here and in other Western advanced nations.[15]

THE FUTURE OF THE ETHNIC IDENTIFICATION JOURNEY

It is not clear whether the Nigerian second generation will always maintain their ethnic distinctiveness from their proximal hosts. The future is hard to predict. It is possible that significant events in the United States and Britain will lead to racial identification increasing in salience, in conjunction with a waning in salience of the ethnic identities held by second-generation blacks. The emergence of the Black Lives Matter movement in the United States, which was birthed out of recent events of police officers shooting and killing unarmed black men, such as the slaying of Tamir Rice in Cleveland, Ohio, and Walter Scott in South Carolina, and which have stirred up debates about race and policing and racial inequality in the judicial system, raises an interesting sociological question about whether such events will have an impact on how the black second generation identifies. These events also raise questions about the salience the black second generation will attach to their racial and/or ethnic identities. Will it be a zero-sum game, where deepening racial consciousness and identification occurs alongside waning ethnic identification, or will it be that such events will lead to increased salience of both ethnic and racial identities?

It is also not clear whether the third and subsequent generations will maintain a similar ethnic distinction from African Americans in the United States and from black Caribbeans in Britain. My respondents told me that they intend to teach their children their ethnic (Nigerian) values. Many of them have married first-generation coethnics, which has had an effect of strengthening their ethnic identities and replenishing their ethnic content. If the adult Nigerian second generation continue these practices, their children will be half second generation and half third generation, and will grow up in transnational social fields that should help maintain a distinct ethnicity that distinguishes the third generation from their proximal hosts. However, what I can say today is that the rapidly growing African population in both countries and the presence of a mixed-age cohort of first-generation African immigrants are helping replenish the ethnicity of group members, especially that of later generation members.

What is clear from my study of the adult Nigerian second generation in the United States and Britain is that their ethnic identities are multiple and overlapping. They move back and forth between their racial and ethnic identities. What is also clear is that they are ethnic hybrids whose observances of ethnic and cultural practices are not as thick as those of their parents, leading me to call my respondents Nigerians with a twist. Furthermore, even as they are embedded in transnational social fields and are influenced by multiple transnational linkages and perspectives, only a minority engage in transnational activities. What this study finds is that even if their ethnic distinction from their proximal hosts becomes attenuated in the future, the interaction between their ethnic and class backgrounds and the positive impact on several of their social outcomes show that blackness does not have to be seen as emblematic of being poor or working class. It does not have to connote having non-goal-oriented identities. It also does not have to be seen as a monolithic mass where national origin, ethnicity, and class cannot be sources of divisions among black people. Rather, the identities black people hold can be fashioned in a multitude of ways.

In the course of writing this book, I have been asked whether given that the adult second generation of Nigerian ancestry interviewed for this study have achieved educational and occupational success, is it possible for them to become white? Or if not white, can they exit the black category and fall on the nonblack side of the black/nonblack color line? My answer to both questions is no. They cannot become white because the notion of whiteness is deeply rooted in Britain's and America's histories and social construction of black people as very different from whites and all other nonblack ethnic minorities.[16] Also, a critical aspect of becoming white is to have the right body. Whiteness is defined as a system of domination that upholds a white identity as an essential something. The meaning and status of whiteness depends on racist structures that associate whiteness with normality.[17] Thus the second generation of Nigerian ancestry, despite their successes, have the wrong body.

So, if not white, can they become honorary whites? An example of the honorary white category is found the tri-racial system, which is similar to the systems found in some Latin American and Caribbean countries. In a tri-racial system, successful Asian groups, light-skinned Latinos, and most multiracials will occupy an honorary white category, which serves as a buffer between a collective black category—comprising a few low-status groups like reservation-bound American Indians, Hmongs, Laotians, and dark-skinned Latinos—and whites, which will expand to include some Asian-origin people and middle-class white Latinos.[18] According to this conceptualization of honorary whiteness, it seems that money can whiten an individual, but it not quite clear whether money or class status can whiten blacks. Indeed, he places black immigrants (both Caribbean and African) in the collective black category. Furthermore, as some scholars have noted, the invitation to become honorary white is at the behest of white people and the invitation can be withdrawn at any time.[19] Thus becoming honorary white does not disrupt the existing ethnoracial hierarchy, which positions whites as the racial center and norm in the United States and Britain. It simply creates a buffer group between white people and collective blacks.

The stubborn line demarcating black people from other races persists even in competing predictions about the future of the U.S. color line. Some claim that a tri-racial model is too optimistic and that race will remain white/nonwhite, with Hispanics and Asians not being assimilated into whiteness as some predict. Others foresee a black/nonblack divide that places Hispanics and Asians on the white side of the divide or a black/nonblack divide where all nonblack groups are positioned, albeit in hierarchical relationships to each other, in contrast to black people. In all these predictions of the future of the U.S. color line, black people remain on one side of the divide or serve as the specter of downward or incomplete assimilation. Even the optimistic take on the future of the U.S. color line, which argues that the upcoming retirement of baby boomers will create sufficient space for nonwhites (immigrants and subsequent generations) to move up into the middle class and mainstream without generating a backlash from white people, finds that black people are lagging behind. In the United States, Asians and Hispanics are integrating into the middle-class mainstream at a much faster rate than black people regardless of their nativity.[20] In Britain, it is not clear if the divide will remain between blacks and whites or between whites and all other nonwhite ethnic groups or if it will evolve into ethnoreligious groupings where the divide is Muslims/non-Muslims and where South Asian Muslims become increasingly racialized and politicized. While we do not know what the future holds in terms of the color/racial divide in both countries, what I argue is that the demographic shifts both countries are undergoing because of continued immigration from nonwhite parts of the world and burgeoning biracial and multiracial populations are creating enough space for the black second generation to create new definitions of blackness.

POLICY IMPLICATIONS

From their own voices, it is clear that some social distance exists between the adult second generation of Nigerian ancestry and members of their communities and their proximal hosts. This is not the best state of affairs for two reasons. First, the Nigerian second generation, despite some of their best efforts and/or desires to be different and to be seen as different from their proximal hosts, live in countries where racial prejudice and racial discrimination against black people exist. Consequently, they also have either experienced discrimination or are at risk of being discriminated against in the future. And these commonalities in past and potential future experiences unite them with their proximal hosts. Second, each of these groups have different strengths that, if leveraged to benefit members across the groups, should help improve the relative position of all black people in these two countries.

For example, Africans, and particularly Nigerians, in both the United States and Britain are well educated. It will be good to think creatively of ways this strength can be leveraged to improve the educational attainment levels of other black groups. In the United States, African Americans wield considerable political power. Even though black immigrants mostly vote for the Democratic Party as African Americans do, how can black immigrants' interests be elevated and introduced into the public arena to receive political attention by African American political leaders? In Britain, Caribbeans earn a higher return on their education than Africans. What lessons can be learned from this, and in what ways can groups collaborate to increase resources and economic opportunities within the black community? If some effort is put into building and nurturing coalitions between members of the different black groups in both countries, at different stages of the life course, such as during K–12 and in college and among professionals and business owners, over time these efforts can contribute to improving the relative position of all blacks in the United States and Britain. Of course greater progress will be made if these efforts are accompanied with changes in structural racism in both societies that disproportionately affect black people.

What also became clear in the course of my research is that the Nigerian second generation in the United States found it much easier to feel and identify as American compared to the Nigerian second generation in Britain. Even though Britain can be viewed as more multicultural than the United States, their roll-out of multicultural projects has not led to increased national identification with Britain among this group of the second generation, and other studies show similar low levels of identification with Britain among second-generation South Asians.[21] Britain is viewed as unwelcoming to immigrants from its nonwhite former colonies. This is a view shared not just by the adult second generation of Nigerian ancestry interviewed for this book, but by all ethnic minorities in Britain.[22] Britain's colonial history and the widespread view among the Nigerian second generation that its relationship with its colonies, now former colonies, is altogether exploitative is a key reason they do not have strong feelings of allegiance to or identification with Britain. It is not because they are economically marginalized, as almost all respondents interviewed are middle-class professionals. Low national identification with Britain among its new citizens is a problem: it poses a security threat to the nation given the observed rise in domestic terrorism around the world, where some naturalized citizens of foreign countries (first-generation) and children of immigrants (second-generation) are showing signs of being susceptible to messages that convince them to carry out heinous crimes against their fellow citizens.

That Britain does not have national myths and a national identity that serve to unify their rapidly growing nonwhite population compounds this problem. Britain has to find a way to revise its national identity so as to unite and inspire an increasingly diverse population, especially members of immigrant groups who have negative memories of British colonialism and more recent racist policies. Comparing the situation in Britain to that of the United States, there is something about America's national identity, about the American Dream, that the black second generation find compelling. There is not an analogous British dream. It may be that policy cannot fix this problem, but Britain has to try, and any attempts to strengthen its national identity and make it more welcoming to its nonwhite citizens must marry a rhetoric of inclusiveness with real implementation.

Last, while first-generation African immigrants are important agents of social and cultural change and economic development in their home countries and the African continent as a whole, it is not really clear what role second-generation Africans will play. The recent visit of President Obama to Kenya, his father's homeland, in July 2015, where he introduced himself as a Kenyan American and the first Kenyan American president of the United States, reveals that second-generation Africans can maintain a connection to their parents' homeland and be powerful agents of change. The fact that second-generation Nigerians in both the United States and Britain hold Nigerian and African identities suggests that they are connected by this identity to the global issues and development challenges confronting Nigeria and the African continent as a whole. This identification suggests that the Nigerian second generation can be persuaded to assist in fostering economic and social development in Nigeria and other places in Africa.

Below I detail some policy initiatives and ideas that might help solve some of the problems mentioned above.

Awakening Kinship: Policy Initiatives for Improving Black-on-Black Relations

For the reasons mentioned above, we need stronger relationships between Nigerians and Caribbeans in Britain and Nigerians and African Americans in the United States. Because I found that college years and college sites were extremely important in the identity formation process of the Nigerian second generation, I believe encouraging closer coalitions at this stage in the life course will have a long-lasting impact in bringing about closer relations and greater understanding between the different black ethnic groups in the future. Established black organizations such as the National Association for the Advancement of Colored People and the United Negro College Fund need to put considerable resources into reaching out to black immigrants (both first and second generation) in colleges to encourage them to become active members and become more socially engaged in a broader black coalition instead of waiting for the first- and second-generation immigrant blacks to seek them out. College administrators in charge of student affairs and student organizations need to encourage cross-black student organization events. This will help prevent African and Caribbean and other nation-specific student associations such as the Nigerian Students Association, which are present at many elite universities, from operating in silos, which entrenches the social distance between black college groups. In Britain, there is a need for more umbrella organizations that serve both Caribbean and African populations to organize members of these groups and advance their interests in the public and private spheres.

In addition, ethnic organizations among Nigerians need to add on to their transnational activities and reach out to working-class and poor blacks in their host country. There is a need for more programs, initiated from within the Nigerian community, that link their members, especially the more successful ones to poorer blacks, be they coethnics or members of the proximal hosts. Such programs will provide role models who can encourage their less fortunate partners; they can provide tutoring help, provide timely information about jobs or other opportunities that will lead to socioeconomic success, and activate links in their own social networks that can assist their partners get better jobs, know what schools to apply to in order to improve their admission success rates, and so on. In these ways, there will be a multiplier effect where the resources possessed by middle-class members help increase the human capital levels of poor and working-class black communities.

Also, closer relations between middle-class and poor blacks should improve understandings about structural racism and the challenges faced by the black poor that should in turn complicate the increasingly widespread view among middle-class blacks that poor blacks are dysfunctional. We see evidence of this viewpoint in the 2007 Pew Survey: it found that over 53 percent of African Americans believe that blacks who do not get ahead are mainly responsible for their situation.[23] Getting firsthand knowledge of the structural challenges facing the black poor through increased personal interaction should help prevent the fraying of ties and encourage empathy between the black middle class and the black poor. Hopefully the result will be a unified political voice among black people to push for changes in America and Britain ensuring a more equitable society.

My findings suggest an opportunity for wider interracial coalitions and better cross-group relations. As I have discussed, the experiences of the Nigerian second generation in both the United States and Britain are quite similar to those of second-generation Asians and Mexicans. All of the groups, as nonwhite, struggle to reconcile their self-given ethnic identities with racial identities imposed by countries' ethnoracial systems.[24] The nonwhite second generation tell very similar stories about how they were brought up—with parents, community, and family members stressing educational achievement and employing multiple strategies to ensure children are upwardly mobile and enter the middle class. A shared story among them is the challenge of gaining full acceptance from whites as they enter middle-class professional settings. It is argued that middle-class minorities have in common cultural elements they put toward navigating discriminatory environments and achieving economic mobility, and that there is space for middle-class minorities to develop a pan-minority identity.[25] If encouraged and nurtured to note the similarities of their experiences, stronger coalitions and greater cross-group understanding can be built. Ethnic community leaders, university college administrators, and youth leaders have an opportunity to break down the walls that limit inter- and intraracial unity.

Loving Your Country: Policy Initiatives to Improve
Low Levels of National Identification

Britishness. What does it mean? What can it mean? How can the sense of it be expanded to become an ideal that is emotionally compelling to an increasingly racially and ethnically diverse British population? This is a debate being had in Britain today. Former Prime Minister David Cameron weighed in forcefully, arguing that Britain should follow America's example in teaching a meaningful sense of what it means to be a Briton just as Americans have succeeded in transmitting a unifying sense of what it means to be an American to its citizens. He has said that British history has to be taught "properly" in schools so that while acknowledging some bad things Britain has done, it celebrates Britain's positive achievements at home and abroad. He has also stated that history lessons should teach British children about the aspects of Britain's current national identity such as the rule of law, adherence to human rights, free speech, freedom of the individual, and parliamentary democracy. However, what we see in this book is that individuals are aware of these aspects of Britain's national identity; it is just that this knowledge does not override or counterbalance their negative perceptions of Britain as an exploiter of nonwhite people and a country that refuses to allow them to become insiders with full rights rather than tolerated as sojourners.

The British government has to comprehensively address Britain's role in past ethnoracial traumas. Teaching British history in school with the intent of celebrating its achievements around the world must be accompanied by not just a mention of some of its racist and exploitative actions, but a true accounting of the historical and long-lasting consequences of these actions in modern-day society. Britain has to confront the institutional racism that exists in its society. The government has to investigate and then understand the reasons ethnic minorities laugh when they are asked if they feel English and respond that only white people can be English. What message is being sent to black immigrants in Britain who are keenly aware that while citizens of white British Commonwealth nations such as Australia, Canada, and the United States and member-states of the European Union are allowed entry into Britain without visas, a privilege not extended to British Commonwealth nations with nonwhite populations? The organizations charged with ensuring equal employment opportunities have to be given more regulatory power to address charges of racial discrimination at work, where many ethnic minorities hit the proverbial glass ceiling. Government agencies such as the National Health Service have to review their hiring processes, as many people charge that black and other ethnic minorities are frequently not hired even when they are as well or better qualified than the white Briton for plum jobs in the service largely because the white Briton is seen as the true citizen of Britain.

Only after these issues are truly addressed, without trying to elide them or sweep them under the rug, will teaching British history properly or having a British day have any impact. Only then would Britain successfully create an emotionally compelling national identity that is perceived by its ethnic minorities to be sincerely inclusive of people of all races, ethnic origins, and religions. And only then will they happily articulate what it means to be British and feel that they are fully and truly, and not just legally, Britons.

Even though the Nigerian second generation interviewed for this book exhibit high levels of identification with the United States, several studies suggest that this is not the case for all second-generation ethnic groups. Second-generation Mexicans are exhibiting low levels of identification with the United States, which is decreasing as they spend more time in the United States. And this diminishing level of national identification with the United States and rising level of identification as Mexican are tied to the hostile reception Mexican Americans, at this time, face in the United States.[26] Thus the United States, like Britain, has some work to do in ensuring that all its people of different races, ethnicities, and religions feel welcome and part of the American immigrant story. The United States needs to draft and pass an immigration bill that successfully achieves its desire to control who is allowed into the country and how many while bringing out of the shadows and granting pathways to citizenship (and as such full rights) to those who are already residing in it. Passing such a comprehensive bill should improve levels of national identification among all its new citizens, an outcome that is increasingly important for the security of the nation, given the emerging link between disaffected new citizens, radicalization, and homegrown terrorism.

Partnering in Nigeria's and Africa's Development: A Policy Initiative to Engage the Second Generation

A simple policy that will engender stronger ties with Nigeria is for parents to take their children on visits to Nigeria more frequently. I found that going back to Nigeria, even for short trips, strengthened the second generation's identification with that country, established an emotional attachment, and engendered a sense of belonging to Nigeria and Africa. It also sensitized them to ways they could foster social and economic development in Nigeria. Parents should be encouraged to take their children back home, and this can be done through private organizations and groups such as transnational Nigerian churches and Nigerian ethnic and professional associations.

Many colleges and universities in the United States and Britain have vibrant African and Nigerian student associations composed of first- and second-generation Africans. These associations can incorporate into their constitutions and charters a charge to give back to their parents' home countries and the African continent as a whole. These associations can commit to sponsoring projects not just in the United States or Britain but also in Nigeria and possibly other African countries where their universities might have partnerships. Sponsoring various student-led, and possibly university-supported, entrepreneurial projects and cultural initiatives back in Africa will be a way for the second generation to become agents of cultural, social, and economic change. In the United States, the Young African Leaders Initiative (YALI), which is supported by the U.S. government, presents a wonderful opportunity for second- generation Nigerians to enhance their knowledge and skills and partner with their African-based YALI counterparts to become involved in developing Nigeria and Africa.

Another policy initiative to get the Nigerian second generation involved in nation building and development in Nigeria is to extend to them current policies that encourage first-generation Nigerian immigrants to return to Nigeria. For example, the Nigerian government has liberalized tax laws and provided tax holidays for a period of years to return migrants who repatriate their assets to set up businesses.[27] Extending such investment incentives to the second generation should increase the number of the second generation engaged in transnational activities and should prove attractive to the second generation who are open to or actively seeking to migrate to Nigeria. Of course, these government policies would only work if the federal government can guarantee the rule of law, safety, transparent transactional practices, and adequate social amenities.

In conclusion, what I have shown in this book is that national origin, the resources African immigrants bring with them, and the ethnicity they have forged in their host country, along with certain national factors of the host country, affect the assimilation outcomes of second- generation blacks. I have provided empirical evidence to show that black people are not a single ethnic group with a monolithic set of cultural practices and identity that too often is characterized as deficient. Nationality, ethnicity, and religion are sources of ethnic distinction among black people just as they are for white people. To make this claim is not to ignore how race, racial prejudice, and racial discrimination affect black people; it is to call attention to the fact that even as racialization processes work to hold black people in a starkly separate position from whites, within different black groups mechanisms and strategies are flourishing to help children attain more positive socioeconomic outcomes. More research needs to be done to study the different strategies being used in different black communities, both immigrant and native, to ensure better outcomes than the largely pessimistic ones predicted by segmented assimilation theory and its variants. As more attention is paid to the variation among black people, greater progress will be made in dismantling the notion in both the United States and Britain that black people are a monolithic mass and that black culture is deficient and characterized by an oppositional culture and identity that devalues schooling and work and that stresses attitudes and behaviors that are often hostile to success in the mainstream economy and that would sway and engulf the black second generation.

Notes on Methods

I conducted my interviews from June 2008 to November 2009. I did fieldwork in Britain from June 2008 to January 2009. My fieldwork in the United States began in February 2009 and ended in November 2009. My primary research sites were the Nigerian embassies in London and New York. I used a screening questionnaire at the embassies to identify individuals who met the sampling criteria: over twenty-two years of age and 1.5- or 1.75- or second-generation individuals of Nigerian ancestry. In the book, following standard convention in immigration literature, I refer to all respondents as second generation. Respondents were asked to indicate whether they would be willing to be interviewed and to provide contact information such as an email address or phone number. I followed up on all those who met the sampling criteria and were willing to be interviewed. While still in the embassy, I immediately scanned the questionnaires upon receiving them and approached those who met the sampling criteria but had not indicated a willingness to be interviewed to ask them to reconsider. This personal appeal netted me many more individuals to interview than I would have otherwise gotten.

There were three main types of visitors to the embassy: those engaged in frequent transnational activities; those who had never visited Nigeria or were infrequent visitors but needed to go because of a critical life event such as a death or wedding in the family; and those who had no business in the embassy or in Nigeria but were serving as escorts to members of their social networks. This great mix of second-generation Nigerians ensured that I did not only sample or oversample individuals actively and seriously engaged in transnational activities. In both the United States and Britain, the embassy was a congregating place for a good representation of the second genera-tion of Nigerian ancestry. In Britain, 62 percent of my respondents were from the embassy. In the United States, 32 percent were from the embassy. The embassy sam-pling worked better in Britain than in the United States because consular clients have to come personally to the Nigerian embassy in London, whereas in the United States, 80 to 90 percent of consular business is done by mail.

After I exhausted the embassy as a site for interviews, I added snowball sampling. I had two different points of entry in both countries: churches and Nigerian organizations. Key informants referred me to others in their organizations and social networks. I was careful to not oversample from any one social network. I diversified the sample so as not to sample on identity issues and to control variation in community involvement. I supplemented the samples by interviewing respondents from social associations expressly created by and for second-generation Nigerians in both countries. I also used my personal contacts within the Nigerian community. As a first-generation Nigerian immigrant, I was able to tap into the social networks of friends and family members on both sides of the pond.

I was worried that sampling from the Nigerian embassy would lead to findings of higher levels of identification with Nigeria than normal because I might have oversampled transnational individuals. However, this worry was quickly dispelled because of the diversity of second-generation adults visiting the embassy and because upon analyzing the data from respondents drawn from the embassies and drawn via the other methods, I found no bias in the findings. Almost all respondents had been greatly influenced by their parents' culture and social networks—an unavoidable influence unless they grew up in households with few or no ties to their parents' home countries.

Among my British respondents, all had finished school, either full-time or part-time. All except two were employed. In the United States, 70 of the 75 respondents had finished school—either full-time or part-time. Five respondents were in graduate school, one was in medical school, one was in law school, and three were in PhD programs. All but one had significant work experience prior to going back to graduate school. Eight of my U.S. respondents were unemployed when I interviewed them but were actively looking for work. Most of them were recent graduates, at the height of the recession that began in 2008.

I had three reasons for sampling adults over the age of twenty-two. First, most studies of the African second generation have focused on children or youths and so could not really investigate questions of intergenerational mobility, which was the motivating question of this study. Most of the other studies focused only on questions of identity formation and acculturation. I wanted to build on these studies while investigating issues of social mobility. Second, literature on identity formation tells us that identities tend to be in flux during childhood and adolescence. I wanted to study the identification journey of the African second generation—tracing it and the mechanisms that shaped their identity choices from childhood to adulthood. This decision to study an older age cohort of the black (African) second generation is, I believe, one reason I found that they hold a multifaceted identity and the emerging coalition among all middle-class blacks regardless of ethnicity. Third, I wanted to find out if these respondents were as transnational as their parents or if transnationalism is more of a first-generation phenomenon.

In Britain, I conducted 40 sit-down interviews and 35 telephone interviews. In the United States, I conducted 20 sit-down interviews and 55 telephone interviews. I paid particular attention to the quality of interviews done by phone and in person, and I found no evidence that the interview medium affected the information received. Respondents I interviewed by telephone were just as engaged as those I interviewed in person. When I called to set up interviews, I told my then potential respondents that I needed between 45 and 90 minutes of their time. I told them that it would be best to set up a time when they could talk to me in private and in comfort. I did not want them to feel constrained by the presence of others or their location when answering questions. Consequently, most of the telephone interviews were done in the evenings when respondents were at home. In Britain I met 20 of the 35 respondents I interviewed over the phone. In the United States, I met 28 of the 55 respondents I interviewed over the phone. I did not meet just under half of them because they lived in cities quite far from me. During my U.S. fieldwork, I was based in Cambridge, Massachusetts, and Philadelphia, Pennsylvania. In Britain, I was based in London.

In Britain, 73 of 75 respondents came from London and its metropolis. One came from Manchester and another from Liverpool. In the United States, the majority of my respondents came from four of the five cities or states with the largest Nigerian population: 25 came from Boston, 20 from New York City, 12 from Texas, and 9 from Maryland. The other 11 respondents came from Atlanta (2), Philadelphia (2), North Carolina (1), Oklahoma (1), Missouri (1), and California (1). I observed no regional differences on the issues of ethnic choices and relations with African Americans. However, there were regional differences in exposure to Caribbeans (those in Texas had limited interaction with them) and exposure to Hispanics (those in Texas had much stronger views about Hispanics).

Comparing the United States and British samples, 56 percent (N = 42) of the Britain sample were female and 44 percent (N = 33) were male; 61 percent (N = 46) of the U.S. sample were female and 39 percent (N = 29) were male. More British respondents had spent time (lived) in Nigeria compared to the U.S. second generation (British sample N = 23; U.S. sample N = 11), primarily because Britain is closer to Nigeria than is the United States. Respondents in Britain were on average five years older than U.S. respondents. Respondents' ages ranged from 21 to 62 (see table A for the sociodemographic breakdown of the sample). I transcribed and analyzed the interviews thematically, using qualitative analysis software. I also created summarizing Excel data sheets to allow for easy and systematic sorting of the data.

TABLE A Sociodemographic Profile of U.S. and British Respondents

Selected Variables	Britain	United States
Period of Parents' Entry*		
1950–1959	1	1
1960–1969	35	3
1970–1979	17	34
1980–1989	18	26
1990–1999	2	9
2000s	0	0
Respondents' Age Cohorts		
21–30	34	61
31–40	30	12
41–50	10	1
51–60	0	1
61 and above	1	0
Average age	32.2	27.2
Generational Status		
1.5 generation (6–13 years)	12	17
1.75 generation (0–5 years)	10	14
2nd generation	53	44
2nd generation who have lived in Nigeria	23	11
Gender		
Male	33	29
Female	42	46
Religion		
Christian	66	70
Muslim	9	5
Sit-down interview	40	20
Telephone interview	35	55
Sample size	75	75

* In both countries, the N is 73 because of two respondents in each country who were went abroad while their parents remained in Nigeria (never migrated to the United States or Britain).

FURTHER DISAGGREGATION
OF THE SECOND-GENERATION CATEGORY

I would recommend, based on my fieldwork, that in future research on the second generation status be further disaggregated to reflect whether the individual spent significant time in his or her parents' country of origin, along with the stage of the life course at which this occurred. I found that the impact on assimilation outcomes was great if living in a parent's country of birth occurred sometime between the ages of seven and sixteen. During these critical formative years, individuals are becoming more aware of themselves and others' perception of them and are more susceptible to being influenced by peers and the social environment. The impact on assimilation outcomes was less pronounced if they lived outside their country of birth after they had finished college or when they were older than twenty-two.

I accepted the immigration literature standard that an individual is second generation if he or she was born in the host country of at least one foreign-born parent. I also agree with Rubén Rumbaut (2004) that, for increased rigor of the study, the first generation could be further split into decimal generations, and I agree that 1.5 and 1.75 immigrants can be merged into the second generation category—which I do because they have spent the majority of their formative childhood years in the receiving country. As such, my sample includes 1.75 generation immigrants, who migrated to the host country between the ages of 0 and 5, and 1.5 generation immigrants, who migrated to the host country between the ages of 6 and 13.

Once I started collecting and analyzing my data, I realized that I had a problem with the second generation immigrant category. I found that there are three subgroups among the second generation (defined as those who are born in the United States or Britain of at least one immigrant parent). The first subgroup is the "born and raised second generation," those who have lived all their lives in their country of birth except for short vacations and out-of-country trips. The second subgroup is the "ambiguous second generation," those who returned to their parents' country of origin as infants, toddlers, or young children, spent a few years in that country, and then returned to their country of birth by their late teens to attend college or university. The third subgroup is the "born-and-returned-to-home-country second generation"; these individuals left their country of birth as infants or toddlers to live in Nigeria and did not return until they had finished university or until they were adults (older than twenty-one). I excluded from my sample the majority of these pseudo-second-generation individuals, specifically, all who had left as infants and returned after the age of twenty-two, because all had spent their entire formative years outside of Britain or the United States. The born-and-returned-to-home-country second generation are much closer on certain dimensions, such as choice of ethnic identification, vibrancy and robustness of cultural practices, and engagement in transnational activities, to the first generation.

On the question of identity, the type of second generation did make a bit of difference, since the born and raised second generation and the 1.75 generation had similar identification patterns, while the born and returned second generation and the 1.5 generation made similar choices. So, going forward, I believe researchers should be aware of this type of diversity among those born in the host country of immigrant parents, which might lead to different assimilation experiences and incorporation outcomes.

It would have been optimal to select my respondents via random sampling, but this was not possible because the populations I was sampling from are hard to find. At the beginning of my fieldwork in Britain, I used telephone registries as sampling frames but found that cold calling individuals with Nigerian ethnic names was not well received. In addition, I was reaching mostly first-generation Nigerians, who were not my target population. Using the telephone directory as the sampling frame also meant that I was excluding Nigerian immigrants with English names and difficult to categorize names. The tri-method I settled on to obtain my sample enabled me to draw a sample that is representative of diasporic Nigerians in the United States and Britain. The educational and age profiles of my respondents and their parents are very similar to what is observed in the U.S. and U.K. census data and other large national data sets.

All respondents lived in major cities in the United States and Britain, which is consistent with the pattern observed for African immigrants in these countries' censuses. Thus it is possible that the experiences of the second generation of Nigerian ancestry in this book differ significantly from the experiences of the African second generation who live in rural areas. However, since the great majority of all African immigrants in both countries live in large cities, drawing respondents only from large cities is not a significant problem. Whether a difference exists between rural and urban second-generation Africans is a question that other researchers may want to pursue.

Frequencies in Each Ethnic Identity Category and Frequencies on Other Questions

	Second Generation in Britain						Second Generation in the United States					
	Nigerian	Nigerian–British	British	Black African	Other	Total	Nigerian	Nigerian–American	American	African	Other	Total
Number of people[1]	(N=48)	(N=2)	(N=8)	(N=13)	(N=4)	(N=75)	(N=29)	(N=28)	(N=9)	(N=3)	(N=6)	(N=75)
Lived in Nigeria for over 1 year[2]	35	1	0	6	1	43 57%	15	12	3	0	0	30 40%
Speak a Nigerian language[3]	20	1	0	3	3	27 36%	17	14	4	0	0	35 47%
Send money, gifts to Nigeria regularly[4]	21	1	0	6	3	33 44%	8	6	0	0	0	14 19%
Visit Nigeria	34	1	3	6	3	47 63%	19	21	11	1	2	50 67%
Member of a Nigerian ethnic association(s)	8	0	0	2	0	10 13%	2	4	0	0	0	6 8%

1 This is a nonprobability sample. The count in each category should not be reified as some judgment calls had to be made during the classification process. This point is especially true for the U.S. second generation on the ethnic categories of Nigerian and Nigerian American. Many of the respondents counted in either of these two categories would be just as happy to be categorized in the other. The goal of the table is to highlight several differences between identificational types and across countries. Such as the importance of living in Nigeria in shaping Nigerian leaning identities and the existence of denser transnational linkages in Britain compared to the United States.

2 This question identifies two different types of the second generation in the United States and Britain. The majority of British respondents who have lived in Nigeria lived in Nigeria during their formative years (defined here as between age 7 to 18). Many of these respondents were born in Britain but returned to Nigeria with their parents as toddlers. In the United States, the majority are 1.75 generation.

3 The second generation, about an additional third, who understand a Nigerian language but cannot speak are not included in the count.

4 The second generation who take gifts and new and used clothes only when they visit Nigeria are not included in the count.

NOTES

INTRODUCTION

1. He recalls the neighborhood as riddled with "crime" and "drug users and dealers."

2. Throughout this book the term *African American* refers to native U.S. blacks, whose ancestors were held as slaves on American soil. African Americans were commonly called black Americans by the African second generation, as "African American" is quite recent.

3. He is referring to a well-known phrase in the book *No Longer at Ease* (p. 152), by Chinua Achebe, one of the best-known Nigerian and African novelists.

4. The general term that covers both solicitors and barristers is *lawyer*. A solicitor is usually the first person a member of the public will go to with a legal problem. Barristers provide specialist legal advice and represent their clients in courts and tribunals. It is very competitive to become a barrister because there are more individuals than open spots in the Bar Professional Course (BPTC), which is for one year full-time, and pupillage, a twelve-month apprenticeship program in a barrister's chamber or other approved legal organization, the two extra stages needed after obtaining a law degree to become a barrister. A solicitor does not need to go through these two stages and only needs to do a one-year full-time legal practice course (LPC).

5. I refer to the individuals who participated in this study interchangeably as "second-generation adults of Nigerian ancestry," "the Nigerian second generation," and "second-generation Nigerians." My preferred term is "the second generation of Nigerian ancestry" because it allows us to discover how they want to be identified, while the other terms seem to assign them a Nigerian or African identity, which is not my intention. But this usage is clumsy, and my use of the other terms should not be read as assigning any specific identity to the second generation.

6. In the United States, the two most influential large-scale studies of the second generation—Children of Immigrants Longitudinal Survey (CILS) and the Immigrant Second Generation in Metropolitan New York—did not include Africans in

their samples. Both surveys have produced influential findings about the second generation (see Kasinitz et al. 2008; Portes and Rumbaut 2001). In Britain, the large-scale Fourth Survey of Ethnic Minorities in Britain did not include black Africans (see Modood, Beishon, and Virdee 1994; Modood et al. 1997). Other notable works on the black second generation that focus solely on the Caribbean second generation are Back 1996; Butterfield 2004; Foner 2011; Portes and Zhou 1993; Warikoo 2011; Waters 1999; and Zephir 2001.

7. I use education as my indicator for class in this book, following the example of prominent scholars such as Robert Putnam (2015) and Douglas Massey (2007). Many indicators for class are used in the social sciences; education, income, occupation, wealth, socioeconomic status (which is usually a composite index of occupational prestige, education, and income), and culture, as well as self-reports. Some of these indices such as occupation, income, and education are closely correlated, although there are cases where an individual might have a high income but a low educational level and/or occupational prestige. Studies on intergenerational mobility show that education is the strongest predictor of a child's social mobility. For individuals, education is also the strongest predictor of the type of occupation held, likelihood of entering the middle class (in terms of occupational prestige and income), and ability to withstand the vicissitudes of the labor market. In terms of the latter, a college graduate who loses his or her job during a recession or labor market restructuring is more likely to get another job that provides an income that keeps him or her in the middle class than an individual with a high school or less than high school diploma. Massey (2007) also operationalizes social class by education. He defines class as "access to human capital—or more specifically, education, the most important resource in today's knowledge based economy" (2007, 252). In addition, education is preferred as an indicator of class over income, because income data tend to contain more errors or missing information: individuals are more likely to lie about how much they earn or refuse to proffer the information.

Consequently, like Putnam (2015), when I talk about middle-class individuals, I am referring to individuals who are college graduates, i.e., who have at least a bachelor's degree. I confirmed with respondents that their own use of "class" was consistent with this definition. As I discuss in chapter 5, some respondents attached some behavioral and attitudinal characteristics to this baseline definition of being middle class.

8. Ogbu 1978, 1987; Ogbu and Simons 1998; Portes and Rumbaut 2001; Portes and Zhou 1993; Waters 1992.

9. Kasinitz et al. 2008.

10. Butterfield 2004; Richards 2008; Zephir 2001.

11. Mittelberg and Waters 1992.

12. For the United States, see U.S. Census Bureau / American FactFinder 2016; For the United Kingdom, see Office for National Statistics Social Survey Division 2015.

13. A diaspora refers to people who have moved from their homelands/countries of origin and settled in a new land.

14. Office for National Statistics 2015a; U.S. Census Bureau / American FactFinder 2016.

15. 2015 IMF Report.

16. I thank John Arthur, a preeminent scholar on African immigrants in the United States, for these insightful comments.

17. Between 1990 and 2000 the African population grew at a pace of 167%, compared to 66.7% for Caribbeans and 13% for African Americans. Between 2000 and 2010, the African population in the United States grew at a rate of 82%, while that of Caribbean blacks increased by only 19% (2010 U.S. Census). According to Waters, Kasinitz, and Asad (2014), at this rate African immigrants are expected to outnumber black Caribbeans by 2050. In Britain, from 2001 to 2011, the African population grew at a rate of 104%. During the same ten-year period, the black Caribbean population remained steady at 1.1% of the total population, increasing by only 29,204 people (2011 U.K. Census). But until now there has been no book-length investigation of second-generation Africans in these countries.

18. My use of the term *black second generation* is strictly descriptive; I am referring to children of immigrants from African and Caribbean nations who have the physical characteristics judged by members of American and British society as denoting their membership in the black racial category. It is in no way intended to reify or essentialize the category.

19. *Proximal hosts* are the group to which new immigrants are assigned in the receiving country—or put another way, the group perceived as the new immigrants' coethnics based on criteria such as race and religion (Mittelberg and Waters 1992, 412–35).

20. Mittelberg and Waters 1992, 412–35.

21. Racialization is both a process of categorization and a practice of racial or cultural discrimination that causes racial/ethnic inequalities. Omi and Winant (2015) define racialization as "emphasiz[ing] how the phenomic, the corporeal dimension of human bodies acquires meaning in social life" (109).

22. In addition to Portes and Zhou 1993 and Portes and Rumbaut 2001, see Ogbu 1978, 1987; Ogbu and Simons 1998; Waters 1999.

23. Schermerhorn 1979, 12.

24. See Lee and Bean 2010; Loewen 1973; Patterson 2005; Vallejo 2012; Yancey 2003.

25. See Kasinitz et al. 2008; Waters, Kasinitz, and Asad 2014.

26. Telles and Ortiz 2008, 15. Ogbu and Simons 1988; Portes and Rumbaut 2001; Portes and Zhou 1993; and Waters 1999 make a similar argument.

27. Isaacs 2008.

28. "Britain" or "Great Britain" refers to the countries of England, Scotland, and Wales, while "United Kingdom" refers to these countries and Northern Ireland. I studied the second generation in Great Britain and not the United Kingdom as none of the second generation who participated in this study were born or lived in

Northern Ireland. I use "Britain" or "Great Britain," except when referring to data (such as the U.K. census) or research on the United Kingdom.

29. This is using the idea of decimal generations in Rumbaut 2004.

30. I discuss in chapter 6 the few instances where generational status made a difference in findings.

31. Among the few exceptions in the United States is Kasinitz et al. 2008, which looked at second-generation adults in New York City. Their sample included West Indians but no second-generation Africans. The studies by Balogun (2011) and Awokoya (2012) look at identity formation among second-generation African adults in university.

32. The majority of the second generation (over 93%) had at least a bachelor's degree and were professionals: doctors, lawyers, engineers, nurses, IT professionals, etc. For the second generation, the majority (over 75%) of their parents had at least a bachelor's degree, but many were not financially well-off, though they possessed middle-class human capital that they transferred to their children.

33. See Arthur 2008, 2010; Vickerman 1999; Waters 1999.

34. From the "I Have a Dream" speech given by the American civil rights activist Rev. Martin Luther King Jr. during the March on Washington for Jobs and Freedom on August 28, 1963.

35. Portes and Rumbaut 2001, 45; my emphasis.

36. Ibid.

37. Chua 2011; Louie 2012; Wu 2015; Zhou and Bankston 1998.

38. Lee and Zhou 2015, 6. "Hyper-selection" refers to a dual positive selectivity where the immigrant group, on average, is more educated than the national average in their country of destination and more educated than the national average in their country of origin.

39. See the work of Vivian Louie (2004, 2012). Also see Lee and Zhou 2015.

40. Wu 2015.

41. Ibid.

42. Bashi Treitler 2013; Kim 1999; Wu 2014.

43. *Institutional racism* is defined as institutional practices that, however unintentionally, have the consequence of systematically operating to the disadvantage of groups seen as racially different.

44. Kim 1999.

45. These scholars offer a cultural explanation for these groups' remarkable achievements and identify three attributes they have in common: (1) a superiority complex, which is a deeply internalized belief in their group's specialness or exceptionality; (2) insecurity, which they define as anxious uncertainty about one's worth or place in society that spurs one to strive harder; and (3) impulse control, which is the ability to resist the temptation to give up in the face of hardship (Chua and Rubenfeld 2014, 8–10).

46. Portes and Rumbaut 2001, 45.

47. See Lee and Zhou 2015; Louie 2004; Modood 2004; Portes and Rumbaut 2001; Portes and Zhou 1993; Zhou and Bankston 1998.

1. Small 1994.

2. Because the black second generation are my primary focus in this book and because of space constraints, less attention is paid to describing the contexts faced by other nonwhite ethnic minorities in both countries, specifically Hispanics in the United States and South Asians in Britain. Discussion of how the national context also affects these groups is tangential. Discussions of the second generation of other ethnic and racial groups are introduced in subsequent chapters when they can lend some crucial analytic insight to understanding the experiences of the black second generation, the second generation of Nigerian/African ancestry in particular.

3. According to the 2010 census, 72.4% of the United States population is white; 12.6%, black or African American; 4.8%, Asian; 0.9%, Native American/Indian; 0.2%, Native Pacific/Hawaiian Islanders; and 6.2%, some other race. Hispanics, who are seen as an ethnic rather than a racial category make up 16.4% of the population. The 2011 U.K census gives the following numbers: 87.1% of the population is white; 6.9%, Asians or Asian British (Indians, 2.3%; Pakistanis, 1.9%; Bangladeshi, 0.7%; Chinese, 0.7%; other Asian, 1.4%; black Britons (a category that consists of black Caribbeans, 1.1%; Africans, 1.7%; black other, 0.2%), 3.0%. The mixed other group in the United Kingdom constitutes 2%.

4. See, to name a few, Bashi Treitler 2013; Bashi and McDaniel 1997; Fryer 1984; Gilroy 1992, 2005; Goulbourne 1998; Pilkington 1994, 2003; Small 1994; Solomos 2003; Steinberg 2001; Telles and Ortiz 2008.

5. Cornell and Hartmann 2007.

6. Omi and Winant 2015, 111.

7. Lacy 2007; Patillo-McCoy 1999.

8. Iceland 2009; Massey and Denton 1993.

9. See, to name a few, Alexander 2010; Charles 2006; Massey and Denton 1993; Pager 2007; Pilkington 1994, 2003; Shapiro and Oliver 2006; Western 2004; Williams and Mohammed 2009.

10. Goulbourne 1998; Omi and Winant 1994; Small 1994; Solomos 2003.

11. Alexander 2010; Goulbourne 1998; Pager 2007; Solomos 2003.

12. Gilroy 2005; Massey and Denton 1993; Omi and Winant 1994.

13. Patterson 2005.

14. See Lee and Bean 2010 and Yancey 2003 for a discussion of the black/non-black color line. See Bonilla-Silva 2004 for a discussion of the tri-racial system that consists of whites, honorary whites, and collective blacks.

15. The use of the term has been criticized as meaningless because South Asians do not define themselves as black. Another criticism is that usage of the term conceals the cultural needs of groups other than those of African and Caribbean origin. See Brah 1993, 197–98. However as Brah notes, during the time it was widely used, the term *black* showed the politics of solidarity between Asians, Caribbeans, and Africans.

16. Brah 1993. She argues that the term *black* became "a political color to be worn with pride against color-based racisms" (197).

17. Bashi Treitler 2013.

18. Gilroy 2004, 102.

19. Alba and Foner 2008; Zolberg and Woon 1999.

20. Modood 2004; Omi and Winant 2015; Tuan 1998; Vickerman 2007; Waters 1999.

21. Omi and Winant 2015.

22. Alba and Nee 2003; Telles and Ortiz 2008, 15.

23. Omi and Winant 1994, 22, 29.

24. Ibid., 22.

25. Ibid.

26. Omi and Winant 1994, 23.

27. See Majors 2001; Modood 2004; Portes and Rumbaut 2001; Portes and Zhou 1993; Sewell and Sowell 1978, 1981.

28. See Modood 2004, 101–2.

29. Pierre 2004, 148.

30. Carter 2005; Gilroy 1992, 2005; Lacy 2007; Lee and Bean 2010; Modood 2004.

31. Alexander 2010; Charles 2006; Massey and Denton 1993; Pager 2007; Shapiro and Oliver 2013.

32. See Ogbu 1987; Ogbu and Simons 1998; Portes and Rumbaut 2001; Waters 1999. The article by Pierre (2004) offers a comprehensive critique of how academic scholarship portrays African Americans and their culture. In Britain, see Modood 2004. Foner (2011) argues that in Britain, black Caribbeans are seen as the country's native blacks, while African Americans are America's native blacks.

33. Modood 2004, 87.

34. Ibid., 102.

35. Ibid.

36. Ibid.

37. Neckerman, Carter, and Lee 1999, 949.

38. Kasinitz et al. 2008; Massey, Duran, and Malone 2003.

39. See Mittelberg and Waters 1992; Modood 2004; Portes and Rumbaut 2001; Waters 1999; Portes and Zhou 1993.

40. Portes and Rumbaut 2001, 271.

41. See the powerful critique of segmented assimilation theory in the article by Neckerman, Carter, and Lee (1999); also see Noguera 2004.

42. Portes and Rumbaut 2001; Portes and Zhou 1993; Telles and Ortiz 2008.

43. Telles and Ortiz 2008, 15.

44. Portes and Rumbaut 2001; Portes and Zhou 1993.

45. Kasinitz et al. 2008.

46. Ibid., 82.

47. Telles and Ortiz 2008; Vallejo 2012.

48. Smith 2003, 319.

49. Jiménez 2010a; Telles and Ortiz 2008; Vallejo 2012.

50. Kim 1999; Lee and Bean 2010; Tuan 1998.

51. Kim 1999; Tuan 1998.

52. Telles and Ortiz 2008.

53. Portes and Rumbaut 2001.

54. Mittelberg and Waters 1992; Waters 1999.

55. Waters 1999. The immigrant identity was held mostly by youths who had recently arrived in the United States. Waters writes, "They did not feel as much pressure to 'choose' between identifying with or distancing from black Americans as did either the American or ethnic respondents and . . . were neutral toward American distinctions between ethnics and Black Americans. They tended to stress their nationality or birth place as defining their ethnicity" (302).

56. Numerous studies on the nonwhite second generation have concluded that many of them are better off remaining ethnic. These studies argued that for today's second generation staying ethnic and resisting certain kinds of Americanization may be the key to upward social mobility. Those who remained tied to their parents communities and networks were more likely to be successful than their ethnic counterparts who become Americanized. See Gibson 1988; Matute-Bianchi 1991; Suárez-Orozco 1987.

57. Waters 1999, 307.

58. Balogun 2011.

59. Richards 2008; Smith 2008; Weiner and Richards 2008.

60. Imoagene 2012; Richards 2008; Zephir 2001.

61. Awokoya 2012; Balogun 2011; Butterfield 2004; Kibona-Clark 2009; Richards 2008; Warikoo 2011.

62. Arthur 2010.

63. Mittelberg and Waters 1992.

64. Kasinitz et al. 2008.

65. Modood et al. 1997.

66. Hutnik 1991, 134.

67. Lam and Smith 2009; Modood, Beishon, and Virdee 1994.

68. Bashi Treitler 2013.

69. Lacy 2007; Patillo-McCoy 1999; Lareau 2003.

70. Cohen 1999.

71. Greer 2013; Smith 2014; Rogers 2006; Kasinitz 1992.

72. See Smith 2014 for a nice discussion of what the black racial identity means. See also Bashi Treitler 2012; Bashi and McDaniels 1997; Greer 2013.

73. Alba 2009; Hochschild et al. 2013; Lee and Bean 2010.

74. From the 2006 Nigerian census, Nigeria's total population was 142 million. The 2015 population estimate is from the CIA World Fact Book.

75. CIA World Fact Book 2015; Central Bank of Nigeria 2010.

76. CIA World Fact Book 2015.

77. Nigeria National Bureau of Statistics 2008.

78. As defined in the 2006 Nigerian census, a literate person is someone who can read and write with understanding a short and simple statement about his or her

daily life in any language (local or foreign). Nigeria counts its literate population from those over the age of six. According to the 2006 census, 113 million individuals of a total population of 142 million were over the age of six. Of 113 million people, 76 million were literate.

79. In Nigeria, 36% of the literate population had no formal educational qualifications; 13% had attended only nursery school; 12% had attended only primary school; 29% had some secondary school or high school diploma. With respect to higher education, 4.3 million Nigerians have a university bachelor's degree (3.8%) and 905,283 (0.7%) have postgraduate degrees.

80. U.S. Census Bureau / American FactFinder 2016.

81. Office for National Statistics 2015a; Office for National Statistics Social Survey Division 2015.

82. Nigeria belongs to what is known as the "Slave Coast" in West Africa, so if seen in this light Nigerians have been in the United States since the seventeenth century.

83. The purpose of these scholarships was to prepare Africans for eventual self-government and create ties with future African leaders. Ette 2012; Fafunwa 1971.

84. Ette 2012; Fafunwa 1971.

85. Nigeria's National Bureau of Statistics 2010 Nigerian Socio-Economic Survey.

86. There is some debate among immigration scholars whether remittances really spur development because most of the money remitted back home is spent on basic consumption and frequently imported consumer goods.

87. In 2007, $16 billion were remitted back to Nigeria. The amount jumped to $40 billion in 2008 and climbed to $42 billion in 2009. The amount of money remitted and classified by the Central Bank of Nigeria as private and home remittances dropped to $38 billion in 2009 and then crept up to $41 billion in 2010. I obtained these figures from the Central Bank of Nigeria in Abuja, Nigeria, in 2012. It is not clear whether these huge amounts include foreign private investments in Nigeria. I was told they did not, but the CBN figures are multiple times larger than the remittance figures compiled by the World Bank for Nigeria. But what is definite is that the CBN and World Bank figures do not capture remittances sent through private channels. All figures are in U.S. dollars.

88. However, many Nigerians had been holding two or even three passports for many years prior to the passage of this law.

89. According to the American Community Survey 2010, 73.4% of Africans were black, 20% were white, and 2% were Asian.

90. Pew Research Center; see Anderson 2015.

91. According to the Migration Policy Institute 2016b.

92. The source for all data in this paragraph is the Migration Policy Institute (2016b).

93. Nigerians' share of the African population has fallen. In 1980 they comprised 37% of the black African population, and in 1990 they comprised 30% of all black African immigrants in the United States.

94. RAD Diaspora Profile, Migration Policy Institute 2016a.

95. Ibid.

96. American Community Survey and Current Population Survey 2014.

97. Ette 2012.

98. Ibid.

99. Ibid.

100. American Community Survey 2014.

101. Chua and Rubenfeld 2014.

102. In the Bronx, Nigerians are found in low- to middle-income neighborhoods that are 40% to over 50% black. In Brooklyn, the largest concentration of Nigerians is in East New York, which is low income and as of 2010 approximately 51% non-Hispanic black, 37% Hispanic, 6.4% Asian, and 1.9% non-Hispanic white. In the 2013 Newest New Yorkers report, "census tracts with a median household income in 25th percentile or lower were labeled lower income, while those in the 75th percentile or higher were categorized as upper income. For New York City, this translated into a median household income under $35,800 for lower income neighborhoods, and above $69,500 for upper income neighborhoods" (NYC Planning 2013, 151).

103. NYC Planning 2013.

104. Ibid.

105. U.K. Census 2001, 2011.

106. Rienzo and Vargas-Silva 2016.

107. In 2005, 56% of Nigerian students got A* to C grades on five or more GCSEs, compared to 55% of white British children and 42% of Black Caribbean students. In 2012, their performance improved to 78% getting A* to C grades on five or more GCSEs, outperforming the national average by 18 percentage points.

108. 2014 British Labor Force Survey.

109. Africans are the largest minority ethnic group in the wards of Peckham in Southwark, Evelyn in Lewisham, and Hackney in King's Park, but residents in these wards are not trapped because there is significant dispersal of ethnic residents out of these neighborhoods into other wards in London and Britain. In King's Park, there was significant net migration into the borough by both ethnic minority and white residents, showing that white residents were not hesitant to move into the area. In 2001 the average index of dissimilarity in Britain for ethnic minorities was about 60, which is the same for the white population. The dissimilarity index score is the percentage of one of the two groups included in the calculation (in this case the ethnic minority group) that would have to move to different geographic areas in order to produce a distribution that matches that of the larger area. According to the 2001 census, the index was highest for Pakistanis (71.7), Bangladeshis (71.6), and Africans (70.6). And the index of dissimilarity for all ethnic minority groups declined over the ten-year period between 1991 and 2001, indicating that ethnic minorities were not marooned in these areas of concentrated ethnic minority populations but were moving out into less ethnically concentrated neighborhoods in Britain.

110. Peckham and Nunhead Community Profile, Southwark Council. http://www.southwark.gov.uk/downloads/download/3861/peckham_and_nunhead_

community_council_area_profile. The report was generated from the 2011 U.K. Census.

111. For example, it ranks in the bottom 25% of all London boroughs in proportion of working age people who are unemployed, homelessness acceptances, proportion of working age population receiving out-of-work benefits, and proportion of nineteen-year-olds without level 3 qualifications. London's Poverty Profile 2016.

112. Ibid.

113. BBC online, "Nigerian London." www.bbc.co.uk/london/content /articles/2005/05/26/nigerian_london_feature.shtml.

114. Muttarak 2004.

115. Ibid. Intermarriage rates for second-generation black Africans compared to first- generation black Africans: for men, first generation = 11.2%; second generation = 20.9%. For women, first generation = 8.3%; second generation = 9.6%. For black Caribbeans, first-generation men = 27.1%; second-generation men = 47.1%. For women, first generation = 16.0%; second generation = 29.0%.

116. Because the 2011 U.K. Census reports educational profile of individuals 16 years old and above, it finds that 56.3% of Nigerian immigrants over the age of 16 have at least a bachelor's degree. I have chosen to use the 2014 British Labor Force Survey's data on education because I can calculate tables for adults over the age of 25, making the data comparable to the U.S. data.

117. The General Household Survey asked country of birth and nativity questions.

118. Arthur 2010.

119. I used Goldthorpe's (1992) 7-class schema plus a variation of it as developed by Heath and McMahon (2005) to classify respondents' and parents' occupation. Horizontal mobility comes into play because Goldthorpe's class schema is only partially ranked. I agree with Heath and McMahon (2005, 400) that classes 2, 3, 4, and 5, routine nonmanual, petty bourgeois, farming, and skilled manual classes respectively, "are all at broadly similar levels." They are lower than positions in the service class but higher than unskilled manual workers and agricultural laborers. Thus upward mobility occurs when movement occurs from class 6 (semi-skilled to unskilled manual workers) and class 7 (agricultural laborers) to any of the higher classes and when movement occurs from classes 2, 3, 4, and 5 to class 1 (the service class). Downward mobility is the opposite. Being stable is when the subject remains in the class position held by his or her father. Horizontal mobility occurs when movement is between classes 6 and 7 or between classes 2, 3, 4, and 5.

120. I did not elicit detailed information of neighborhoods to be able to geocode my data on respondents' neighborhood—i.e., match it to U.S. census information. So it is impossible for me to give precise information on racial composition, degree of residential segregation, or poverty or affluence of the neighborhood. However, I did ask my respondents about the racial composition of their neighborhoods, along with the city or cities and states they had lived in.

121. McLanahan 2002.

122. Author's analysis of the Early Childhood Longitudinal Survey (ECLS-K) restricted sample.

123. Glick Schiller, Basch, and Blanc-Szanton 1995, 50.

124. Nursing was the most common/modal occupation of mothers of respondents interviewed in this study.

CHAPTER TWO. "YOU ARE NOT LIKE ME!"

1. Mittelberg and Waters 1992, 413. We see evidence of the ethnicity paradigm in operation, as Mittelberg and Waters conflate race and ethnicity as the same thing for the black (Haitian) immigrants.

2. Ibid., 416.

3. Ibid.

4. The title of the speech comes from the line, "As I look ahead, I am filled with foreboding; like the Roman, I seem to see 'the River Tiber foaming with much blood.'"

5. Pilkington 2003.

6. These groups are seen regardless of the racial or ethnic composition as part of the different waves of the African diaspora, with contemporary African immigrants being the most recent wave and forming the postcolonial African diaspora. For more about the different waves of the African diaspora and the linkages between the groups, see Zeleza 2009.

7. African refugees seem to be the exception, especially if they are African Muslims. The response of British and American natives has been hostile in several cities.

8. Ispa-Landa 2014. Ispa-Landa studied black teenagers in the MECO program in Boston and found that black boys are having an easier time assimilating into the suburban, predominantly white schools. They have white girlfriends, while the black girls do not have white boyfriends but instead are isolated. In this arena, the experiences of African and African American girls were similar, even though boundaries of different black ethnicities were being drawn.

9. But this view is not limited to Britain and the United States. Even in Africa, and focusing here on Nigeria, white people tend to be highly esteemed—sometimes more than similarly deserving blacks. Biracial children (with one white and one black parent) are often very popular in schools and in their neighborhoods. Among darker-complexioned women, there is widespread use of bleaching creams to lighten the skin; some men also use bleaching creams. In many minds, taking such measures makes these people more attractive. These bleachings, straightenings, and other actions to achieve an idealized (white) standard of beauty happen not only in the United States and Britain but also play out in different forms in other parts of the world, including Africa.

10. One of the legacies of slavery, it has been argued by Jan Rogozinski (2000) is that blacks with white blood are preferred by both whites and other blacks and enjoy a higher status than their darker-skinned brethren.

Orlando Patterson (1982) argues that in slave societies, domestic slaves who lived in and near the homestead had higher status than plantation field slaves because they were viewed as being closer to the seat of power, the white slave owner. In the same vein, "mulatto" children born of black female slaves and white men had a higher social status and many were freed by their white fathers. The end result of these developments is that in the past and still in present-day former slave societies lighter-skinned blacks have higher social status; they are more likely to be upwardly mobile, and they have better life chances than darker-skinned blacks.

11. This practice is dying out in cities and among the middle and upper classes.

12. Bashi Treitler 2004. Bashi Treitler argues that we can see an antiblack position in most Western advanced democracies that is manifested in their restrictive policies on black immigrants, specifically immigration policies.

13. Kasinitz et al. 2008, 319.

14. Ibid., 318.

15. See also Waters 1999.

16. Frazier 1957; Lacy 2007; Landry 1987; Pattillo-McCoy 1999; Rollock et al. 2015.

CHAPTER THREE. "IT'S UN-NIGERIAN NOT TO GO TO COLLEGE"

1. See the powerful critique of segmented assimilation theory in Neckerman, Carter, and Lee 1999; also see Noguera 2004. As discussed in chapter 1, this is also the view held by Tariq Modood about blacks in Britain.

2. See Lee and Zhou 2014, 2015; Louie 2004; Modood 2004; Portes and Rumbaut 2001; Portes and Zhou 1993; Zhou and Bankston 1998.

3. Blau and Duncan 1967; Haveman and Wolfe 1995; Steelman and Powell 1989; Teachman 1987.

4. Blau and Duncan 1967; Heath and McMahon 1997, 2005.

5. Coleman 1988.

6. Borjas (1992) found in his empirical study of the effects of ethnic capital on intergenerational mobility that ethnic capital has a positive and significant impact on the educational attainment of respondents in the GSS, holding constant the fathers' educational attainment. A one-year increase in the average schooling level of an ethnic group increases the average schooling of the next generation by about 0.2 years. He also found that ethnic capital plays as important role as the father's human capital in determining the skills of the next generation (137). He also argues that the significant role played by ethnic capital in the intergenerational transmission process delays the economic convergence of ethnic groups across generations.

7. Borjas 1992, 125–26.

8. Ibid.

9. Kao and Tienda 1995.

10. There is an achievement gap between whites and blacks in reading and math scores in average grade point average (GPA); in passing rates on standardized exams;

in high school graduation rates; and in both high school and college drop-out rates. National Center for Education Statistics 2013.

11. National Center for Education Statistics 2013.

12. Hills et al. 2010.

13. See John Ogbu and his collaborator in cultural ecology theory (Ogbu 1987; Ogbu and Simons 1998) and Alejandro Portes's and his collaborators thesis on the negative consequences of reactive ethnicity on academic performance (Portes and Rumbaut 2001; Portes and Zhou 1993).

14. Carter 2005, 7.

15. Ogbu and Simons 1998.

16. Ibid.

17. Stepick 1998; Warikoo 2011, 10; Waters 1999.

18. Carter 2005.

19. See Sewell 1997; Sewell and Majors 2001; Small 1994; Solomos 2003.

20. Ainsworth-Darnell and Downey 1998; Morgan and Methta 2004.

21. Carter 2005.

22. Ibid., 12–13.

23. Warikoo 2011.

24. Carter 2005; Imoagene 2008; Noguera 2004; Warikoo 2011.

25. Imoagene 2008; Pew Research Center, www.pewsocialtrends.org /2015/04/09/chapter-1-statistical-portrait-of-the-u-s-black-immigrant-population/.

26. Cheung and Heath 2007; Hills et al. 2010; Modood 2004.

27. Chua 2011; Louie 2012; Zhou and Bankston 1998.

28. See Louie 2004, 2012; see also Zhou and Lee 2015.

29. Carter 2005; Lee and Zhou 2014; Louie 2012.

30. Excerpt from an interview with Vivien Louie by Rohan Mascarenhas, Russell Sage Foundation, about her book, *Keeping the Immigrant Bargain,* September 10, 2012, www.russellsage.org/news/immigrant-success-america-interview-vivian-louie.

31. Louie 2012.

32. Ibid.; see also Kasinitz et al. 2008.

33. Lee and Zhou 2014.

34. Ibid., 3.

35. Ibid., 4.

36. Ibid.

37. A similar scenario is a second-generation Laotian from a very poor background who benefits from higher teacher expectations and differential treatment because of the racial stereotype that obscures the heterogeneity among Asian groups and sees Asian Americans as high-achieving model minorities.

38. Coleman 1988.

39. Schermerhorn 1979.

40. Lareau 2003.

41. Lee and Zhou 2014, 2015; Modood 2004; Shah, Dwyer, and Modood 2010.

42. Mason 2000; Pilkington 2003.

43. Portes and Rumbaut make a similar point in their book *Legacies* (2001).

44. Lee and Zhou 2014, 2015.

45. Carter 2005; Warikoo 2011; Ainsworth-Darnell and Downey 1998.

46. Carter 2005; Warikoo 2011.

47. Lareau 2003.

48. Chua 2011; Lee and Zhou 2014, 2015; Modood 2004; Shah, Dwyer, and Modood 2010; Zhou 2005; Zhou and Bankston 1998.

49. Lee and Zhou 2015, 70–89.

50. Ibid.

CHAPTER FOUR. FORGING A DIASPORIC NIGERIAN ETHNICITY IN THE UNITED STATES AND BRITAIN

1. Portes and Rumbaut 2001, 148.

2. Ibid., 148–49.

3. Bourdieu 1986, 243.

4. Ibid., 244.

5. In Nigeria, many of the second generation would be called *akata* because in this context they would be foreigners, but in America and Britain these terms are used to draw symbolic cultural and moral boundaries against African Americans and British Caribbeans.

6. Studies on the second generation in the United States find that parents worry that they will lose their children to American ways. See Awokoya 2012; Portes and Rumbaut 2001; Suárez-Orozco and Suárez-Orozco 2001; Waters 1999.

7. Lareau (2003) found that children of middle-class parents were raised according to the logic of concerted cultivation, which encourages children to negotiate with adults in positions of authority, including their parents.

8. Coleman 1988.

9. Lacy 2007.

10. Waters 1999.

11. Cornell and Hartmann 2007; Jenkins 2008.

12. Barth 1969; Cornell and Hartmann 2007; Jenkins 2008; Tilly 2006.

13. CIA World Fact Book 2015.

14. Lamont 1992, 4.

15. Greer 2013; Rogers 2006; Waters 1999.

16. Modood et al. 1997.

17. Feagin and Sikes 1994; PEW Research Center 2008.

18. A recent book by Chua and Rubenfeld (2014) includes Nigerians among the most successful cultural groups in the United States.

19. See, e.g., Bashi Treitler 2013; Lieberson 1981; Loewen 1977.

20. Followers of Rastafarianism wear dreadlocks in the Caribbean. It is seen as partly a desire to reconnect with African roots. African Americans co-opted dread-

locks as a way to celebrate their blackness. Among Nigerians, dreadlocks have negative symbolic meaning. A special ceremony has to be conducted for children with matted hair before the hair is cut for fear of the child dying. This tradition is observed among southwestern Nigerians, especially the Yoruba. Natural dreadlocks have fetish undertones. Consequently, southern Nigerians do not see dreadlocks as fashionable and frown at Nigerians who adopt the style. Dreadlocks are an example of a symbol that has different meanings for three different black groups and is an illustration of the different contexts of blackness in which these groups operate.

21. Ignatiev 1995; Lieberson 1981; Roediger 1994, 2005.

22. Loewen 1977; Wu 2015.

23. Foner 2000, 226.

24. Bashi Treitler 2013; Omi and Winant 2015; Steinberg 2001.

25. Bakalian and Bozorgmehr 2009; Wu 2015.

26. Dodoo 1999.

27. Model 2008.

28. Omi and Winant 2015, 148.

29. Rios 2011.

30. Ibid., 40.

31. Ibid, 81.

32. Omi and Winant 2015, 153.

33. Rollock and Gillborn 2014.

34. Goulbourne and Chamberlain 2001; Modood et al. 1997.

35. Warikoo 2011.

36. For comparative discussions of Caribbeans, African Americans, and Africans in the United States, see Dodoo and Takyi 2002; Logan and Deane 2003. For a discussion of Caribbeans' relative rank among ethnic minorities in Britain, see Cheung and Heath 2007; Hills et al. 2010; Modood et al. 1997.

37. Foner 1979; Steinberg 2001.

38. Greer 2013.

39. Pierre 2004, 150. The authors Pierre identifies in her essay are Mary Waters (1999) and her scholarship on West Indians in New York; Philip Kasinitz in his book *Caribbean New York;* and Milton Vickerman in his book *Crosscurrents.*

40. Chua and Rubenfeld 2014.

41. Chua and Rubenfeld 2014, 8–10. These scholars offer a cultural explanation for these groups' remarkable achievements and identify three attributes they have in common: (1) a superiority complex, which is a deeply internalized belief in their group's specialness or exceptionality; (2) insecurity, which they define as anxious uncertainty about one's worth or place in society, which spurs one to strive harder; and (3) impulse control, which is the ability to resist temptation to give up in the face of hardship a difficult task.

42. He actually said to the crowd in a Houston rally sometime in October 2013, "Have you all noticed, you know, the Nigerian email scammers? They've been a lot less active lately because they've all been hired to run the Obamacare websites."

43. Indeed, in 2015 Nigeria ranked 136 out of 168 countries in Transparency International's Corruption Perception Index.

44. See Barth 1969; Smith 1996.

45. Schermerhorn 1979.

46. Smith 1996, 189.

47. Barth 1969, 14.

48. Bonilla-Silva 2004.

49. Pierre 2004, 158.

50. Morrow 1992.

CHAPTER FIVE. ON THE HORNS OF RACIALIZATION

1. Feagin 1992; Kasinitz et al. 2008; Lacy 2007; Pattillo-McCoy 1999.

2. Ben Carson, a retired neurosurgeon, was the first to successfully separate twins conjoined at the head. He was awarded the Presidential Medal of Freedom by President George W. Bush in 2008. He was one of seventeen candidates for the Republican Party's nomination for president in the 2016 U.S. election.

3. I was still at Harvard University during this time.

4. Dawson 1995.

5. Lacy 2007; Lee and Bean 2010.

6. Neckerman, Carter, and Lee 1999, 946.

7. Brubaker, Loveman, and Stamatov 2004, 39.

8. Ibid.

9. Benjamin 2005; Collins 1997; Feagin and Sikes 1994.

10. Waters 1999.

11. Massey et al. 2003.

12. Greer 2013; Rogers 2004; Waters 1999.

13. Waters 1999.

14. Vickerman 1999.

15. Parrillo and Donaghue 2005. The authors did not indicate whether the scores indicating level of prejudice were statistically significant, but Model (2008) argues that the large sample size of 2,916 makes it likely that they are significant.

16. Waters 1999.

17. Model 2008. Model used queue theory to operationalize the white favoritism thesis. As she explains it, queue theory basically argues that workers are lined up/arranged so that in the eyes of employers members of the most desirable minority stand at the head, members of the second most desirable stand next, etc. Thus, "in a single labor market, the larger the proportion of the labor force ranked below a given group (or the smaller the proportion above), the more successful that group will be" (132).

18. Djamba 1999.

19. Benjamin 2005; Collins 1989; Feagin and Sikes 1994; Fleming, Lamont, and Welburn 2012.

20. Omi and Winant 1994.

21. Portes and Rumbaut 2001; Portes and Zhou 1993; Waters 1999.

22. Greer 2013.

23. Arthur 2000; Greer 2013; Humphries 2009.

24. Kasinitz et al. 2008.

25. See Alba 2009; Myers 2007.

26. Kasinitz et al. 2008.

27. Ibid., 326–27.

28. Kasinitz et al. 2008.

29. Feagin and Sikes 1994, 135.

30. Jackman 1994, 130.

31. However, I found evidence of differentiation in U.S. respondents' racial identity. I found evidence of three types: racial pragmatists, racial coalitionists, and racial conservatives. This finding will be further developed in a forthcoming article.

32. Lacy 2007.

33. Cohen 1999.

34. Wamba 1999.

35. Sean Combs, known as P. Diddy and other names, is a successful rap artist, record label owner, and fashion mogul in the United States.

36. My sample is different from the breakdown in Nigeria where the total population is split 45 percent Christian and 45 percent Muslim and 10 percent traditional religion worshipers. However, most Muslims in Nigeria are from the North—Hausas and Fulanis—and they have extremely low out-migration rates to the United States and the United Kingdom compared to Nigerians from the South—Yorubas and Ibos (see Dustmann and Theodoropoulos 2006).

37. Frazier 1957; Lacy 2007.

38. Lacy 2007; Pattillo-McCoy 1999.

39. Harris and McKenzie 2011.

40. Lee and Bean 2010, 187.

41. Kasinitz et al. 2008.

42. Cheung and Heath (2007, 524) define ethnic penalties as estimates of the extent to which ethnic minorities are disadvantaged in comparison to people belonging to the charter population, in this case whites of British ancestry, who have the same age, educational qualifications, and marital status.

43. Cheung and Heath 2007.

44. Ibid.; Berthoud 2000; Carmichael and Woods 2000; Heath and McMahon 1996.

45. Jackman 1994.

46. Gilroy 1992, 2004.

47. Foner 2011.

48. Gilroy 2005.

49. Gilroy 1992, 2004; Small 1994; Winder 2004.

50. Charles 2006; Finney and Simpson 2009; Massey and Denton 1993; Peach 1996.

51. See Lacy 2007; Pattillo-McCoy 1999.

52. Pew Research Center 2007. Among African Americans, 67 percent say that blacks often or almost always face discrimination when applying for a job, 65 percent say the same about renting an apartment or buying a house, 50 percent say this about eating at restaurants and shopping, and 43 percent say it about applying to a college or university. By contrast, whites, by majorities of two to one or larger, believe blacks rarely face bias in such situations (5).

CHAPTER SIX. FEELING AMERICAN IN AMERICA, NOT FEELING BRITISH IN BRITAIN

1. Modood 1992, 2010; Modood, Beishon, and Virdee 1994; Modood et al. 1997.
2. Jenkins 2008, 5.
3. Ibid.
4. According to Vertovec and Wessendorf (2010), the countries most known for their implementation of policies deemed, officially or not, multicultural are Australia, Canada, the United States, Great Britain, Sweden, and the Netherlands.
5. Kymlicka 2001, 2004, 2010; Parekh 2009; Vertovec and Wessendorf 2010.
6. Bloemraad 2006, 2007; Kymlicka 2001, 2010; Yuval-Davis 2004.
7. Fomina 2006; Phillips 2006; Prins and Saharso 2010; Schlesinger 1991.
8. Kymlicka 2001.
9. Ignatieff 1995; Kymlicka 2001; Tamir 1993.
10. Anderson 1993, 6.
11. Kymlicka 2001, 212.
12. Smith 1996.
13. Yuval-Davis 2004.
14. Ibid.; Handlin 1973; Spillman 1997.
15. Hochschild 2001, 35.
16. Lareau 2003; Levy 1998; MacLeod 1987; Oliver and Shapiro 2006.
17. Primarily from the work of Patterson (2001).
18. Gilroy 1992, 2004, 2005, 2007; Weight 2002. The institutions of slavery and colonialism were maintained on an ideology of white supremacy and black inferiority. Uprisings were often quelled with brutal acts (Rogozinski 2000; Williams 1970). However, these systems of governance were delegitimized after World War II and with the passage of conventions on human rights.
19. Weight 2002, 727.
20. Powell 2002; Weight 2002.
21. Gilroy 2007; Weight 2002.
22. Gilroy 2007, 102, 111.
23. Parekh Report 2000.
24. Cheung and Heath 2007; Heath and McMahon 1996, 2005.
25. Gilroy 2007, 114.

26. It remains to be seen how Britain's national identity will be affected by its exit from the European Union.

27. Cantle Report 2001; Crick Report 1998; Parekh 2009, 39; Parekh Report 2000.

28. Kymlicka 2001, 212.

29. Gordon 1964.

30. The second generation in the United States identified as American or hyphenated American or confidently straddled Nigerian and Nigerian American.

31. Gilroy 2004; Rodney 1972; Williams 1970.

32. Heath and McMahon 1996.

33. Gilroy 2005.

34. Patterson 2001.

35. Modood et al. 1997, 329–31.

36. Lam and Smith 2009.

37. This is Jay-Z's view. Cited in "Jay-Z Becomes a Broadway Producer for 'Fela,'" by Steven Roberts, www.mtv.com/news/articles/1626972/20091124/jay_z.jhtml.

38. Modood, Beishon, and Virdee 1994; Portes and Rumbaut 2001; Portes and Zhou 1993; Stopes-Roe and Cochrane 1990; Tuan 2002.

39. Carter 2005.

40. Foner 2011; Kasinitz et al. 2008; Modood et al. 1997; Richards 2008; Warikoo 2011.

41. I show that for the Nigerian second generation ethnic identities as Nigerian are entangled with a class identity, to the extent that to be Nigerian is to be successful. This raises the question, how would nonsuccessful or non-middle-class second-generation Nigerians identify? I found no difference in respondents' class status and their likelihood to identify or not identify as Nigerian. My sample includes individuals who came from lower- and working-class backgrounds and respondents who have less than a bachelor's degree. None of these respondents were less likely to identify as Nigerian. I attribute the reason their class background does not have an impact on whether or not they identify as Nigerian to the powerful mechanism of cultural embedding (see chapter 4), which ensured that Nigerian values were transmitted from the parental generation to the second generation.

42. Portes and Rumbaut 2001; Roth 2012; Tuan 1998; Waters 1999.

43. Espiritu 1992.

44. Several value points on the axial line are from Parekh 2009, 33.

45. Modood et al. 1997, 330.

46. By "generational cohorts," I mean the 1.5, 1.75, and second generation. By "second-generation subsets," I mean those who had spent all their lives in the United States and Britain versus those who had spent some of their formative years in Nigeria.

47. Regardless of generational status, respondents who have spent significant time in Nigeria engage in transnational activities. They are, in most cases, planning

to live in Nigeria, if not in the near future, then by retirement age. They feel that they belong to Nigeria. Breaking down the sample into generational status subsets, respondents who had spent significant time in Nigeria identified as Nigerian at a higher rate than respondents who had spent no significant time in Nigeria. There was more variation in the primary ethnic choices of the second generation with no time spent in Nigeria. The identification patterns of the 1.75 generation subset are similar to the second generation who spent no significant time in Nigeria, in that only a minority identify as Nigerian. However, the increasing Nigerian and African populations in the United States and Britain, rapid replenishment of those populations with new immigrants, and the mixing of birth and generational cohorts are making the second generation more Nigerian.

Waters and Jiménez (2005) discuss how the mixture of generations and age cohorts affect integration outcomes for the second generation. Jiménez (2010b) discusses how recent immigrants help replenish the ethnicity of later generation immigrants of the same ethnic group.

CONCLUSION

1. Portes and Rumbaut 2001, 45.

2. Haller, Portes, and Lynch 2011a, 736–37.

3. See Espiritu 2002; Modood et al. 1997; Portes and Rumbaut 2001; Stopes-Roe and Cochrane 1990; Tuan 1998, 2002.

4. Min and Kim 2002.

5. Kasinitz et al. 2008; Lee and Zhou 2015; Louie 2004, 2012.

6. Lee and Zhou 2014; Modood 2004.

7. Alba 2009; Lee and Bean 2010; Patterson 2005; Yancey 2003.

8. See Lee and Bean 2010; also see Fryer 1984; Gilroy 1992, 2005; Yancey 2003.

9. See Modood 2004; Portes and Rumbaut 2001; Portes and Zhou 1993; Tuan 1998; Vickerman 2007; Waters 1998.

10. Harris and McKenzie 2011.

11. Pew Research Center 2010.

12. Charles 2006; Logan and Deane 2003; Massey and Denton 1993; Pattillo-McCoy 1999.

13. Pattillo-McCoy 1999.

14. This is an argument made by other studies on the black middle class; see, e.g., Lacy 2007.

15. This study did not focus on how religion might affect the identity formation process of the Nigerian second generation because among those I interviewed being Muslim or Christian did not have a significant impact or differential effect on their identity formation process. None of the Muslim second-generation respondents interviewed proffered a Muslim identity as their primary or strongest identity. I examined my data to see whether religious status played a significant role in how respondents identified and in their assimilation trajectories and did not find any

effects. What I found was that being religious—whether Christian or Muslim—was more likely to lead respondents to have a strong Nigerian-centric self-given primary identity but that there was no difference between Muslims and Christians in their narrations about the critical events that shaped how they identify and their ethnic identification endpoints. I also investigated whether being Muslim affected how respondents viewed America or Britain and found that my Muslim respondents' responses were not appreciably different from my Christian respondents. This might be due to the fact that I had few Muslim respondents in the sample. It is possible that other studies on the adult Nigerian second generation with a larger Muslim sample might discover that religion plays a much more significant role in views of the nation and in identity formation. I expect that religion will play a much greater role in identity formation among the children of African refugees who are also Muslim.

16. Pinder 2013; Yancey 2003.

17. Pinder 2013.

18. Bonilla-Silva 2004.

19. Kim 1999; Pinder 2013.

20. Alba 2009.

21. Modood 2005; Parekh 2009.

22. See, e.g., Fryer 1984; Gilroy 1992, 2005; Modood et al. 1997; Parekh 2009.

23. Pew Research Center 2007.

24. Espiritu 2002; Kibria 2002; Lee and Zhou 2015; Min and Kim 2002; Tuan 2002; Vallejo 2012.

25. Neckerman, Carter, and Lee 1999.

26. Portes and Rumbaut 2001; Telles and Ortiz 2008.

27. Arthur 2010.

REFERENCES

Achebe, Chinua. 1963. *No Longer at Ease*. London: Heinemann.

Ainsworth-Darnell, James, and Douglas Downey. 1998. "Assessing the Oppositional Culture Explanation for Racial/Ethnic Differences in School Performance." *American Sociological Review* 63: 536–53.

Alba, Richard. 2008. "Blurred vs. Bright Boundaries: Second Generation Assimilation and Exclusion in France, Germany, and the United States." *Ethnic and Racial Studies* 28(1): 20–49.

———. 2009. *Blurring the Color Line: The New Chance for a More Integrated America*. Cambridge, MA: Harvard University Press.

Alba, Richard, and Nancy Foner. 2008. "Immigrant Religion in the U.S. and Europe: Bridge or Barrier to Inclusion?" *International Migration Review* 42(2): 369–92.

Alba, Richard, Philip Kasinitz, and Mary C. Waters. 2011. "The Kids are (Mostly) Alright: Second Generation Assimilation, Comments on Haller, Portes and Lynch." *Social Forces* 89(3): 763–74.

Alba, Richard, and Victor Nee. 2003. *Remaking the American Mainstream: Assimilation and Contemporary Immigration*. Cambridge, MA: Harvard University Press.

Alexander, Michelle. 2010. *The New Jim Crow: Mass Incarceration in the Age of Color Blindness*. New York: New Press.

Anderson, Benedict. 1991. *Imagined Communities: Reflections on the Origins of Nationalism*. 2nd ed. London: Verso.

Apraku, Kofi. 1991. *African Émigrés in the United States: A Missing Link in Africa's Social and Economic Development*. New York: Praeger.

Arthur, John. 2000. *Invisible Sojourners: African Immigrant Diaspora in the United States*. Westport, CT: Praeger/Greenwood Press.

———. 2008. *The African Diaspora in the United States and Europe: The Ghanaian Experience*. Aldershot: Ashgate.

———. 2010. *African Diaspora Identities: Negotiating Culture in Transnational Migration*. New York: Lexington.

Arthur, John A., Joseph Takougang, and Thomas Owusu, eds. 2012. *Africans in Global Migration: Searching for Promised Lands*. Aldershot: Ashgate.

Ashmore, Richard D., Kay Deaux, and Tracy Mclaughlin-Volpe. 2004. "An Organizing Framework for Collective Identity: Articulation and Significance of Multidimensionality." *Psychological Bulletin* 130(1): 80–114.

Awokoya, Janet. 2012. "Reconciling Multiple Black Identities: The Case of 1.5 and 2.0 Nigerian Immigrants." In *Africans in Global Migration: Searching for Promised Lands*, ed. John A. Arthur, Joseph Takougang, and Thomas Owusu, 97–116. Lanham, MD: Lexington Books.

Back, Les. 1996. *New Ethnicities and Urban Culture: Racism and Multiculture in Young Lives*. New York: St. Martins.

Balogun, Oluwakemi M. 2011. "No Necessary Tradeoff: Context, Life Course, and Social Networks in the Identity Formation of the Second-Generation Nigerians in the USA." *Ethnicities* 11(4): 436–66.

Bankston III, Carl L. 2004. "Context and Contradictory Consequences." *Sociology of Education* 77(2): 176–79.

Bankston III, Carl L., Stephen J. Caldas, and Min Zhou. 1997. "The Academic Achievement of Vietnamese American Students: Ethnicity as Social Capital." *Sociological Focus* 30: 1–16.

Banton, Miles. 1977. *The Idea of Race*. London: Tavistock.

Barth, Fredrik. 1969a. Introduction to *Ethnic Groups and Boundaries: The Social Organization of Cultural Difference*, ed. Fredrik Barth, 9–38. Boston, MA: Little, Brown.

———. 1969b. "Pathan Identity and Its Maintenance." In *Ethnic Groups and Boundaries: The Social Organization of Culture Difference*, ed. Fredrik Barth, 117–34. Boston, MA: Little, Brown.

Bashi, Vilna, and Antonio McDaniel. 1997. "A Theory of Immigration and Racial Stratification." *Journal of Black Studies* 27(5): 668–82.

Bashi Treitler, Vilna. 2004. "Globalized Anti-Blackness: Transnationalizing Western Immigration Law, Policy, and Practice." *Ethnic and Racial Studies* 27(4): 584–606.

———. 2013. *The Ethnic Project: Transforming Racial Fictions in Ethnic Factions*. Stanford, CA: Stanford University Press.

Batson, Christie D., Zhenchao Qian, and Daniel T. Lichter. 2006. Interracial and Intraracial Patterns of Mate Selection among America's Diverse Black Populations." *Journal of Marriage and Family* 68(August): 658–72.

Bean, Frank D., and Stephanie Bell-Rose, eds. 1999. *Immigration and Opportunity: Race, Ethnicity and Employment in the United States*. New York: Russell Sage Foundation.

Bean, Frank D., Cynthia Feliciano, Jennifer Lee, and Jennifer Van Hook. 2009. "The New U.S. Immigrants; How Do They Affect Our Understanding of the African American Experience?" *Annals of the American Academy of Political and Social Science* 621(January): 202–20.

Bean, Frank D., and Gillian Stevens. 2003. *American's Newcomers and the Dynamics of Diversity*. New York: Russell Sage Foundation.

Benjamin, Lois. 2005. *The Black Elite*. Lanham, MD: Rowman & Littlefield.

Berthoud, R. 2000. "Ethnic Employment Penalties in Britain." *Journal of Ethnic and Migration Studies* 26: 389–416.

Bhattachayyara, G., L. Ison, and M. Blair. 2003. *Minority Ethnic Attainment and Participation in Education and Training: The Evidence*. London: DfES.

Blau, Peter, and Otis Duncan. 1978. *American Occupational Structure*. New York: Free Press.

———. [1967] 2001. "The Process of Stratification." In *Social Stratification: Class, Race & Gender,* ed. David B. Grusky, 390–402. Boulder, CO: Westview Press.

Bloemraad, Irene. 2006. *Becoming a Citizen: Incorporating Immigrants and Refugees in the United States and Canada*. Berkeley: University of California Press.

———. 2007. "Citizenship and Pluralism: The Role of Government in a World of Global Migration." *Fletcher Forum of World Affairs* 31: 1.

Bonilla-Silva, Eduardo. 2004. "From Bi-racial to Tri-racial." *Ethnic and Racial Studies* 27(6): 931–50.

Borjas, George, J. 1985. "Assimilation, Changes in Cohort Quality, and the Earnings of Immigrants." *Journal of Labor Economics* 3(4): 463–89.

———. 1987. "Self-Selection and the Earnings of Immigrants." *American Economic Review* 77(4): 531–53.

———. 1992."Ethnic Capital and Intergenerational Mobility." *Quarterly Journal of Economics* 107(1): 123–50.

Bourdieu, Pierre. 1986. "Forms of Capital." In *Handbook of Theory and Research for the Sociology of Education,* ed. J. Richardson, 241–58. New York: Greenwood Press.

Brah, Anthony. 1996. *Cartographies of Diaspora: Contesting Identities*. London: Routledge.

Brah, Avtar. 1993. "Difference, Diversity, Differentiation: Processes of Racialisation and Gender." In *Racism and Migration in Western Europe,* ed. John Solomos and John Wrench, 195–214. Oxford: Berg.

British Broadcasting Corporation Online. 2014. "Nigerian London." 13 November. www.bbc.co.uk/london/content/articles/2005/05/26/nigerian_london_feature .shtml.

Brown, Jacqueline Nassy. 2005. *Dropping Anchor, Setting Sail: Geographies of Race in Black Liverpool*. Princeton, NJ: Princeton University Press.

Brubaker, Rogers. 2009. "Ethnicity, Race, and Nationalism." *Annual Review of Sociology* 35: 21–42.

Brubaker, Rogers, and Frederick Cooper. 2000. "Beyond 'Identity.'" *Theory and Society* 29(1): 1–47.

Brubaker, Rogers, Mara Loveman, and Peter Stamatov. 2004. "Ethnicity as Cognition." *Theory and Society* 33: 31–64.

Bryce-Laporte, R. S. 1972. "Black Immigrants: The Experience of Invisibility and Inequality." *Journal of Black Studies* 3: 29–56.

Butterfield, Sherri-Ann. 2004. "'We're Just Black': The Racial and Ethnic Identities of Second Generation West Indians in New York." In *Becoming New Yorkers:*

Ethnographies of the New Second Generation, ed. Philip Kasinitz, John H. Mollenkopf, and Mary C. Waters, 288–312. New York: Russell Sage Foundation.

Cantle Report. 2001. *Community Cohesion: A Report of the Independent Review Team.* Chair Ted Cantle. London: Home Office.

Capps, Randy, Kristen McCabe, and Michael Fix. 2011. *New Streams: Black African Migration to the United States.* Washington, DC: Migration Policy Institute.

Carmichael, F., and R. Woods. 2000. "Ethnic Penalties in Unemployment and Occupational Attainment: Evidence for Britain." *International Review of Applied Economics* 14: 71–98.

Carter, Prudence. 2005. *Keepin' It Real: School Success beyond Black and White.* New York: Oxford University Press.

Casanova, Jose. 2009. "Immigration and the New Religious Pluralism: A European Union–United States Comparison." In *Secularism, Religion and Multicultural Citizenship,* ed. Geoffrey Brahm Levey and Tariq Modood, 139–63. Cambridge: Cambridge University Press.

Charles, Camille Zubrinsky. 2003. "The Dynamics of Racial Residential Segregation." *Annual Review of Sociology* 29(1): 167–207.

———. 2006. *Won't You Be My Neighbor? Class, Race, and Residence in Los Angeles.* New York: Russell Sage Foundation.

CIA World Factbook. 2015. Washington, DC: Central Intelligence Agency.

Central Bank of Nigeria. Annual Report and Statement of Accounts for the Year Ended 2010. Lagos: Central Bank of Nigeria.

Cheng, Yuan. 1997. "The Chinese: Upwardly Mobile." In *Ethnicity in the 1991 Census: The Ethnic Minority Populations of Great Britain,* vol. 2, ed. Ceri Peach, 161–80. London: HMSO.

Cheung, Sin Yi, and Anthony Heath. 2007. "Nice Work If You Can Get it: Ethnic Penalties in Great Britain." In *Unequal Chances: Ethnic Minorities in Western Labor Markets,* ed. Anthony F. Heath and Sin Yi Cheung with Shawna Smith, 507–50. Oxford: Oxford University Press.

Chin, Margaret M. 2005. *Sewing Women: Immigrants and the New York City Garment Industry.* New York: Columbia University Press.

Chiswick, Barry. 1978. "The Effect of Americanization on the Earnings of Foreign-Born Men." *Journal of Political Economy* 86(5): 897–921.

Christian, M. 2005. "The Politics of Black Presence in Britain and Black Male Exclusion in the British Education System." *Journal of Black Studies* 35(3): 327–46.

Chua, Amy. 2011. *Battle Hymn of the Tiger Mother.* New York: Penguin Press.

Chua, Amy, and Jed Rubenfeld. 2014. *The Triple Package: How Three Unlikely Traits Explain the Rise and Fall of Cultural Groups in America.* New York: Penguin Press.

Cohen, Cathy J. 1999. *The Boundaries of Blackness: AIDS and the Breakdown of Black Politics.* Chicago: University of Chicago Press.

Cohen, Phil. 2002. "Psychoanalysis and Racism: Reading the Other Scene." In *A Companion to Racial and Ethnic Studies,* ed. D. T. Goldberg and John Solomos, 170–201. Oxford: Blackwell.

Cohen, Robin. 1994. *Frontiers of Identity: The British and the Others.* Harlow: Longman.

Coleman, David, and John Salt, eds. 1997. *Ethnicity in the 1991 Census: Demographic Characteristics of the Ethnic Minority Populations.* London: HMSO.

Coleman, James. 1988. "Social Capital in the Creation of Human Capital." *American Journal of Sociology* 94: 95–120.

Collins, Sharon M. 1989. "The Marginalization of Black Executives." *Social Problems* 36: 317–31.

———. 1993. "Blacks on the Bubble: The Vulnerability of Black Executives in White Corporations." *Sociological Quarterly* 34(3): 429–47.

———. 1997. *Black Corporate Executives: The Making and Breaking of a Black Middle Class.* Philadelphia, PA: Temple University Press.

Conley, Dalton. 1999. *Being Black, Living in the Red: Race, Wealth, and Social Policy in America.* Berkeley: University of California Press.

Cornell, Stephen, and Douglas Hartmann. 2007. *Ethnicity and Race: Making Identities in a Changing World.* London: Pine Forge Press.

Crick Report. 1998. *Education for Citizenship and the Teaching of Democracy in Schools.* London: Qualifications and Curriculum Authority [QCA].

Croom, Adam M. 2011. "Slurs." *Language Sciences* 33: 343–58.

———. 2013. "How to Do Things with Slurs: Studies in the Way of Derogatory Words." *Language & Communication* 33: 177–204.

Dalal, Farhad. 2002. *Race, Colour and the Process of Racialization: New Perspectives from Group Analysis, Psychoanalysis and Sociology.* Hove: Brunner-Routledge.

Daley, Patricia. 1997. "Black-African: Students Who Stayed." In *Ethnicity in the 1991 Census: The Ethnic Minority Populations of Great Britain,* vol. 2, ed. Ceri Peach, 44–65. London: HMSO.

Demi, F. 2001. "Ethnic and Gender Differences in Educational Achievement and Implications for School Improvement Strategies." *Educational Research* 43 (1): 91–106.

Demireva, Neli. 2006. "Examining the Differential Job Search Methods of Ethnic Groups in the U.K.: How First and Second Generation LFS Subjects of Immigrant Descent Use Their Social Resources and Institutional Settings to Overcome Labor Market Disadvantage?" Paper presented at the Harvard Oxford Stockholm Conference, Oxford University, April 22–24.

Department of Education and Skills (DfES). 2003. *Aiming High: Raising the Achievement of African Caribbean Pupils: Guidance for Schools.* London: DfES.

———. 2004. "Permanent Exclusions from Schools and Exclusion Appeals, England 2002/2003." Provisional report. DfES, London.

Devine, Fiona. 1997. *Social Class in America and Britain.* Edinburgh: Edinburgh University Press.

Djamba, Yanyi K. 1999. "African Immigrants in the United States: A Socio-Demographic Profile in Comparison to Native Blacks." *Journal of Asian and African Studies* 34(2): 210–15.

Dodoo, F. Nii-Amoo. 1997. "Assimilation Differences among Africans in America." *Social Forces* 76(2): 527–46.

Dodoo, F. Nii-Amoo, and Baffour K. Takyi. 2002. "Africans in the Diaspora: Black-White Earnings Differences among America's Africans." *Ethnic and Racial Studies* 25(6): 913–41.

Dodoo, Frank. 1991. "Earnings Differences among Blacks in America." *Social Science Research* 20(2): 93–108.

Dowell, Myers. 2007. *Immigrants and Boomers: Forging a New Social Contract for the Future of America.* New York: Russell Sage Foundation.

Durr, Marlese, and Adia Harvey Wingfield. 2011. "Keep Your 'N' in Check: African American Women and the Interactive Effects of Etiquette and Emotional Labor." *Critical Sociology* 1–15.

Dustmann, Christian, and Nikolaos Theodoropoulos. 2006. "Ethnic Minority Immigrants and Their Children in Britain." Discussion paper. Centre for Research and Analysis of Migration. Department of Economics, University College London.

Eberhardt, Jennifer, and Susan Fiske. 1996. "Motivating Individuals to Change: What's a Target to Do?" In *Stereotypes and Stereotyping,* ed. N. Macrae, C. Stangor, and M. Hewston, 369–418. New York: Guilford Press.

Edin, Kathryn, and Maria Kefalas. 2005. *Promises I Can Keep: Why Poor Women Put Motherhood before Marriage.* Berkeley: University of California Press.

Elam, Gillian, and Martha Chinouya. 2000. "Feasibility Study for Health Surveys among Black African Populations Living in the U.K.: Stage 2—Diversity among Black African Communities." Manuscript prepared for the Department of Health, National Centre for Social Research, London.

Ellis, Mark 2001 "A Tale of Five Cities? Trends in Immigrant and Native-Born Wages." In *Strangers at the Gates: New Immigrants in Urban America,* ed. Roger Waldinger, 117–58. Berkeley: University of California Press.

Embrick, David G., and Kasey Henricks. 2013. "Discursive Colorlines At Work: How Epithets And Stereotypes Are Racially Unequal." *Symbolic Interaction* 36(2): 197–215.

Erikson, Robert, and John Goldthorpe. [1992] 2001. "Trends in Class Mobility: The Post-War European Experience." In *Social Stratification: Race, Class, and Gender in a Sociological Perspective,* ed. David Grusky, 344–72. Boulder, CO: Westview Press.

Espiritu, Yen Le. 1992. *Asian American Panethnicity.* Pennsylvania: Temple University Press.

———. 1994. "The Intersection of Race, Ethnicity, and Class: The Multiple Identities of Second Generation Filipinos." *Ethnicity* 1: 249–73.

———. 2002. "The Intersection of Race, Ethnicity, and Class: The Multiple Identities of Second-Generation Filipinos." In *Second Generation: Ethnic Identity among Asian Americans,* ed. Pyong Gap Min, 19–52. Walnut Creek, CA: Alta Mira Press.

Ette, Ezekiel Umo. 2012. *Nigerian Immigrants in the United States: Race, Identity and Acculturation*. Lanham, MD: Lexington Books.

Fafunwa, A. Babs. 1971. *A History of Nigerian Higher Education*. Yaba, Nigeria: Macmillan.

Fanon, Frantz. 1967. *The Wretched of the Earth*. Harmondsworth: Penguin.

Farley, Reynolds, and Richard Alba. 2002. "The New Second Generation in the United States." *International Migration Review* 36(93): 669–701.

Feagin, Joe, R. 1992. "The Continuing Significance of Race: Antiblack Discrimination in Public Places." *American Sociological Review* 56: 101–16.

Feagin, Joe, and Karyn McKinney. 2003. *The Many Costs of Racism*. Lanham, MD: Rowman and Littlefield.

Feagin, Joe R., and Melvin P. Sikes. 1994. *Living with Racism: The Black Middle-Class Experience*. Boston: Beacon Press.

Finney, Nissa, and Ludi Simpson. 2009. *"Sleepwalking to Segregation?": Challenging Myths about Race and Migration*. Bristol: Policy Press.

Fleming, Crystal M., Michele Lamont, and Jessica S. Welburn. 2012. "African Americans Respond to Stigmatization: The Meanings and Salience of Confronting, Deflecting Conflict, Educating the Ignorant and 'Managing the Self.'" *Ethnic and Racial Studies* 35(3): 400–417.

Foley, M., and D. Hoge. 2007. *Religion and the New Immigrants: How Faith Communities Form Our New Citizens*. New York: Oxford University Press.

Fomina, Joanna. 2006. "The Failure of British Multiculturalism: Lessons for Europe." *Polish Sociological Review* 456: 409–24.

Foner, Nancy. 1979. "West Indians in New York City and London: A Comparative Analysis." *International Migration Review* 13(2): 284–313.

———. 1985. "Race and Color: Jamaican Migrants in London and New York City." *International Migration Review* 19: 708–27.

———. 2000. *From Ellis Island to JFK: New York's Two Great Waves of Immigration*. New Haven, CT: Yale University Press; New York: Russell Sage Foundation.

———. 2005. *In a New Land: A Comparative View of Immigration*. New York: New York University Press.

———. 2007. "How Exceptional Is New York? Migration and Multiculturalism in the Empire City." *Ethnic and Racial Studies* 30(6): 999–1023.

———. 2011. "Black Identities and the Second Generation: Afro-Caribbeans in Britain and the United States." In *The Next Generation: Immigrant Youth in a Comparative Perspective,* ed. Richard Alba and Mary C. Waters, 251–68. New York: New York University Press.

———. 2014. "Reflections on Reflections of the Future of Ethnicity." *Ethnic and Racial Studies* 37(5): 786–89.

Foner, Nancy, and Richard Alba. 2010. "Immigration and the Legacies of the Past: The Impact of Slavery and the Holocaust on Contemporary Immigrants in the United States and Western Europe." *Comparative Studies in Society and History* 52(4): 798–819.

Foner, Nancy, and George M. Fredrickson. 2004. *Not Just Black and White: Historical and Contemporary Perspectives on Immigration, Race, and Ethnicity in the United States.* New York: Russell Sage Foundation.

Frazier, Franklin E. 1957. *Black Bourgeoisie.* New York: Collier Books.

Fryer, Peter. 1984. *Staying Power: Black People in Britain since 1504.* Atlantic Highlands, NJ: Humanities Press.

Gans, Herbert. 1992. "Second-Generation Decline: Scenarios for the Economic and Ethnic Futures of the Post-1965 American Immigrants." *Ethnic and Racial Studies* 15(2): 173–92.

Garcia, Linda C. 1976. "Ethnic Slurs in Chinese-Cebuano Relations." *Philippine Quarterly of Culture and Society* 4: 93–100.

Geertz, Clifford. 1963. "The Integrative Revolution: Primordial Sentiments and Civil Politics in the New States." In *Old Societies and New States: The Quest for Modernity in Asia and Africa,* ed. Clifford Geertz, 105–57. New York: Free Press.

Gibson, Margaret. 1988. *Accommodation without Assimilation: Sikh Immigrants in an American High School.* Ithaca, NY: Cornell University Press.

———. 1997. "Conclusion: Complicating the Immigrant/Involuntary Minority Typology." *Anthropology and Education Quarterly* 28: 431–54.

Giddens, Anthony, Mitchell Duneier, Richard P. Applebaum, and Deborah Carr. 2012. *The Essentials of Sociology.* 4th ed. New York: Norton.

Gillborn, D., and H. Mirza. 2000. *Educational Inequality: Mapping Race, Class and Gender: A Synthesis of Research Evidence.* London: Office for Standards in Education.

Gillborn, D. 1990. *"Race," Ethnicity and Education: Teaching and Learning in Multi-Ethnic Schools.* London: Unwin-Hyman.

Gilroy, Paul. 1992. *There Ain't No Black in the Union Jack.* London: Routledge.

———. 2004. *After Empire: Melancholia or Convivial Culture.* Abingdon: Routledge.

———. 2005. *Postcolonial Melancholia.* New York: Columbia University Press.

———. 2007. *Black Britain: A Photographic History.* London: Saqi.

Glazer, Nathan, and Daniel P. Moynihan. 1975. Introduction to *Ethnicity: Theory and Experience,* ed. Nathan Glazer and Daniel P. Moynihan, 1–26. Cambridge, MA: Harvard University Press.

Glick Schiller, Nina, Linda Basch, and Cristina Blanc-Szanton. 1995. "From Immigrant to Transmigrant: Theorizing Transnational Migration." *Anthropological Quarterly* 68: 48–63.

Goddard, Cliff, and Anna Wierzbicka. 2004. "Cultural Scripts: What Are They and What Are They Good For?" *Intercultural Pragmatics* 1–2: 153–66.

Gordon, Milton M. 1964. *Assimilation in American Life: The Role of Race, Religion, and National Origins.* New York: Oxford University Press.

Goulbourne, Harry. 1998. *Race Relations in Britain since 1945.* Basingstoke: Palgrave Macmillan.

Goulbourne, Harry, and M. Chamberlain. 2001. *The Caribbean Family in a Trans-Atlantic Context.* London: Macmillan.

Gould, Stephen Jay. [1981] 1996. *The Mismeasure of Man.* New York: Norton.

Graham, Sandra, April Z. Taylor, and Cynthia Hudley. 1998. "Exploring Achievement Values among Ethnic Minority Early Adolescents." *Journal of Educational Pyschology* 91: 606–20.

Greater London Authority (GLA). 2005. *London's Changing Population, Diversity of a World City in the 21st Century.* Greater London Authority Data Management and Analysis Group Briefing 2005/39. London: GLA.

Greer, Christina M. 2013. *Black Ethnics: Race, Immigration, and the Pursuit of the American Dream.* Oxford: Oxford University Press.

Grodsky, Eric, and Devah Pager. 2001 "The Structure of Disadvantage: Individual and Occupational Determinants of the Black-White Wage Gap." *American Sociological Review* 66: 542–67.

Hacker, Andrew. [1992] 1995. *Two Nations: Black and White, Separate, Hostile, Unequal.* New York: Ballantine Books.

Hall, Stuart. 1996. "Politics of Identity." In *Culture, Identity and Politics: Ethnic Minorities in Britain,* ed. Terence Ranger, Yunas Samad, and Ossie Stuart, 129–35. Aldershot: Avebury.

————. 1997. "The Local and the Global: Globalization and Ethnicity." In *Culture, Globalization, and the World System: Contemporary Conditions for the Representation of Identity,* ed. Anthony D. King, 19–40. Minneapolis: University of Minnesota Press.

Haller, William, Alejandro Portes, and Scott M. Lynch. 2011a. "Dreams Fulfilled, Dreams Shattered: Determinants of Segmented Assimilation in the Second Generation." *Social Forces* 89(3): 733–62.

————. 2011b. "On the Dangers of Rosy Lenses: Reply to Alba, Kasinitz, and Waters." *Social Forces* 89(3): 775–82.

Halter, Marilyn. 2007. "West Africans." In *The New Americans: A Handbook to Immigration since 1965,* ed. Mary Waters and Reed Ueda, 283–94. Cambridge, MA: Harvard University Press.

————. 2010. "Young, Gifted, and West African: Transnational Migrants Growing Up in America." In *Helping Young Refugees and Immigrants Succeed,* ed. Gerald Holton and Gerhard Sonnert, 113–127. New York: Palgrave Macmillan.

Handlin, Oscar. 1973. *The Uprooted.* Boston, MA: Little, Brown.

Harper, Sam, John Lynch, Scott Burris, and George Davey Smith. 2007. "Trends in the Black-White Life Expectancy Gap in the United States, 1983–2003." *JAMA* 297: 1224–32.

Harris, Fredrick C., and Brian D. McKenzie. 2011. "Still Waters Run Deep: The Complexities of African-American Identities and Political Attitudes." Unpublished manuscript.

Haveman, Robert, and Barbara Wolfe. 1995. "The Determinants of Children's Attainments: A Review of Methods and Findings." *Journal of Economic Literature* 33: 1829–78.

Haynes, Jo, Leon Tikly, and Chamion Caballero. 2006. "The Barriers to Achievement for White/Black-Caribbean Pupils in English Schools." *British Journal of Education* 27(5): 569–83.

Heath, Anthony, and Dorren McMahon. 1997. "Education and Occupational Attainments: The Impact of Ethnic Origins," In *Ethnicity in the 1991 Census: Employment, Education and Housing among the Ethnic Minority Populations in Britain,* vol 4, ed. Valerie Karn, 91–113. London: HMSO.

———. 2005. "Social Mobility of Ethnic Minorities." In *Ethnicity, Social Mobility and Public Policy: Comparing the USA and U.K.,* ed. Glenn C. Loury, Tariq Modood, and Steven M. Teles, 393–413. Cambridge: Cambridge University Press.

Hedger, Joseph A. 2013. "Meaning and Racial Slurs: Derogatory Epithets and the Semantics/Pragmatics Interface." *Language Communication* 33: 205–13.

Hills, John, Mike Brewer, Stephen Jenkins, Ruth Lister, Ruth Lupton, Stephen Machin, Collin Mills, Tariq Modood, Teresa Rees, and Sheila Riddell. 2010. "An Anatomy of Economic Inequality in the UK: Report of the National Equality Panel." Government Equalities Office, London.

Hochschild, Jennifer. 1995. *Facing up to the American Dream: Race, Class, and the Soul of the Nation.* Princeton, NJ: Princeton University Press.

———. 2001. "Public Schools and the American Dream." *Dissent* (Fall): 35–42.

Hochschild, Jennifer, Vesla Weaver, and Traci Burch. 2012. *Creating a New Racial Order: How Immigration, Multiculturalism, Genomics, and the Young Can Remake Race in America.* Princeton, NJ: Princeton University Press.

Holtzman, Jon. 2007. *Nuer Journeys, Nuer Lives: Sudanese Refugees in Minnesota.* Boston, MA: Allyn and Bacon.

Humphries, Jill. 2009. "Resisting Race." In *The New African Diaspora,* ed. Isidore Okphewho and Nkiru Nzegwu, 31–60. Bloomington: Indiana University Press.

Hutnik, Nimmi, 1991. *Ethnic Minority Identity: A Social Psychological Perspective.* Oxford: Clarendon Press.

Iceland, John. 2009. *Where We Live Now: Immigration and Race in the United States.* Berkeley: University of California Press.

Ignatieff, Michael. 1995. *Blood and Belonging.* New York: Noonday Press.

Ignatiev, Noel. 1995. *How the Irish Became White.* New York: Routledge.

Imoagene, Onoso. 2008. "Comparing Educational Outcomes of Second Generation Immigrants to Natives from Kindergarten to Fifth Grade." In *Ethnicity and Social Divisions: Contemporary Research in Sociology,* ed. Karin Hallden, Elias le Grand, and Zenia Hellgren. Newcastle: Cambridge Scholars Publishing.

———. 2012. "Being British vs. Being American: Identification Choices among the Nigerian Second-Generation." *Ethnic and Racial Studies* 35(12): 2153–73.

———. 2015. "Broken Bridges: An Exchange of Slurs between African Americans and Africans and Its Impact on Identity Formation among the Second Generation of Nigerian Ancestry." *Journal of Language Sciences.* doi 10.1016 /j.langsci.2015.03.010.

Isaacs, Harold R. 1975. *Idols of the Tribe: Group Identity and Political Change.* Cambridge, MA: Harvard University Press.

Isaacs, Julia B. 2008. "Economic Mobility of Families across Generations." Paper prepared for Brookings Institution.

Ispa-Landa, Simone. 2014. "Gender, Race, and Justifications for Group Exclusion: Urban Black Students Bused to Affluent Suburban Schools." *Sociology of Education* 86(3): 218–33.

Iyall Smith, E. Keri. 2008. "Hybrid Identities: Theoretical Examinations." In *Hybrid Identities: Theoretical and Empirical Examination,* ed. Keri E. Iyall Smith and Patricia Leavy, 1–9. Leiden: Brill.

Jackman, Mary. 1994. *The Velvet Glove.* Berkeley: University of California Press.

Jenkins, Richard. 2008. *Social Identity.* London: Routledge.

Jiménez, Tomás R. 2010a. "Affiliative Ethnic Identity: A More Elastic Link between Ancestry and Culture." *Ethnic and Racial Studies* 33(10): 1756–75.

———. 2010b. *Replenished Ethnicity: Mexican Americans, Immigration, and Identity.* Berkeley: University of California Press.

Jiménez, Tomás R., and Adam L. Horowitz. 2013. "When White Is Just Alright: How Immigrants Redefine Achievement and Reconfigure the Ethnoracial Hierarchy." *American Sociological Review* 78(5): 849–71.

Jones, Edward W., Jr. 1973. "What It's Like to Be a Black Manager." *Harvard Business Review* (July–August): 108–16.

Kaba Amadu, Jacky. 2009. "Africa's Migration Brain Drain: Factors Contributing to the Mass Emigration of Africa's Elite to the West." In *The New African Diaspora,* ed. Isidore Okpewho and Nkiru Nzegwu, 109–23. Bloomington: Indiana University Press.

Kalmijn, Matthijs. 1996. 'The Socioeconomic Assimilation of Caribbean American Blacks.' *Social Forces* 74: 910–30.

Kao, Grace. 1995. "Asian-Americans as Model Minorities? A Look at Their Academic Performance." *American Journal of Education* 103: 121–59.

Kao, Grace, and Marta Tienda. 1995. "Optimism and Achievement: The Educational Performance of Immigrant Youth." *Social Science Quarterly* 76: 1–19.

———. 1998. "Educational Aspirations of Minority Youth." *American Journal of Education* 106(3): 349–84.

Karn, Valerie, ed. 1997. *Ethnicity in the 1991 Census: Employment, Education and Housing among the Ethnic Minority Populations in Britain.* London: HMSO.

Kasinitz, Philip. 1992. *Caribbean New York: Black Immigrants and the Politics of Race.* Ithaca, NY: Cornell University Press.

Kasinitz, Philip, John Mollenkopf, and Mary C. Waters. 2002. "Becoming American / Becoming New Yorkers: Immigrant Incorporation in a Majority Minority City." *International Migration Review* 36(4): 1020–36.

———. 2004. *Becoming New Yorkers: Ethnographies of the New Second Generation.* New York: Russell Sage Foundation

Kasinitz, Phillip, John H. Mollenkopf, Mary C. Waters, and Jennifer Holdaway. 2008. *Inheriting the City: The Children of Immigrants Come of Age.* New York: Russell Sage Foundation.

Kellner, Peter. 2009. "What Britishness Means to the British." In *Britishness: Perspectives on the British Question,* ed. Andrew Gamble and Tony Wright, 63–65. Oxford: Wiley Blackwell.

Kibona-Clark, Msia. 2009. "Questions of Identity among African Immigrants in America." In *The New African Diaspora,* ed. Isidore Okpewho and Nkiru Nzegwu, 255–70. Bloomington: Indiana University Press.

Kibria, Nazli. 2002. "College and Notions of 'Asian Americans': Second-Generation Chinese Americans and Korean Americans." In *Second Generation: Ethnic Identity among Asian Americans,* ed. Pyong Gap Min, 183–208. Walnut Creek, CA: Alta Mira Press.

Kim, Claire. 1999. "The Racial Triangulation of Asian Americans." *Politics and Society* 27(1): 103–36.

Kivisto, Peter, and Georganne Rundblad. 2000. "Overview: Multicultural America in the Post–Civil Rights Era." In *Multiculturalism in the United States: Current Issue, Contemporary Voices,* ed. Peter Kivisto and Georganne Rundblad, xxi–xlvi. Thousand Oaks, CA: Pine Forge Press.

Kollehon, Konia T., and Edward E. Eule. 2003. "The Socioeconomic Attainment Patterns of Africans in the United States." *International Migration Review* 37(4): 1163–90.

Kymlicka, Will. 2001. *Politics in the Vernacular.* Oxford: Oxford University Press.

———. 2004. "Justice and Security in the Accommodation of Minority Nationalism." In *Ethnicity, Nationalism and Minority Rights,* ed. Stephen May, Tariq Modood, and Judith Squires, 144–75. Cambridge: Cambridge University Press.

———. 2010. "The Rise and Fall of Multiculturalism? New Debates on Inclusion and Accommodation in Diverse Societies." In *The Multiculturalism Backlash: European Discourses, Policies, and Practices,* ed. Steven Vertovec and Susanne Wessendorf, 32–49. London: Routledge.

Lacy, Karyn R. 2007. *Blue-Chip Black: Race, Class, and Status in the New Black Middle Class,* Berkeley: University of California Press.

Lam, Virginia, and Gordon Smith. 2009. "African and Caribbean Adolescents in Britain: Ethnic Identity and Britishness." *Ethnic and Racial Studies* 32(7): 1248–70.

Lamont, Michele. 1992. *Money, Morals, and Manners: The Culture of the French and the American and Upper-Middle Class.* Chicagon: University of Chicago Press.

———, ed. 1999. *The Cultural Territories of Race: Black and White Boundaries.* Chicago: University of Chicago Press.

Lamont, Michele, and Virag Molnar. 2002. The Study of Boundaries in the Social Sciences." *Annual Review of Sociology* 28: 167–95.

Landry, Bart. 1987. *The New Black Middle Class.* Berkeley: University of California Press.

Lareau, Annette. 2003. *Unequal Childhoods: Class, Race, and Family Life.* Berkeley: University of California Press.

Lee, Jennifer "Who We Are: America Becoming and Becoming American." *Du Bois Review* 2(2): 287–302.

Lee, Jennifer, and Frank D. Bean 2004. "America's Changing Color Line: Immigration, Race/Ethnicity, and Multiracial Identification." *Annual Review of Sociology* 30: 221–42.

———. 2010. *The Diversity Paradox: Immigration and the Color Line in 21st Century America*. New York: Russell Sage Foundation.

Lee, Jennifer, and Min Zhou. 2014. "The Success Frame and Achievement Paradox: The Costs and Consequences for Asian Americans." *Race and Social Problems* 6: 38–55.

———. 2015. *The Asian American Achievement Paradox*. New York: Russell Sage Foundation.

Levitt, Peggy. 2001. *The Transnational Villagers*. Berkeley: University of California Press

Levy, Frank. 1998. *The New Dollar and Dreams: The Changing American Income Distribution*. New York: Norton.

Lieberson, Stanley. 1981. *A Piece of the Pie: Blacks and White Immigrants since 1880*. Berkeley: University of California Press.

Loewen, James. W. 1971. *The Mississippi Chinese: Between Black and White*. Cambridge, MA: Harvard University Press.

Logan, John R., and Glenn Deane. 2003. "Black Diversity in Metropolitan America." Lewis Mumford Center for Comparative Urban and Regional Research, University at Albany. Unpublished manuscript.

London's Poverty Profile. "Overview of London Boroughs." Accessed June 2, 2016. www.londonspovertyprofile.org.uk/key-facts/overview-of-london-boroughs/.

Louie, Vivian S. 2004. *Compelled to Excel: Immigration, Education, and Opportunity among Chinese Americans*. Stanford, CA: Stanford University Press.

———. 2012. *Keeping the Immigrant Bargain: The Costs and Rewards of Success in America*. New York: Russell Sage Foundation.

Loury, Glenn C., Tariq Modood, and Steven M. Teles, eds. 2005. *Ethnicity, Social Mobility and Public Policy: Comparing the USA and U.K.* Cambridge: Cambridge University Press.

MacLeod, Jay. 1987. *Ain't No Makin' It: Aspirations and Attainment in a Low-Income Neighborhood*. Boulder, CO: Westview Press.

Manning, Patrick. 2009. *The African Diaspora: A History through Culture*. New York: Columbia University Press.

Manyika, S. 2001. "Negotiating Identities: African Students in British and American Universities." Dissertation Abstracts International, Section A: Humanities & Social Sciences, vol. 62, no. 1, p. 97.

Marrow, Helen. 2009. "New Immigrant Destinations and the American Color Line." *Ethnic and Racial Studies* 36(6): 1037–57.

Mason, David. 2000. *Race and Ethnicity in Modern Britain*. Oxford: Oxford University Press.

Massey, Douglas. 2008. *Categorically Unequal: The American Stratification System*. New York: Russell Sage.

Massey, Douglas S., Camille Z. Charles, Garvey Lundy, and Mary J. Fischer. 2003. *The Source of the River: The Social Origins of Freshmen at America's Selective Colleges and Universities*. Princeton, NJ: Princeton University Press.

Massey, Douglas S., and Nancy Denton. 1993. *American Apartheid: Segregation and the Making of the Underclass*. Cambridge, MA: Harvard University Press.

Massey, Douglas S., Jorge Durand, and Nolan J. Malone. 2003. *Beyond Smoke and Mirrors: Mexican Immigration in an Era of Economic Integration.* New York: Russell Sage.

Matute-Bianchi, Maria Eugenia. 1991. "Situational Ethnicity and Patterns of School Performance among Immigrants and Nonimmigrant Mexican-Descent Students." In *Minority Status and Schooling: A Comparative Study of Immigrant and Involuntary Minorities,* ed. Margaret Gibson and John U. Ogbu, 205–47. New York: Garland.

Maxwell, Rahsaan. 2009. "Caribbean and South Asian Identification with British Society: The Importance of Perceived Discrimination." *Ethnic and Racial Studies* 32(8): 1449–69.

May, Stephen, Tariq Modood, and Judith Squires. 2004. "Ethnicity, Nationalism, and Minority Rights: Charting the Disciplinary Debates." In *Ethnicity, Nationalism and Minority Rights,* ed. Stephen May, Tariq Modood, and Judith Squires, 1–26. Cambridge: Cambridge University Press.

McLanahan, Sara. 2002. "Life without Father: What Happens to Children?" *Contexts* 1(1): 35–44.

McLanahan, Sara, and Gary Sandefur. 1994. *Growing Up with a Single Parent: What Hurts, What Helps.* Cambridge, MA: Harvard University Press.

Migration Policy Institute. 2016a. "Select Diaspora Populations in the United States." Accessed May 29, 2016. http://www.migrationpolicy.org/research /select-diaspora-populations-united-states.

———. 2016b. "U.S. Immigration Trends." Accessed June 2, 2016. www .migrationpolicy.org/programs/data-hub/us-immigration-trends#history.

Miles, Robert. 1989. *Racism.* London: Routledge.

———. 1993. *Racism after "Race Relations."* London: Routledge.

Min, Pyong Gap, and Rose Kim. 2002. "Formation of Ethnic and Racial Identities: Narratives by Asian American Professionals." In *Second Generation: Ethnic Identity among Asian Americans,* ed. Pyong Gap Min, 153–82. Walnut Creek, CA: Alta Mira Press.

Mirza, Heidi. 1992. *Young, Female and Black.* London: Routledge.

———. 2006. "'Race,' Gender and Educational Desire." *Race, Ethnicity and Education* 9(2): 137–58.

Mittelberg, David, and Mary C. Waters. 1992. "The Process of Ethnogenesis among Haitian and Israeli Immigrants in the United States." *Ethnic and Racial Studies* 15(3): 412–35.

Model, Suzanne. 1999. "Ethnic Inequality in England: An Analysis Based on the 1991 Census." *Ethnic and Racial Studies* 22: 966–90.

———. 2005. "Non-White Origins, Anglo Destinations: Immigrants in the US and Britain." In *Ethnicity, Social Mobility and Public Policy in the USA and U.K.,* ed. Glenn C. Loury, Tariq Modood, and Steven M. Teles, 363–92. Cambridge: Cambridge University Press.

———. 2008. *West Indians: A Black Success Story?* New York: Russell Sage Foundation.

Model, Suzanne, and Gene Fisher. 2001. "Black-White Unions: West Indians and African Americans Compared." *Demography* 38(2): 177–85.

Model, Suzanne, Gene Fisher, and Roxane Silberman. 1999. "Black Caribbeans in Cross-National Perspective." *Journal of Ethnic and Migration Studies* 25: 183–208.

Modood, Tariq. 1992. *Not Easy Being British: Colour, Culture and Citizenship.* Stoke-on-Trent: Runnymede Trust; Trentham Books

———. 2004. "Capitals, Ethnic Identity and Educational Qualifications." *Cultural Trends* 13(2): 87–105.

———. 2005. *Multicultural Politics: Racism, Ethnicity, and Muslims in Britain.* Minneapolis: University of Minnesota Press.

———. 2010. *Still Not Easy Being British: Struggles for a Multicultural Citizenship.* Stoke-on-Trent: Trentham Books.

———. 2011. "Capitals, Ethnic Identity, and Educational Qualifications." In *The Next Generation: Immigrant Youth in a Comparative Perspective,* ed. Richard Alba and Mary C. Waters, 185–206. New York: New York University Press.

Modood, Tariq, Sharon Beishon, and Satnam Virdee. 1994. *Changing Ethnic Identities.* London: Policy Studies Institute.

Modood, Tariq, Richard Berthoud, Jane Lakey, James Nazroo, Patten Smith, Satnam Virdee, and Sharon Beishon. 1997. *Ethnic Minorities in Britain: Diversity and Disadvantages.* London: Policy Studies Institute.

Morgan, S., and J. Mehta. 2004. Beyond the Laboratory: Evaluating the Survey Evidence for the Disidentification Explanation of Black-White Differences in Achievement." *Sociology of Education* 77(1): 82–101.

Morrow, Lance. 1992. "Africa: The Scramble for Existence." *Time,* September 7, 40–46.

Murji, Karim, and John Solomos. 2005. *Racialization: Studies in Theory and Practice.* Oxford: Oxford University Press.

Muttarak, Raya. 2004. "Marital Assimilation: Interethnic Marriage in Britain." Paper presented at the 12th Biennial Conference of the Australian Population Association, 15–17 September, Canberra.

Muttarak, Raya, and Anthony Heath. 2010. "Who Intermarries in Britain: Explaining Diversity in Intermarriage Patterns." *British Journal of Sociology* 61(2): 275–305.

Myers, Dowell. 2007. *Immigrants and Boomers: Forging a New Social Contract for the Future of America.* New York: Russell Sage Foundation.

Nagel, Joanne. 1994. "Constructing Ethnicity: Creating and Recreating Ethnic Identities and Culture." *Social Problems* 41: 152–76.

National Center for Education Statistics. 2015. "The Condition of Education 2013." Accessed August 20, 2015. https://nces.ed.gov/.

Nassir, Na'Ilah Suad. 2012. *Racialized Identities: Race and Achievement among African American Youth.* Stanford, CA: Stanford University Press.

Neckerman, Kathryn M., Prudence Carter, and Jennifer Lee. 1999. "Segmented Assimilation and Minority Cultures of Mobility." *Ethnic and Racial Studies* 22: 945–65.

Nee, Victor, and Jimy Sanders. 2000. "Understanding the Diversity in Immigrant Incorporation: A Forms-of-Capital Model." *Ethnic and Racial Studies* 24: 386–411.

Newman, Katherine S. 1999. *No Shame in My Game: The Working Poor in the Inner City.* New York: Russell Sage.

NYC Planning. 2013. *The Newest New Yorkers: Characteristics of the City's Foreign born Population.* New York: Department of City Planning, City of New York.

Nigeria National Bureau of Statistics. 2008. *Nigeria Core Welfare Indicators Questionnaire Survey 2006.* Abuja, Nigeria: National Bureau of Statistics.

Noguera, Pedro A. 2004. "Social Capital and the Education of Immigrant Students: Categories and Generalizations." *Sociology of Education* 77(2): 180–83.

Office for National Statistics. Social Survey Division, Northern Ireland Statistics and Research Agency. Central Survey Unit. 2014. Labour Force Survey 2014 [data accessed November 20, 2015]. UK Data Service, http://ukdataservice.ac .uk/.

———. 2015a. Census 2011: Country of Birth, Table QS203UK.

———. 2015b. Census 2011: Ethnic Groups, Table CT0071.

Ogbu, John U. 1978. *Minority Education and Caste: The American System in Cross-Cultural Perspective.* New York: Academic Press.

———. 1987. "Variability in Minority School Performance: A Problem in Search of an Explanation." *Anthropology and Education Quarterly* 18: 312–34.

———. 1990. "Minority Status and Literacy in Comparative Perspective." *Daedelus* 119 (2): 114–18.

Ogbu, John U., and Herbert D. Simons. 1998. "Voluntary and Involuntary Minorities: A Cultural-Ecological Theory of School Performance with Some Implications for Education." *Anthropology and Education Quarterly* 29(2).

Okihiro, Gary Y. 1994. *Margins and Mainstreams: Asians in American History and Culture.* Seattle: University of Washington Press.

Oliver, Melvin, and Thomas Shapiro. 2006. *Black Wealth, White Wealth: A New Perspective on Racial Inequality.* New York: Routledge.

Olssen, Mark. 2004. "From the Crick Report to the Parekh Report: Multiculturalism, Cultural Difference, and Democracy: The Re-Visioning of Citizenship Education." *British Journal of Sociology of Education* 25(2): 179–92.

Omi, Michael, and Howard Winant. 1994. *Racial Formation in the United States: From the 1960s to the 1990s.* New York: Routledge.

———. 2015. *Racial Formation in the United States.* 3rd ed. New York: Routledge.

Osbourne, J. 1997. "Race and Academic Disidentification." *Journal of Educational Psychology* 89: 728–35.

Osler, A., and H. Starkey. 2001. "Citizenship Education and National Identities in France and England: Inclusive or Exclusive?" *Oxford Review of Education* 27(2): 287–305.

Owens, Jayanti, and Scott M. Lynch. 2012. "Black and Hispanic Immigrants' Resilience against Negative-Ability Racial Stereotypes at Selective Colleges and Universities in the United States." *Sociology of Education* 85(4): 303–25.

Pager, Devah. 2007. *Marked: Race, Crime, and Finding Work in an Era of Mass Incarceration.* Chicago: University of Chicago Press.

Parekh, Bhiku. 2006. *Rethinking Multiculturalism: Cultural Diversity and Political Theory.* New York: Palgrave Macmillan.

———. 2009. "Being British." In *Britishness: Perspectives on the British Question,* ed. Andrew Gamble and Tony Wright, 32–40. Oxford: Wiley Blackwell.

Parekh Report. 2000. *The Future of Multi-Ethnic Britain.* London: Runnymede Trust / Profile Books.

Park, Julie, and Dowell Myers. 2010. "Intergenerational Mobility in the Post-1965 Immigration Era: Estimates by and Immigrant Generation Cohort Method." *Demography* 47(2): 369–92.

Park, Robert E. 1950. *Race and Culture.* Glencoe, IL: Free Press.

Parrillo, Vincent N., and Christopher Donaghue. 2005. "Updating the Bogardus Social Distance Studies: A New National Survey." *Social Science Journal* 42(2): 257–71.

Patterson, Orlando. 1982. *Slavery and Social Death: A Comparative Study.* Cambridge, MA: Harvard University Press.

———. 2001. "The American View of Freedom: What We Say, What We Mean." *Society* 38(4): 37–45.

———. 2005. "Four Modes of Ethno-Somatic Stratification: The Experiences of Blacks in Europe and the Americas." In *Ethnicity, Social Mobility and Public Policy: Comparing the USA and U.K.,* ed. Glenn C. Loury, Tariq Modood, and Steven M. Teles, 67–121. Cambridge: Cambridge University Press.

Pattillo-McCoy, Mary. 1999. *Black Picket Fences: Privilege and Peril among the Black Middle Class.* Chicago: University of Chicago Press.

Peach, Ceri. 1996. "Does Britain have Ghettos?" *Transactions, Institute of British Geographers* 21(1): 216–35.

———. 1997. "Black-Caribbeans: Class, Gender, and Geography." In *Ethnicity in the 1991 Census: The Ethnic Minority Populations of Great Britain,* vol. 2, ed. Ceri Peach. London: HMSO.

Pettit, Becky, and Bruce Western. 2004. "Mass Imprisonment and the Life Course: Race and Class Inequality in U.S. Incarceration." *American Sociological Review* 69 (April): 151–69.

Pew Research Center. 2007. "Optimism about Black Progress Declines: Blacks See Growing Values Gap between Poor and Middle Class." Accessed August 9, 2015. www.pewsocialtrends.org/2007/11/13/blacks-see-growing-values-gap-between-poor-and-middle-class/.

———. 2010. "Blacks Upbeat about Black Progress, Prospects a Year after Obama's Election." Accessed August 2, 2015. www.pewsocialtrends.org/2010/01/12/blacks-upbeat-about-black-progress-prospects/.

———. 2015. "Chapter 1: Statistical Portrait of the U.S. Black Immigrant Population." Accessed January 13, 2016. www.pewsocialtrends.org/2015/04/09/chapter-1-statistical-portrait-of-the-u-s-black-immigrant-population/.

Phillips, Deborah. 2006. "Parallel Lives? Challenging Discourses of British Muslim Self-Degregation." *Environment and Planning D: Society and Space* 24: 25–40.

Pierre, Jemima. 2004. "Black Immigrants in the United States and the 'Cultural Narratives' of Ethnicity." *Identities: Global Studies in Culture and Power* 11: 141–70.

Pilkington, Andrew. 1984. *Race Relations in Britain.* Slough: University Tutorial Press.

———. 2003. *Racial Disadvantage and Ethnic Diversity in Britain.* Houndmills: Palgrave Macmillan.

Pinder, Sherrow. 2013. *Whiteness and Racialized Ethnic Groups in the United States: The Politics of Remembering.* Lanham, MD: Lexington Books.

Portes, Alejandro, Patricia Fernandez-Kelly, and William Haller. 2005. "Segmented Assimilation on the Ground: The New Second Generation in Early Adulthood." *Ethnic and Racial Studies* 28(6): 1000–1040.

Portes, Alejandro, and Rubén Rumbaut. 1996. *Immigrant America.* Berkeley: University of California Press.

———. 2001. *Legacies: The Story of the Immigrant Second Generation.* Berkeley: University of California Press.

Portes, Alejandro, and Min Zhou. 1993. "The New Second Generation: Segmented Assimilation and Its Variants." *Annals of the American Academy of Political and Social Science* 530: 74–96.

Powell, David. 2002. *Nationhood and Identity.* London. I. B. Tauris.

Prins, Baukje, and Sawitri Saharso. 2010. "From Toleration to Repression: The Dutch Backlash against Multiculturalism." In *The Multiculturalism Backlash: European Discourses, Policies, and Practices,* ed. Steven Vertovec and Susanne Wessendorf, 72–91. London: Routledge.

Putnam, D. Robert. 2015. *Our Kids: The American Dream in Crisis.* New York: Simon and Schuster.

Reynolds, T. 2006. "Caribbean Families, Social Capital, and Young People's Diasporic Identities." *Ethnic and Racial Studies* 29(6): 1087–1103.

Richards, Nicola Bedelia. 2008. "Hybrid Identities in the Diaspora: Second-Generation West Indians in Brooklyn." In *Hybrid Identities: Theoretical and Empirical Examination,* ed. Keri E. Iyall Smith and Patricia Leavy, 264–89. Leiden: Brill.

Rienzo, Cinzia, and Carlos Vargas-Silva. 2016. "Migrants in the UK: An Overview." 5th ed. Migration Observatory at the University of Oxford. www.migration observatory.ox.ac.uk./resources/briefings/migrants-in-the-uk-an-overview/.

Rios, Victor, M. 2011. *Punished: Policing the Lives of Black and Latino Boys.* New York: New York University Press.

Rodney, Walter. 1972. *How Britain Underdeveloped Africa.* Washington, DC: Howard University Press.

Rodriguez, Gregory. 2007. *Mongrels, Bastards, Orphans, and Vagabonds: Mexican Immigration and the Future of Race in America.* New York: Pantheon.

Roediger, David R. 1994. *Towards the Abolition of Whiteness: Essays on Race, Politics, and Working Class History.* London: Verso.

———. 2005. *Working towards Whiteness: How America's Immigrants Became White: The Strange Journey from Ellis Island to the Suburbs.* New York: Basic Books.

Rogers, Reuel. 2004. "Race-Based Coalitions among Minority Groups: Black-Caribbeans and African-Americans in New York City." *Urban Affairs Review* 39: 283–317.

———. 2006. *Afro-Caribbean Immigrants and the Politics of Incorporation: Ethnicity, Exception, or Exit*. New York: Cambridge University Press.

Rogozinski, Jan. 2000. *A Brief History of the Caribbean: From the Arawak and the Carib to the Present*. New York: Plume.

Rollock, Nicola, David Gillborn, Carol Vincent, and Stephen J. Ball. 2015. *The Colour Class: The Educational Strategies of the Black Middle Classes*. New York: Routledge.

Roscigno, Vincent J., Lisa M. Williams, and Reginald A. Byron. 2012. "Workplace Racial Discrimination and Middle-Class Vulnerability." *American Behavioral Scientist* 56(5): 696–710.

Roth, Wendy 2012. *Race Migrations: Latinos and the Cultural Transformation of Race*. Stanford, CA: Stanford University Press.

Rumbaut, Rubén G. 2004. "Ages, Life Stages, and Generational Cohorts: Decomposing the Immigrant First and Second Generations in the United States." *International Migration Review* 38(3): 1160–1205.

Rumbaut, Rubén G., Douglas Massey, and Frank Bean. 2006. "Linguistic Life Expectancies: Immigrant Language Retention in Southern California." *Population and Development Review* 32(3): 447–60.

Schermerhorn, Richard A. 1979. *Comparative Ethnic Relations: A Framework for Theory and Research*. Chicago: University of Chicago Press.

Schlesinger, Arthur, Jr. 1991. *The Disuniting of America: Reflections on a Multicultural Society*. Knoxville, TN: Whittle Communications.

Schmid, Carol L. 2001. "Educational Achievement, Language-Minority Students, and the New Second Generation." *Sociology of Education* 74 (Extra Issue): 71–87.

Scholz, John, Karl Levine, and Kara Levine. 2004. "U.S. Black-White Wealth Inequality: A Survey." In *Social Inequality,* ed. Kathryn M. Neckerman, 895–929. New York: Russell Sage Foundation.

Sewell, Tony. 1997. *Black Masculinities and Schooling: How Black Boys Survive Modern Schooling*. Stoke-on-Trent: Trentham Books.

Sewell, Tony, and Richard Majors. 2001. "Black Boys and Schooling: An Intervention Framework for Understanding the Dilemmas of Masculinity, Identity and Underachievement." In *Educating Our Black Children: New Directions and Radical Approaches,* ed. Richard Majors, 183–202. London: Routledge.

Shah, Bindi, Claire Dwyer, and Tariq Modood. 2010. "Explaining Educational Achievement and Career Aspirations among Young British Pakistanis: Mobilising 'Ethnic Capital'?" *Sociology* 44(6): 1109–27.

Shapiro, Thomas, and Melvin Oliver. [1997] 2013. *White Wealth/Black Wealth: A New Perspective on Racial Inequality*. New York: Scribner's.

Shaw-Taylor, Yoku, and Steven A. Tuch, eds. 2007. *The Other African Americans: Contemporary African and Caribbean Immigrants in the United States*. Lanham, MD: Rowman and Littlefield.

Sheridan, Lorraine. 2006. "Islamophobia Pre– and Post–September 11, 2001." *Journal of Interpersonal Violence* 21(3): 317–36.

Small, Mario, and Monica McDermott. 2006. "The Presence of Organizational Resources in Poor Urban Neighborhoods: An Analysis of Average and Contextual Effects." *Social Forces* 84: 1697–1724.

Small, Stephen. 1994. *Racialised Barriers: The Black Experiences in the United States and England in the 1980s.* New York: Routledge.

Smith, Anthony, D. 1995. *Nations and Nationalism in a Global Era.* Oxford: Polity Press.

———. 1996. "Chosen Peoples." In *Ethnicity,* ed. John Hutchinson and Anthony D. Smith, 189–96. Oxford: Oxford University Press.

Smith, Candis Watts. 2014. *Black Mosaic: The Politics of Black Pan-Ethnic Diversity.* New York: New York University Press.

Smith, James P. 2003. "Assimilation across Latino Generations." *American Economic Review* 93(2): 315–19.

———. 2006. "Immigrants and the Labor Market." *Journal of Labor Economics* 24(2): 203–33.

Smith, Robert Courtney. 2005. *Mexican New York: Transnational Lives of New Immigrants.* Berkeley: University of California Press.

Solomos, John. 2003. *Race and Racism in Britain.* 3rd ed. Basingstoke: Macmillan.

Song, Miri. 2010. "What Happens after Segmented Assimilation? An Exploration of Intermarriage and 'Mixed Race' Young People in Britain." *Ethnic and Racial Studies* 33(7): 1194–1213.

Sowell, Thomas. 1978. "Three Black Histories." In *Essays and Data on American Ethnic Groups,* ed. Thomas Sowell, 7–64. Washington, DC: Urban Institute.

———. 1981. *Ethnic America: A History.* New York: Basic Books.

Spillman, Lyn. 1997. *Nation and Commemoration: Creating National Identities in the United States and Australia.* Cambridge: Cambridge University Press.

Steelman, Lala Carr, and Brian Powell. 1989. "Acquiring Capital for College: The Constraints of Family Configuration." *American Sociological Review* 54: 844–55.

Steinberg, Stephen. 2001. *The Ethnic Myth: Race, Ethnicity, and Class in America.* Boston: Beacon Press.

Stepick, Alex. 1998. *Pride against Prejudice: Haitians in the United States.* New York Immigrants Series. Boston: Allyn and Bacon.

Stone, John, and Howard Lucas. "Immigration and Ethnic Relations in Britain and America." In *Race Relations in Britain: A Developing Agenda,* ed. Tessa Blackstone, Bhiku Parekh, and Peter Sanders, 221–38. London: Routledge.

Stopes-Roe, Mary, and Raymond Cochrane. 1990. *Citizens of This Country: The Asian British.* Clevedon, U.K.: Multilingual Matters.

Strelitz, Jason. 2004. "Second Generation Immigrants to the UK: Outcomes in Early Adulthood and Patterns of Social Mobility." Paper presented to European Association of Population Studies.

Suárez-Orozco, Carola E., and Marcelo M. Suárez-Orozco. 1995. *Trans-formations: Immigration, Family Life, and Achievement Motivation among Latino Adolescents*. Stanford, CA: Stanford University Press.

———. 2001. *Children of Immigration*. Cambridge, MA: Harvard University Press.

Suárez-Orozco, Marcelo M. 1987. "Becoming Somebody: Central American Immigrants in U.S. Inner-City Schools." *Anthropology and Education Quarterly* 18(4): 287–99.

Suárez-Orozco, Marcelo M., and Carola E. Suárez-Orozco. 1995. "The Cultural Patterning of Achievement Motivation: A Comparison of Mexican, Mexican Immigrant, Mexican American and Non-Latino White American Students." In *California's Immigrant Children: Theory, Research, and Implications for Educational Policy*, ed. Rubén G. Rumbaut and Wayne A. Cornelius, 161–90. San Diego: Center for U.S.-Mexican Studies, University of California, San Diego.

Swidler, Ann. 2001. *Talk of Love: How Culture Matters*. Chicago: University of Chicago Press.

Takaki, Ronald T. 1979. *Iron Cages: Race and Culture in Nineteenth-Century America*. Seattle: University of Washington Press.

Takyi, Baffour K. 2009. "Africans Abroad: Comparative Perspectives on America's Postcolonial West Africans." In *The New African Diaspora*, ed. Isidore Okpewho and Nkiru Nzegwu, 236–54. Bloomington: Indiana University Press.

Tamir, Yael. 1993. *Liberal Nationalism*. Princeton, NJ: Princeton University Press.

Taylor, Charles. 1994. *Multiculturalism: Examining the Politics of Recognition*. Princeton, NJ: Princeton University Press.

Teachman, Jay D. 1987. "Family Background, Educational Resources, and Educational Attainment." *American Sociological Review* 52: 548–57.

Telles, Edward. 2004. *Race in Another America: The Significance of Skin Color in Brazil*. Princeton, NJ: Princeton University Press.

Telles, Edward E., and Vilma Ortiz. 2008. *Generations of Exclusion: Mexican Americans, Assimilation, and Race*. New York: Russell Sage Foundation.

Thomas, Kevin J. A. 2011 "What Explains the Increasing Trend in African Emigration to the US?" *International Migration Review* 45(1): 3–28.

Tilly, Charles. 2006. *Identities, Boundaries, and Social Ties*. New York: Paradigm Publishers.

Tuan, Mia. 1998. *Forever Foreigners or Honorary Whites? The Asian Ethnic Experience Today*. New Brunswick, NJ: Rutgers University Press.

———. 2002. "Second-Generation Asian American Identity: Clues from the Asian Ethnic Experience." In *Second Generation: Ethnic Identity among Asian Americans*, ed. Pyong Gap Min, 209–38. Walnut Creek, CA: AltaMira Press.

Tyson, Karolyn, William Darity, and Domini Castellino. 2005. "It's not 'a Black Thing': Understanding the Burden of Acting White and Other Dilemmas of High Achievement." *American Sociological Review* 70(4): 582–605.

United States Census Bureau / American FactFinder. 2016. 2014 American Community Survey 1-Year Estimate, Tables S1501, S15002B, S0201. U.S. Census Bureau American Community Survey Office, 2015. http://factfinder2.census .gov.

Vallejo, Jody Agius. 2012. *Barrios to Burbs: The Making of the Mexican American Middle Class.* Stanford, CA: Stanford University Press.

Vasquez, Jessica. 2011. *Mexican Americans across Generations: Immigrant Families, Racial Realities.* New York: New York University Press.

Vertovec, Steven, and Susanne Wessendorf. 2010. "Introduction: Assessing the Backlash against Multiculturalism in Europe." In *The Multiculturalism Backlash: European Discourses, Policies, and Practices,* ed. Steven Vertovec and Susanne Wessendorf, 1–31. London: Routledge.

Vickerman, Milton. 1999. *Crosscurrents: West Indian Immigrants and Race.* New York: Oxford University Press.

———. 2007. "Recent Immigration and Race: Continuity and Change." *Du Bois Review* 4(1): 141–65.

Waldinger, Roger, ed. 2001. *Strangers at the Gates: New Immigrants in Urban America.* Berkeley: University of California Press.

Wamba, Philippe. 1999. *Kinship: A Family's Journey in Africa and America.* New York: Penguin.

Warikoo, Natasha K. 2011. *Balancing Acts: Youth Culture in the Global City.* Berkeley: University of California Press.

Waters, Mary C. 1990. *Ethnic Options: Choosing Identities in America.* Berkeley: University of California Press.

———. 1992. "The Construction of a Symbolic Ethnicity: Suburban White Ethnics in the 1980s." In *Immigration and Ethnicity: American Society—"Melting Pot" or "Salad Bowl"?,* ed. M. D'Innocenzo and J. P. Sierefman, 75–90. Westport, CT: Greenwood Press.

———. 1999. *Black Identities: West Indian Immigrant Dreams and American Realities.* Cambridge, MA: Harvard University Press.

Waters, Mary C., and Tomás R. Jiménez. 2005. "Assessing Immigrant Assimilation: New Empirical and Theoretical Challenges." *Annual Review of Sociology* 31: 105–25.

Waters, Mary C., Philip Kasinitz, and Asad L. Asad. 2014. "Immigrants and African Americans." *Annual Review of Sociology* 40: 369–90.

Waters, Mary C., Van Tran, Philip Kasinitz, and John H. Mollenkopf. 2010. "Segmented Assimilation Revisited: Types of Acculturation and Socioeconomic Mobility in Young Adulthood." *Ethnic and Racial Studies* 33(7): 1168–93.

Weight, Richard. 2002. *Patriots: National Identity in Britain, 1940–2000.* Oxford: Macmillan.

Weiner, F. Melissa. 2008. "Bridging the Theoretical Gap: The Diasporized Hybrid in Sociological Theory." In *Hybrid Identities: Theoretical and Empirical Examination,* ed. Keri E. Iyall Smith and Patricia Leavy, 101–15. Leiden: Brill.

Western, Bruce. 2006. *Punishment and Inequality in America.* New York: Russell Sage Foundation.

William, William J. 1980. *The Declining Significance of Race: Blacks and Changing American Institutions.* Chicago: University of Chicago Press.

Williams, David R., and Selina A. Mohammed. 2009. "Discrimination and Racial Disparities in Health: Evidence and Needed Research." *Journal of Behavioral Medicine* 32: 20–47.

Williams, Eric. 1970. *From Columbus to Castro: The History of the Caribbean, 1492–1969.* London: Deutsch.

Wilson, William Julius. 2010. *More than Just Race: Being Black and Poor in the Inner City.* New York: Norton.

Wimmer, Andreas. 2008. "Elementary Strategies of Ethnic Boundary Making," *Ethnic and Racial Studies* 31(6): 1025–55.

———. 2009. "The Making and Unmaking of Ethnic Boundaries: A Multilevel Process Theory." *American Journal of Sociology* 113(4): 970–1022.

Winder, Robert. 2004. *Bloody Foreigners: The Story of Immigration to Britain.* New York: Little, Brown.

Womack, Ytasha L. 2010. *Post Black: How a New Second Generation Is Redefining African American Identity.* Chicago: Lawrence Hill Books.

Wong, Paul Chienping, Faith Lai, Richard Nagasawa, and Tieming Lin. 1998. "Asian Americans as a Model Minority: Self Perceptions and Perceptions by Other Racial Groups." *Sociological Perspectives* 41(1): 95–118.

Wu, Ellen D. 2014. *The Color of Success: Asian Americans and the Origins of the Model Minority.* Princeton, NJ: Princeton University Press.

Yancey, George. 2003. *Who Is White? Latinos, Asians, and the New Black/NonBlack Divide.* Boulder, CO: Lynne Rienner.

Yeboah, E. A. Ian. 2008. *Black African Neo-Diaspora: Ghanaian Immigrant Experiences in the Greater Cincinnati, Ohio, Area.* Lanham, MD: Lexington Books.

Young, Iris M. 1997. "Polity and Group Difference: A Politics of Ideas or a Politics of Presence?" In *Contemporary Political Philosophy,* ed. Robert E. Goodin and Philip Pettit, 256–72. Oxford: Blackwell.

Yuval-Davis, Nira. 2004. "Borders, Boundaries, and the Politics of Belonging." In *Ethnicity, Nationalism and Minority Rights,* ed. Stephen May, Tariq Modood, and Judith Squires, Cambridge: Cambridge University Press.

Yuval-Davis, Nira, Kalpana Kannabiran, and Ulrike M. Vieten. 2006. *The Situated Politics of Belonging.* London: Sage.

Zeleza, Paul Tiyambe "Diaspora Dialogues: Engagements between Africa and Its Diasporas." In *The New African Diaspora,* ed. Isidore Okphewho and Nkiru Nzegwu, 31–60. Bloomington: Indiana University Press.

Zephir, Flore. 2001. *Trends in Ethnic Identification among Second-Generation Haitian Immigrants in New York City.* Westport, CT: Bergin and Garvey.

Zhou, Min, and Carl L. Bankston III. 1998. *Growing Up American: How Vietnamese Children Adapt to Life in the United States.* New York: Russell Sage Foundation.

Zhou, Min, and Jennifer Lee. 2007. "Becoming Ethnic or Becoming American? Reflecting on the Divergent Pathways to Social Mobility and Assimilation among the New Second Generation." *Du Bois Review* 4(1): 189–205.

Zolberg, Aristide, and Long Litt Woon. 1999. "Why Islam Is like Spanish: Cultural Incorporation in Europe and the United States." *Politics and Society* 27(5): 5–38.

INDEX

Italic page numbers indicate tables and figures.

African diaspora. *See* diaspora, African

African identity, in multifaceted identity of Nigerians, 5, 201, 203–4, 205–6

African population: in Britain, 4–5, 43–44, 239n17; in U.S., 4–5, 41–42, 239n17, 244nn89,93

aggression, black, perceptions of, 160–61

ajereke, 103

akatas (foreigners), 102–3, 250n5

Alex (pseudonym), 159

Amara (pseudonym), 63, 92, 214

American Community Survey (ACS), 41, 42, 244n89

American Dream, 145, 178, 181, 184, 190–91, 222

American identity (of individuals), 176–209; embraced by immigrants, 177–78, 184, 190–95, 255n30; in ethnic hybrids, 197–200; freedom in, 191–92; frequencies of, *236*; in multifaceted identity, 206–9; opportunities in, 190–92; patterns of British identity compared to, 194–96, *195*, 206–8; rejected by immigrants, 192–93; strategies for improving immigrant reception of, 225–26. *See also* national identity of U.S.

Americanization, social mobility linked to resistance to, 243n56

Anna (pseudonym), 199

AP classes, 85–86

Asad, L. Asad, 239n17

Asian immigrants: on black ethnic differences in U.S., 145; cross-group coalitions with, 224; distancing themselves from African Americans, 121; educational attainment of (*See* educational attainment of Asians); ethnic capital of, 96–97, 212; as ethnic hybrids, 212; ethnicity as social capital for, 15, 28, 212; hyper-selectivity of, 17, 240n38; in middle class, 220; as model minority, 16–17, 32, 74, 77; population in U.S., 41; in racial hierarchy, 17; segmented assimilation theory on, 15, 28; in tri-racial systems, 219. *See also specific groups*

assimilation, definition of, 26. *See also* identificational assimilation

assimilation of second generation, 14–18; among European vs. nonwhite immigrants, 14–15, 30; immigrant selectivity in, 4; theories on, 30–37

assimilation theories: ethnicity and race conflated in, 26, 28; ethnicity paradigm in, 26–27; on second generation, 30–37; straight-line model in, 14–15. *See also* segmented assimilation theory

assimilative strategy of self-identification, 35

Australia, visa requirements for citizens of, 183, 225

Awokoya, Janet, 240n31

Azikiwe, Nnamdi, 38

baby boomers, 220

balkanization, ethnic, 180

Balogun, Oluwakemi M., 240n31

barristers, 237n4

Barth, Frederik, 133

Bashi Treitler, Vilna, 248n12

Bayo (pseudonym), 169

beauty, standards of, 61–64, 247n9

Bello (pseudonym), 127

belonging, in national identity, 180–81, 207–8

"better blacks," 122, 146, 168, 174

beyond racialization theory, 9–10, 210–11; application to other groups, 216–17; ethnicity as factor in, 10, 16, 71–72, 211; proximal hosts as factor in, 10, 16, 54, 211; transnational linkages as factor in, 10, 100–101, 211. *See also specific factors*

Bidemi (pseudonym), 164–65

bigotry of low expectations, 88–90

Bimpe (pseudonym), 81

biracial individuals, in racial hierarchy, 247nn9–10

black, as ethnic vs. racial identity, 205. *See also* black racial identity

black, category of. *See* black racial category

black Americans. *See* African Americans

black British. *See* British blacks

black Caribbeans. *See* Caribbeans, black

black culture: as deficient, 16, 27–29, 30, 228; as oppositional, 3, 16, 29, 36, 75; of working-class British blacks, 28–29, 199; in workplace, 151, 165

black ethnic diversity: African American
views on, 143, 145; Nigerian views on,
120, 214–15; sociological theories
minimizing, 25–29; white American
views on, 139–41, 145–46
black ethnicity, reactive: Nigerians' lack
of, 3, 7, 9, 69, 131, 144, 210–11;
segmented assimilation theory on, 15,
29, 33, 68–69, 100
black identity. *See* black racial identity
Black Lives Matter, 217
blackness: creation of new definitions for,
214–15, 220; definition and use of term,
36–37; equated with poverty and
criminality, 13–14, 27, 170; as
monolithic, 14, 36, 72, 141, 156, 210;
"one-drop rule" of, 36
black/nonblack color line, 24, 133, 219
Black Power movement, 24
black racial category: vs. black as ethnic
category, 205; in Britain, 24, 36–37,
241–42nn15–16; class lines in, 137–38;
hierarchy within, 70; multiple
ethnicities within (*See* black ethnic
diversity); new divisions with, 214–17;
possibility of exit from, 8, 219;
recognition of diversity within, 215–16;
in U.S., 24, 36–37, 120–21
black racial identity: vs. African American
identity, 1–2, 117, 205; vs. black ethnic
identity, 205; among Caribbeans,
126–127; definition and use of term,
36–37; future of, 217–18; among
Haitians, 34; as "just black," 16, 68, 87,
215; in multifaceted identity, 3, 5, 152,
201, 204; oppositional culture in, 3, 16,
36; pan-ethnic, 100; racial solidarity in
U.S. based on, 151–52; among West
Indians, 33–34, 126–127, 243n5
black second generation: identity of, 33–37;
meaning and use of term, 239n18. *See
also* Caribbeans; second-generation
Nigerians
black-white gap. *See* racial gaps
bleaching creams, 247n9
BNP. *See* British National Party
Bode (pseudonym), 108
Bolade (pseudonym), 189

Bonilla-Silva, Eduardo, 133
"booty scratchers, African," 57–60
Borjas, George J., 248n6
Bose (pseudonym), 64, 119
boundaries, types of, 112. *See also specific
types*
Bourdieu, Pierre, 81, 101
Brah, Avtar, 241–42nn15–16
"brain drain," 39
Britain, vs. United Kingdom, use of terms,
239n28
British black identity: among Caribbeans,
35, 126–127; as pan-ethnic identity, 205;
rejected by Nigerians, 3, 109, 176
British blacks: ethnicity theory on
assimilation of, 27; segmented
assimilation theory on, 27–28;
working-class culture of, 28–29, 199.
See also Caribbeans
British-born Nigerian identity, 3
British Empire, in national identity, 182–83.
See also colonial history
British identity (of individuals), 176–209;
in ethnic hybrids, 197–200; frequencies
of, *236*; instrumental view of, 185–86;
multicultural narrative of, 185, 187; in
multifaceted identity, 206–9; patterns
of American identity compared to,
194–96, *195*, 206–8; rejected by immigrants, 2–3, 176–77, 184–90; strategies
for improving immigrant reception of,
221–22, 224–26. *See also* national
identity of Britain
British National Party (BNP), 25, 59,
157–58, 183, 189, 208
British street (youth) culture, 127, 170
Brown, James, 197
"bubus, African," 59–60
Bukola (pseudonym), 124–25
bullying, in Britain, 2, 56
"bush babies," 59, 61

CAAPS/ABC News Black Politics Study,
215–16
California, ethnic conflicts in, 100
Cameron, David, 39, 131, 196, 224–25
Canada, visa requirements for citizens of,
183, 225

capital, ethnicity as, 71–73, 212; and educational achievement gap, 79; extension of framework of, 16, 19, 30; sociological explanations of, 72–73. *See also* cultural capital; ethnic capital; human capital; social capital

Caribbeans, black, in Britain, 53–70; as *akatas* (foreigners), 102, 250n5; class schema in relations with, 138, 170–73; colonial experience of, 168–69, 174; educational achievement gap among, 74–76, 128–29; education as ethnic boundary with, 93–94; as focus of previous studies, 3, 237n6; identity of, 33–37, 35, 126–127, 196; in interracial marriages, 45, 108, 171; moral and cultural boundaries with, 94, 99–100; as native blacks, 168, 242n32; Nigerian parents' discrimination against, 107–8; origin as ethnic boundary with, 56–61; physical differences as ethnic boundary with, 61–63; population of, 5, 43, 239n17; as proximal hosts, 6; racial discrimination by, 2, 56, 59–61; racial solidarity with, 168–70; stereotypes of, 108; strategies for improving relations with, 221, 222–24; style as ethnic boundary with, 63–64; symbolic boundaries with, 123–28; timing of immigration by, 129, 168; views on, vs. in U.S., 128–30; working-class culture of, 28

Caribbeans, black, in U.S.: on black ethnic differences, 145; ethnic boundaries with, 120–21; as focus of previous studies, 3, 237n6; identity of, 33–37; immigrant selectivity among, 122; population of, 41, 239n17; timing of immigration by, 129; views on, vs. in Britain, 128–30

Carson, Ben, 136, 252n2
Carter, Prudence, 76, 92
CBN. *See* Central Bank of Nigeria
census forms: British, 206, 215; U.S., 145, 205–6
Central Bank of Nigeria (CBN), 244n87
Cheung, Sin Yi, 253n42
Chiamaka (pseudonym), 191

childhood: attempts to erase cultural markers in, 64–68; influence on identity formation, 69–70, 95; relations with proximal hosts in, 54, 56–64

children, biracial, in racial hierarchy, 247nn9–10

Children of Immigrants Longitudinal Survey (CILS), 237n6
Chimkamtu (pseudonym), 189
Chinedum (pseudonym), 58, 82
Chinelo (pseudonym), 104–5, 200
Chinese immigrants: educational attainment of, 27–29, 78, 96–97; ethnic capital of, 96–97
Christians, Nigerian, 37, 45, 154, 253n36, 256n15
Chua, Amy, 240n45, 250n18, 251n41
Chuka Eke (pseudonym), 88, 89, 125, 160, 176–77, 187
churches. *See* religious practices
CILS. *See* Children of Immigrants Longitudinal Survey
citizenship: vs. belonging, 180–81; British, in British identity, 185; dual, Nigerians with, 40, 244n88; education about, 179, 224; U.S., immigration policies on, 25; U.S., in American identity, 193
Civil Rights movement, U.S., 121–22
class. *See* social class
class reproduction, 181
class schemas, *172*; in Britain, 138, 170–73; definition of, 138; in U.S., 138, 153–56
clothing, erasing markers of difference in, 65
coalitionists, racial, 253n31, 255n42
coalitions: of middle-class blacks, 8, 136–37; of proximal hosts and Nigerians, 220–21, 222–24
Coleman, James, 72, 79
college: black ethnic diversity in admissions to, 139; solidification of identities in, 109–10; strategies for improving black-on-black relations during, 222–23; student associations in, 223, 226–27
Colombian immigrants, 78
colonial history of Britain: in assimilation outcomes, 9, 29, 187–88; in national identity, 176–77, 179, 182–83, 213–14,

221; in racial discrimination, 9, 29, 168–69, 174

color lines: as black/nonblack, 24, 133, 219; in Britain vs. U.S., 24; future of, 219–20; movement in, 36–37

Combs, Sean (P. Diddy), 153, 253n35

Commonwealth of Nations, 183, 225

concerted cultivation, 250n7

Conservative Party (Britain), 59, 169

conservatives, racial, 253n31, 255n42

Constitution, U.S., 181, 192

contact theory, 155

contamination effect, 75, 77

corruption, Nigerian, perception of, 131, 252n43

cosmopolitanism, 180

"cricket test," 186

criminality, blackness equated with, 13–14, 27, 170

criminalization, of minority youth, 123, 160

Cruz, Ted, 131, 251n42

cultural boundaries: in Britain, 94, 99–100, 112, 123–28; class schemas in, 138; definition of, 112; in U.S., 99, 112, 113–18

cultural capital: in educational attainment, 91, 95, 96; forms of, 101; in workplace, 165

cultural creativity, 31

cultural ecology theory, 74–75

cultural embedding: definition of, 7; in diasporic Nigerian ethnicity, 7, 101–10; and social class, 255n41

cultural frames, 78–79

cultural hybrids, 197–200

cultural mainstreamers, 76, 92

cultural markers: attempts to erase, 64–68; examples of, 22

cultural straddlers, 76

culture: British street (youth), 127, 170; in definition of ethnic groups, 7–8; in explanations of educational achievement gap, 74–78. See also black culture; oppositional culture

cultures of mobility, minority, 29, 96, 137

Daniel (pseudonym), 192, 202–3

Dapo (pseudonym), 125–26, 186

Dara (pseudonym), 149–50, 151, 152

dating, interracial, 62, 247n8

Dayo (pseudonym), 126

Declaration of Independence, U.S., 181, 192

Deji (pseudonym), 146

Democratic Party (U.S.), 152, 221

Demola (pseudonym), 159–60

Deola (pseudonym), 117

Desola (pseudonym), 61

diaspora, definition of, 238n13

diaspora, African: in Britain, 43–44; in U.S., 41–42; waves of, 203, 247n6

diaspora, Nigerian, 37–47; in Britain, 38–39, 44–47; Nigerian government engagement with, 40–41; origins of, 38–39, 244n82; return migration in, 195; in U.S., 38–39, 42–43

Diaspora, Nigerian Department of, 40

Diaspora Commission, 40

diasporic Nigerian ethnicity, 7, 98–134; cultural embedding in, 7, 101–10; definition of, 111, 212; in multifaceted identity, 5, 201, 202–3, 209; proximal hosts in formation of, 101–2; vs. reactive black ethnicity, 7, 69; solidification in early adulthood, 109–10; subjective factors defining, 132–33; symbolic boundaries in, 111–28

Dimeji (pseudonym), 160

discrimination. See racial discrimination

dissimilarity index, 245n109

dissociative strategy of self-identification, 35, 196

Diversity Visa Lottery program, 39, 42

domestic terrorism, 221, 226

dominant achievement ideology, 76, 92

Dominican immigrants, 78

Donaghue, Christopher, 252n15

dreadlocks, 121, 250n20

Ebola, 134

Eche (pseudonym), 64–65

economy of Nigeria: oil and gas in, 37, 39; overview of, 39–41; policy initiatives for development of, 222, 226–27; remittances to, 40, 47, 236, 244nn86–87 education: about British history, 224–25; citizenship, 179, 224; multicultural, 179

educational attainment, 71–97; cultural explanations for racial gaps in, 74–78; effects of ethnic capital on, 80, 84, 87, 96–97, 248n6; as indicator for class, 238n7; status attainment model of, 72; structural explanations for racial gaps in, 77–79

educational attainment of Asians, 27–29; ethnic capital in, 96–97, 212; in model minority thesis, 16–17, 74, 77; racialization of, 91; structural explanations for, 77–78

educational attainment of Caribbeans, 74–76, 128–29

educational attainment of Nigerians, 79–97; in Britain, 4, 17–18, 38, 44, 45–48, *46, 48*, 245n107; as ethnic boundary, 71–73, 79, 82, 91–97; institutional support in Britain for, 88–91, 94; institutional support in U.S. for, 84–88; and model minority thesis, 17–18; in Nigeria, 4, 37–38, 244n79; as social norm, 7, 73, 80–84, 95; of study respondents, 11, 47–49, 72, 230, 240n32; as symbolic boundary with proximal hosts, 117–18; in U.S., 4, 38, 42, *48*, 48–49

Ehi (pseudonym), 107

elders, respect for, 104–5, 118–19

email scammers, 131, 251n42

embodied state, cultural capital in, 101

Emem (pseudonym), 108, 161

emotional attachment: in belonging, 181; to national identity of Britain, 184–86, 190, 207; to national identity of U.S., 190, 192–93, 207

English identity, 190, 225. *See also* British identity

English language, in national identity of Britain, 183, 190

Enitan (pseudonym), 185

ethnic balkanization, 180

ethnic boundaries: based on cultural markers, 22, 63–68; based on education, 71–73, 79, 82, 91–97; based on origin, 56–61; based on physical differences, 61–64; based on style, 63–64; moral and cultural boundaries as, 94, 99; rigidity of, in U.S. vs. Britain, 101, 112–13. *See also* symbolic boundaries

ethnic capital: of Asians, 96–97, 212; definition of, 73, 147; in educational attainment, 80, 84, 87, 96–97, 248n6; in workplace, 147–49, 174

ethnic conflicts, ethnic identities strengthened after, 100

ethnic differences: decline of, in assimilation, 26; Nigerian strategy of minimizing, 138, 150–51; signaling, in ethnic identity, 110–11. *See also* black ethnic diversity

ethnic groups: definition of, 7–8, 80, 132; of Nigeria, 37, 100, 111; subjective factors defining, 132–33

ethnic hybrids, 34, 197–200, 212, 218

ethnic identity: black as, 205; of black Caribbeans, 196; future of, 217–20; of Haitians, 34; hybrid, 34, 197–200, 212, 218; multifaceted (*See* multifaceted identity); signaling difference and establishing similarity in, 110–11; social mobility linked to, 34, 243n56; strengthening of, after ethnic conflicts, 100; of U.S. vs. British Nigerians, 178, 194–96, *195, 236*; values as foundation of, 200; of West Indians, 33–34. *See also specific identities*

ethnic identity formation: childhood experiences in, 69–70, 95; class in, 8, 35; endpoints of, 19, 136; ethnogenesis theory on, 55; future of, 217–20; proximal hosts in, 6–7, 35, 54, 68–70; social class in, 173–74

ethnicity: in beyond racialization theory, 10, 16, 71–72, 211; among blacks, 25–30; as capital (*See* capital); as choice for white groups, 15; identity conflated with, 16; race conflated with, 16, 26, 28, 247n1; situational, 34–35, 202. *See also specific ethnic groups*

ethnicity paradigm, in assimilation theories, 26–27

ethnic minorities: British, self-identification strategies among, 35, 196; pan-

identity formation *(continued)*
proximal hosts in, 6–7, 35; social actors shaping, 55; social class in, 8, 35, 173–74. *See also* ethnic identity formation
Idowu Damola (pseudonym), 1–2, 114–15, 116, 148–49, 150
Ike (pseudonym), 65, 80–81, 102, 105–6, 113–14, 119
Ima (pseudonym), 144
immigrant(s): in national identity of Britain, 25, 128–129, 157, 183, 207; in national identity of U.S., 25, 157, 178, 181. *See also specific groups*
immigrant identity, among West Indians, 33, 243n55
Immigrant Second Generation in Metropolitan New York, 237n6
Immigration and Nationality Act of 1965, 30
immigration policy of Britain: rise of restrictive, 59, 129, 189; vs. U.S. policy, 25; visa requirements in, 39, 129, 183, 194, 225
immigration policy of U.S.: vs. British policy, 25; future of, 226; visa requirements in, 39, 42, 129
imperialism. *See* colonial history
income levels: of Nigerians in Britain, 44; of Nigerians in U.S., 42; of study respondents, 14
India, national identity of white Britons in, 177
Indians. *See* South Asians
individualism, in U.S., 191
institutional racism: in Britain, 168, 183, 225; definition of, 240n43; effects of, 27; in U.S., 17
instrumental view of British identity, 185–86
intermarriage. *See* marriage, interracial
International Monetary Fund, 39
interracial dating, 62, 247n8
interracial marriage, in Britain, 45, 108, 171, 246n115
involuntary minorities, educational achievements of, 75–77
Ispa-Landa, Simone, 247n8

Jackman, Mary, 151
Jamaicans, in Britain: conflict in Africans' relations with, 59; as largest Caribbean group, 59; slavery in history of, 60; symbolic boundaries with, 123–26; and white nationalists, 158
Jay-Z, 197, 255n37
Jibola (pseudonym), 80, 109–10
Jide (pseudonym), 155, 197–98
Jiménez, Tomás R., 256n48
Johnson, Boris, 196
Jonathan, Goodluck, 40
judicial system: British, 160–61, 183; U.S., 217
"just black" identity, 16, 68, 87, 215

Kasinitz, Philip, 150, 160, 239n17, 240n31, 251n39
Kemi Olotu (pseudonym), 53–54, 57, 80, 85, 102, 146
Kenya, Obama's visit to, 222
Kike (pseudonym), 65
King, Martin Luther, Jr., 14
Korean Americans, 100
Kunle (pseudonym), 203–4

Labor Force Survey, 47
labor market, discrimination in. *See* workplace discrimination
Labor Party (Britain), 59, 169
Lamide (pseudonym), 99–100
languages: English, 183, 190; Nigerian, 37, 197, *236*
Laotians, 74, 249n37
Lareau, Annette, 250n7
Latinos. *See* Hispanic immigrants
Laura (pseudonym), 61–62, 143
lawyers: British, 2, 164, 237n4; U.S., 143–44
Lee, Jennifer, 78–79
Linda Okpara (pseudonym), 57, 62, 98–99, 142, 148
linked fate, 137, 151–52
literacy rates, in Nigeria, 38, 243n78
Lola (pseudonym), 107
London: Nigerians in, 44–45, 196; poverty in, 45, 246n111; residential patterns of Africans in, 245n109
Los Angeles, ethnic riots in, 100
Louie, Vivian, 78
low expectations, bigotry of, 88–90

national identity of Britain *(continued)*
and ethnic hybrids, 197–200;
multicultural policies in, 179–80, 207;
and multifaceted identity, 206–9;
national myths in, 184, 187, 190; need
for revisions to, 221–22; place of
immigrants in, 25, 128–129, 157, 183, 207;
recent changes to, 182, 254n18; rejected
by immigrants, 2–3, 176–77, 184–90;
strategies for improving immigrant
reception of, 221–22, 224–26; U.S.
national identity compared to, 221–22
national identity of U.S., 176–209; British
national identity compared to, 221–22;
embraced by immigrants, 177–78, 184,
190–95, 255n30; and ethnic hybrids,
197–200; freedom in, 181–82, 191–92;
multicultural policies in, 179–80, 207;
and multifaceted identity, 206–9;
national myths in, 181–82, 184, 190–92;
opportunities in, 181, 190–92; place of
immigrants in, 25, 157, 178, 181; rejected
by immigrants, 192–93; strategies for
improving immigrant reception of,
225–26
nationalism: definition of, 180; white, in
Britain, 157–58
national myths: of Britain, 184, 187, 190;
role of, 180; of U.S., 181–82, 184,
190–92
National Party, British (BNP), 25, 59,
157–58, 183, 189, 208
National Resource Fund (Nigeria), 40–41
National Survey of Ethnic Minorities,
Fourth, 196, 238n6
Native Americans, 74
native blacks: African Americans as, 168;
black Caribbeans as, 168, 242n32; black
second generation as, 69–70
"naughty" students, 88–89
Ndubusi (pseudonym), 118
Nena (pseudonym), 109
New York, Nigerians in, 43, 245n102
NIDO. *See* Nigerians in the Diaspora
Organization
Nigeria: *akatas* (foreigners) in, 250n5;
beauty standards in, 247n9; ethnic
groups of, 37, 100, 111; influence on

other African nations, 5; languages of,
37, 197, *236*; overview of nation, 37–41,
111; population of, 5, 37, 243n74; return
migration to, 195, 255n48; return visits
to, 50, 91, 105–6, 195–96, 226–27
Nigerian diaspora. *See* diaspora, Nigerian
Nigerian Diaspora Day, 41
Nigerian ethnicity: denial of, by youth, 65;
in Nigeria vs. diaspora, 7, 100, 111;
subjective factors defining, 132–33. *See
also* diasporic Nigerian ethnicity
Nigerian first generation: selectivity of, 7,
18, 80, 132; transnational linkages
among, 199. *See also* parents
Nigerian National Volunteer Service
(NNVS), 40
Nigerian second generation. *See* second-
generation Nigerians
Nigerians in the Diaspora Organization
(NIDO), 40
Nigerian Students Association, 223
Nigerian third generation, 218
Nnamdi (pseudonym), 191
NNVS. *See* Nigerian National Volunteer
Service
No Longer at Ease (Achebe), 237n3
nonblack/black color line, 24, 133, 219
noncompliant believers, 76
nonwhite immigrants, assimilation of,
14–18; theories of, 30–33; vs. white
immigrants, 14–15, 30. *See also specific
groups*
norms. *See* social norms
nursing, 51, 142, 247n124

Obama, Barack, 136, 140, 152, 169, 193–94,
222
"Obama effect," 169
Obasanjo, Oluwasegun, 40
Obiageli (pseudonym), 199
occupational achievements: schema for
classifying, 49, 246n119; as social
norm, 7; of study respondents, 47–49,
48
Ogbu, John, 74–75, 76, 77
oil exports, from Nigeria, 37, 39
Omi, Michael, 26, 122–23, 239n21
"one-drop rule," 36

Onyinye (pseudonym), 83, 84, 145–46
opportunities, in national identity of U.S.,
181, 190–92
oppositional culture: black culture as, 3,
16, 29, 36, 75; in educational
attainment, 75; segmented assimilation
theory on, 29
origin, ethnic boundaries based on, 56–61
"other," as race, 3
Oye (pseudonym), 88–89, 124, 159, 166, 203
Oyinkan (pseudonym), 65–66, 103, 117–18

Pakistanis. *See* South Asians
Pamela (pseudonym), 109
pan-ethnic African identity, 35; in Britain
vs. U.S., *195*, 215; in multifaceted
identity, 5, 201, 203–4, 205–6
pan-ethnic black identity, 100, 205
pan-ethnicity, class-based, 173–74
pan-minority identity, 224
parents, Nigerian: in cultural embedding
process, 101–10; in educational
attainment of children, 71, 80–84, 96;
in identity formation of children, 55;
racial discrimination by, 107–8; vs.
U.S. parents, 103–4, 250n7
Parrillo, Vincent N., 252n15
passports: British, 177, 185–86, 189; U.S.,
192
Patterson, Orlando, 182, 192, 247n10
Pauline (pseudonym), 88, 165, 166, 187
P. Diddy (Sean Combs), 153, 253n35
penalties, ethnic, 162, 163, 183, 253n42
people of color, 24
Pew Research Center, 155, 175, 215, 216, 223
physical differences, ethnic boundaries
based on, 61–64
Pierre, Jemima, 251n39
Pinkett-Smith, Jada, 197
police shootings, 217
policy initiatives, 220–27; for improving
black-on-black relations, 220–21,
222–24; for improving national
identification, 221–22, 224–26; for
partnering in African economic
development, 222, 226–27
political party affiliations: in Britain, 169;
in U.S., 152, 221

political power, of African Americans, 221
poor, the. *See* poverty
population of Britain: African immigrants
in, 4–5, 43–44, 239n17; black
Caribbeans in, 5, 43, 239n17; Nigerian
immigrants in, 44; percentages by
race/ethnicity, 241n3
population of Nigeria, 37, 243n74
population of U.S.: African immigrants
in, 4–5, 41–42, 239n17, 244n89; black
Caribbeans in, 41, 239n17; Nigerian
immigrants in, 42, 244n93;
percentages by race/ethnicity, 241n3
Portes, Alejandro, 100
postcolonialism, in national identity of
Britain, 183, 188
postmodernism, and nationalism, 180
poverty: blackness equated with, 13–14, 27,
170; distance between middle-class and
poor blacks, 155–56, 174–75, 216; in
London, 45, 246n111; in Nigeria, 39;
strategies for improving relations with
poor blacks, 223–24
Powell, Enoch, 59, 247n4
pragmatists, racial, 253n31, 255n42
"preferred blacks," 122, 130, 139, 146, 168,
174
presidential elections, U.S.: of 2008, 152,
169, 193–94; of 2016, 131, 252n2
Proposition 187 (California), 100
proximal hosts, 6–7, 53–70; in beyond
racialization theory, 10, 16, 54, 211; in
context of reception, 16, 29, 68–69;
definition of, 6, 239n19; in diasporic
Nigerian ethnicity formation, 101–2;
education as ethnic boundary with,
91–97; erasing markers of difference
with, 63–68; in ethnic identity
formation, 6–7, 35, 54, 68–70;
ethnogenesis theory on, 55; lasting
impact of relations with, 67–70; moral
and cultural boundaries with, 99–100;
origin as ethnic boundary with, 56–61;
physical differences as ethnic boundary
with, 61–64; racial discrimination by,
56–61, 67–68; slavery in history of, 59,
60, 67; social class of, 8, 86, 137–38;
social distance between Nigerians and,

proximal hosts *(continued)*
53–54, 57, 62, 66, 220; strategies for improving relations with, 220–21, 222–24; style as ethnic boundary with, 63–64; symbolic boundaries in Britain against, 123–28; symbolic boundaries in U.S. against, 113–23. *See also* African Americans; Caribbeans, black
pseudonyms, use of, 12
public spaces, racial discrimination in, 149, 157–59
Putnam, Robert, 238n7

queue theory, 252n17

Rabi (pseudonym), 186
race: definition of, 22–23; ethnicity conflated with, 16, 26, 28, 247n1; in ethnicity theory, 26–27; identity conflated with, 16; in second-generation assimilation, 14–18; as social boundary, 112
racelessness, 3, 34
racial classification: in tri-racial systems, 24, 219; in U.S., evolution of, 141, 145, 219–20. *See also* color lines; racial hierarchy
racial coalitionists, 253n31, 255n42
racial conservatives, 253n31, 255n42
racial discrimination: in contexts of reception, 51; by representatives of the state, 67–68, 160–61
racial discrimination in Britain, 156–73; by black Caribbeans, 2, 56, 59–61; colonial history in, 9, 29, 168–69, 174; covert, 158–59, 165–66; failure to address history of, 168; gender dynamics in, 159–62, 166; by Nigerian parents, 107–8; origins and history of, 23–24; prevalence of, 2, 156–57, 167; in public spaces, 157–59; racial solidarity in response to, 168–70; by teachers, 88–91; vs. U.S., 156, 167–68, 174–75; by white nationalists, 157–58; by white peers in childhood, 58–59; by working- vs. middle-class whites, 158–59. *See also* workplace discrimination

racial discrimination in U.S., 138–52; by African Americans, 56–58, 142–43; African American vs. Nigerian responses to, 116–17; black vs. white perceptions of, 254n52; vs. Britain, 156, 167–68, 174–75; by Nigerian parents, 107; origins and history of, 23–24; racial solidarity in response to, 146, 151–52; by teachers, 142; against West Indians, 139–40; by white peers in childhood, 58. *See also* workplace discrimination
racial gaps: in American Dream, 181; in educational achievement, 74–79, 248n10; in mentoring, 143–44
racial hierarchy: African Americans in, 17, 121; Asian Americans in, 17; biracial children in, 247nn9–10; within black category, 70; in Britain vs. U.S., 22, 24, 36; Haitians in, 65; honorary whites in, 133, 219
racial identity, black. *See* black racial identity
racial inequality, origins and history of, 23–24
racialization: British vs. U.S. processes of, 51; complexity of responses to, 54; definition of, 239n21; of educational attainment of Asians, 91; of ethnic minorities, 6. *See also* racial discrimination
racialization theory, on second-generation assimilation, 30–32. *See also* beyond racialization theory
racial pragmatists, 253n31, 255n42
racial segregation: legacy of, in African American experience, 114; residential, in Britain, 44, 45, 49, 171; residential, in U.S., 23, 49
racial solidarity: in Britain, 168–70; in U.S., 146, 151–52
racism. *See* institutional racism; racial discrimination
rainbow underclass, 31, 137
Rastafarianism, 250n20
RCCG. *See* Redeemed Christian Church of God

reactive black ethnicity. *See* black ethnicity, reactive

reception, context of: in Britain vs. U.S., 3–4, 22–25; national history in, 29; proximal hosts in, 16, 29, 68–69; racial discrimination in, 51; in segmented assimilation theory, 15, 29

Redeemed Christian Church of God (RCCG), 167, 196

refugees, African, hostility toward, 247n7

religious practices of Nigerians: in Britain, 45, 167, 196; in class schema, 154; effects on identity formation, 256n15; in Nigeria, 37, 253n36; in U.S., 154, 196

remittances, to Nigeria, 40, 47, *236*, 244nn86–87

Republican Party (U.S.), 25, 152

residential patterns of Nigerians: in Britain, 44–45, 245n109; in U.S., 43

residential segregation: in Britain, 44, 45, 49, 171; in U.S., 23, 49

respect, for elders, 104–5, 118–19

respondents. *See* study respondents

return migration, 195, 255n48

Rice, Tamir, 217

Rios, Victor, 123

riots, race/ethnic: in Britain (1981), 160, 168; in California (1992), 100

Rogozinski, Jan, 247n10

role models, 7, 87, 89

roots, ancestral, 113–14

Rubenfeld, Jed, 240n45, 250n18, 251n41

Rufiat (pseudonym), 171

Rukhe (pseudonym), 81

Rumbaut, Rubén, 100, 233

Sade Bankole (pseudonym), 62, 65, 154, 177–78, 190

Sam Echekoba (pseudonym), 89–91, 105, 108, 163, 170–71, 188–89, 195–96

schemas, definition of, 138. *See also* class schemas

schools: factors affecting Nigerian experiences in, 66–67; institutional support from, in Britain, 88–91, 94; institutional support from, in U.S.,

84–88; as key site of interaction with proximal hosts, 55. *See also* college

Scott, Walter, 217

second-generation Nigerians: definition of, 10–11, 233; gaps in study of, 2, 11; as model minority, 17–18, 131–32; population of, 4–5, 42; terms used for, 237n5

segmented assimilation theory, 15–16, 212; applied to Britain, 27–29; on Asian immigrants, 15, 28; context of reception in, 15, 29; critique of black culture in, 16, 27–29, 30; on educational attainment, 75; ethnicity as choice in, 15; origins of, 15; racialization theory compared to, 31; on rainbow underclass, 31, 137; on reactive black ethnicity, 15, 29, 33, 68–69, 100

segregation: based on race (*See* racial segregation); based on social class, 112

selective acculturation, 15, 198

selectivity of immigrants: among Asians, 17, 240n38; in assimilation outcomes, 4; among black Caribbeans, 122; among Nigerian first generation, 7, 18, 80, 132

self-identification strategies, of British ethnic minorities, 35, 196

Seun (pseudonym), 63–64, 65, 154–55

Shawn (pseudonym), 167, 185–86, 187

Shubby (pseudonym), 118

Sikes, Melvin P., 150–51

Simisola (pseudonym), 85–86

Simons, Herbert D., 75

situational ethnicity, 34–35, 202

Skin (pseudonym), 119–20

skin color: bleaching creams and, 247n9; discrimination based on darkness of, 140–41; ethnic boundaries based on, 61–62, 64, 247nn9–10

"slave babies," 59

Slave Coast, 244n82

slavery: within Africa, 113; in African American identity, 1, 113–14, 214, 237n2; in British vs. U.S. national contexts, 23; hierarchy of slaves, 247n10; in relations between Africans and proximal hosts, 59, 60, 67

Smith, Will, 197
social boundaries: definition of, 112; in delineation of ethnic boundaries, 112
social capital, ethnicity as, 72, 211–12; for Asians, 15, 28, 212; human capital created from, 18, 72, 80; segmented assimilation theory on, 15
social class: in American Dream, 181; in black racial category, 137–38; and cultural embedding, 255n41; in educational attainment, 85–86; in identity formation, 8, 35, 173–74; indicators used for, 238n7; in multifaceted identity, 8, 201, 204, 255n41; of proximal hosts, 8, 86, 137–38; in racial discrimination in Britain, 158–59; of rainbow underclass, 31, 137; as schema for black-on-black relations, 138, 153–56, 170–73, *172*; segregation based on, 112; as social boundary, 112; working-class culture of British blacks, 28–29, 199. *See also* middle class
social development in Nigeria, policy initiatives for, 222, 226–27
social distance, between proximal hosts and Nigerians, 53–54, 57, 62, 66, 220
social education, 161
social mobility: ethnic identity linked to, 34, 243n56; in national identity of U.S., 181; segmented assimilation theory on, 15–16. *See also* middle class
social norms: educational attainment as, 7, 73, 80–84, 95; occupational achievements as, 7
socioeconomic boundaries: in Britain, 112; class schemas in, 138; definition of, 112; in U.S., 112
socioeconomic class. *See* social class
solicitors, 237n4
solidarity. *See* racial solidarity
South Asians: as black, 24, 241n15; educational attainment of, 27–29; Muslim, 220; pan-ethnic identity of, 205; population in Britain, 44; and white nationalists, 158
sports: participation in, 67; stereotypes about, 88

state: racial discrimination by representatives of the, 67–68, 160–61; role in racial system, 122–23
status attainment model, 72
stereotypes: of African Americans, 98–99, 107, 108, 118, 136, 153; of Africans, 57, 88; of Asians, 30; of black Caribbeans, 108
street (youth) culture, British, 127, 170
structural factors, in educational achievement gap, 77–79
student associations, 223, 226–27
study methodology, 10–14, 229–34
study respondents, 47–51, 229–34; educational attainment of, 11, 47–49, 230, 240n32; family life of, 49–50; income levels of, 14; neighborhood context of, 49, 246n120; sociological profile of, *232*; transnational linkages of, 50–51, 229–30, *236*
style, ethnic boundaries based on, 63–64
subjective factors, in defining ethnic groups, 132–33
success frames, 78–79, 81, 84, 212
symbolic boundaries, 111–28; in Britain, 112, 123–28; definition of, 112; in delineation of ethnic boundaries, 111–12; types of, 112; in U.S., 112, 113–23

Tabira (pseudonym), 85
Tami (pseudonym), 161, 163
tax laws, 227
teachers, British: in identity formation, 55; institutional support from, 88–91, 94; racial discrimination by, 88–91
teachers, U.S.: in identity formation, 55; institutional support from, 84–88; racial discrimination by, 142
Tea Party (U.S.), 25
Tebbit, Norman, 186
Temitayo Tella (pseudonym), 56–57, 83, 135–36, 142
terrorism, domestic, 221, 226
Thatcher, Margaret, 186
third-generation Nigerians, 218
threading, hair, 2, 63–64

Titi Ajayi (pseudonym), 21, 85, 86–88, 93, 115–16, 142
Tokunbos, 195
transnationalism: definition of, 50; as response to racial discrimination in Britain, 167
transnational linkages: in beyond racialization theory, 10, 100–101, 211; in Britain vs. U.S., 194–96; in diasporic Nigerian ethnicity, 101–10; among first- vs. second-generation Nigerians, 199; of study respondents, 50–51, 229–30, 236
tribal marks, 64, 248n11
tri-racial systems, 24, 219
Tunji Mills (pseudonym), 58, 152, 193

Uju (pseudonym), 107
Uloma (pseudonym), 147–48
underclass, rainbow, 31, 137
unemployment, in Nigeria, 39
United Kingdom, vs. Britain, use of terms, 239n28
United Negro College Fund, 223
universities. See college

values: as foundation of Nigerian identity, 200, 202; in national identity of Britain, 183–84, 190; as symbolic boundary in U.S., 118–23
Vertovec, Steven, 254n4
Vickerman, Milton, 251n39
Vietnamese immigrants, 96–97
visas: British, 39, 129, 183, 194, 225; U.S., 39, 42, 129
voluntary minorities, educational achievements of, 75–77

Warikoo, Natasha, 75
Waters, Mary C., 239n17, 243n55, 247n1, 251n39, 256n48
Weight, Richard, 182
Wessendorf, Susanne, 254n4
West Indians, in Britain, identity of, 126–127
West Indians, in U.S.: identity of, 33–34, 243n55; racial discrimination against,

139–40; success in workplace, 140–41; timing of immigration by, 129
white, category of: expansion of, 121, 219; honorary whites in, 133, 219; Nigerians barred from, 133, 219
"white, acting," 75–77, 92–95
white Americans: on black ethnic differences, 139–41, 145–46; discrimination by (See racial discrimination); educational attainment of, explanations for, 74–79; as percentage of population, 241n3
white Britons: discrimination by (See racial discrimination); educational attainment of, explanations for, 74–79; national identity of, after emigration to India, 177; as percentage of population, 241n3; white nationalism among, 157–58
white favoritism thesis, 140, 252n17
white immigrants in U.S.: distancing themselves from African Americans, 121; ethnicity as choice for, 15; ethnicity theory on, 26–27; vs. nonwhite immigrants, assimilation of, 14–15, 30; segmented assimilation theory on, 15
white nationalists, in Britain, 157–58
whiteness, meaning of, 219
white supremacy, in Britain, 23, 183, 254n18
Winant, Howard, 26, 122–23, 239n21
Winfrey, Oprah, 136
Wole (pseudonym), 142–43, 191
working-class culture, of British blacks, 28–29, 199
workplace discrimination in Britain, 161–68; colonial legacy in, 188; cultural capital and, 165; gender dynamics in, 161–62, 166; in hiring laws, 189; Nigerian strategies for dealing with, 138–39; policy initiatives to address, 225; responses to, 165–67; return on education in, 129
workplace discrimination in U.S., 138–51; by African Americans, 142–43; ethnic capital and, 147–49; perceptions of, 142–44; queue theory on, 252n17; responses to, 149–51; return on